Political Capacity and Economic Behavior

The Political Economy of Global Interdependence
Thomas D. Willett, Series Editor

Political Capacity and Economic Behavior

EDITED BY

Marina Arbetman and Jacek Kugler

WestviewPress

A Division of HarperCollins*Publishers*

For Hannah, Joshua, and Tad, whose world it is

Copyright © 1997 by Westview Press, A Division of HarperCollins Publishers, Inc.

Published in 1997 in the United States of America by Westview Press, 5500 Central Avenue, Boulder, Colorado 80301-2877, and in the United Kingdom by Westview Press, 12 Hid's Copse Road, Cumnor Hill, Oxford OX2 9JJ

A CIP catalog record for this book is available from the Library of Congress.
ISBN 0-8133-3073-4   ISBN 0-8133-3364-4 (pbk.)

The paper used in this publication meets the requirements of the American National Standard for Permanence of Paper for Printed Library Materials Z39.48-1984.

10   9   8   7   6   5   4   3   2   1

Contents

Tables and Figures

FIGURES

Acknowledgments

This work was inspired by the challenge of Samuel Huntington's (1968, 1) brilliant contention that the "...most important distinction between nations concerns not their form of government, but their degree of government." This work is the result of two decades of research. In the interim many scholars contributed to the development of the notion of political capacity. We are particularly grateful to Richard Musgrave for pointing us in the right direction; to Raja Chelliah who contributed his insight during a marvelous meeting in Oxford, England; to Margaret Kelly who provided data that made the early efforts possible; to Eliott Morss and Roy Bahl for their enormous insights during our conference in Ann Arbor, Michigan; to William Domke who was the first to expand this approach to a long term historical analysis. We wish to thank in particular Thomas Borcherding, Bruce Bueno de Mesquita, Patricia Dillon, Christine Ries, Scott Gates, Douglas Lemke, King Banion, Young-Bae Hwang, Subrada Mitra, John Odell, Paul Perez, and Randolph Siverson for their very helpful suggestions during the 1993 Claremont Conference on Political Capacity and Economic Behavior. Robert Jackman deserves special recognition for his careful review of the manuscript and his invaluable comments. Many students who are now our colleagues helped in the development of these ideas. Major contributions were made at different stages by Youssef Cohen, Glenn Palmer, Ben Hunt, Frances Oneal, Doris Fuchs, David Hopson, Mark Abdollahian, Carole Alsharabati, and Murat Kalaora. The typescript would not be finished without the organization and editorial skills of Sandra Seymour, Gwen Williams, Ruth Carter, and Roichelle and Jay Winderman. Sharon Freeman designed and formatted the manuscript, which turned out to be no easy task. Alisa Newman patiently and promptly typed the many versions of this manuscript. Ruth Carter and Brian Buford-Efird coordinated the project and were instrumental in keeping all the chapters up-to-date and protected against a variety of computer mishaps. Our special appreciation goes to Thomas Willett, who must be given credit for the patience he exercised as we attempted to redefine economics in political terms.

Academic work can seldom be completed without support. We were very fortunate to have received support from the Ford Foundation, DARPA, and the Earhart Foundations in the early stages of this research. The current volume could never have been completed without the support of the Lincoln Foundation and we are particularly grateful to Kathryn Jo Lincoln and Carolyn Denham, who gave the go-ahead on this project. Equal credit must be given to the Murphy Institute of Political Economy at Tulane University for its financial backing in every stage of this project. Our thanks also goes to Daniel Mazmanian who always found resources when they were most needed.

Finally, thanks are due to our spouses Ian Rabinowitz and Cheryl Kugler for their forbearance with our obsession with political capacity and for their willingness to share in the opportunity cost of this effort.

Marina Arbetman
Jacek Kugler

Introduction

Marina Arbetman, Jacek Kugler

The overall aim of this book is to explore how the political capacity of governments affects economic and political performance. It is our contention that capable governments resolve the challenges associated with development and preserve domestic stability far more effectively than less capable governments do under similar circumstances. This book will show that political capacity plays a critical role in economic, demographic and social changes that characterize the process of national development.

Political capacity captures the ability of political systems to carry out the tasks chosen by the nation's government in the face of domestic and international groups with competing priorities. Organski and Kugler (1980: 72), who first introduced this concept, argued that "it is evident to us that a highly capable political system need not be free, democratic, stable, orderly, representative, participatory or endowed with any of the other desiderata" frequently associated with normative conceptions of political capacity. While "one may well argue that non-democratic, non-participatory or non-representative systems could not be regarded as developed," yet such governments can be politically capable. Seen in this light, political capacity is an expression of the political effectiveness of an elite in achieving governmental goals, and does not imply acceptance or support for the means by which such goals are attained. This normative free evaluation of political capacity provides a general, gross benchmark for any political system, regardless of regime type.

Kugler and Arbetman (Chapter 1) define political capacity as two distinct but complementary dimensions. Relative Political Reach (RPR)[1] focuses on human resources and measures the scope and breadth of government influence on the population. Relative Political Extraction (RPE) centers on material resources and gauges the flexibility of the government to gather revenues required to implement a desired policy. Governments increase their political capacity by expanding reach over the population or by extracting more from groups already mobilized. In the initial stages of development it is far easier to gain additional capacity by

1

reaching relatively unorganized portions of a population. Organski (Chapter 2) points out that as economic development progresses, it is more effective to extract additional resources from already mobilized groups than to incorporate groups increasingly reluctant to support the government. The reason is political costs (Organski et al. 1984; Arbetman 1995). In developing societies large portions of the population are not organized for political purposes, and governments can easily tap new resources by expanding the population base. In developed societies, on the other hand, governments have already accessed most of the population. Moreover, these populations are organized into political groups around a multitude of interests and can effectively oppose further governmental mobilization. Thus in developing societies governments can look outside a limited group of supporters to expand their resources, while in developed societies they have no choice but to reach into the pockets of already well-organized groups for additional revenues. At each stage of economic development, then, costs incurred by governments to gather additional resources and advance their policy goals are conditioned by changing economic circumstances.

A major aim of this book is to provide gross comparisons of aggregate political performance similar to those obtained with *GDP* for economic output.[2] Political capacity is an appropriate tool because it measures the overall performance of governments across societies over time, regardless of political regimes, ethnic compositions, religious characteristics, or cultural differences.[3] Like *GDP*, *RPC* is a gross map that outlines the key components of political performance without providing details about how each country has achieved such outputs. The aggregate measures of political capacity and economic output share advantages and drawbacks. Economists have made us well aware of the multiple definitions and distortions associated with *GDP*-type aggregate measures of economic performance. The main problems include inconsistent reporting, distorted cross-national comparability due to the use of different baskets of goods to calculate purchasing power across countries and over time, and ineffective calculation of the public sector output. Moreover, cross-temporal comparability is further suspect due to inflation and technology changes over time (Madison 1988; Summers and Heston 1991).

Such distortions are present and even magnified in measures of political capacity. Estimates of tax revenues used to measure extraction are poorly reported and seldom provided consistently across nations for a given fiscal year. Likewise, measures of labor participation used to approximate reach are distorted by incomplete reporting and wide definitional differences. Again, inflation affects capacity estimates because it distorts revenue figures used to control services delivered by the public sector. Finally, although we do not take them into account, prior political choices made by different nations regarding the provision of public services affect the validity of the base used to obtain relative extraction and reach in the same way the basket of goods affects *GDP* comparisons. Many of these drawbacks can be overcome with refinements in the data, but some cannot.

While such drawbacks must be noted, these difficulties should not obscure the advantages of an aggregate measure of political capacity. Indeed, despite measurement problems, *GDP* remains an extraordinarily useful first approximation of the overall economic performance of a nation and an efficient first-cut indicator of average individual performance. Likewise, *RPC* provides a benchmark index of the aggregate performance of political systems, and when disaggregated it captures the effectiveness of national, state, or local governments. There is, however, one fundamental drawback that differentiates *GDP* and political capacity. *GDP* and equivalent measures provide absolute estimates of overall economic productivity. This allows direct comparisons between societies at all levels of economic production. Political capacity, on the other hand, reflects only the relative success or failure of a government to extract and reach resources in a society, compared to other societies within an economic cross section and over time. Unlike economic output, therefore, political capacity measures the shadow of politics and does not directly disclose the aggregate political components that generate that performance by sector. In sum, *RPC* reports on the variation in reach and extraction relative to the performance of other societies endowed with similar levels of material and human resources. For this reason, comparisons across societies and over time within one society are valid only within a narrow range of economic development. Such comparisons become increasingly suspect for societies with different economic endowments.[4]

POLITICAL CAPACITY AND ECONOMIC AND POLITICAL BEHAVIOR

In this volume the contributors show that a politically capable government that is an active economic participant can positively intervene to shape an environment. Specifically, such postive interventions by capable governments are shown by Adji, Ahn, Holsey, andWillett (Chapter 7) and by Feng and Chen (Chapter 5) to attract investments; by Arbetman and Ghosh (Chapter 8) to minimize the gap between official and black market exchange rates; by Leblang (Chapter 6) to foster economic growth; by Snider (Chapter 12) to enhance distributive commitments; by Benson,

Kugler, Panasevich, and Hira (Chapter 11) to limit domestic violence; by Al-Marhubi (Chapter 3) to reduce inflation pressure; by Alcazar (Chapter 4) to stabilize monetary flows; by Arbetman, Kugler, and Organski (Chapter 10) to reduce population growth; and by Ponder (Chapter 9) to secure more funds from the federal government for local requirements than the average. In each case capable governments are more effective in implementing governmental goals than their weaker counterparts.

Another theme that runs through this volume is the importance of constraints that governments face in their efforts to increase revenues. Alcazar (Chapter 4) accurately indicates that governments cannot increase taxes at will because of "a struggle between the government and its constituency (the public)." This reinforces the notion that governments want to maximize resources but are constrained by the increasing political costs generated by opposition to such extraction within the selectorate (Organski et al. 1984; Arbetman 1995). Without the provision of public goods made possible by these resources, however, the economic development of a country will be hindered,[5] and this in turn will make it more difficult to provide stability. In contrast, a political environment in which uncertainty is minimized will foster economic activity and attract private investment. This is precisely the argument put forth by Feng and Chen (Chapter 5). In their view, macropolitical certainty increases as the variance in political capacity decreases. Investors react to such changes because "the lack of consistency" in government's capacity to rule the nation or to organize its society will create uncertainty in the market place.

A third theme underlying this volume is that state intervention can benefit society, but that positive intervention varies with levels of development. A successful active state is one that goes in and out of the market as required. It is difficult to assess a priori optimal levels of intervention, but we expect these to be nonlinear and correlated with levels of economic development. The state is clearly a key actor for countries in the developing stages, when governments have to provide the most public goods, and also convince the population of the direction of policy. As countries develop, the marginal cost of collecting additional funds increases, making it more difficult to manipulate economic output. For example, Leblang (Chapter 6) argues that a "politically capable government is able to provide a market conducive to economic growth." Further, the idea that effective governments are flexible is most clearly put forward by Snider (Chapter 12), who ascertains that "state capacity is more strongly associated with policy effectiveness when adjusted for the differential flexibility of governments to act." In this case flexibility refers to "the ability to implement domestic policy changes or to respond to shocks from the international environment." In sum, flexible governments can act, and they act to preserve power and to benefit society.

This volume will also show that in peacetime the state is an autonomous and responsive contributor to economic growth. Three chapters in particular highlight the idea that capable governments pursue the long-term growth of the state. First, Al-Marhubi (Chapter 3) demonstrates that efficient states minimize the fiscal deficit, even if this means less short-term monetary flexibility, and that efficient governments are able to control inflation by reducing the fiscal deficit. Second, Alcazar (Chapter 4) shows that highly capable governments do not make use of seigniorage to gather resources, but instead use tax revenues that are less regressive. Finally, Adji, Ahn, Holsey, and Willett (Chapter 7) argue that lower political capacity indicates less ability to extract resources, implying higher budget deficits and an increase in uncertainty. They further suggest that faced with low capacity, "a country is more likely to create new taxes or increase existing ones, thereby reducing the return on investments." In sum, from three different perspectives the contributors to this volume find that capable governments align their policies with sound macroeconomic criteria, while weak governments stress political survival. As expected, therefore, capable governments successfully implement policies that ensure growth, while weak, constrained governments cannot bear the political costs of painful macroeconomic adjustments and act as if they were predatory.

The fifth theme of this volume is that political effects are unevenly distributed. The presence of nonlinear patterns is also revealed in Arbetman, Kugler, and Organski's contribution on demography (Chapter 10), where they show that for developing economies political capacity is a main determinant of declines in fertility and mortality. Only in societies with high levels of development are the effects of political capacity overtaken by choice factors. Similar nonlinear structures are shown by Arbetman and Ghosh (Chapter 8) for black market premiums. Political capacity has a stronger effect at lower levels of capacity, where increases in capacity are most useful for advancing the government's economic policy. Paradoxically, it is precisely the weak governments, who could do so much, that have most difficulty in increasing capacity and are impotent to act.

The sixth theme of this volume opens a whole new arena of research by exploring political effects within rather than across nation states. Although tax effort models applied to local governments have been a traditional focus of the public finance literature (Break 1980), most political applications have been across nation states.[6] Ponder (Chapter 9) measures the relative political capacity of each state in the United States to assess levels of intergovernmental transfers. Here political capacity is used to reflect the administrative efficiency of states, whereas high *RPE* is "related to the employment of superior mechanisms for seeking grants-in-aid, project grants and carrying out programs which are required as a condition of receiving federal funds." Ponder (Chapter 9) finds that as *RPE* increases, the "transaction costs associated with securing federal funds decreases," challenging his own expectation that high levels of extraction would be counterproductive for state governments seeking to gain hold of unrestricted federal moneys.

Assessments of political capacity refer also to comparisons among countries faced with serious challenges. The question of who holds the power and how unified the government is can be answered by aggregate estimates of capabilities. Within the public choice tradition, Alcazar (Chapter 4) discusses confrontations between the government and the public, while Leblang (Chapter 6) addresses the government as the aggregation of individual interests where opposition comes from within the government. Snider (Chapter 12) posits the issue of problem solving indirectly by conceptualizing a government unable to be flexible in confronting policy changes. He states that as economies develop "proliferation of distributive commitments ... made to an expanding number of constituencies [it] undermines their ability to act flexibly in times of crisis." Benson, Kugler, Panasevich, and Hira (Chapter 11) pose the stability problem. Using domestic conflict as a dependent variable, they conceive of political capacity as a determinant of the level of domestic stability. They posit that for a conflict situation to arise, the opposition's resources have to match the government's, and concurrently the opposition has to reject the status quo. They then show that domestic conflict emerges from "a complex relationship between the level of political extraction a government has achieved and the increase or decrease in the extraction compared with the relative strength of the opposition." Again, capable governments are able to insure stability, while their weak counterparts are exposed to challenges.

The final part of this volume proposes means to extend the measures of political capacity. Edwards (Chapter 13) suggests that a measure of absolute political capacity can be constructed by empirically estimating the "economic frontier," since market forces at different levels of economic development differentially restrict the ability of decision-makers to extract resources from populations. Holsey and Cao (Chapter 14) provide an empirical approximation of these new estimates. Willett (Chapter 15) challenges us to look beyond current structures and explore the political elite's ability to increase political capacity. Finally, Kugler and Arbetman (Chapter 16) provide a guide to future research on political capacity.

This short journey through the analytical results supports the contention that politically capable governments that extract human and material resources to advance their goals are more successful than others in a number of political and economic dimensions. This work also supports the notion that autonomous governments primarily preserve stability and political continuity and also advance macroeconomic policies designed to attain long-term sustained economic growth. Furthermore, this investigation shows that political capacity varies with economic development and adapts in response to new challenges in the process of development.

In sum, government capacity is a critical, yet still widely overlooked, element of national development. We hope these contributions will enhance the current debate and encourage further study.

NOTES

1. In previous work, Relative Political Reach *(RPR)* is labeled as Relative Political Penetration *(RPP)*. Reach is used here because it captures more effectively than penetration the concept of mobilizing a population. Moreover, previous work does not always distinguish clearly between Relative Political Extraction *(RPE)*, which measures the government's ability to capture material resources, and Relative Political Capacity *(RPC)*, which is the aggregate of Extraction and Reach. We hope the consistent terminology adopted here will clarify these important distinctions.

2. Deutsch (1966), Rokkan (1970), Gurr (1970), and Cutright (1971) proposed social indicators that are now contained in the annual publication of the World Bank's Social Indicators of Development. These measures of political performance reflect societies' well-being with a large number of indexes and aggregates constructed from such measures. In general, these measures replicate behavior already monitored by *GDP* or alternative measures of economic performance. They do not distinguish political performance across levels of economic development.

3. An alternative measure of political performance is suggested by institutional comparisons, which are the concrete expressions of governmental authority and produce regulations for a society. Following in the tradition of Max Weber, Douglas North's pathbreaking work details at length the formal constraints imposed by institutions on the economic and political elites in society. Many ways to define institutions exist, but Nordingler (1981) seems to have captured their essence in his description of "those individuals who occupy offices that authorize them, and them alone to make and apply decisions that are *binding* [italicized for emphasis] on any and all segments of society," institutions are the regulatory arm of the state that has the authority to pursue and enforce governmental goals. However, different institutional configurations and changes in such configurations make it very difficult to use this concept to measure political capacity across time and space. Current discussion on this subject is informative but discursive. For example, Knight (1992, 107) explicitly argues that "we cannot see, feel, touch or even measure institutions; they are constructs of the human mind." If this is true, institutions are a poor basis for comparison since they are vaguely specified, and one must consider formal as well as informal and unspecified aspects of institutions.

4. Work on absolute measures of political capacity is reported in Organski et al (1984). The chapters by Edwards and by Holsey et al. overcome in part this limitation.

5. This point is one in which Willett and Edwards greatly contributed to the discussion.

6. An exception is Rouyer's (1987) application to India, where he focuses on the state's capacity to implement family planning programs.

PART ONE

The Concept of Political Capacity

1

Relative Political Capacity:
Political Extraction and Political Reach

Jacek Kugler, Marina Arbetman

THE CONCEPT OF POLITICAL CAPACITY

In the following pages we shall ask a number of questions about the relation between political capacity, domestic conflict, and patterns of socio-economic and demographic change that are instumental in the process of political development. The central proposition explored is that under certain conditions structural political change directly and significantly shapes patterns of development. Our aim is to develop an accurate measure of political structures. We contend that this work allows researchers for the first time to compare the performance of the political institutions of the United States with those of, say, China or Iran. If the structural answers that we formulate are persuasive, systematic political research that has not been possible thus far will at last be within reach. One would be able, for example, to make direct comparisons of strength between the great powers, and between them and the small nations. One could contrast directly the political performance of democracies and authoritarian regimes. One could assess across time the importance of political structures in the process of development. Since the validity of proposed political measures cannot be taken for granted, this book elaborates the impact of measures of political capacity using a number of empirical applications across a variety of topics central to political economy. The empirical implications drawn from these applications provide an extended laboratory test of the validity of the political measures. The reader can also concentrate on chapters that identify the theoretical and empirical differences in the political performance of political systems during the process of development, gaining unsuspected insights into the structure of politics throughout the development process.

Finally, the reader may choose to combine these two perspectives and build the basis for a much wider range of questions regarding the role that structural capacity of political systems plays in the overall process of socio-economic development.

There is little disagreement that political decisions play a critical role in the process of national development. Were this not the case, competition over the selection of the governing elite would be simply an interesting but inconsequential process. Therefore we take it for granted that politics is an important component of development. In order to understand the effects of politics, however, it is necessary to measure its presence and assess its structural effects as constraints faced by the governing elite. Unfortunately, the development of structural measures of politics lags far behind the development of aggregate theoretical structures or measures of policy (Jackman 1993). This volume begins to fill a large vacuum that has prevented the development of comparative analysis in the field of political economy in particular and development studies in general.

The aggregate performance of governments can be approximated as political capacity, or the ability of political systems to carry out the tasks chosen by the nation's government in the face of domestic and international groups with competing priorities. Recall that this conception can be broken down into two distinct but complementary components: political reach and political extraction.

Relative political reach (*RPR*) focuses on human resources and measures the scope and breadth of government influence on the population. Relative political extraction (*RPE*) centers on material resources and gauges the flexibility of the government in gathering revenues required to implement a desired policy. Political capacity is therefore the conjunction

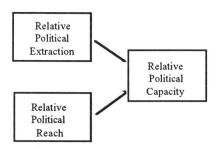

FIGURE 1.1 The Structure of Political Capacity

between reach and extraction.

The extractive element reflects most accurately efforts by the government to mobilize the material resources available in the society and use them in turn to advance its goals. The reach element reflects efforts by the government to mobilize human resources and increase the allocation of time and effort in pursuit of governmental goals. Governments increase their political capacity by expanding reach over the population or by extracting more from groups already mobilized. We anticipate that there is a relation between the level of economic development and the potential for increasing political capacity. In the initial stages of development it is far easier for the government to gain additional capacity by reaching relatively unorganized portions of a population. As economic development progresses, however, it is more effective to extract additional resources from already mobilized groups than to expand demands or incorporate new groups that are reluctant to support the government. The reason for this is political costs (Organski et al. 1984). In developing societies large portions of the population are not organized for political purposes, and governments can easily tap new resources by expanding the population base. In developed societies, on the other hand, governments have already mobilized most of the population, and these populations are organized into political groups around a multitude of interests that can effectively oppose further governmental mobilization. Thus, in developing societies governments can look outside a limited group of supporters to expand their resources, while in developed societies they have no choice but to reach into the pockets of already well-organized groups for additional revenues. The costs incurred by governments to gather additional resources and advance their policy goals are therefore conditioned by changing economic circumstances.

The study of political capacity implicitly assumes that political elites are autonomous actors who can implement their goals. Of course, elites enjoy differing degrees of political flexibility determined by peace or war conditions, and choose diverse means to achieve their aims. These key elements are elaborated below.

THE GOALS OF GOVERNMENT

Our conception of political capacity assumes that governmental elites are goal motivated. Across cultures political elites pursue multiple political goals that vary over time. However, without a primitive identification of overriding common goals, it is difficult to conceive of maximization. To solve a similar but less complex problem, economists assume, for simplicity's sake, that firms are profit maximizers, even though profit is clearly not the only objective of a firm. Likewise, although governments pursue a multitude of complex objectives, we suggest that the primary concern of government is to stay in power for as long as possible while maintaining stability, and the secondary goal is to sustain long-term economic growth. The political goals take precedence over economic objectives, but in the absence of direct challenges to the government's authority the economic goal is maximized (Downs 1975; Bueno de Mesquita and Siverson 1995). Like profit maximization among firms, political stability and sustained economic growth do not exhaust the objectives of governments. Indeed, during domestic and international upheavals—such as wars, revolutions, or national breakdowns—governing elites will disregard both growth and stability as they seek to gain political dominance for religious, ideological, or ethnic priorities. However, while these upheavals distort goal maximization in the short term, in the long run governments seek to ensure political permanence and stability and to insure these with sustained long-term growth. Figure 1.2 describes the relationship between these two goals of government.

The primary goal of political elites is to preserve power (Geddes 1991). Totalitarian and authoritarian governments have a strong hold on power, but face uncertain rules of succession. In such regimes confrontation over governance is rare, while conflict over political succession is frequent. Democracies, on the other hand, have common rules that allow the electorate to decide political succession by majority rule. Therefore, in democracies, confrontations over governance are frequent, but conflict over succession is rare. The subsidiary goal of political elites is sustained long-term economic growth (Londregan and Pool 1990). Governments attempt to maintain steady economic growth in order to minimize domestic instability and avoid the prospect of defeat in international war. In the absence of external threats, steady long-term economic growth ensures political stability (see Figure 1.2; Organski, Kugler, and Abdollahian 1995).

We will show that under stress political goals take precedence over economic priorities, as governments facing external or internal threats sacrifice economic stability to maintain their political standing. Further-

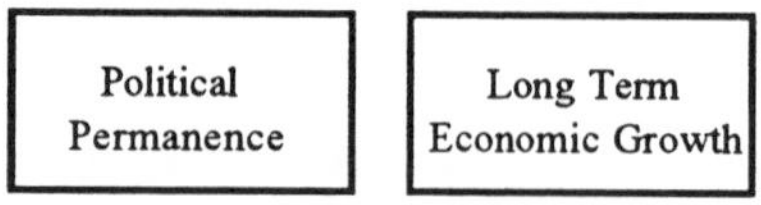

| Political Permanence | Long Term Economic Growth |

FIGURE 1.2 The Long Term Goals of Government

more, we will show that in total war extraction and reach are maximized with the unique goal of preserving the political structures, regardless of economic implications. Under stress, then, politics dominate economic considerations. While it is not as easy to demonstrate, we believe that political goals continue to take precedence in peacetime as well.

THE ACTIVE STATE

A fundamental deduction derived from public choice is that to maximize its goals the government must be an active agent who influences the national agenda, often becoming the arbitrator between governmental policy goals and those of individuals and firms. Clearly governments are not totally independent active agents, but are constrained by the mandate of key stakeholders.[1] This conception of government rejects the "laissez-faire" conception of the state, which views government actions as interfering with economic efficiency, implying that the least government is the best government. Concurrently, this conception of government also rejects the notion of a predatory state, which seeks to maximize its own interests at the expense of the wider interest of society. Instead, we conceive of the government as an active agent that advances an agenda of sustained growth and political stability independently from those of key financial stakeholders, religious or ethnic groups, and, in the case of democracies, the electorate. This conception of capable governments falls in the middle of the following continuum.[2]

To construct measures of political capacity we need to accept the premise that governments have autonomy to pursue their own goals separate from those of other groups in society. Economists commonly hold the notion that a capable government is also a minimal government. While we agree with Coase (1966) that political regulations increase transaction costs, thereby reducing economic efficiency, we reject the unwarranted but often made implication that market mechanisms will be most effective under minimal political regulations. Indeed, we are persuaded by the

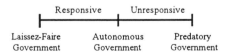

FIGURE 1.3 The Continuum of Government Autonomy

cumulative evidence that market exchanges cannot be sustained without enforcement of property rights, regulation of monetary transactions, provision of public services, regulation of the distribution of information, or preservation of domestic stability. By assuming such responsibilities governments undoubtedly increase transaction costs, but concurrently make the existence of markets possible, and as complexity increases they become cost efficient (Whitley 1986; North 1981, 1990). To execute the goals set by a political elite, the absolute size of government should not be thought of as small or large, but rather of the optimal size and scope to allow efficient market operations without crowding out competing private interests. In addition to market efficiency, governments have their own agenda that takes into account the mandate of selectorates and is constrained by the goals of the key stakeholders in society who decide on political permanence. But within these constraints, governmental choices regarding the function of the market are autonomous (Caporaso and Levine 1992).

This autonomous, goal-seeking conception of government is also in stark contrast to that of a predatory state. Political analysts, particularly those with an interest in world politics, usually assume anarchy and easily conceive of the state as a predatory actor. In this view a government is an anarchic institution bent on maximizing power to advance the selfish ends of the political elite (Holt and Turner 1966; Huntington 1968; Skocpol 1986; Levi 1988). (For an effective review of this tradition see Jackman 1993.) Predatory governments do not look beyond the short term and reach as far as is feasible into the population to extract as much of the available resources as possible, stopping only when the marginal costs of further extraction and additional reach are greater than the marginal gains.[3] Indeed, as Mancur Olson suggests, a predatory government would only be effective for a roving band that has no need to insure the continuity of support from its population base. However, when such a band settles down, the shadow of the future looms large and prior experience is recalled. The head of such a government ensures political permanence and stability with economic performance. Thus, a predatory government of a roving band would not list sustained growth among its highest priorities, and would disregard challenges from the selectorate for as long as it is incapable of defeating the leader by force. A government in a stationary group, however, cannot afford to be predatory and strive to achieve sustained growth to meet the expectations of the selectorate and avoid overt and covert opposition.

An extension of the predatory argument suggests that political elites strategically choose to extract resources beyond sustainable levels, not because the government is inefficient or has no alternative, as is the case in many developing countries, but to pursue a political strategy that hurts the incoming or prospective government. Following this logic, strategic predators encourage extensive public spending and generate large budget deficits with the explicit objective of constraining the options of successor governments and forcing them to face crowding-out effects (Cukierman et al. 1989). By such actions, strategic predator governments knowingly destroy the possibility of long-term sustained growth. Examples of such behavior in developing societies are frequently drawn from Latin American governments prior to the debt crisis, or, in developed societies, from the United States' willingness to incur military and social spending that eventually combine to create lasting budget deficits that constrain steady growth.

Although many instances of seemingly predatory action can be illustrated, we find such arguments theoretically unconvincing. Note that contrary to our assumption that capable governments will sustain growth and political stability, the policy choices of both predators and strategic predators, regardless of their political capacity, are detrimental to long-term growth and directly or indirectly induce political instability. We contend that cases of predatory governmental activity are overwhelmingly exemplars of governments with low political capacity. In developing nations, where predatory practice is most frequently noted, many governments act as if they were predatory not because they have excess capacity that can be strategically allocated to destroy the political future of competing governments, but simply to survive in the short term. In Argentina and Brazil, for example, the military governments responsible for the debt crises were replaced by democratic regimes, and in Mexico the PRI lost much of its political control because of the debt crisis. In developed societies, where strategic options for budget reallocations abound and predatory practices should be most frequent, such actions are in fact rare. Their occurrence indicates political weakness. In the United States, for example, Johnson's attempt to wage the Vietnam War on credit while building a social net failed and led to a Republican revival. Likewise, Reagan's desire to build up the military without raising revenues led to an economic downturn and limited the re-election prospects of his successor, Bush. If such actions were strategically calculated, they certainly seem to have backfired.

Far more persuasive from our perspective is the proposition that governments that appear to be or are predators or strategic predators are also incapable governments. Such governments are unable to persuade the population to pay for their priorities, and are forced to borrow in order to implement chosen policies. Indeed, this is precisely the definition of incapable government.

To summarize, a capable autonomous government is an autonomous source of regulations with the primary goals of long-term economic growth and political permanence while responding to the mandate of the selectorate and key interest groups.[4] But capable autonomous governments do not extract as much as possible because taxation and mobilization generate resistance. At the same time, capable autonomous governments do not extract as little as possible because without resources, implementation of goals is ineffective and chaos prevails (Alesina and Drazen 1991). Instead, capable autonomous governments limit their attempts to extract and reach to the levels required to implement their desired policies.

From the perspective of political capacity, political economy is the continuous interplay between the political rules that impose political choices, and the market forces that determine outcomes based strictly on price considerations. We postulate that there exists an optimal level of government capacity that maximizes economic effectiveness and political stability in societies, and that this level differs with economic productivity. However, these relations are only beginning to be understood, and our work is but a first step in defining these critical relations.

EMPIRICAL CHARACTERISTICS OF POLITICAL CAPACITY

Relative political capacity measures extraction of material resources and population reach. In this section we start with the specification of political extraction, followed by political reach.

Relative Political Extraction

Extraction deals with the transfer of resources from the population to the government to allow the government to advance its policy goals. We turn to the field of taxation to transform the theoretical concept of extraction into an operational measure. Organski and Kugler (1980: 74) explained why the fiscal system is representative of government capacity: "[T]axes are exact indicators of governmental presence. Few operations of governments depend so heavily on popular support—or on fear of punishment. Revenues affect directly the lives of most individuals in society, and few activities are avoided so vigorously. Without some form of tax revenue, there is no national unity, and no control. Failure to impose and extract taxes is one of the essential indicators of governmental incapacity to obtain and maintain support." In sum, governmental operation depends on resources extracted from the population. Without such resources governments do not and cannot govern (Levi 1988).

The concept of political extraction concerns political efficiency and not the size of the tax revenue. The impetus for the development of this concept comes from studies carried out by IMF economists concerned with the "tax effort" made by different societies. Their goal was to assess the ability of nations to qualify for and repay loans. To do so Jorgen Lotz and Elliott Morss (1971) proposed estimating the government's ability to extract resources based on economic production characteristics, and contrasting this potential extraction with the actual extraction, creating a "tax effort ratio." They argued that it was possible to produce an effective estimate of tax effort by considering: (1) the ability to export goods; (2) level of agricultural productivity, distinguishing between subsistence and market-oriented production; (3) the availability of minerals that could be produced for export; and (4) the overall economic output of a society. Raja Chelliah, Hanssel Baas, and Margaret Kelly (1974), and Roy Bahl (1971) added constraints and provided the first cross-sectional and cross-temporal estimates for developing nations, later extended by Alan Tait, W. Gratz, and B. Eichengreen (1979). In addition, differential allocation of expenditures should be directly considered for developed societies. When estimates were restricted to developing nations, it was far easier to assume that choices on the expenditure side—including welfare, national health, universal education beyond elementary school, and unemployment compensation—were limited. Therefore, only controls for the input side of revenues were needed. Once the estimates included developed nations, controls for the expenditure side were imperative because policy choices are not necessarily constrained by inadequate resources.

The extension of this research by political scientists was motivated by different concerns. Organski and Kugler (1980) argued that the tax effort approximated the unspecified political capacity that governments were making in pursuit of their own goals. Works by Kugler and Domke (1985), Organski et al. (1984), Rouyer (1987), Snider (1988) and Arbetman (1990, 1995) developed this notion further and tested its use empirically by accounting for fertility and mortality, the outcome of war, the evaluation of the debt crisis, the expropriation of multinational corporations, the recovery from war and the onset of domestic violence. (Arbetman [1990] carefully details the development of political effort estimates in the last two decades.)

Political extraction does not explicitly specify the political components that produce different levels of adjusted revenue across countries. Rather, it measures politics by the difference between the expected economic performance and the real performance of governments. Since this indirect process is controversial, before turning to the estimates used to evaluate political capacity we address two interrelated concerns. First, can cross-national work be done? Second, does political extraction measure political elements?

Richard Bird (1992) is perhaps the most prominent critic of cross-national tax effort measures and, by extension, political extraction measures. He contends that cross-national comparisons of tax structures cannot be performed because each society's tax practices are embedded in a long and unique cultural tradition. Moreover, he argues that the use of tax effort to rank countries as high or low performers is inadequate, and laments that "poor" performers are denied access to IMF resources that they desperately need. Faced with the stark choice between compliance or no loan, such nations are forced to impose taxes on populations that lead to the collapse of already weak economic systems. We believe that Bird's policy implication is correct, but his reasoning is not.

Bird is incorrect when he contends that cross-national differences make it impossible to compare revenue flows across societies. If Bird were correct, GNP comparisons would be as flawed as comparisons of tax levels. Total revenue, like total output, originates in different patterns of extraction and production, but despite these differences societies create strong coalitions to support efficient tax collection as well as competitive production patterns. Precisely for this reason, as indicated earlier, political extraction captures the pool of resources acquired by governments, and not the means by which such resources are gathered. Bird also argues that economic uses of tax effort are designed to measure the slack that governments have within their own societies to extract additional taxes. He accurately points out that governments that fail to meet the norms established by others at similar levels of development are asked to make a larger "effort." From a political perspective Bird is correct when he decries the practice of asking "weak" governments to extract more from populations before they can penetrate them effectively. When such governments extract more they expose themselves to instability. Bird intuitively understands that non-performers are not reserving resources; rather, they are unable to gather such resources to advance their goals.

Our second query refers to the ability of political extraction to account for politics (Cheibub 1994). Political extraction as well as political reach are measured by deviations from expected economic performance. Such deviations could be attributed to cultural differences, sociological differences or regime differences. They could also be the result of random noise. Kugler (1983) shows formally that one cannot dismiss these claims outright. By construction these aggregate measures of politics are attenuated. There is, however, substantial empirical support for the contention that politics dominates all other factors responsible for the generation of revenues after economic controls are applied. Organski and Kugler (1980), Organski et al. (1984), Snider (1988, 1990), Arbetman (1995), and Rouyer (1987), among others, provided a number of empirical tests of such measures in very diverse political contexts. The tests presented in this volume strongly indicate that political variations are captured by these indicators. Therefore, although we have not captured the political process explicitly, we are capturing the shadow of politics.

Let us now proceed with characteristics of the model and data used to calculate political extraction. For this book we put together a data set from 1960-1992 that incorporates control for both revenues and expenditures for all nations. For the first time, a common equation for political extraction is used for all members of the international system. Thus unlike previous efforts where the pooled cross sections were partial, these estimates are comprehensive and current.[5]

We extend previous work by IMF economists and our own research to account adequately for inter-country differences in the economic potential that provides the base for taxation. We have retained controls that balance our desire for simplicity and comprehensiveness. The level of productivity of the economy is accounted for by GNP per capita. It is expected to have a positive effect on levels of taxation, for the larger the economic output per capita the more a government can potentially extract. Exports and mineral production provide the government with easy money that can be accessed without exercising political pressure over the population. Health expenditures that disclose commitments by previous governments are used to control large differences in the public-private sector allocations. Concurrent controls for education and military expenditures add little to this element (Arbetman 1990). Finally, a variable distinguishing the most developed from the developing nations is added to enhance the differences between these sets of countries. Table 1.1 summarizes the base evaluations used in our construction of political extraction:

Where:

TAX RATIO	= total government revenues - total non-tax revenues - Social Security/GNP
TIME	= Year - 1959
GDP.CAP	= GDP per capita adjusted by terms of trade in constant 1985 dollars
MIN/GDP	= mineral production/GDP
EXPORT/GDP	= exports/GDP in current national currency
HEALTHEX	= health expenditures/GDP in current national currency
OECD	= dummy variable. OECD = 1, others = 0

Note that in Table 1.1 economic inputs account for slightly over one third of the variance in tax ratios and could easily be improved upon by including additional control variables (Cheibub 1994). Yet the aim is not to reduce variance, but to reduce variance caused by differences in economic priors. For example, adding defense expenditures as a control variable accounts for a substantial portion of the variance among large nations. The

TABLE 1.1 Estimate of Predicted Extraction, 1960—1992[6]

Variables	Coefficient	Std. Error	T-Stat
TAX RATIO			
TIME	.0008	.00013	6.7[**]
GDP.CAP	1.23e-06	4.28e-07	2.8[*]
MIN/GDP	.1390	.01231	11.3[**]
EXP/GDP	.0552	.00601	9.1[**]
HEALTHEX	1.531	.09549	16.0[**]
OECD	.0428	.00507	8.4[**]
Constant	.0831	.002821	29.4[**]
R²	.357		
Number of Observ.	3580		

[*] Significant at .005 percent level.
[**] Significant at .001 percent level.

All Data is in National Currency.

Sources: IMF. *Government Financial Statistics Yearbook,* Table VA, Line III; Table A, Line 5; Table A, Line 2; Consolidated General Government, Table B, Line 5. R. Summers and A. Heston. 1988. "A New Set of International Comparisons of Real Product and Price Level Estimates for 130 Countries, 1950-1985." *Review of Income and Wealth* 25:1-25. World Bank. *World Debt Tables.* Table on Use and Origin of Resources. IMF. *International Financial Yearbook.* National Accounts Table, Line 90c.

reason is that in recent decades societies like the United States, China, and Russia spend a far larger proportion of their resources on defense than societies like Japan, Belgium, or developing societies that do not face the threat of ideological or international conflict. From our perspective, however, the differences in military expenditures capture political decisions regarding security and hegemonic responsibility, and do not capture economic disparities. For this reason we do not include such controls. Likewise, adding controls for levels of domestic and international violence produces substantial improvements in fit. Such differences emerge because societies like Israel, Iraq, Iran, Cambodia, Peru, Chile, Vietnam, or the two Koreas make efforts to safeguard themselves against domestic or international threats. Again, this is an aspect of the political capacity to mobilize that we wish to capture. Indeed, controlling out such differences would capture portions of political effort and would diminish the value of the overall index.

In past work Organski and Kugler (1980) used two different controls to calculate political extraction. One was based on output per capita and was deemed more effective in societies where the marketplace is already well-instituted. The second used agricultural production controls, a more sensitive control in societies where subsistence economy is widespread.[7] Over time, perhaps because of global development or improvements in reliability of the basic data, these two indicators have converged.[8] The measure of political extraction is constructed as the following ratio:

$$Relative\ Political\ Extraction\ =\ \frac{Actual\ Extraction_{ti}}{Predicted\ Extraction_{t}}.$$

This measure contrasts the performance of societies at similar levels of development. As such, an index of one indicates that the society extracts the mean or average from its population given the resource base. High capacity is indexed by ratios above one, and low capacity is reflected by indexes of less than one. A society whose political extraction is 2 reflects a political performance twice that of the average society in that economic pool, while an index of 0.5 indicates a society whose political performance is half that of the average society. Note that such inferences cannot be made across levels of economic productivity, since this is a relative and not an absolute measure of political performance. Therefore, the meaningful comparisons are across similar levels of development.

General characteristics of political behavior emerge in Figure 1.4, which considers the performance of countries at different levels of economic performance.

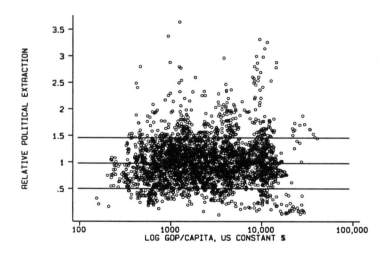

FIGURE 1.4 Cross Section *RPE* and *GDP* per Capita US Constant Dollars, 1960—1990

By construction, the mean performance of societies in the sample is very close to the average 1.0 theoretically anticipated, but there is an enormous variation in the political capacity of societies. The weakest societies extract 12 percent of what is normal for their group, while the strongest societies manage to extract more than 350 percent of what is expected from them. The highest outliers—such as North Vietnam or Israel—are usually associated with domestic or international conflict. Note that most nations fall somewhere between 50 and 150 percent of the expected average. Extreme efforts are seldom maintained over more than a decade, presumably because the government is not only taxing from current product but is using some of society's wealth to fund its efforts.

On the low side, very weak societies—such as Nepal—extract a fraction of the available product, suggesting that the government captures little and can deliver little in return. In general, the performance of Latin American societies is low relative to all other nations. The performance of Mexico, for example (detailed in Figure 1.7), is typical and falls consistently below average. We believe that the relatively low political performance of Latin American societies in the period 1960-1990 may have contributed to the economic slowdown and rise in international debt in the region far more than domestic endowment or international intervention.

Steps to refine the measure of political extraction over the last three decades have concentrated on a more effective specification of the economic controls (Kugler 1983; Arbetman 1990; Snider 1996; Tait et al. 1979). This process is extended in the latter chapters of this book. Edwards (Chapter 13) and Holsey and Cao (Chapter 14) propose ways of approaching an absolute measure of political extraction by disintegrating the random elements from the systematic components embedded in the residual term, and setting an economic frontier from which derivations can be estimated. If such efforts succeed, nations at all levels of economic development could be compared directly, and the relative measures presented here would be dramatically improved. Further extensions include a direct specification of the political components that constitute political extraction, but this infant work is the task of future research.

Relative Political Reach

The government's incapacity to reach human resources is captured by the extent the unofficial or black market labor force contributes to the productivity of the overall society. The general concept of unofficial markets refers to any activity performed outside the control of the government by individuals who may otherwise observe the law. We concentrate on black market activity of the labor force because it provides a good indicator of how much human activity escapes government scrutiny. The unofficial labor force includes all functions in the economic sphere where the objective of individual actors is to evade taxes and other governmental regulations.

The number of black market activities performed outside the channels established by the state in its role as regulator of citizens' actions is vast. Such activities include economic transactions that are clearly illegal, such as drug trafficking, fraudulent labor practices, and criminal activity; semi-legal activities, such as household work, part-time activities not reported for tax purposes; and legal activities, such as charity work. Clearly, not all unofficial activities that go unregistered are defined in monetary terms. Barter transactions embody aggregate value but are difficult to evaluate and register in the national accounts (Smith 1986). Conceptually, the distinction between illegal, unregistered, or legal activity is relatively clear, but empirically the distinction is blurred. We assume that the bulk of unregistered activity is of the illegal variety and affects the government's ability to govern.

Why do people engage in the unofficial economy? There are different motives. Some individuals enter the black market to increase their total income by avoiding taxes; others do so as a result of trading in illegal products, such as drugs, that cannot be sold otherwise. In other cases, societal conditions make the decision to "go underground" acceptable, as is the case of the Mafia in Italy, foreign currency dealers in Israel, and smugglers in Zaire (Laughlin 1981). However, the willingness of individuals to risk legal reprisals for their actions indicates the government's inefficiency in coopting the population and implementing its goals. When a government is able to enforce laws that impose greater costs on individuals than the benefits they can obtain from underground activities, black market activities cease.

All governments have the right to enforce laws by applying financial penalties, including monetary sanctions or fines, or by imposing prison sentences. In order to advance governmental goals that involve distributing resources among the population, political elites must first be able to levy them. Yet the more prevalent underground activities are, the less control governments have over the population's activities and the attached monetary resources produced. Consequently, the bigger the informal sector, the weaker the government.

The unofficial economy has economic and social consequences. Public revenue losses, from direct tax, social security contributions, and health insurance, are the most important short-term economic consequences. The fewer resources available to the state, the less it is able to deliver in public services. Another consequence refers to the structure of the national output, which will differ according to the opportunities of the black market. An unofficial economy makes possible the survival of factories with very low productivity, when excess demand is high enough to permit the existence of unregistered producers of goods and services (Contini 1982).[9] Indeed, extensive activities in the black market are carried out only if certain institutional and technological conditions are present. Skolka (1987) argues that in a black market the required technology cannot be too sophisticated, since "off the books" producers cannot rely on the insurance, qualified service, or maintenance that sophisticated technology requires. All these services are very expensive outside formal channels. Black market producers cannot appeal to the courts and must rely on the word of their partners or resort to vendettas to settle their disputes. For an unofficial economy to exist, the institutional framework has to be permissible, the risk of fines must be low and profits high. All these conditions indicate a government that is not capable of imposing its own rules. In sum, informal economic transactions that are untaxed, unmeasured, and unregulated reflect the inability of governments to persuade populations to function under the official umbrella (Smith 1986).

Two standard approaches are available to measure the informal economy. First, one can trace the amount of money in the black market and compare it to the overall product.[10] Second, one can measure the relative number of individuals who work outside official channels. Since our intent is to capture the human resources that defy government reach, the second approach is most appropriate.

Measuring human resources in the informal sector is not straightforward. Human resources are important not only because individuals produce most of the resources in society, but also because populations can be mobilized to support policy goals. Yet, to mobilize the population, the government has to be able to reach individuals in society first.

As in the case of *RPE*, levels of economic development also have an impact on the government's ability to reach populations. In the early stages of development, it is difficult to reach the population. In subsistence agricultural economies it is difficult to separate individuals from the land, or gain a portion of the resources produced for self consumption. Of the limited resources produced in such societies, most are destined for immediate consumption, not for trade. In advanced stages of development, more of the population has been reached, but other organized clusters, such as trade unions or business groups, prevent governments from fully reaching such populations. To capture the effects of unreported subsistence production, one can gauge the size of the informal labor market by establishing a labor profile under conditions where the informal sector is non-existent.[11] Using this information as a base, one can calculate the inconsistencies between reported product and the estimated results to infer the size of the unofficial economy (Fua 1976; Gaetani D'Aragona

1981; Pettenati 1979; Tokman 1982).[12] As in the case of political extraction, the main limitation is that this approach only indirectly measures the government's reach over the population.

From the perspective of political reach, a good approximation of the number of people who refuse to abide by government regulations can be calculated directly from labor statistics. Assuming that countries with similar levels of development have equivalent active population profiles, Pettenati (1979) proposes a more direct way to gauge the size of the informal sector. He states that the difference between the average proportion of active population in countries with similar levels of development and the actual active population in a given country can be attributed to the informal labor sector. Simply stated, given an average active population required to produce similar levels of product, the unexplained differences between the actual active population among similar economic structures are due to differences in the labor supply, rather than differences in output. Therefore, differences in the size of the active labor force in countries at equivalent levels of development reflect the effects of black market economies.

Pettenati proposes a simple index to estimate the share of full-time or part-time employment not officially recorded. In the European context this index was originally calculated using the informal labor sector as a proxy for unemployment, and comparing each individual OECD country's activity rate for a specific year to the average activity rate for all the OECD countries for the same year. Pettenati argues that this index would capture black market activity and confirms his suspicions with several local surveys.[13] Using similar assumptions, we calculated a simple index to determine the share of full-time or part-time employment that is not officially recorded. To avoid negative numbers and bind the index to zero, the index of political reach is calculated as follows:[14]

$$\textit{Relative Political Reach} \ = \ \frac{\textit{Actual Activity Rate}_{ti}}{\textit{Average Activity Rate}_t}.$$

where Activity Rate is the crude activity participation rate reflected by the active population above the specific minimum legal age, including all officially recorded sectors of the economy adjusted for levels of unemployment. The average activity rate is calculated for five different average levels of development: developed, developing, underdeveloped, historically planned economies, and oil exporting countries. These averages are computed across time and across countries. An *RPR* above one means that the conditions for disguised unemployment do not exist, because there is an excess demand for labor compared to other countries with a similar level of development. When the index is less than one, an excess labor

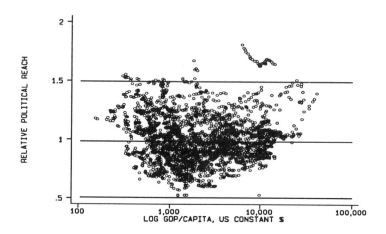

FIGURE 1.5 Cross-section of *RPR* and *GDP* per capita in U.S. Constant Dollars, 1960—1990

supply exists and concealed labor is expected. Figure 1.5 provides a summary of the characteristic distribution of *RPR* for all countries.

The statistics reported in Figure 1.5 show two cross sections. *RPR* refers to all nations except those in the former components of the Soviet Union. Like *RPE*, the extremely high numbers in *RPR* are associated with mobilization during conflict, while slightly less high numbers are often related to swift changes in policy. For example, upward movements in *RPR* were recorded in West Germany during the 1960s, when major reforms in the welfare state took place, and in Mozambique during the de-colonization process of the 1970s. The lowest *RPR* levels are present in countries in times when the population is excluded or ignored by the political process. For example, low levels of *RPR* are present in Algeria, Jordan, or Egypt before 1980.

A contrast between the distribution of *RPR* (Figure 1.5) and *RPE* (Figure 1.4) shows that *RPR* is less volatile. Indeed, the maximum level of *RPR* is slightly above 1.80, while for *RPE* the maximum is close to 3.5. As expected, the very poor nations can reach high levels of *RPR*, but show relatively low levels of *RPE*. Moreover, few developed societies fall below the average in reach, while a large number under-perform in extraction.

The level of *RPR* is not a function of regime type. In the case of

Argentina, for example, President Illia's democratic government in the 1960s attained high levels of reach (*RPR* = 1.2). This trend was reversed in 1966 after a military coup headed by General Ongania. The opposite occurred in Chile, where the Allende government had limited and declining reach, while the military ruler Pinochet reversed this trend and achieved high levels of reach. On the other hand, Egypt's *RPR* remained below average after the death of Nasser in 1970 despite a smooth constitutional transition by Vice President Sadat, and when Sadat was assassinated *RPR* was not dramatically altered by the peaceful transfer of power to Mubarak. The type and continuity of a political system and its economic stability are not necessarily related. Until 1985 Costa Rica, a democratic country, had slightly below average *RPR*, albeit with an upward trend. Like democracies and governments in transition, authoritarian governments have also shown a wide variety of patterns in *RPR*. For example, the South African government effectively coopted the population before 1970, but with the exception of the Soweto uprisings in 1976 the country's *RPR* has been below average. This case shows *RPR* changing over time under an authoritarian regime whose goals were eroding. Since the democratic election of President Mandela, South Africa has recovered *RPR* but has not yet reached the levels prior to 1970.

In general, authoritarian regimes seem to perform at average levels. In the Philippines, President Marcos, who gained power in 1966, maintained below average *RPR* throughout his time in office. The 1973 referendum that imposed martial law was associated with the lowest level of *RPR* in the thirty-year period analyzed. Perhaps it was because of this weakness that the democratic revolution led by Corazon Aquino in 1986 was so successful and bloodless. Finally, the Indonesian federation under President Sukarno from 1959 to 1965 was below average by *RPR* standards. When General Suharto took power in 1965 political reach did not initially increase, but in the last decade *RPR* levels in Indonesia have risen to above-average levels. (*RPE* also increased in the 1970s, around the time that oil was found). Indonesia today is a politically capable country, with both indicators of political capacity above average.

RPR is not related to *RPE*, and it does not follow that high levels of reach are related to high levels of economic performance. Indeed, authoritarian-military governments are most prone to a high dislocation between economic performance and mobilization of populations. For example, between 1968 and 1973, frequently labeled the "miracle" years, Brazil experienced economic growth, but its levels of *RPR* remained below average. Obviously, the decision not to "divide the cake before it rises" (Dillon Soares 1986, 291) failed to attract popular support. Authoritarian governments are sometimes able to reach their populations. China's *RPE* has been above average since 1960, except for the period of the Cultural

Revolution, when levels of **RPR** decreased dramatically. With economic mobilization under Deng's regime **RPR** has been on the rise.

The relation between reach and economic development, regime type and political extraction is complex. The mobilization of populations follows from the ability of governments to persuade or coerce their subjects into compliance with established goals. Some nations, such as China, manage to reach populations despite low levels of economic performance, while others, including Brazil, fail to mobilize populations despite economic success. A look at the aggregate relation between political capacity indicators and levels of growth and size will provide a sense of the relatively unexplored interrelation between these factors.

Contrasting Reach With Extraction

The performance of reach and extraction vary with the size of nations. Figure 1.6 shows that societies with small populations vary dramatically in their ability to extract, and to a lesser degree in their ability to reach populations.

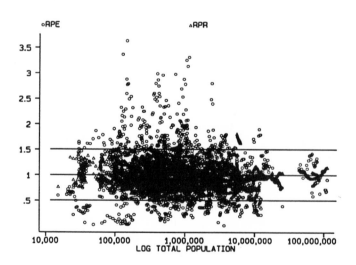

Figure 1.6 Distribution of *RPE* and *RPR* Given Total Population

Figure 1.6 also shows that societies with the largest total populations fall much closer to average performance. Thus China, India, and Indonesia do not show the volatility associated with smaller nations in the process of development. Perhaps a minimum level of governmental organization is required to maintain political continuity in a country of such size.

A number of specific cases were chosen to illustrate differences in performance. Consider first the case of Mexico.

Figure 1.7 shows that Mexico has the characteristic trajectory found in Latin America; that is, it underperforms both in terms of reach and extraction. Note also that the fluctuations in extraction are closely related to crisis periods. In the post-1970 period the oil boom is responsible for the *RPE* rise, only to collapse before the strong political intervention by President Salinas. Extensions of this data to the present would no doubt show a second major decline reflecting the crisis conditions under President Zedillo's government.

Consider now the case of South Africa. Figure 1.8 shows that the white South African government was able to capture resources, but slowly lost its grip over the population. The high levels of extraction maintained even during crisis suggest that resources were available. For this reason the transition to Mandela's government may have been stable, as the new government could fund many of its new priorities.

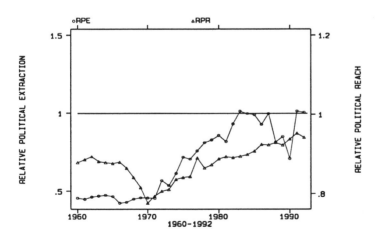

Figure 1.7 Political Capacity of Mexico—1960-1992

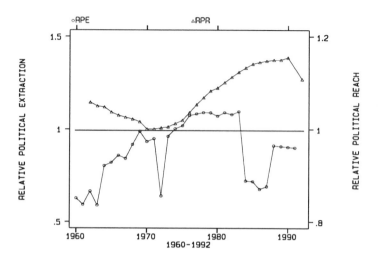

Figure 1.8 Political Capacity of South Africa: 1960—1992

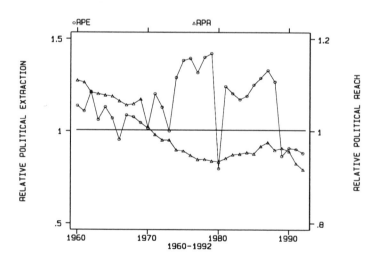

Figure 1.9 Political Capacity of China, 1960—1992

China's summary shows the volatility of the political system in that society. Figure 1.9 indicates that China's government succeeded more than most in mobilizing its population, but has a mixed record on extraction. The effects of the Cultural Revolution are apparent, as is the movement towards privatization. This distinct pattern indicates that while the government has substantial control over human resources, its ability to extract revenues to advance policy goals is limited.

Finally, consider the case of India. Figure 1.10 shows that India's government in 1960 was losing support from the population. Extractive ability remained high despite wide fluctuations until the late 1980s, when India started a pronounced and continuous political decline, halted only after 1989. The economic transformation that India is now experimenting with is perhaps a reaction to the previous government's inability to maintain its hold over society.

These illustrations provide a sense of the variability in *RPE* and *RPR* measures, which are also associated with major political fluctuations. More sensitive evaluations require the controlled analysis found in this volume.

ALTERNATE CONCEPTUALIZATIONS AND USES OF POLITICAL CAPACITY

At this point it is appropriate to ask how the two components of relative political capacity, *RPE* and *RPR*, interact, and how they can be combined. Organski and Kugler (1980) conceived of political capacity as requiring both human and material resources. They argued that reach was the stronger variable during the early stages of development, as governments first mobilized populations and then extracted resources from the organized groups. Because for many years extraction was the only component measured, the ability of governments to extract resources became a surrogate for the whole concept. Once Arbetman (1990) developed measures for reach, however, the full conception of political capacity could be estimated. As expected, replications of previous work using both variables improved previous results (see Arbetman, Kugler, and Organski, Chapter 10).

Political capacity is a complex variable. To capture the effects of political reach and extraction we propose two basic constructs. The first simply measures the independent linear effects of *RPR* and *RPE* by incorporating both into the explanatory side of the equation. The second captures in addition the nonlinear interaction between reach and extraction. These nonlinear effects can be captured for each independent variable (e.g., RPE^2 or RPR^2), or for the combined *RPC* measure (e.g., $[RPC = \alpha_o + \alpha_1 RPE + \alpha_2 RPR + \alpha_3 (RPR \times RPE)]$), implying that political development varies

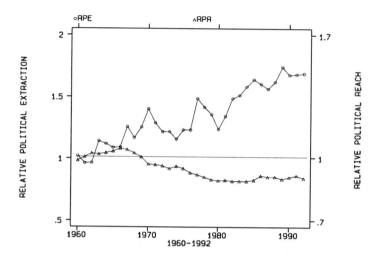

Figure 1.10 Political Capacity of India: 1960—1992

along levels of economic development or other independent variables (e.g., *RPC*GDP* or *RPR*GDP*). Finally, the standard deviation in *RPC* can capture the variation in political performance over time. These formulations allow for a full exploration of the effects of each political component by conceiving of independent as well as interactive components. None has been adopted as a final standard.

Applications in this book use various aspects of political capacity in their analysis. *RPE* is used in most empirical economic applications because of the direct interpretation of extraction on resource availability (Al-Marhubi, Chapter 3; Leblang, Chapter 6; Snider, Chapter 12; Ponder, Chapter 9; and Kugler, Benson, Panasevich, and Hira, Chapter 11). Other contributions use both variables (Alcazar, Chapter 4; Adji, Ahn, Holsey, and Willett, Chapter 7; Arbetman and Ghosh, Chapter 8; Arbetman, Kugler, and Organski, Chapter 10), and report that such inclusions improve results. Finally, the variance in *RPE* is successfully used to capture political uncertainty (Feng and Chen, Chapter 5).

Simple versions prove useful. Kugler, Benson, Panasevich, and Hira (Chapter 11) use *RPE* and change in *RPE* to explain levels of domestic violence. Alcazar (Chapter 4) establishes that the effects of *RPR* are stronger than *RPE* on seigniorage. Alcazar finds, as expected, that when she divides the sample between developed and developing countries, both measures perform better in the former. Arbetman and Ghosh (Chapter 8) show that *RPR* has a stronger effect than *RPE* on premiums, and that *RPE* ceases to be significant at high levels of development. Feng and Chen (Chapter 5) use *RPE* standard deviations from the mean for each country to measure changes in political stability, and show that private investments are directly affected by such variations. However, nonlinear versions reflecting political interactions prevail. Al-Marhubi (Chapter 3) justifies the need for a quadratic *RPE* model, since "beyond some threshold increases in *RPE* can be detrimental to the economy's performance because of incentives that arise from rent seeking, corruption, and other wasteful activities." The empirical evidence supports this specification. Leblang (Chapter 6) posits that as countries develop, *RPE* contributes less to economic growth, and reflects this insight by applying a curvilinear model (expressed as a function of *GDP — RPE*GDP* and *RPE*GDP²*) to growth. Again, in poor countries high *RPE* has a stronger effect on growth than in more developed countries. Likewise, Snider (Chapter 12) posits nonlinear relations to explain economic growth. To reflect such patterns he divides the sample into four different levels. His specification of *RPE* includes *RPE*, inverse *RPE*, percentage change *RPE*, and log *RPE²*. While the results are less straightforward for less developed countries than for advanced developing countries, he finds that the coefficients are larger for developed than for less developed countries. These results are somewhat unexpected, since other works suggest that the effects of political capacity are attenuated by economic and political development. Finally, Ponder (Chapter 9) uses a nonlinear version of *RPE* constrained by the relative level of economic development to show how governmental transfers are affected across the United States.

Two chapters apply the interactive version of $[RPC = \alpha_o + \alpha_1 RPE + \alpha_2 RPR + \alpha_3(RPR \times RPE)]$). Adji, Ahn, Holsey, and Willett (Chapter 7) find that *RPE* and *RPR* have similar effects on nominal foreign direct investment, but the interactive term is not significant and loses power when applied to real investments. Lastly, Arbetman, Kugler, and Organski (Chapter 10) find that as countries develop economically the marginal effects of *RPE* and *RPR* on births decrease. In the case of births, *RPE* and *RPR* have similar coefficients at low levels of economic development, but *RPR* becomes stronger than *RPE* as countries develop. Both are less important when nations achieve high economic output.

The empirical results of all these chapters give us a hint of the potential of political capacity. The two dimensions, extraction and reach, are important in the model specification. Results also indicate that it is fruitful to investigate nonlinear relations between political and economic variables. These results further suggest that the real world is, as expected, quite complex and dynamic.

GOALS OF GOVERNMENT AND VARIATIONS
IN POLITICAL CAPACITY

It has been argued that political considerations are primary and supersede economic priorities. Here we demonstrate that under the stress of war this relation is clear. Under crisis conditions, all governments mobilize resources, and the most capable reach limits that cannot be approximated in peacetime. In each case they abandon economic growth to preserve political continuity and insure stability. The effects of serious challenges to governmental continuity are shown in Table 1.2, which traces the variations in political extraction for a substantial cross section of governments waging total war at different levels of economic development.[15]

Consider first the main developed societies. Contrary to expectations, Germany was not the most capable government in the early stages of World War II; rather, Britain earned this rank. This difference, despite a smaller economic base, produced the unexpected stalemate during the 1940 Battle of Britain. Furthermore, in relative terms Japan extracted far more than any other belligerent nation from its population base in its losing effort during 1943-1945. The United States also mobilized resources, but attained relatively low levels of political extraction.

Among developed societies, note first that the unexpected stalemate between Russia, an established Western power, and Japan during the 1904-1905 bilateral war can be accounted for by the high level of political extraction attained by Japan. It is perhaps for this reason that the Czar of Russia was forced to face the unpleasant surprise that this mere "distraction" from domestic purposes turned into a international debacle of major proportions. Finally, during the long domestic struggle over political integration, North Vietnam managed to extract far more from a smaller resource base than did South Vietnam, which received massive aid from the United States. Thus, political disparity and not military might account for the unexpected outcome of the Vietnam War.

It is important to note that among developing nations war can produce major variations in political capacity. In fact, the overall highest one-year performance recorded was attained by Germany during the last year of World War I, and the second highest was that of Japan at a similar stage of World War II. In general, as countries develop, the degree of potential mobilization diminishes simply because resources have already been tapped by previous governments. To this degree developing societies are more "flexible" than developed societies. Yet wide variations in perfor-

Table 1.2 Relative Political Extraction During Total War

War	Year	Japan AUT/TOT	Russia AUT/TOT	Germany AUT/TOT	UK (DEMO)	France (DEMO)	Italy	USA** (DEMO)	North Vietnam TOT	South Vietnam AUT
Russo-Japanese	1904	2.36	.83							
	1905	**4.40**	**1.06**							
WWI	1913	.90	.61	.55	.50	.68	.65	.31		
	1914	.87	.96	2.13	1.95	1.30	.67	.30		
	1915	.84	**2.13**	5.84	3.10	2.00	.71	.33		
	1916	.73	1.61	5.24	**4.89**	**3.26**	1.14	.36		
	1917	.92	n.a.	**5.92**	3.86	2.06	1.28	1.33		
	1918	.88	*	4.69	3.16	3.15	**1.51**	**2.51**		
WWII	1939	1.98	1.46	1.55	1.43	1.18	.73	.63		
	1940	2.18	1.33	2.05	2.30	**2.00**	1.15	.63		
	1941	2.51	1.55	2.43	2.31	n.a.*	.90	.84		
	1942	2.95	1.82	2.58	**2.58**	n.a.*	**1.31**	1.41		
	1943	4.09	1.62	**2.61**	2.38	n.a.*	.84	**2.51**		
	1944	**5.43**	1.69	2.47	2.46	n.a.*	.27*	2.24		
	1945	n.a.	**1.85**	n.a.	2.34	n.a.*	.39*	1.95		
Vietnam	1960								4.40	.94
	1967								**4.70**	.91
	1973								4.16	.80
	1979								4.20	.80

* Nation surrendered
** Data reflect U.S. government's fiscal years (move up half a year) N.A. = not ascertained.

mance over time cannot simply be explained by development levels. For example, France mobilized effectively for World War I, but failed to replicate the effort during World War II. Conversely, Russia could not generate its many resources under the Czars, but was a capable contender under Stalin's communist rule. Indeed, political capacity captures not only the systematic constraints facing governments, but also the performance of individual governments given the constraints they face.

Finally, Table 1.2 shows that under extreme stress almost all governments exceed average performance. As one would anticipate, in response to the realization that survival is at stake governments try to gather as many resources as possible to avoid occupation and dismantlement (Organski and Kugler 1980; Kugler and Domke 1985; Kugler and Arbetman 1989). While major variations in capacity are apparent, the reasons for these disparities are not. It is common in the field to associate performance with regime type. However, note that in Table 1.2 democracies,[16] including the United Kingdom, France, and the United States; totalitarian regimes, including North Vietnam as well as Japan, Germany, the Soviet Union, and Italy during World War II; and various shades of authoritarian regimes,[17] such as Japan and Germany before World War II, Russia, and South Vietnam, sometimes perform well and sometimes do not. Indeed, authoritarian Germany, the top performer in the set, outperforms democratic Britain in World War I, but totalitarian Germany performs worse than democratic Britain at the outset of World War II, resulting in the reversal during the Battle of Britain. Once totalitarian Germany is defeated the scale changes once more. We already noted the up and down pattern in democratic France, and the variation in the performance of authoritarian Russia and the totalitarian Soviet Union. Finally, totalitarian North Vietnam clearly outperforms authoritarian South Vietnam. In sum, regime type is a poor guide to political performance.

Under the stress of total war it is difficult to conceive that political elites sometimes choose failure, even when such outcomes mean not only their removal from government but also banishment or death for the leaders. Consequently, this overview of nations under stress shows that political capacity does not measure "good" states, but measures politically capable states that can perform under duress. Perhaps testing nations under stress is inappropriate; still, one is drawn to the conclusion that differences in governmental performance are not related to regime type, but rather to the quality of government.

HOW GOVERNMENTS GENERATE POLITICAL CAPACITY

The means governments use to increase political capacity are not reflected directly by current measures of extraction and penetration, but are important in the study of political capacity. Governments can reach their populations and extract material resources by persuasion or coercion. By persuasion, political elites earn trust and ease eventual implementation of desired policies. For this reason we anticipate that persuasion is the cost-effective political alternative to coercion. We agree with Jackman (1993), who elaborated the drawbacks faced by political elites who rely on coercion to prop up a government. Governments that fail to persuade the population to abide by the law lose not only resources, but political influence as well. In general, individuals will enjoy the public goods provided by government, but will attempt to avoid paying the costs of such services. For example, the black market economies and limited tax revenues in Russia since 1991 have drained that society of much needed resources and limit the government's ability to implement new economic policies. A major reason for the slow pace of economic reform is the loss of popular trust. Yeltsin's government failed to persuade the population of the need to make further sacrifices. Persuasion, then, relies on the population's adherence to the rules, and its willingness to pay taxes and abide by the government's policy choices.

Coercive extraction of resources, like deterrence, relies on fear. Unlike accommodation, which is associated with persuasion and mutual trust, governments base coercion on the expectation of non-compliance with goals advanced by the state (Kugler and Werner 1994). In political interactions coercion and persuasion are always present, but heavy reliance on coercion indicates that domestic groups do not support governmental goals and actively avoid paying to support them. Again, like deterrence, coercion is costly, but political compliance can be enhanced by the fear of punishment. Yet coercive regimes are not necessarily stable. Indeed, coercion, so effective under Stalin, was less effective under Brezhnev and may have contributed to the Soviet Union's decline in capacity. Over the long term, as the costs associated with coercion increase, political effectiveness declines, while with persuasion the levels of political effectiveness achieved can be maintained or increased. This may account for the resiliency of democratic systems, where non-coercive policies and changes of government are common.

The debate as to whether persuasion and coercion are the most useful means available to governments that wish to reach and extract resources from their populations is raised but not resolved. Hints and insights suggest that persuasion has been superior, but such statements do not amount to findings. The measures of political capacity presented in this work do not explicitly include ways to distinguish between coercion and persuasion, and the exploration of such means remains an open field.

LIMITATIONS OF RELATIVE INDEXING

Estimates of extraction and reach reflect the relative performance of governments, but must be used in conjunction with other considerations appropriate for each research question. For example, the extension of primary education is a common goal in most societies, yet only a fraction of the population of the developing world is literate, and an even smaller proportion has completed mandatory levels of primary or secondary education. Thus, one expects that in developing nations an increase in reach and extraction will substantially increase compliance with levels of education. However, in the developed world, where literacy is almost universal and secondary education is commonly completed, variations in the capacity of governments will have minimal impact on education. The relative performance of governments across levels of economic development, therefore, tells little about specific policy performance.

The general insight derived from this example is that in developing societies existing regulation is the central concern, while in economically developed countries the concern shifts to the degree of regulation. Consider the rise and fall of Japan's MITI. In the post-World War II period MITI helped develop Japan's economy through subsidies and by targeting economic sectors. This agency is routinely credited with transforming Japan from a developing to a leading developed society. Today MITI's interventions, by contrast, are far more controversial. For example, MITI's selection of a particular computer chip (486) that led to a temporary advantage produced a market gloat and resulted in Japan's retrenchment and loss of technical lead within a year. In complex market economies it is very difficult to assure that state intervention is useful, and the possibility of overextension of governmental regulation looms large, but in simpler market economies state intervention appears far more useful.

It should be clear, however, that while regulations in developed societies are at issue, in such societies regulations are already far more comprehensive and intrusive than in developing countries. Economic complexity multiplies regulation; regulation of electronic monetary transactions, investment plans, property rights, patents, or information distribution all increase with the complexity of the economy.[18] In general, economic and political elements are related along non-linear patterns that correspond with levels of economic development, and controls are required to capture political variance with relative measures of political capacity. This volume starts to explore these interactions.

NOTES

1. This statement runs contrary to classic economic perspective and modernization theories, which posit that the individual, especially the entrepreneur, is the key to fostering innovation. Once the process of modernization is triggered, positive effects will soon follow. Moreover, some authors hold that pre-industrial development in Europe is inversely related to government participation, because governments would use resources meant for private investment in an inefficient manner (Gerschenkron 1966).

2. Concern with democratic regimes has driven much of the literature in the political arena. This tradition leans heavily toward a mandate view of government, associating political capacity with the efficient aggregation and reflection of individual voter preferences. The central question posed is whether elites effectively represent the public interest, provide full information on voters' choices to decision makers, and create institutions that permit such political elites to use this information to make policy choices (Campbell, Converse, Miller and Stokes 1960; Verba, Nye, and Petrocik 1972; Florina 1981; Segura and Kuklinski 1995). Within this literature the autonomy of a government is of small concern, and capacity indicates the extent to which the state represents the aggregation of individual or private interests where the government plays a subsidiary role to the wishes of an electorate. This is not consistent with our view of government. We postulate that political elites extract resources to further their own goals, and that such goals may well differ from those held by the majority of the electorate and key actors in the selectorate. Indeed, the expression of continuous disagreement between government, business, and the mass public centers on the extraction of taxes. The population expects and demands services and security but is seldom willing to pay for such services, and firms wish to minimize taxes but advocate the rule of law and frequently demand subsidies and extensions. Indeed, individuals avoid taxes by taking refuge in black market activities while taking advantage of public services. Likewise, firms press and lobby for the reduction of taxes and limitations of labor regulations. We do not consider such actions to be a rejection of government, but simply the expression of a difference between the goals held by individuals, firms, and the government. In sum, representing capacity with the level of representation of the government introduces a normative bias that prevents comparisons of performance across political regimes.

3. Classic examples of predatory governments are totalitarian regimes with strong ideological structures, or absolute monarchies that derive their right to rule from divine mandates, bent on imposing their goals on the population. Manifestations range from religious fundamentalism, as in Khomeini's Iran, extreme nationalism and racism, as in Nazi Germany, or divine-right rulers such as the Russian Czars or the Saud family in Saudi Arabia.

4. The selectorate is the group of individuals that has critical influence on the political decisions made by the ruling elite. In democratic countries the selectorate is composed of all participants in elections plus pressure groups. In authoritarian

governments the selectorate is composed of key groups without whose support the government cannot exist. In monarchies the selectorate is composed of supporters or a royal claim. In totalitarian governments the selectorate is restricted to the key actors required to coerce the population into agreement with the government. All governments, regardless of their overt regime, are eventually responsive to the mandate of their selectorate. Recent work by Bueno de Mesquita and Siverson (1995) suggests a political framework that makes these aggregate comparisons politically meaningful. These authors conceive of governments as units led by a political leader responsive to selectorates of different sizes. Totalitarian leaders and absolute monarchs make divine or ideological claims to legitimize authority, but respond in reality to a narrow selectorate of political stakeholders. This selectorate includes the nobility, clan, or party members that can veto the leader's political decisions. Authoritarian leaders respond to a wider selectorate composed of business, political and/or military stakeholders. Finally, democratic leaders respond to the widest selectorate of enfranchised voters, mediated by business and labor interests that lobby to advance their causes.

5. Overlapping structures used in Organski and Kugler (1990) were 1960—1972 and Arbetman (1990) were 1970—1985 to account for differences in reporting from the IMF and the World Bank.

6. When the control for OECD is removed, the stability of the coefficients is not greatly affected. The GDP.CAP coefficient becomes 5.59e-06, which is slightly larger than the one for the full equation.

Variables	Coefficient	Std. Error	T-Stat
TAX. RATIO			
TIME	.0009	.00013	6.9**
AGR.GDP	-0.09	.0095	-10.1*
MIN/GDP	.12	.0106	11.6**
EXP/GDP	.03	.0061	5.2**
HEALTHEX	1.31	.0959	14.0**
OECD	.04	.0046	8.7**
Constant	.12	.0048	25.4**
R^2	.36		
Number of Observ.	3651		

* Significant at .005 percent level.
** Significant at .001 percent level.

7. The alternative specification using agricultural production as a control in developing countries is illustrated in the above table.

8. The distributional characteristics of these two ratios are also quite similar:

Variable	Obs.	Mean	Std. Dev.	Min.	Max.
RPE.AGR	3651	.996	.405	.113	3.721
RPE.GDP	3580	.995	.410	.124	3.653

These alternatives are useful to preseve continuity with past research and could be used to assess the sensitivity of the estimates where outliers exist. Unless otherwise stated, the cross-national work reported in this book relies on political extraction using controls for individual productivity, not agricultural output.

9. In general, unofficial activity that increases the production of goods and services has positive short-term distributive effects.

10. Monetary approaches to measuring the informal economy assume that black market transactions leave traces in the economy, and set a point in time when black market activities were non-existent. Most of these models assume that transactions in the informal sector are made in cash and try to trace the discrepancies between cash and other indicators or between different points in time. The main drawback is the lack of data for developing countries. A further theoretical problem is that all the monetary approaches to measuring the unofficial economy make strong assumptions about the stability of the velocity of circulation of money. These calculations are rendered meaningless in situations of high inflation or in developing economies that rely more on subsistence or barter systems. Other approaches, such as the causal approach, that try to include causal determinants of the informal economy have the problem of a soft data base. Another indirect approach compares production from different angles–output, expenditures, and income–assuming that discrepancies are due to the existence of unrecorded activities. For these last two methods data is available only for a handful of countries. As for the econometric and monetary approaches, there are a number of variations in the models tailored to each case study that make them difficult to calculate and to compare. For an extensive review of monetary methods, see Arbetman 1990.

11. Several authors have attempted to model the size of the black market labor sector. For example, Michael Hopkins (1983) developed an underemployment model; Victor Tokman (1982, 1985) tried to measure the underutilization of labor, equating this to the presence of unofficial labor markets; Gabriele Gaetani D'Aragona (1981) modeled the informal labor sector in developed countries; Portes (1984; Portes et al. 1986) looked at the informal labor sector in developing countries; and Contini (1979, 1981a) looked specifically at the size of the informal labor sector in Italy. For an extensive analysis of these models, see Arbetman 1990.

12. According to Pettenati, the categories of people most likely to participate in the informal economy are: housekeepers, pensioners, unemployed, migrants, self-employed, and some groups of the services and industry sectors. However, this information is very difficult to get across time, much less across countries.

13. In surveys of Italy it became evident that between 15 and 20 percent of the

population worked in the Italian informal economy. Pettenati used this difference to account for the apparent differences between the Italian activity rate and that of the rest of the developed countries.

14. We tested the reliability of the Hopkins, Tokman, D'Aragona, Portes, and Pettenati models and found that they are all highly correlated. We choose to use Pettenati's approach since it is parsimonious and does not have the data constraints that other models impose (see Arbetman 1990).

15. Total war is a conflict in which both parties are fully engaged, and the outcome threatens each other's territorial existence (Organski and Kugler 1980; Vasquez 1994).

16. Much work on "state" strength has a heavy ideological component. Particularly common is the distinction made between democratic and non-democratic political structures, where the former are judged "superior" and the latter "inferior." We do not dispute that democratic competitive regimes are "superior," for they provide means to replace governments through voting and revealing the wishes of the electorate, or by the absence of war between democracies (Bueno de Mesquita and Siverson 1995). Nor do we dispute that the life of individuals in democratic systems is "superior," because they are assured of human rights and freedom of expression far more frequently than under alternate governments. Yet such regimes are not necessarily more politically "capable." Democracies require costly duplication of political elites to generate political competition. There is no indication that democracies are less aggressive in general, as they wage war just as often or more frequently than others against non-democratic regimes. Finally, human rights are preserved by relatively liberal governments, and this characteristic of democracy may not hold when extreme disparity of preferences is present, as is the case in Northern Ireland over time or currently in the Bosnian remnant of the Yugoslav state.

17. Centralized regimes are sometimes considered "superior," because by limiting the level of political distention their elites can act decisively when major policy transitions take place. The relatively authoritarian political elites of Chile, Korea, and Japan, to a lesser extent, are given credit for the rapid and sustained economic growth that these societies underwent following World War II. It is noted that economic growth slowed substantially as these societies moved towards competitive democracy. Such examples are persuasive, particularly in Latin America, where Chile achieved stable and sustained growth under the military rule of Pinochet. However, most Latin American nations had the unenviable record of Argentina under a succession of dictators and military juntas that managed to stifle growth, induce spiraling inflation, and maintain a steady decline in economic output. This vicious circle was reversed only after democracy was established by Menem's Peronist government. Such experiences are repeated frequently. Authoritarian regimes face serious difficulties when leadership replacement is required. In sum, it is not hard to show that periods of growth are associated with both authoritarian and non-authoritarian regimes, but it is difficult to show that growth periods are associated with particular regime types over time. We propose that regime considerations are not a central concern in understanding the process of economic and social development; rather, development is associated with variations in political capacity across regimes and over time.

18. Note that although regulation of speed limits was removed, New York still regulates traffic far more than Montana, simply because its road systems are used more heavily.

2

Theoretical Link of Political Capacity to Development

A. F. K. Organski

INTRODUCTORY REMARKS

Political development and the resulting rise in capacity are rooted in two dynamics: one propelling the growth of the state and the other the expansion of the political system to include the mass of the people. It is these two expansions, which occur in sequence over the developmental trajectory, that are responsible for the massive increase in the size and capacity of government. We shall examine this process and present propositions to account for both, keeping in mind that there is nothing inevitable about the process of development and that failure is frequent. This chapter also aims to explore how closely the measures of relative political capacity (RPC) presented in this book reflect the rise in the size and performance of government (see Chapter 1).

THE SETTING FOR POLITICAL GROWTH

Massive increases in government's political capacity do not occur in isolation. They are part and parcel of an *interconnected* set of changes among elements of the economy, the social structure, and the political, demographic, and value systems. Taken together, these changes make up the developmental process or, as others have called it, the massive transformation of societies that produce the modern nation state (Tilly 1975; Chapter 1).

Two points should be noted. Different models of development are the result of various sequences (Nordlinger 1981; Binder 1971) in which the critical subsystems of a society (political, economic, demographic, etc.) change. In the Western model, for example, economic change in the form of the agricultural and first industrial revolution proved to be the locomotive driving urbanization and leading to a change of social values, a drop in vital rates, and a further expansion of the political system. This Western experience led to the view that economic change is (and should be) the engine of the developmental process. The Soviet model differed. In the Soviet experience it was political change that drove industrialization and urbanization, and in turn, depressed birth and death rates. In China also it was political change that drove changes in other sectors of national life. The sequence in China, however, differed from the Soviet case in a critical respect. Government capacity expanded, creating conditions for a profound decline of vital rates in advance of economic development. Then, government's power propelled forward the opening of private markets and economic development with lower fertility easing economic growth. The Western and the Soviet-Chinese models appear to be the major models of development to date, although other sequences have been recorded. Clearly the sequence in which the changes in question occur determines the course of development in the society.

To date, the process has always begun with the building of the state. State building had consequences—most often unintended—that started, prodded and shielded the social, economic, and psychological components of the developmental process. State building stimulates the interplay of changes within and across socioeconomic and demographic sectors and pushes the process to levels where social transformation is self-sustaining. Development in the modern era, then, has always begun with a massive transformation of the political sector. The building of the state always precedes all other changes, no matter in what order these other changes follow.

One wonders why development is usually viewed primarily, if not entirely, as a socioeconomic process, with government playing a dependent role.[1] This view appears at variance with experience. For example, the history of the relations between politics and economics makes clear the dynamic created by government in mobilizing the human and material resources essential for economic growth. Government leaders make the critical decisions in apportioning resources between production and consumption, dividing the latter between support for standards of living and state security. Government decisions and actions, directly or indirectly, help move economies from agriculture to manufacture (and at a later time from manufacture into services, and from services to the information sector), by initiating and in many cases regulating the flow of rural to urban migration. This migration supplies the new economy with the labor essential for growth. This shift, in turn, creates conditions for the change in values, where instrumental and scientific beliefs replace magical ones. This change is essential to the development of science and technology. Urbanization is again critical in lowering the costs of political control, fueling the expansion of the political system.

Most important government decisions and actions are critical to the creation of savings and capital. Savings, the life blood of economic development, are the difference between production and consumption. Governments play a central role in augmenting the first and controlling and/or minimizing the second. Where private markets rule economic decisions, governments manipulate economies indirectly. Where economies have been centralized, the full force of political power is used directly to expand savings and investment and reduce consumption. *Mutatis mutandis*, the entire history of economic growth confirms these basic points. (Toynbee 1956; North 1981, 1990; Polanyi 1944; Cole 1961).

In short, government's role is central in every important change that society makes in conjunction with economic development. The role political power plays in the development of economies begins with, but goes far beyond, defining property rights. Economic markets are central, but they do not operate by themselves. Political markets and bureaucracies are also essential. One cannot understand the operation of one unless one understands the role played by the other (North 1981; Organski 1965, Chapters 2-5; Ardant 1972).

THE SOURCE OF STATE GROWTH AND POLITICAL EXPANSION

The growth of the political system is part of the overall shift we have described, but it is guided by its own dynamics and can be looked at separately. There is no need to summarize the history of state expansion or the literature on enlargement of the political system to include mass publics. Rather, what is required is to identify the essential factors that expand the political system and increase its capability. The process that began in Western Europe and has now spread across the face of the globe is enormously complex. As it moved it varied across societies and over time. Regardless of differences, however, wherever development has occurred political systems have transformed themselves into bureaucracies with high capacity to mobilize human and material assets of the society. (Organski et al 1984, Chapters 1, 2; Organski and Kugler 1980, Chapter 2). The increase in capacity is extraordinary; it is comparable to the massive enhancements in economic productivity and geographic mobility that have been part of the developmental process.

Two circumstances fueled the rise of states and nations in preindustrial Europe, and still fuel the initial process of state building today in the developing world. First, elites attempt to defray the costs of providing themselves with security against actual and potential adversaries that only reliable military and paramilitary forces can provide. Second, the central elites must have the means to maintain a coalition of supporters that, together with reliable military forces, grants stability to their rule. This second need for resources never abates; it only grows and grows. We shall deal with the problem of maintaining a coalition of supporters later in this chapter. In both dynamics, failure to obtain resources means governmental leaders become vulnerable to removal from their positions, or even worse.

For purposes of study it is convenient to view the governmental system as a gigantic mechanism ever pressing to reach into the society, extract resources from it, pool such resources, and then allocate them to undertakings the governing elites have chosen to pursue. The resources sought after are both human and material, tangible and intangible; the reach of government into the population and revenue extraction are convenient indicators, but they are only indicators of the broader array of resources elites seek and obtain from their societies. Figure 2.1 presents the dynamic we have described.

Political elites do all in their power to squeeze every bit of resources they can from their populations. Why then can't they extract more? A number of explanations are advanced. For example, it can be argued that the elites' drive to collect as much revenue as possible is can be restrained by their realization that if they do so, they will destroy the source of their wealth. Or, it can be argued that the operation of the principal-agent relationship is at play. The power of the elite to implement policies that will extract the resources they need is limited by conflicting interests.

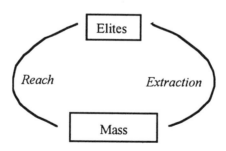

FIGURE 2.1 Elite Mass Dynamics Interaction

However, the *productivity* of the policies in raising the needed revenue and the level of *resistance* the measures in question create are loosely related. We propose a different hypothesis. The governmental elites' drive to collect resources is constrained by resistance from the coalition of their supporters. If that resistance is ignored, the coalition could unravel. Resistance generates political costs the governing elite must sustain if it is to implement its policy goals. The calculation of political costs are a key factor in leaders' decision making process. If the government calculates that political costs will threaten basic support, it will restrain its tax collectors.

The mix of resources the elites need and the way they put them to use also varies with circumstances. The allocation of resources changes predictably over the developmental trajectory. Prior to economic development, the preoccupation of government is security, and the major governmental allocation of disposable resources goes to defray the costs of the military and paramilitary forces and governmental administration. During the initial phase of economic development, economic investment becomes an additional item on the agenda. Political and economic resources are channeled, directly or indirectly, to the increase of production and control of consumption. After the initial phase of economic development is completed, more governmental resources are spent to promote the social welfare of the mass publics who are recent entrants into the political system. Hence the sobriquet of "welfare state."

In short, before economic development, government elites offer few gains other than security to their populations in exchange for the resources they extract. In part this is so because many nonsecurity resources (e.g., education, health, etc.) are not available, and channels do not exist for the masses to demand the few that are available. After economic development progresses the allocation of resources changes profoundly for two reasons: Mass publics have elbowed themselves into the political system; and with the increased economic productivity there are more resources to be shared.

THE BUILDING OF THE STATE

Obtaining essential revenue is never easy, and indebtedness is a constant in the building of states and nations. The instruments developed for the mobilization of resources link elites to masses. These links make it possible for elites to reach the masses and compel or convince them to change their behavior and share a portion of their possessions with government.

The robustness and effectiveness of these bureaucratic linkages is the critical factor in distinguishing levels of capacity of states. If these bureaucracies are very weak, (e.g., countries in South Asia or Africa, such

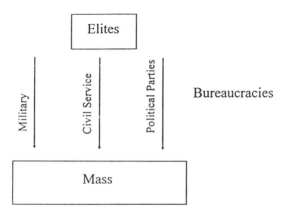

FIGURE 2.2 Bureaucracies that Link Mass and Elite

as Afghanistan or Uganda) the capability of the political system is very low. On the other hand, if the bureaucracies are very robust, as they were in North Vietnam and Israel during the wars these nations fought, political capability is high (Organski et al. 1984; Organski and Kugler 1980). In short, the robustness of the *political* links by which elites can mobilize the resources of the nation are a critical predictor of governmental capability and performance.

Let us now turn to a discussion of those political bureaucracies that make governments capable to act.

Figure 2.2 shows that the bureaucracies that link central elites and masses, and enabling elites to mobilize the resources of the polity and impose order and stability on the system are the military, the body of administrators who collect and allocate resources,[2] and the political party. Let us briefly discuss each in turn.

The Military

We already noted that the costs of maintaining military forces are a major impetus for the *initiation* of state building. The building of the state is a process requiring the cooperation and subjugation of a very large number of local elites. State building involves an increase in the power of the central leadership, and a sharp reduction of the autonomy and power of regional and local elites, whose share of the resources they had previously disposed is thereby reduced (Tilly 1975). Thus, the initial phases of state building internal strife is constant. Domestic challengers are as troubling as international ones. Resistance and rebellion are eventually crushed when advantage in military power enables the center to prevail, suppress rebellion and establish controls.

The transformation of the military forces from an admixture of relatively small forces of retainers and mercenaries in the pre-industrial era into the national citizen armies of the developed world is a major element in the growth of the state. It is an immensely costly, long, and complex process shaped by socioeconomic, political, and technological factors.

The Civil Administration

The civil bureaucracy is one of two tools that reach into society, collect resources, and allocate these material resources to advance elites' policies. There are variations over time and across countries in the experience of this growth in political capacity; however, some important similarities exist.[3]

As in the case of military forces, the establishment of a civil administration that is an effective, dutiful, and subservient instrument for central elites is costly and tortuous, continuing through most of the developmental process. At the beginning of state building expanding the civil service is an awesome task for rulers. The marginal political costs for maintaining the civil administration and the military forces, however, decrease as development progresses.

Central political leaders lacking an effective central control must build the civil service from scratch or coopt the civil administration that local elites possess. In the European experience in the centuries preceding the industrial revolution, the crown sought to induce parts of the church bureaucracy, as well as regional or local bureaucracies, to shift allegiance (Fisher and Lundgreen 1975). Today, in a number of developing countries struggling to develop their political systems, central governments seek to wean existing civil servants away from their allegiance to tribe, family, religion, or all three.

The role of civil administration changes with economic development. Before economic development this institution is almost exclusively a tool to collect resources and to administer law and order. After the industrial revolution is completed, large portions of the resources collected by the government are returned in the form of services. The shift occurs because, with the completion of the economic transformation, the mass of the population working in the new economy elbow their way into the political system. Led by new leaders, they demand resources in exchange for their support. In response, government ceases to invest political and economic resources solely on the productive machine and security forces, and begins to invest heavily in the national welfare as well. The bureaucracy is slowly transformed into a civil service. The civil service continues as a mechanism for the collection of resources, but it also becomes the major tool to monitor the economy and redistribute resources as well (Fisher and Lundgreen 1975).

The Political Party

The political party is the instrument responsible for mobilizing the masses. The political party differs from the civil bureacracy in the resources it mobilizes. The civil bureaucracy primarily mobilizes material resources, while the political party focuses primarily on the mobilization of human resources, ushering in an era of mass politics. Mobilization consists of obtaining the consent of the masses to the policies the elites have formulated. Without mass parties the government is largely impotent. The Russian experience after the fall of communism is a case in point.

This distinction, however, should not be pushed too far. The civil service is also used to regulate human resources. For example, the civil service regulates the labor force and recruits and provisions the military forces. Political parties can also take on some roles of the administration. In the command economies of China and the Soviet Union, political parties have played major roles in directing the economies. Be that as it may, political parties usher in the era of modern politics wherein the masses become potent political resources in intra-elite struggles.

The emergence of these new political institutions are clearly connected to the changes in the socioeconomic environment: the agricultural and industrial revolutions, mass urbanization, and economic growth. Parties are rooted in society's inherent social cleavages and the expanding class divisions that result from industrialization and urbanization (Rokkan et al. 1970; Duverger 1951; Lipset and Rokkan 1967, Part 1). It is these divisions and the agonies and inequities of industrialization, that predispose mass publics to political mobilization. This process in turn creates counter-elites who mobilize the masses, cut the costs of such mobilization, and create a challenge to incumbent elites. Unions and political parties organize and discipline the new labor force, ushering it into the political arena. They demand that standards of living, devastated by industrialization and urbanization, be improved. The entrance of mass publics into national politics expands the political market place. Sectors of the masses become available for membership in constituencies and potentially for alliances with members of the elite political coalitions backing or opposing the leadership. Elites compete for a share of this market, seeking to gain leverage in the governing coalitions. I shall turn to the management of these coalitions later in this chapter.

We should note that where mass parties emerge in advance of economic development and are associated with the centralization of economies, governing elites have used parties to impose economic privations on the masses. Under such circumstances, issues of welfare are addressed only symbolically. After industrialization is completed, it is difficult to use political parties as channels for reform, as in the West. The experiences of Communist countries are cases in point.

Political development is a process driven by the interests of elites. Parties, even in democratic societies, are not principally enforcers of mass preferences on elites. Their primary effect is the other way around. They provide a channel for elite preferences to reach and be adopted by mass publics. That is what we mean when we talk of mobilization of mass publics. Of course, there is interaction between elites and masses; the process could never be solely a one-way street. But the focus on the interaction should not divert attention from the fact that the decisive net consequence of party operation is not to enable mass preferences to shape the preferences of elites but for the preferences of elites to shape the preferences and the behavior of mass publics.

Mass consent, or at least acquiescence to elite preferences, is a prerequisite for elite policies to become reality. The reason for this is simple. The costs of coercing the masses to comply with elite policies become increasingly expensive as the economy is transformed and masses become engaged in the manufacturing and service sectors. They become prohibitively expensive in the information age. Even in the most repressive regimes elites can be stymied. Remember the bitter joke in Moscow: "They make believe they pay us; we make believe we work." It speaks volumes about the critical role of mass acquiescence or consent in economic performance.

THE TWO DYNAMICS OF POLITICAL DEVELOPMENT

State Growth

We have argued that the growth of the state is self-sustaining. We should indicate conditions that favor this dynamic. We noted earlier that the major reason the process of state building begins at all is that the elites must pay for the military forces that guarantee their safety and their right to rule. If this is to be accomplished, political elites must *reach* the people making up the society they rule, and *extract* resources from them.[4] In the last analysis it is the government's reach into the society and extraction of resources from it that reveals the capacity of government to govern. It is for that reason that measures of the government's reach and extraction are the two central components of the measure of relative political capacity.

It is the process of reach and extraction that sets off a dynamic leading to self-sustaining state growth. A general outline of the progression involved goes as follows. As central elites begin to penetrate the society and find the revenues needed to fulfill their needs, they meet resistance from regional and local elites who resent this intervention. To sustain the effort to overcome such resistance, central elites must obtain even more resources to expand the military forces and to enhance the bureaucracy that collects those resources. This expansion of the state capacity requires, in turn, more resources and drives the central elites to reach further into the society and find additional sources for the required revenues. That effort renews the resistance, with still more regional and local elites rising in opposition. When the central elites are thus stymied from getting the resources they seek, they attempt to squash the opposition, which, in turn, requires additional armed forces, additional capability to obtain resources, and, of course, additional collection of revenues. The self-sustaining dynamic undergirding the growth of the state and its power should be clear.

In short, the growth of the state system is rooted in conflicting forces: pressure by central elites to obtain resources, the resistance to elite extraction, attempts to reduce the autonomy of local leaders, and the increasing costs of suppressing that resistance.

The Expansion of the Political System

Security and safety are not the only preoccupations of governing elites; there is a second concern. Central elites must maintain a coalition to support their claim to power. The management of that coalition requires resources in ever larger amounts. The consequence of that management process is the enlargement of the political selectorate that ends up including the mass of the population (see Chapter 1).

This dynamic of inclusion is central to political development and capacity. We have noted over and over again that the increase of government capacity is a function of the government's ability to increase its reach into the society and mobilize its *human* resources. We have just described the role parties play in this process. The effort is rendered possible because the masses have been predisposed to political mobilization by tidal changes in the economy and social structure. The dynamic that underpins elites' increasing ability to extend their reach is rooted in the process of including new groups into the political system.

Again, the fuel that moves the process of inclusion forward is elites' need for resources to maintain the support of a coalition. This should come as no surprise, since all politics at the national level are a matter of coalitions being constructed, undone, and reconstructed. The coalition central leaders put together must be strong enough to enable the central elite to deter or defeat any opposition challenge to the established regime.

Managing such a coalition is a constant preoccupation of central leaders. If national leaders fail in this task and allow opponents to gain the upper hand, sooner or later there will be successful challenges and the incumbent leadership will be removed from power. For central elites, keeping the coalition together in support of their regime is a matter of political life or death.

Once again, the key to keeping the coalition together is the availability of resources to buy the support of the members. This demand for resources frequently overtakes the demands of the state apparatus and continues to grow through the developmental process. There is a cost and benefit calculation in the management of the coalition that has the unintended consequence of transforming the state structure and enlarging the political system. This second dynamic is key to the mobilization of new sectors of the population; elite politics become mass politics.

THE COSTS OF COALITIONS

Our attempt to explain the dynamic involves a complex procedure. Membership in the coalition provides a wide range of benefits to the members in exchange for their support. The list of benefits that the central political elite provides is almost endless. Illustrations would include tax abatements, grants, monopolies, contracts, access to lucrative business dealings in the private sector, favorable rules in the market place, and on and on. Of course, benefits are not limited to economic gains but extend to a long list of social and political benefits.

It is in the interest of central elites to give away as little as possible of their resources in return for the necessary support from each member of the coalition. *Inter alia,* a major concern is to avoid strengthening any group or sub-coalition of groups to the point that it can challenge or control the central leadership.

The interests of each member oppose those of the central political elite. That is, members maximize their position by receiving as many resources as they can for as little support as possible. In addition, each member competes with every other, seeking advantages and avoiding as much as possible being disadvantaged in the distribution of benefits or in the payment of support to the central elite.

There is a cardinal rule in the distribution of resources by the central leadership. Resources will be dispensed in proportion to the utility members have in supporting the central leadership. The stronger the coalition member, the more valuable the member's support to the central leadership. On the other hand, the more powerful and valuable a coalition member happens to be, the more it can demand in return for its continued support. In short, the length of time in the coalition reflects on the power of the member, and, in turn, on the price asked for its support.

COALITIONS AND THE GROWTH OF THE POLITICAL SYSTEM

Understanding the expansion of the state system is rooted in the set of positive relations we have just mentioned. The value of a member is the contribution it can make to the defense of the government. The longer a member stays in the coalition, the more powerful the member will become, and the higher the price demanded of the leadership for its support. It is in the interest of members to increase their price if they can, since they will be pressed for resources by their constituencies to whom commitments have been made. Failure to deliver would threaten their constituencies' support and their own power and influence in the coalition.

The central political leadership has an interest in selectively replacing members who cost as much or more than any benefits they bring the coalition. The advantage of a new member to the central elites should be plain. The benefits of its support should be substantially greater than such support should cost. For a time the new members are likely to be satisfied with fewer and cheaper resources. This will change over time as the new group gains the advantages of membership, becoming a more powerful and more expensive coalition partner.

One illustration may help illuminate what we mean. The entrance of women into the political arena in the United States (Klein 1984) initially led to demands by the feminist movement for symbolic resources (e.g., changes in forms of address and the like). These were followed by demands for proscription of sexual harassment in the workplace and abuse in the family environment, access to professional positions, removal of glass ceilings, and equal pay for equal work. These demands required some, but not much expenditure of resources by the government. As this coalition becomes more powerful, at least in part because of government help, more expensive demands—support for child care, for example— should be in the offing.

In short, initially new coalition members will make modest demands that can be satisfied with cheap resources. However, their demands escalate as they become more powerful, until some point where they become vulnerable to being replaced. The frequent need of the elites in power to find relatively inexpensive supporters is key to the recruitment into the system, the formation of new coalitions, and the expansion of the political system.[5]

When most of the population is included in the political system, the entrance of new groups becomes less frequent and more costly, and the expansion of the political system inevitably decelerates. That is the reason for the second inflection and the S shape of the developmental trajectory. Even after this governmental power keeps growing, however, and the jockeying for support of groups in the system becomes more intense. Resources to reward key supporters are found by demoting less powerful groups, thereby freeing up benefits for the leaders of the coalition. Most of the OECD nations are now in this situation. The tilt of the U.S. government away from protecting labor organizations is an illustration of the demotion of groups and the transfer of resources away from them.

CAPACITY AND COMPARISON

But if development leads to political capacity and capacity is the determinant of government's ability to govern, surely this dimension is central to any comparisons of political systems. Indeed, we argue that such comparison is both most inclusive and theoretically more productive than any involving *forms* of government. Comparisons of levels of democracy or representativeness reflect far more quality of life issues than does comparing the way systems work. Moreover, the use of these dimensions severely limits the number of cases for meaningful comparison. Huntington was so right in the opening salvo in his famous treatise *Political Order*: "The most important of political distinctions among countries concerns *not their form of government but their degree of government.*"[6]

We noted early in this chapter that the transformation in the political system and the resulting massive rise in the capacity of the system is connected to changes in the economic, social and demographic structures. How demographic, economic, and social changes effect political behaviors has long been explored. Research questions have usually asked how economic, demographic, social, and psychological changes affect political behavior. The study of the influence going the other way has been greatly handicapped by the lack of any way to effectively measure differences in the development and capacity of political systems.

The measure of relative political capacity (*RPC*) has begun to address this problem. The chain of reasoning underpinning this measure goes like this: Political development produces political capacity; capacity is the determinant of government performance in obtaining the resources it needs to translate its goals and promises into reality; resources can be described as collection of revenue and the government's ability to reach the population. We should emphasize that a major resource is government's reach into society and the control it exercises over the behavior of its citizens. Indeed, it is this reach over citizens' behavior that, in a large number of situations, proves the more important aspect of the capacity of government. Thus, political capacity can be described successfully by a measure reflecting government performance in these two functions.

One should note that governmental reach and extraction, the two components of the measure of relative political capacity (*RPC*) reflect precisely the dynamic that generates political capacity. The component indicating political extraction (*RPE*) monitors the government's performance in raising revenue. The component of political reach (*RPR*) identifies the performance of government in mobilizing the population. The measure as a whole captures the very core of the process of development and, therefore, of the capacity of political systems.[7]

We do not mean to say that the form of a government has no bearing on its capacity. If one controls for levels of capacity, what difference will form of government make in governmental elites' ability to extract the resources they require? In the context of our discussion the issue of form is best addressed as the degree of limitation imposed on the power of government. It is usually thought that governments with no limitations on their power have an advantage, because they are able to control their people and obtain resources even in the face of resistance from their populations. But such plausible beliefs are really quite unsupported. The connection between political form and capacity is far more complicated.

Using the measure of relative political extraction (*RPE*) as their measure of political capacity Kugler and Domke (1985) demonstrated that the performance of political systems in obtaining resources was related principally to level of development, with form unrelated to capacity. In their test exploring the relation between capacity and performance in major conflicts, major combatants in World War II differed radically from expectations based on assumptions that democracies and limited governments were less capable of obtaining resources than dictatorial systems. They showed, *inter alia,* that both Britain and France did better than Nazi Germany, and all three did better than the Soviet Union. This was the inverse of what was expected. Their data led to the conclusion that political form and capacity were unrelated. Democratic systems were not disadvantaged by the self-imposed limitations on their governments' power. The authors were not unaware of the implications of their findings for the relationship between form and capacity. More recent research by Schultz and Weingast (1995) establishes important micro-foundations for the Kugler-Domke findings. They proposed that limitations on governmental power might aid rather than hinder in obtaining resources. The essence of the argument is that, in the case of borrowing, limitations on governmental power should reassure lenders that the government cannot arbitrarily renege on its debts. Therefore, movement toward limited government lowers the lenders' risks and interest rates, and thus increases the availability of loans (Schultz and Weingast 1995; Bueno de Mesquita and Siverson 1995).

How, then, do limitations of governmental power affect the level of resources governmental elites obtain? The process is clearly complex. We suggest that performance in raising revenue is influenced by the political and economic costs elites need to pay in raising revenue by either borrowing or taxation.

In short, the costs of the two methods move in opposite directions. The economic costs of borrowing should decrease slowly until governmental power is substantially limited. It takes time for a government to establish credibility that it will keep its word. In addition, initial increases in military power are too small to grant security to potential investors. Once power and credibility are established, economic costs should decrease quite rapidly. The political costs due to taxation ought to move in the opposite way, rising slowly from low to high levels. Limitation of governmental power should be pronounced before government elites are made to pay a significant political price for taxation. Once it is clear that it is safe to resist governmental exactions, political costs should rise rapidly. Overall costs, i.e., political plus economic costs, should rise very slowly if at all until substantial limitations of governmental power have been imposed. Then, they should rise significantly (see Figure 2.3).

Overall costs would behave differently if the economic costs were to fall more rapidly than the political costs, or the other way around. In the first case the overall costs should proceed evenly and then decrease rapidly. Should the political costs rise faster than the economic costs, overall costs should rise steeply. One should also note that for political elites, the economic costs of borrowing should be less salient than the political costs they pay until a time when opponents succeed in transforming the economic costs of servicing the loans and repaying principal into political costs. On the other hand, when taxes are imposed the economic costs would be less troublesome to political elites than the political costs. Also, such costs increase as opponents are permitted to voice their dissatisfaction with increased limitations on governmental power (Lust-Okar and Organski, forthcoming).

CONCLUSION

Political development produces governmental capacity and ability to govern. Capacity to govern is entirely dependent on the ability of the system to mobilize the resources necessary for what the government wants to do. It makes sense, therefore, to infer governments' capacity by their

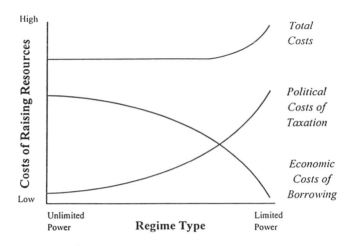

FIGURE 2.3 Effects of Forms of Governments on Costs to Raise Resources

performance.

Two dynamics make up the process that results in the rise in political capacity. The government's extraction of resources is connected with the growth and strengthening of state structures, and governmental reach into civil society is connected with both the dynamic promoting state growth and the progressive enlargement of the political system to include an increasing share of the mass of the people. Both dynamics cause a massive rise in political capability to mobilize the human as well as the material resources of the nation. Both dynamics are self-sustaining, fueled by elite needs to defray the costs of security and obtain support. The elites' efforts to obtain resources generate resistance that requires greater effort to control, which in turn generates additional resistance. Each step in the escalation requires more resources and further escalation. The bureaucracies that carry on the process grows, and with them grow the capacity of the state to mobilize resources. The self-sustaining nature of the process is evident. The strategy of indexing the performance of government in reaching into society and extracting resources from it as a measure of capacity seems entirely appropriate.

The second self-sustaining dynamic, also fueled by an escalating need for resources, undergirds the expansion of the political system to include ever more people. The elites' calculus of the costs and benefits coalition memberships is the source of the dynamic that explains why members of the coalition are replaced and new groups are recruited. It is this recruitment of new groups that expands the system.

Finally, consequences of differences in governmental performance across nations and over time are telling indications of the importance of the study of the capacity and development of political systems. The literature of development, and comparative and international politics is replete with discussions of strong and weak states. Such terms do not have much meaning however, unless one can measure how strong is strong and how weak is weak, and therefore tell one from the other. The measure of relative political capacity (*RPC*) is a major step in that direction.

NOTES

1. It has been a tenet of economic history that governmental power and economic growth are negatively related. The argument is that strong governments deplete the tax base of a society, depriving economic elites of the savings necessary for investment. See for example the classic work of Alexander Gershenkron (1962). The weakness of the Crown in England was thought a major condition in facilitating the decentralized process of economic growth that accompanied the agricultural and industrial revolutions in the UK. The hypothesis is plausible and widely accepted. An empirical test, however, casts serious doubt on this proposition. A. F. K. Organski , J. Kugler, J. T. Johnson, Y. Cohen (1984: 38-43); A. Thomas (1948, 1955); A. Toynbee (1956); D. North (1981, 1990); K. Polanyi (1944); G. D. H. Cole (1961).

2. It would be incorrect to view this bureaucracy as a civil service. The idea of service to the mass is very recent. For most of the development process this bureaucracy has no mission to serve. It is almost exclusively an instrument to collect resources.

3. Within limitations one can contrast the experience of pre-industrial European monarchs with leaders in the developing world today. There are immense differences, but there are also essential similarities. To students of the developing world today the picture we have sketched of elites' reasons for and problems in raising resources for state building in Europe in the first portion of this millennium should not be altogether unfamiliar. The study of development began in earnest soon after World War II. Shaky assumptions were used to support hypotheses about how the developmental dynamic functioned. It was assumed that the developing societies of the time reflected in some sense the preindustrial experience of societies that had made it to the developed level. Given this assumption one could use cross national empirical research (data had become available after World War II for developing societies) as proxies for European experience for which data were unavailable at the time. When such data were developed they showed the assumption was distorted and there developed a tendency to proscribe such comparisons even if done with reason and caution. Such a research strategy wastes the opportunity to learn from fundamental similarities of state building in the two epochs.

4. Throughout the developmental process external resources are no substitute for domestic resources. Most resources must be generated from within. This

is particularly so in the development of government bureaucracies.

5. Powerful centrifugal forces—fast-moving technologies revolutionizing warfare and economic production—are eroding the structure of the nation state. The relative power of major coalitions of actors within national systems are undergoing change. The power of the masses is being eroded by the increasing automation of production. Economic elites are less dependent on the masses to produce goods and services for their markets. However, masses are still essential as consumers of the goods produced and as taxpayers for the bills of government. Governments are less dependent on the masses to fight because of nuclear and missile technologies. But they are still dependent on masses to pay the bills for war making. And masses can no longer depend on elites for security. Nuclear and missile technology makes the elite of any nation unable to guarantee security for its population. Safety guarantees are in the hands of the elites of adversaries. One's own government cannot promise protection should it fail to dissuade opponents from attacking. They can only promise to avenge the attack (Organski 1965, Chapter 7).

6. The rest of the statement is worth quoting. "The differences between democracy and dictatorship are less than differences between those countries whose politics embodies consensus, community, legitimacy, organization, effectiveness, stability and those countries whose politics are deficient in these qualities." Samuel Huntington (1976,1). Political capacity was also clearly the missing component for any satisfactory measurement of national power. (Organski 1958, Chapter 8).

7. The political costs of obtaining resources, however, behave in curvilinear fashion, moving from high to low, and then again from low to high, over the developmental trajectory of a society. (Organski et al. 1984, 55-59).

PART TWO

Economic Applications

3

Political Capacity and Economic Determinants of Inflation

Fahim Al-Marhubi

INTRODUCTION

In recent years, a convergence has taken place in economic theory with regard to the causes of inflation. As long as inflation is defined as a sustained increase in the general price level, almost all economists agree that it is a monetary phenomenon because inflationary pressures must be accommodated by monetary expansion (Mishkin 1984, 1; Friedman 1968, 39). This view, however, does not address the question of what factors actually determine the behavior of monetary authorities.

Recognition of the crucial linkage between inflation and monetary policy has led to a resurgence of interest in the political economy of inflation and monetary policymaking. One element germane to an understanding of this linkage is the fact that political and institutional constraints can both initiate and perpetuate inflationary pressures (Dornbusch and Edwards, 1991). Therefore, analyses of the causes and control of inflation must go beyond merely technical economic considerations. Whether demand-pull or sustained cost-push, inflation remains a political phenomenon because it cannot occur without acceptance by the monetary authorities of a higher rate of monetary growth.

At the same time, a small but growing theoretical literature has formulated a positive approach to exploring how policy makers behave under various political incentives and constraints. Central to this approach is an outline of the ways in which macroeconomic policy and performance are influenced by the organizational strengths of different decision makers and by the political and institutional environments in which they operate. With respect to debt and inflation, this literature has concentrated on two different types of political incentive constraints. As Alesina and Tabellini

(1990, 342) suggest, "in the first line of research emphasizing unified governments alternating over time, debt and inflation are caused by political instability, that is, by frequent turnover of governments with different preferences. In the second group of papers on decentralized government, on the other hand, a myopic policy does not reflect a deliberate choice, but rather the inability to take collective decisions. The incentive constraint here is caused by fragmentation of power among different decision makers."

In models based on individual rationality that satisfy intertemporal financing constraints, Alesina and Tabellini (1990), Tabellini and Alesina (1990), Persson and Svensson (1989), and Cukierman et al. (1989) have recently shown how public debt and inefficient tax collection systems can be used to influence and constrain the policies of future governments. Further, Willett (1988), Cukierman et al. (1989), Roubini and Sachs (1989), Edwards and Tabellini (1990), Roubini (1990) and Grilli et al. (1991) use empirical evidence from both industrial and developing countries to indicate that political incentives and political institutions are significant determinants of economic policy outcomes.

This chapter shows that there is empirical support for a political economy explanation of inflation. While traditionally countries with lax fiscal and monetary policies generate inflation, the ability of a nation to maintain fiscal and monetary discipline depends on certain features of its particular political system. One such feature is the level of the nation's political development measured in terms of the capacity of the political system to extract resources from the society. The results, although not definitive, suggest that relative political extraction affects budget deficits and that budget deficits are accommodated by monetary expansion.

THEORETICAL OVERVIEW: RELATIVE POLITICAL EXTRACTION AND BUDGET DEFICITS

This theoretical overview suggests both that the political capacity of governments to extract resources should affect budget deficits, and that potential links exist between budget deficits and money creation. The objective of this chapter is to investigate empirically the relationship between the relative political extraction *(RPE)* of governments (see Chapter 1) and their inflation performance. Relative political extraction influences the rate of inflation indirectly through its effect on governments' budgetary positions. To develop a political economy analysis of economic policy outcomes, *RPE* is used as a broad measure of political behavior because it approximates the capacity of the state to mobilize, aggregate, and direct the requisite human and material resources of its society to fulfill national objectives.

This research concentrates on fourteen Latin American economies during the years 1972—1985. A significant rationale for the longstanding fiscal imbalances and chronic inflation which have plagued many Latin American economies derives from the region's continued pattern of political instability, political polarization, and distributional conflict (Dornbusch and Edwards 1991; Haggard and Kaufman 1992). That is, in the effort to accommodate the demands of various interest groups to maintain or increase their income shares, these nations typically fail to reach a social consensus on the distribution of national income. And even if such a consensus is achieved, inability or unwillingness on the part of government to enforce the distributional pact can likewise lead to unsustainable budget deficits and inflation (Baer 1991; Bresser and Dall'Acqua 1991; Feijo and de Carvalho 1992).

Success in initiating, implementing, and sustaining stable public budgetary policies hinges not only on the ability of a government to design a technically consistent policy package, but also on its capacity to mobilize support for its policies. Additionally, the government must resist pressure from the opposition and special interest groups to boost wages and implement other similarly popular but unsustainable fiscal policies. In summary, after all other economic factors which may affect fiscal deficit performance have been controlled for, increases in relative political extraction should lead to lower public deficits and lower rates of monetary accommodation.

Over the last decade, the causal influence of budget deficits on interest rates and monetary expansion was the subject of considerable controversy. Accordingly, the relationship between monetary expansion and the government's budgetary position has been investigated empirically in a number of studies of the United States (King and Plosser 1985; Joines 1985; Grier and Neiman 1987; Willett et al. 1988), of other industrial countries (Demopoulos et al. 1987; Protopapadakis and Siegel 1987; Burdekin and Laney 1988; Willett et al. 1988) and, recently, of developing countries as well (De Haan and Zelhorst 1990).

Conventional wisdom argues that, whereas debt monetization is not an automatic process in industrial countries, budget deficits have a much stronger link with inflation in developing countries. It is argued that the inflationary consequences of budget deficits in developing countries derive from the absence of well-developed capital markets to absorb newly issued debt, which in turn constrains the ability of the monetary authorities to engage in discretionary monetary policy. The direct control of the central bank by the government in most developing countries may also make debt monetization more likely. In addition, the choice of central bank operating procedures may influence the degree of monetary accommodation of budget deficits.[1] For example, pressures to hold down interest rates in many developing countries in the 1970s may have increased the likelihood of monetary accommodation of deficit pressures. It is therefore argued that under such circumstances, monetary growth depends primarily upon fiscal policy.

The recent literature has identified other possible links between government deficits and money creation (De Haan and Zelhorst 1990; Protopapadakis and Siegel 1987). First, political pressures may exist which impel the monetary authorities to accommodate budget deficits, especially in countries which lack effective independent central banks. Second, as the recent public finance literature has highlighted, an optimal level of seigniorage or inflation tax may exist such that those countries with relatively rudimentary tax structures should experience relatively high optimal rates of anticipated inflation.[2]

A third potential link between public debt and monetary policy is through the "time inconsistency problem" facing monetary policy makers, which has been analyzed by Kydland and Prescott (1977). The existence of nominal fixed interest rates on government debt creates incentives for policy makers to inflate at a rate greater than that which bondholders have initially anticipated, thus reducing the real value of the debt and the government's future tax liabilities. In essence, unanticipated inflation acts as a lump-sum tax on holders of government debt. However, Protopapadakis and Siegel (1987, 36) state that this channel of the monetization relationship predicts that the incentive to monetize debt is related to the *level* and not the rate of growth of government debt. Consequently, although such incentives are important for the United States and other industrial countries whose debts are denominated in their own currencies, such inflation surprises have limited usefulness for the Latin American economies, most of whose debts are denominated not in their own currencies but in U.S. dollars.

Incentives to inflate at rates greater than the public anticipates can also be traced to a government's attempts to exploit potential short-run inflation-unemployment tradeoffs associated with the Phillips curve in order to lower unemployment (Barro and Gordon 1983). Another possible connection between deficits and money growth, known as the "fiscal dominance hypothesis," has been identified by Sargent and Wallace (1981). Assuming that there exists a long-term constraint which imposes an upper limit on the debt-to-*GDP* ratio, Sargent and Wallace argue that if the time paths of both government spending and tax revenue are fixed, and if the real interest rate exceeds the rate of economic growth, government debt will expand faster than real income. At some future date, the public will no longer be willing to absorb additional government debt. The monetary authorities will then be forced to monetize the debt.

The following analysis provides empirical evidence concerning the effects of political extraction on government financing decisions and monetary expansion in fourteen Latin American economies. The analysis departs from previous analyses in two important respects. First, the rate of monetary expansion and the size of the budget deficit are specified as endogenous variables within a system of equations describing the fiscal and monetary policy reaction functions. The existence of potential links between budget deficits and money growth makes the single-equation approach inappropriate, as this approach would lead to biased parameter estimates in cases where the monetary authorities decide to monetize all or some portion of the fiscal authorities' deficit. Under such conditions, growth of the money supply would be partially determined by the size of the deficit, and the budget deficit variable would have a significant positive effect on monetary expansion. Consequently, the monetary and fiscal policy reaction functions are estimated simultaneously. Second, the fiscal policy reaction function is respecified by adding relative political extraction of states as an additional determinant of the behavior of budget deficits, along with the typical macroeconomic variables which influence the responses of fiscal authorities.

Using these arguments I develop a more complex model that incorporates political considerations to account for the inflationary process.

MODEL AND DATA DESCRIPTION

A three-equation system was employed to analyze the relationship among state extraction, budget deficits, monetary growth, and inflation for a sample of fourteen Latin American economies for the years 1972—1985.[3] Unlike previous studies, which examined the link between government deficits and money growth in a single-equation framework, the current model allows for possible simultaneity in the monetary and fiscal policy reaction functions. Thus, I posit the following system of equations to capture the behavior of the fiscal and monetary authorities:

$$DEF_t = f[GAP_{t\text{-}1}, SEIGN_t, RPE_t, RPE^2_t],$$ (1)

$$M_t = f[GAP_t, INFLATION_t, RES_t, DEF_t],$$ (2)

$$INFLATION_t = f[M_t, RGDP_t].$$ (3)

where:

DEF	= Budget deficit as percent of *GDP*. Source: *Economic and Social Progress in Latin America* by Inter-American Development Bank, various issues.
GAP	= Deviations of real *GDP* from trend, calculated as Real *GDP* growth minus average real *GDP* growth. Data on real *GDP* were obtained from the IFS of the IMF (line 99 b.p.).
INFLATION	= Growth rate of CPI, calculated as annual percentage change in the Consumer Price Index (CPI). Raw data were obtained from the IFS of the IMF (line 64) and *Economic and Social Progress in Latin America* by Inter-American Development Bank, various issues.
RES	= Growth rate in international reserves. Raw data were obtained from the IFS of the IMF, various issues. International Reserves are Total Reserves minus Gold (line 1I.d).
SEIGN	= Change in base money as percent of *GDP*, calculated as change in base money as percentage of *GDP*. Data on base money and *GDP* were obtained from the IFS of the IMF (line 14 and line 99b).
RPE	= Relative Political Extraction, defined as the ratio of actual tax extraction to expected tax extraction. Data were provided by the editors.
M	= Growth rate of *M1* money supply, calculated as annual percentage change. Raw data were obtained from the IFS of the IMF, various issues (line 34). Base Money (line 14).
RGDP	= Growth rate of real *GDP*, calculated as annual percentage change in real *GDP*.[4] Raw data were obtained from the IFS of the IMF (line 99b.p.), various issues.

The first equation specifies the policy reaction function for the fiscal authorities. The budget deficit is considered to be influenced by the state of the economy, partly because of built-in automatic stabilization. The rate of real growth above trend, summarized by the *GAP* variable, takes into account the automatic cyclical effects of recessions and booms on budget deficits, and also the response of the fiscal authorities to the level of economic activity. Consequently, if the fiscal authorities follow a counter-cyclical policy, a negative relationship between the output *GAP* variable and the budget deficit is expected. The output *GAP* variable is entered with a one-period lag in order to capture the lengthy lag between making a policy decision for fiscal policy in the legislative process and its actual implementation.

The measure of fiscal deficits includes nominal interest payments but does not correct for seigniorage taxation. To deal with this problem, the methodology proposed by Roubini (1991) was adopted. That is, seigniorage is included as an additional variable in the deficit equation. According to Roubini's (1991, 69) rationale, its inclusion "directly captures the effects on the nominal deficit of seigniorage taxation and indirectly controls for the nominal component of interest payments. In fact, if nominal interest payments are high because of a high inflation rate, this measure of seigniorage will also be high and will therefore partially control for this inflationary effect on interest payments."

RPE is included in the deficit equation in order to test the primary hypothesis that, in addition to the conventional fiscal policy reaction function variables, there also exists a relationship between the political extraction of governments and budget deficits. RPE^2 is also included to show that, beyond some threshold, increases in relative extraction allowing government command over an economy's resources become detrimental to an economy's performance because of the incentives which arise in such an economic environment for rent seeking, corruption, and other wasteful activities (Krueger 1993).

The second equation specifies the policy reaction function for the monetary authorities. For the countries under review, results are presented using both $M1$ and base money, or high-powered money, as indicators of monetary policy. Many monetary policy reaction function studies employ some interest rate as the dependent variable and only use monthly or quarterly data. Although this approach is appropriate for the analysis of short-run behavior of the monetary authorities, a more appropriate approach for the analysis of persistent accommodation over long-time horizons must focus on annual money supply. (For further discussion, see Willett et al. 1988.)

The monetary authorities are also hypothesized to respond in a feedback manner to the general state of the economy. If monetary policy is directed toward the objective of price stability, increases in inflation rate and real output above trend should lead to decreases in money growth. However, economies with a long history of inflation are likely to have powerful inflation-feedback or inertial mechanisms which tend to perpetuate the inflationary spiral. For example, the existence of backward wage and price indexation can lead to inertia so that the money supply simply follows price changes. In such a case, one would expect to find a positive relationship between inflation and changes in the money supply. In addition, a pro-cyclical policy instituted in order to maintain a constant purchasing power in the face of increased demand for nominal cash balances, which arises from increases in the inflation rate, would also give rise to a positive association between inflation and money growth.

Given the low degree of financial market development exhibited by most of the countries in the sample, it is often argued that the monetary authorities are typically unable to effectively sterilize reserve flows resulting from balance of payments disequilibria. Therefore, the growth of international reserves is included in the model to take into account the effects of changes in reserves on overall money supply. Consistent sterilization of reserve flows, however, would lead to minimal correlation between reserve flows and monetary aggregates. Finally, the deficit variable represents the fiscal authorities' revenue requirements in excess of revenue generated from non-borrowed sources, and thus reflects the potential interdependence of fiscal and monetary policy.

In addition to these two-policy reaction functions, the third equation defines inflation in terms of the simple quantity theory approach, as a negative function of real output growth and a positive function of the rate of monetary growth (Burdekin and Laney 1988, 653).

In summary, the channels of influence from state extraction to inflation are as follows: Low state extraction is associated with large budget deficits, large deficits imply high money growth, and high money growth is associated with high rates of inflation.

EMPIRICAL RESULTS

Table 3.1 presents results obtained using *M1* and high-powered base money as indicators of monetary policy.[5]

The estimated fiscal policy reaction functions in the table show that all the posited variables—lagged output gap, seigniorage, and relative political extraction—are significant determinants of budget deficits at the 10% level or better. The negative coefficient on the output above trend variable indicates that the effect of automatic stabilizers (counter-cyclical policy) in the fiscal authority's expenditure and revenue functions during recessions lead to increasing budget deficits and booms to decreasing budget deficits. The positive and significant coefficient of seigniorage shows that countries with less efficient tax systems are more likely to experience large fiscal deficits.

This finding is consistent with that obtained by Roubini (1991). Because of the positive correlation between seigniorage and the inflation rate, the positive and significant coefficient of seigniorage suggests the existence of the Olivera-Tanzi effect in which high rates of inflation reduce the real proceeds of taxes and thereby lead to a positive correlation between seigniorage and budget deficits.

TABLE 3.1 Channels of Influence of Politics to Deficits, Money and Inflation Using M1 and Base Money (1972-1985); Generalized Method of Moments Using M1 and Base Money

Variables	(1.1)			(1.2)		
	Coefficient	Std. Error	T-value	Coefficient	Std. Error	T-value
M1 or BASE MONEY						
Deficit Equation:						
LAGGED OUTPUT GA	-0.08	0.04	2.09*	-0.07	0.04	1.79
SEIGNIORAGE	0.16	0.06	2.47*	0.24	0.06	3.69**
RPE	-18.86	4.74	3.97**	-20.31	5.46	3.72**
RPE²	9.08	2.77	3.27**	10.01	3.06	-3.27**
CONSTANT	10.90	1.93	5.63**	11.23	2.31	4.86**
R²	0.26			0.26		
Number of Observ.	196			196		
Money Equation:						
OUTPUT GAP	-0.04	0.28	0.14	-0.04	1.85	0.02
INFLATION	0.63	0.03	21.50**	0.41	0.82	4.96**
RESERVES	-0.02	0.01	1.20	0.26	0.16	1.59
BUDGET DEFICIT	3.32	0.95	3.47**	43.05	11.30	3.81**
CONSTANT	5.75	3.95	1.46	-87.65	33.30	2.63**
R²	0.95			0.72		
Number of Observ.	196			196		
Inflation Equation:						
MONEY GROWTH	1.55	0.09	17.64**	1.27	0.11	11.38**
REAL GDP GROWTH	-0.34	0.35	0.97	-2.61	0.84	3.11**
CONSTANT	-18.60	4.06	4.57**	-3.19	6.19	0.52
R²	0.94			0.78		
Number of Observ.	196			196		

* Significant at 5 percent level.   ** Significant at 1 percent level.

Finally, the negative and positive significant coefficients of *RPE* and *RPE*^{2} suggest that, after other factors have been taken into account, increases in political extraction have a negative but declining effect on fiscal deficits. This result is consistent with the a priori expectation that politically capable governments will be able to implement consistent and sustainable demand management policies because they possess the capacity to extract resources and deliver them to their intended ends.

Examination of the money growth equations shows that lagged inflation and current budget deficits exert statistically significant pressure on the rate of monetary expansion. With respect to inflation rates, the positive coefficient of the inflation variable indicates the existence of a pro-cyclical policy to meet the increased demand for nominal cash balances and/or cost-push accommodation that will maintain a constant purchasing power. As noted previously, the positive coefficient of lagged inflation could also indicate the presence of powerful inflation-feedback or inertial mechanisms, such as backward-looking wage and price indexation. Changes in international reserves do not appear to affect the money supply, which implies that most of the changes in monetary growth are attributable to domestic rather than external developments. Finally, the positive and significant coefficient of the budget deficit variable shows that deficits lead to increased rates of monetary growth.

As expected, the inflation equation shows that higher rates of monetary expansion are associated with higher rates of inflation. Real *GDP* growth, however, exerts a significant negative influence only on base money, not on the growth of *M1*.

In summary, the results indicate that countries with low levels of political extraction experience large budget deficits, high monetary growth, and high rates of inflation. To a degree, then, political choices account for the inflationary process.

CONCLUSION

This chapter provides an empirical examination of the relationship among relative political extraction, budget deficits, money creation, and inflation for fourteen Latin American economies for the years 1972—1985. To allow for endogeneity, the budgetary position of the fiscal authorities and the monetary policy reaction functions are specified as endogenous variables within a simultaneous-equation framework. The evidence supports the view that fiscal deficits in Latin American economies are partly determined by political factors; in particular, cross-country differentials in fiscal deficits depend upon differences in relative political extraction. In turn, deficit monetization leads to increased rates of monetary expansion and inflation.

Future research should examine an even broader body of data in order to shed light on the variety of ways in which politics and economics interact. For example, in evaluating the effects of political extraction on economic policy outcomes, further studies could concentrate on the specification of more refined policy reaction functions that would take into account external as well as internal developments. Finally, based on the promising initial results detailed here, future empirical work could explore the possibility that there exists a quantifiable two-way causality between political actions and economic outcomes.

NOTES

1. For specific discussions and empirical analysis of the link between the choice of operating procedures and the degree of monetary accommodation, see Laney and Willett (1983).

2. The optimal inflation tax is that rate which taxes the holdings of cash balances such that the marginal excess burden from the inflation tax equals the marginal cost of the most efficient alternative method of raising government revenue. The empirical evidence from developing countries, however, rejects the implications of the optimal inflation tax theory (Roubini 1991; Edwards and Tabellini 1991a).

3. The sample is comprised of the following countries: Argentina, Bolivia, Brazil, Chile, Colombia, Costa Rica, Dominican Republic, Ecuador, El Salvador, Guatemala, Honduras, Mexico, Uruguay, and Venezuela.

4. In the second model tested, M_t is replaced by Base Money$_t$.

5. The central bank and fiscal authority policy functions were estimated using annual data for the years 1972—1985. The entire system of three equations was estimated using the Generalized Method of Moments (GMM) estimator. The GMM estimates are consistent and asymptotically efficient and the standard errors of the estimates are heteroskedastic-consistent and robust to serial correlation.

4

Political Capacity and the Use of Seigniorage

Lorena Alcazar

INTRODUCTION[1]

By treating policy makers as machines that minimize the excess burden of all forms of taxation, traditional economic theory has failed to fully explain the differences in the use of seigniorage across countries. These differences may exist because of crucial political constraints that affect policy makers' decisions. A political economy literature has been developed to address this issue. However, most of the relevant studies are only theoretical in character and are based solely on developed countries. This chapter incorporates political constraints to explain the use of seigniorage. In particular, it uses political capacity as a proxy for government strength to explain the tendency of policy makers to use seigniorage to finance large fiscal deficits and consequently inflate the economy.

The political science literature has extensively documented the use of political capacity, particularly with the objective of predicting the results of international wars. Within this body of literature, Organski and Kugler (1978, 1980) and Arbetman (1990) developed a measure of relative political extraction (*RPE*) based on the ability of the state to gather resources and the authority of the state to use these resources to implement political decisions. However, only recently has this index begun to be used to explain economic policies (Snider 1988; Arbetman 1995; this volume).[2]

The central idea to be modeled can be stated as follows: Governments with lower political capacity are relatively more concerned about political approval than about economic efficiency. This, together with a pressure to implement expansionary policies, results in constraints against politically costly policies such as increasing taxes, and consequently a higher tendency to use seigniorage. A politically constrained government is unable to increase taxes to satisfy expenditure demands, and therefore must rely more heavily on seigniorage.

The chapter is organized as follows. First, there is an introduction of the main political-economic models that analyze seigniorage by considering political incentives and constraints. Second, an alternative political-economic approach is developed to explain differences in the use of seigniorage across countries, and how government capacity can play a significant role in this model is discussed. The next section tests the empirical implications of the model using econometric panel data analysis. Empirical evidence from a panel of 65 developed and developing countries for the years 1967—1985 supports the predictions of the current model. Finally, conclusions are drawn.

DEFINING SEIGNIORAGE

Seigniorage is the ability of the government to finance its expenditures by printing money. This ability derives from the government's sovereign monetary monopoly. It is one of the sources of government revenue and an alternative to higher ordinary taxation or interest-bearing public debt. It accounts for about 0.5% of GNP in low-inflation industrialized economies, and for a much greater percentage in most developing countries, ranging from 0.6% to 9% of the GNP (De Haan et al. 1993). In the case of nations experiencing extreme hyperinflation, it becomes the only source of government revenue (Blanchard and Fisher 1989).

Given that money creation causes inflation, which in turn reduces the real value of money balances, seigniorage acts as a tax on monetary holdings or money-denominated assets. Although there is no agreement on how best to measure seigniorage, it is generally defined as the rate of growth of the money supply multiplied by the real monetary balances.[3]

POLITICAL-ECONOMIC MODELS OF SEIGNIORAGE

Economic models of optimal seigniorage presented in Appendix A are based on a framework in which a "benevolent dictator" chooses the policy that maximizes a social utility function. The empirical evidence does not provide solid support for the implications of any of the theories presented, especially in the case of developing countries. For this reason this work is based on an alternative political-economic approach suggesting that the inclusion of political institutions, incentives, and constraints is crucial in modeling and predicting policymakers' decisions.

Two main alternative approaches that focus on political constraints to explain the use of seigniorage (or inflation) can be distinguished in the literature (see Chapter 3): myopic models and inability models. The so-called "myopic models" are based on the tradition of two-party systems and assert that governments *choose* to pursue high levels of seigniorage because they do not expect to be reappointed and therefore to benefit from a tax reform (Cukierman et al. 1989). On the other hand, there are several models of decentralized policy making which assert that high levels of seigniorage are inevitable because weak governments are *unable* to make a collective decision (Alesina and Drazen 1991, Aizenman 1989, among others). The fundamental difference between these two approaches is that the first emphasizes strategic behavior, reflected by a willingness to inflate the economy, whereas the second views the government as powerless to change the status quo and forced to rely on seigniorage.

The central idea of the strategic or myopic models is that governments deliberately engage in inefficient economic policies in order to worsen the state of the world inherited by their successors. Using this model, Cukierman, Edwards, and Tabellini (1989) predict that in more polarized and unstable political systems (where political instability is defined as the likelihood of a change in the executive, either by constitutional or unconstitutional means), the party in office deliberately refrains from reforming the tax system in order to constrain the next party's spending, and therefore relies more heavily on seigniorage. The implications of this model are tested using a cross section analysis of 58 developing countries. Their dependent variable is seigniorage. Independent variables include: proxies for the ease of taxation (size of agricultural sector, size of the external trade sector, etc), a proxy of the government's perceived probability of being re-elected,[4] and a proxy of political polarization (frequency of coup attempts). Their empirical results are encouraging. However, the applicability of this model to developing countries presents some problems. For the model to be applicable, a certain consensus and certainty about "the rules of the game" is required (i.e., a regular alternation of political parties should be observed). These assumptions seem too strong in the case of most developing countries, where political parties usually are personalized and short-lived. Additionally, the interpretation of their political instability variable, reflecting frequency of government change, may be misleading. For example, the estimated political instabilities of Mexico (0), Nicaragua (0.07), and Brazil (0) are much lower than those of the United States (0.15), Denmark (0.31), and the Netherlands (0.38).

The central idea of inability models or decentralized policy making models is that inflation is unavoidable rather than a choice. According to these models, the more polarized the government (i.e., the weaker the government), the more conflict will there be among the different policy makers and the more seigniorage will be used. Edwards and Tabellini (1991b) test this implication and find no empirical support. However, this lack of empirical support may be explained by the inaccuracy of the interpretation of political weakness as a political struggle *within* the government. I argue that a struggle *between* the government and its selectorate is what forces the government to avoid increasing taxes to satisfy public demands. Therefore, the proxies of political weakness used by Edwards and Tabellini (whether the party in office has a majority of seats in the parliament or the number of parties in the governing coalition) are not appropriate. A measure of political capacity that relates government to its constituents is a more appropriate alternative to test the inability hypothesis.

POLITICAL CONSTRAINTS AND THE USE OF SEIGNIORAGE: AN ALTERNATIVE POLITICAL-ECONOMIC FRAMEWORK

The central hypothesis proposed here is straightforward: Weak governments avoid using politically costly economic policies because they fear disrupting the fragile political equilibrium. The selectorate's approval is the basis of the government's power. Within this framework, given strong pressure for expansionary policies, the government faces political pressure not to increase taxes, and consequently relies more heavily on residual forms of financing such as seigniorage. Therefore, the lower the political capacity of the government, the stronger the incentive to use seigniorage.

This argument implicitly assumes that the Central Bank is not completely independent. Second, it assumes that countries with higher use of seigniorage have limited alternative sources of fiscal revenue and possess inefficient tax systems, poor government bonds markets and consequently constrained access to foreign debt. Third, it assumes that in the short run the government chooses tax and seigniorage rates within the framework of the tax system already in place, since to implement a tax reform requires a long time. Finally, the argument posits that increasing taxes carries a higher political cost than increasing seigniorage. The public is seen as partially myopic because it observes only the immediate effects of seigniorage on income (higher fiscal spending), but does not recognize the pervasive longer effects that seigniorage will have on inflation.[5] This public myopia is due to agents' faulty perceptions and the imperfect information that the public utilizes in making decisions. While there is a diffuse cost of seigniorage, there is a clear and immediate cost of taxes.[6]

The hypothesis is that a weak goverment is politically unable to increase taxes and, instead, is "forced" to rely on seigniorage. This alternative approach may be interpreted as a variant of the inability type of models. Recall that those models argue that weak governments (polarized political systems) are unable to make an efficient policy decision and resort more often to the use of seigniorage. I argue that weak governments do tend to use more seigniorage but use a different interpretation of government weakness: government's political strength with respect to its constituents. Recall from Chapter 1 that political capacity has two dimensions: (1) the ability of the government to extract resources, and (2) the ability to penetrate society and exercise its authority over as many subjects as possible. The first dimension *(RPE)* is estimated by measuring the extractive capabilities of a government with respect to its taxable capacity. The second dimension *(RPR)* is proxied by estimates from the size of the informal sector.[7] The idea is that when governments lack the capacity to penetrate society, they become untrustworthy, encouraging people to act outside the law with little fear of being caught (see Chapter 1).

The effects of the political constraints on policy makers' decisionmaking process can be included in a simple version of a traditional model of optimal seigniorage and taxes. Assume the following intertemporal maximization problem,[8] where the government maximizes the function

$$W_t = E_t\{\Sigma \beta^k[U(c_{t+k}) + H(g_{t+k})]\}$$

subject to the following constraints:

$$g_t^2 \leq \tau_t + s_t$$
$$c_t^2 \leq 1 - \tau_t - s_t - \mu(\tau_t) - \delta(s_t)$$

where:

c = private consumption
g = public consumption
τ = tax collection
s = seigniorage collection
$\mu(\tau)$ = deadweight loss to private sector from tax
$\mu'(\tau) > 0$ and $\mu''(\tau) > 0$
$\delta(s)$ = deadweight loss to private sector from seigniorage
$\delta'(s) > 0$ and $\delta''(s) > 0$.

All the variables are expressed in per capita terms. E_t denotes the expectations operator, and every individual is endowed with one unit of output in each period.

From the first-order conditions, the following equations are derived:

$$H'(g) = U'(c)[1 + \delta'(s)], \tag{1}$$
$$U'(c) [1 + \delta'(s)] = U'(c) [1 + \mu'(\tau)], \text{ and} \tag{2}$$
$$[1 + \delta'(s)] = [1 + \mu'(\tau)]. \tag{3}$$

The implications of these first-order conditions are the same as those obtained in Appendix A. In particular, equation (3) equates at the margin the distortions associated with the last dollar collected from each source of revenue (traditional Ramsey Rule).

Now, a new variable is introduced in the government constraint: $\alpha [\tau(P)]$.[9] It denotes the political cost of increasing taxes.[10]

$$g_t^2 \leq \tau_t + s_t\, \alpha\,(\tau_t(P))$$

where:
P = political capacity of government (proxied by **RPC**).
$\alpha\,(\tau = 0) = 0$
$\alpha'(\tau) > 0$
$d\alpha(t)/dP < 0$ (the political cost of taxes is a decreasing function of the relative political capacity of the government).

From the new first-order conditions, the following equations are obtained:

$$H'(g) = U'(c)[1 + \delta'(s)], \tag{4}$$

$$H'(g)[1 - \alpha'(\tau)] = U'(c)[1 + \mu'(\tau)], \text{ and} \tag{5}$$

$$[1 + \mu'(\tau)] / [1 - \alpha'(\tau)] = [1 + \delta'(s)]. \tag{6}$$

It can be derived from equation (6) that seigniorage is positively associated with the political cost of taxes $(ds/d\alpha\,(\tau) > 0)$,[11] and because $d\alpha(\tau)/dP$ is by assumption negative it can be inferred that $ds/dP > 0$. Therefore, a testable implication of the model is: *Countries characterized by politically stronger or more capable governments are expected to exhibit relatively lower seigniorage.*

Results from Panel Analysis

A panel data set is employed to test the significance of the political features that were identified to determine the differences in the use of seigniorage across countries. The data base includes 65 developed and developing countries from all continents[12] (see Appendix B for a complete list). The years considered are 1967-1985. The following simple specification (using a FEM) is estimated:

$$s_{it} = \alpha_i + \beta x_{it} + \delta Z_{it} + \mu_{it} \qquad i = 1,..., N \qquad t = 1,...,T \qquad (7)$$

where s_{it} (the policy maker instrument) denotes the level of seigniorage; α_i is a scalar representing the effects of those time-invariant variables peculiar to the ith country; X_{it} is a vector of economic variables; Z_{it} is a vector of political variables; and u_{it}, the error term, represents the effects of the omitted time-variant variables.

For this panel data set, the fixed effects model (FEM) is preferred over the random effects model (REM) for two main reasons (Cheng Hsiao 1986; Judge, et al. 1988). First, the FEM is used when conditional inferences will be made on the sample, which is the case here, while the REM is recommended when unconditional inferences will be made with respect to a much larger population. Second, if the unmeasurable country fixed effects are correlated with the explanatory variables, the REM estimated parameters will be biased. Whenever such a correlation is suspected, the FEM should be chosen. In this case, it is likely that country-specific attributes (such as population characteristics) may be correlated with some of the explanatory variables. In addition, note that FEM is especially valuable when cross-section dummies account for all the time-invariant specific attributes of every country in the sample as is the case here.

Dependent Variables:
* *SEIGN./REVEN:* This is the change in money (reserve money) as a percentage of total government revenues (Source: IFS, line 14).
* *INF TAX/REV:* This is inflation rate multiplied by reserve money as a percentage of total government revenues. As can be seen in the next table, both variables are highly correlated. This index is chosen because the objective is to explain seigniorage, as opposed to ordinary taxation, as an instrument used to finance government expenditures.[13]

			CORRELATION MATRIX		
	MEAN	STD.DEV.	SEIGN./REV.	SEIGN./GDP	INF.TAX/REV
SEIGN./REVEN.	10.98	12.78	1.00	0.77	0.80
SEIGN./GDP	2.88	7.01	0.77	1.00	0.64
INF.TAX/REVEN.	8.65	12.81	0.80	0.64	1.00

Explanatory Variables:
* *Relative Political Capacity (RPC):*[14] See Chapter 1 (Data provided by the editors).

Correlations between *RPE* and *RPR*, the two dimensions of political capacity is only around 10%, showing that they represent different dimensions of political power.

• *REAL GDP PER CAPITA*: This is a proxy for the level of economic development. It is expected that less developed countries will have less efficient tax systems. Consequently, *GDP* per capita will reflect the efficiency of the tax system (see endnote 6). A negative coefficient is expected. (Source: Summers and Heston 1988)

• *Variables of the sectoral structure of GDP*: Traditionally these variables are included to account for differences in the cost of ordinary tax collection. Thus, *AGRICULTURE/GDP* (Source: The World Bank), considered as the hardest sector to tax, is expected to have a positive coefficient, and the ratio of foreign trade to *GDP* (*OPENNESS*) (Source: Summers and Heston 1988), is expected to have a negative coefficient because exports and imports are considered politically easy to tax.

• *FISCAL DEFICIT*: : This equals the difference between government revenues and expenditures as a percentage of *GDP*. It is used to control for fiscal constraints. (Source: IFS)

Before presenting the final results, let us recall the expectations of the impact of each element on seigniorage:

SEIGNIORAGE/REVENUES

EXPLANATORY VARIABLES:	SIGN
RPE	(-)
RPR	(-)
RGDP PER CAPITA	(-)
FISCAL DEFICIT	(+)
OPENNESS	(-)
AGRICULTURE/GDP	(+)

Results

Tables 4.1, 4.2, and 4.3 report the results of different specifications of equation (7). Table 4.1 presents the results obtained by including the two indices of political capacity in the basic model. The first column (1.1) includes *RPE*, and the second (2.2) includes both *RPE* and *RPR*. The negative signs show that the lower the government's political capacity, the higher the tendency of governments to use seigniorage. The coefficients of the political capacity proxies are highly significant in all cases. All the variables have the expected signs. The fiscal deficit and agriculture as a percentage of *GDP* are significant, while *RGDP PER CAPITA* and *Openness* are not. The model explains approximately 60% of the

TABLE 4.1 A Political Economic Model of Seigniorage Including Relative Political Capacity (1967-1985): Fixed Effects Model

Variables	(1.1)			(1.2)		
	Coefficient	Std. Error	T-value	Coefficient	Std. Error	T-value
SEIGNIORAGE/						
GOV. REVENUE						
RGDP PER CAPITA	-0.001	0.0004	-1.39	-0.00	0.0004	-0.925
FISCAL DEFICIT	1.158	0.0812	14.27**	1.118	0.0817	13.69**
OPENNESS	-0.025	0.0315	0.78	-0.032	0.0319	-1.015
AGRICULTURE/GDP	0.456	0.0915	4.98**	0.414	0.0919	4.51**
RPE	-3.244	1.6476	-1.97**	-3.147	1.6349	-1.93*
RPR				-19.805	6.1813	-3.20**
R^2	0.61		0.614			
Number of Observ.	874		874			

* Significant at 10 percent level.
** Significant at 1 percent level.

TABLE 4.2 A Political Economic Model of Seigniorage using Lagged Political Variables and Correcting for Autocorrelation; Fixed Effects Model

Variables	(2.1) Lagged Model			(2.2) AR1		
	Coefficient	Std. Error	T-value	Coefficient	Std. Error	T-value
SEIGNIORAGE/ *GOV. REVENUE*						
RGDP PER CAPITA	-0.001	0.0005	-1.51	-0.0002	0.0005	-0.39
FISCAL DEFICIT	1.132	0.0828	13.67**	0.7375	0.0766	9.63**
OPENNESS	-0.029	0.0325	-0.91	-0.0333	0.0365	-0.91
AGRICULTURE/GDP	0.471	0.0962	4.90**	0.4167	0.1000	4.16**
RPE	-3.687	1.6219	-2.27**	-3.1315	1.6954	-1.85*
RPR	-18.023	6.3866	-2.82**	-12.713	6.6386	-1.92*
R^2	0.635			0.506		
Number of Observ.	828			828		

* Significant at 10 percent level.
** Significant at 1 percent level.

TABLE 4.3 A Political Economic Model of Seigniorage for Developing and Developed Countries

Variables	(3.1) Developing Countries			(3.2) Developed Countries		
	Coefficient	Std. Error	T-value	Coefficient	Std. Error	T-value
SEIGNIORAGE/ *GOV. REVENUE*						
RGDP PER CAPITA	-0.0007	0.001	-0.62	0.0004	0.0002	-1.97*
FISCAL DEFICIT	1.2647	0.112	11.40**	0.0116	0.067	0.17
OPENNESS	0.0411	0.525	0.52	0.0116	0.012	0.95
AGRICULTURE/GDP	0.4781	0.126	3.79**	-0.1001	0.142	0.71
RPE	-3.3207	2.005	-1.66*	0.3834	1.432	0.27
RPR	-22.802	8.540	-2.67**	-2.905	4.566	-0.64
REAL GDP GROWTH	0.0113	0.096	0.12	0.2047	0.060	3.43**
R^2	0.536			0.618		
Number of Observ.	551			323		

* Significant at 10 percent level.
** Significant at 1 percent level.

differences in seigniorage.

A possible limitation of these results is that the relation between political capacity and seigniorage could be due to reverse causation, that is, higher inflation may produce lower political capacity. Against this objection, it can be argued that political capacity is normally a response to many different political, social, and economic variables. Further, the variable observed by the public is inflation, not seigniorage. In any case, an instrument of the political capacity variable (Lagged Political Capacity) is tested to avoid this possible problem in the relation between current political capacity and seigniorage.

The first regression of Table 4.2 (2.1) reports the results of re-estimating the second regression of Table 4.1 using one-year lagged political capacity. The previous results hold. All the variables remain strongly significant. If inflation affects political capacity, this effect should occur in the same period (if not in the next one). Therefore, if there is a joint endogeneity problem, it should be corrected (or at least substantially reduced) by the use of a lagged political capacity variable.

The validity of these results may also be disputed because of the possible presence of autocorrelation within each country and/or hetero-skedasticity among countries. To confront the first problem the FEM is re-estimated using an AR1 specification. The last regression of Table 4.2 (2.2) reports the new estimations. All the previous results hold.[15]

Recall that myopic models may face some problems when applied to developing countries and I suggested an alternative approach. To test the hypothesis that this alternative approach is more appropriate in the case of developing countries, Table 4.3 presents the results after dividing the sample between developing and developed countries. The outcomes are very interesting. In the case of developing countries, previous results hold. Both are significant political capacity variables. On the other hand, in the estimated regression for developed countries, the *RPE* and *RPR* indexes lose their significance while some other economic variables, including *RGDP PER CAPITA* and *OPENNESS*, become more significant.

To summarize, the empirical evidence presented in this section supports the predictions that *the relative political capacity of governments is a significant determinant of differences in the use of seigniorage across developing countries.*

CONCLUSIONS

The objective of this chapter was to explain differences across countries in the use of seigniorage by taking into acount both economic variables and political constraints. The results confirm the existence of a link between the political and economic policies which a nation promulgates—in this case, its use of seigniorage (Arbetman and Kugler 1995). The chapter also provides substantial supporting empirical evidence for the hypothesis that differences in the use of seigniorage across countries and time are explained by differences in government political capacity. In all cases, the proxies for political constraints were highly significant and robust to alternative model specifications.

Empirical evidence has been provided supporting the modified version of the inability hypothesis, where weak governments avoid facing a political struggle with the public by choosing seigniorage over taxation policy. Indeed, relative political extraction and relative political reach were significant determinants of seigniorage. Additionally, the results suggest that the approach adopted here is more appropriate for developing than for developed countries.

APPENDIX A: OPTIMAL SEIGNIORAGE IN THE THEORY OF PUBLIC FINANCE

In an ideal monetary world, where there are only lump-sum taxes, the only distortion would be the tax on currency. This distortion may be eliminated by applying the so-called "Friedman Rule," whose policy prescription is: Produce money at the rate which makes its opportunity cost zero. That is, make the real interest rate equal to the deflation rate.

Once it is recognized that distortionary taxes are being employed, the determination of optimal seigniorage becomes an objective of public finance theory. Phelps (1973) introduced the analysis of seigniorage as an alternative distortionary tax. One of the main points of his work was to prove that the Friedman Rule is wrong and that a positive rate of inflation may be optimal. In Phelps' model, revenue from seigniorage comes from a wedge between the consumer's price and the producer's price, just as in the case of any other tax. Therefore, by applying differential tax analysis (as suggested by Ramsey in 1927), Phelps concluded that the optimal inflation tax is positive.

Manikow (1987) extends earlier work and analyzes the use of seigniorage in an intertemporal optimization problem. The monetary and fiscal authority chooses a sequence of tax rates and money growth rates so as to minimize the excess burden of taxation, subject to the constraint that the present value of government obligations does not exceed the present value of their revenues. There are two sources of revenue: taxes on output and seigniorage. Both sources of revenue cause deadweight social losses. The policy objective is to minimize the present value of that social loss function. Thus, the choice between income taxation and seigniorage depends on the relative marginal social costs of these two forms of taxation. Specifically, given that τ is the tax rate on output, the revenue raised through taxes is equal to τY. The deadweight loss associated with this tax revenue is $f(\tau)Y$, where

$f'>0$ and $f''>0$. The inflation tax rate is π. The revenue raised through seigniorage is $(\pi + y)Yk$, where y is the growth rate of output and k is the constant coming from the money demand equation $(M/P = Y\,k)$. The social cost of inflation is $h(\pi)Y$, where $h'>0$ and $h''>0$. Consequently, the present value of the total social losses from both types of revenue, to be minimized by the policy-maker, is:

$$E_t \int_0^\infty e^{-\beta s}\,[f(\tau) + h(\pi)]Y\,ds \tag{8}$$

subject to the budget constraint

$$\int_0^\infty e^{-\beta s}\,Gds + B_t = \int_0^\infty e^{-\beta s}\,[\tau + \pi k + yk]\,Y\,ds. \tag{9}$$

The first-order conditions of this intertemporal minimization problem are

$$E_t\{f'(\tau_{t+s})\} = f'(\tau_t), \tag{10}$$

$$E_t\{h'(\pi_{t+s})\} = h'(\pi_t), \tag{11}$$

$$h'(\pi_t) = kf'(\tau_t). \tag{12}$$

The optimal tax rate and inflation rate should satisfy these three equations. The first two equations imply "tax smoothing" of the policies, that is, equating the marginal cost of the present and future tax rates—of the tax rate in equation (10) and of the inflation rate in equation (11). Equation (12) equalizes the marginal cost of raising revenue through ordinary taxation and through seigniorage.

Therefore, this theory implies specific testable conditions. The marginal cost of taxation and inflation should be martingales, and if $f'(\tau)$ and $h'(\pi)$ are quadratic, the tax and inflation rates themselves should also be martingales. Further, equation (12) implies that an increase in government revenue requirements should increase the use of both instruments. Thus, the level of taxation should move together with the level of inflation. The main implication of this theory is that in the presence of distortionary taxation, it is optimal to tax money.[16] Note that when inflation uncertainty is taken into account this lowers the optimal rate (Banian et al. 1994; Banian 1995b).

Maximizing Government Revenues from Seigniorage

Up to now, it has been assumed that the government maximizes a social welfare function and is constrained by limited resources. However, one can also assume a predatory government whose objective is to maximize revenues. In this case, the relevant question would be: What is the maximum amount of seigniorage that the government can collect? The usual answer is that seigniorage is maximized when the elasticity of the tax base (real balances) with respect to the tax rate is equal to -1, as in any monopoly case. As Tanzi (1991) illustrates, even assuming no Central Bank independence where the government has control of the money printing mechanism, there is a limit to the amount of real fiscal deficit that can be financed by monetary expansion. As the government increases the rate of money growth to finance its deficit, the rate of inflation increases while the holdings of real balances fall. Initially, the positive effect on revenues coming from a higher inflation tax compensates for the negative effect coming from the fall in real balances. At some point (when the elasticity of the *demand for* real balances is 1), the combination of these two variables (tax rate and base) is *maximized*, limiting the size of the fiscal deficit that can be financed by money creation.[17]

Friedman (1971) presents a modified model. He argues that the former analysis is only correct in a stationary economy and that it is misleading in the case of a growing economy. In such an economy, by issuing money the government obtains a yield from two sources: the tax on existing real cash balances and the tax on the additional real cash balances that are demanded as income rises. As the rate of prices increases, the second source of yield decreases. Therefore, in these economies the inflation tax that maximizes revenues is lower than the unit-elasticity rate.

Empirical Evidence

Optimal seigniorage in the theory of public finance implies that money growth and inflation are determined by government revenue requirements. The implications of the theory are testable.

Manikow (1987) tests whether inflation rates and tax rates move together in the United States. He estimates two regressions using American data for the years 1952-1985. First, he uses the nominal interest rate as the dependent variable and a proxy for tax rates as the independent variable. Because the real interest rate is assumed constant in the model, the nominal interest rate should move together with inflation. Second, he directly regresses inflation rates on tax rates.[18] His results provide some support for the theory that the average tax rate is positively related to the nominal interest rate and to the inflation rate, but that only the first relationship is significant.[19]

With a similar model, Poterba and Rothemberg (1990) test the implications of the theory using annual data from a sample of five OECD countries: the United States, Britain, France, Germany, and Japan. Their findings confirm Manikow's results for the United States. However, the significant positive association found in U.S. data cannot be generalized: French and British data show a significant negative relation between the two relevant variables, there is no significant relation in the German case, and only in the Japanese case is the theory supported at all.

Using a large sample of developing countries, Roubini (1991) rejects the empirical implications of the theory of optimal seigniorage. As in Manikow (1987) and Poterba and Rothemberg (1990), he tests a simple regression of the inflation rate on the tax rate and a time trend for 75 developing countries for the years 1950-1988. His results show that only fifteen countries present a significant positive relation between the tax rate and the inflation rate. He also tests the model by means of an alternative approach. First, he performs unit-root tests on the inflation and tax rates to see if they are nonstationary variables, as suggested by the first-order conditions of the minimization problem. Then, he tests for the presence of cointegration between the two variables, to determine whether they move together as predicted by the theory. The results, obtained using this new approach, also reject the theory. The unit-root hypothesis is accepted for only 22 countries out of 75. Finally, the hypothesis of no cointegration is rejected for only three countries (see also Burdekin 1991).

Edwards and Tabellini (1991a) also test the implications of optimal taxation theory. Working with a data sample from 21 developing countries for the years 1954-1987, they provide a strong rejection of the hypothesis. Moreover, their work indicates that the inflation tax often behaves as a residual source of government revenue; i.e., any change in government spending is reflected one-for-one in higher inflation.

Having evaluated the implications of the optimal taxation theory and proceeding under the conception that the objective of the government is to maximize revenues, Friedman (1971) estimates the rates of inflation that would maximize the government's revenue according to his model. He finds that those optimal rates do not correspond with what is observed in most developing countries.

Edwards and Tabellini (1991a) also estimate the relation between the rate of inflation and the logarithm of the inflation tax revenue for a sample of developing countries (Turkey, Argentina, Brazil, and Chile). They find that in these countries there is indeed a Laffer curve type of relationship between the rate of inflation and the revenues obtained from this tax. They also find that these countries have passed the top of the curve; i.e., the inflation tax has been higher than the one required to maximize revenues from this source.

APPENDIX B: COUNTRIES INCLUDED IN MAIN SAMPLE*

(listed alphabetically by geographical region)

1. Cameroon	23. Argentina	45. Australia
2. Egypt	24. Bolivia	46. New Zealand
3. Ghana	25. Brazil	47. Austria
4. Kenya	26. Chile	48. Belgium
5. Malawi	27. Colombia	49. Cyprus
6. Mauritius	28. Ecuador	50. Denmark
7. Morocco	29. Guyana	51. Finland
8. Senegal	30. Paraguay	52. France
9. S. Leone	31. Peru	53. Germany
10. Tunisia	32. Uruguay	54. Greece
11. Zaire	33. Burma	55. Iceland
12. Zambia	34. India	56. Ireland
13. Barbados	35. Israel	57. Italy
14. Canada	36. Japan	58. Malta
15. Costa Rica	37. Jordan	59. Netherlands
16. Dominican Repub.	38. South Korea	60. Norway
17. El Salvador	39. Malaysia	61. Spain
18. Guatemala	40. Pakistan	62. Sweden
19. Mexico	41. Philippines	63. Switzerland
20. Nicaragua	42. Singapore	64. Turkey
21. Panama	43. Sri Lanka	65. United Kingdom
22. United States	44. Thailand	

*The sample corresponds to the one used by Barro (1991), "Economic Growth in a Cross-Section of Countries," except for the countries for which no political variables and/or seigniorage were available.

NOTES

1. I want to thank Art Denzau, Steve Fazzari, Douglass North, Paul Rosthein, and Hugo Santa Maria for very helpful comments and discussions.

2. The empirical work in the area of political economy has only utilized indirect measures of political constraints, such as frequency of government change, number of political disorders, and whether the party in office has a majority of seats in the parliament.

3. Alternative measures commonly used in the literature are: inflation rate times real balances and nominal interest rate multiplied by real balances. It is important to note the difference between seigniorage and the inflation tax. The inflation tax is imposed on money holders as a consequence of inflation (the loss of real value of money), and is equal to the inflation rate multiplied by the real balances. Seigniorage is the same as the inflation tax only when the inflation rate is equal to the money growth rate; that is, when there is no output growth.

4. To proxy the perceived probability of being re-elected, they estimate a probit equation. The dependent variable is actual frequency of government change (regular or irregular), and the explanatory variables include indicators of economic performance, political variables (riots, political executions, executive adjustments, and coup attempts), and structural variables (dummies to account for democracy, elections, and majoritarian democracies).

5. However, at high levels of inflation agents may learn about and identify the pervasive costs of inflation, change their preferences, and press for anti-inflationary policies.

6. Also, in low-income countries a very large percentage of the population spends most of its budget on staple foods. Therefore, the government can hide the costs of inflation from the public by shielding some staple foods with subsidies or price controls.

7. An alternative method using tax structures is proposed by Snider. The idea is that direct tax collection requires higher bureaucratic skills and higher levels of compliance than does indirect tax collection. Therefore, weaker governments would rely more heavily on indirect tax revenue than on direct.

8. This simple model is inspired by the one used in Cukierman et al. (1989).

9. The political variable is introduced as part of the constraint and not in the utility function because this approach argues in favor of a government inability to increase taxes over a government unwillingness to do it (myopic models).

10. Seigniorage also may have a political cost, but as explained before, it would be smaller than the political cost of taxation. Therefore, in the interest of simplification, the political cost of seigniorage is assumed to be equal to zero.

11. This result is obtained by applying the implicit function theorem to equation (6).

12. Middle Eastern and former Soviet countries are excluded, as are some countries for which data is missing.

13. *SEIGN/GDP* and *INFL.TAX/REV* are used to test the robustness of the results.

14. See Chapter 1 of this volume for a complete description of the estimation and interpretation of the indices of political capacity.

15. Regarding the other possible statistical problem, heteroskedasticity, it may be argued that the errors may be correlated with some of the independent variables because of their possible correlation with the size of the country. However, this is unlikely here because the variables that may be related to the size of the country are scaled (estimated as a percentage of *GDP*, or some other scale variable). In addition, a plot of the residuals with the population variable did not show any pattern of correlation.

16. These results are not universally accepted. The model critiques are mostly based on a different interpretation of money. Lucas (1986) argues that money should not be taxed like any other good because, "it is only the means to a subset of goods that an income tax has already taxed once." In general, Lucas and others (Kimbrough 1986; Faig 1988) argued that money should not be included in the utility function, and reexamined the theory of optimal seigniorage by treating money only as an intermediate good. These alternative models show that a positive seigniorage is not optimal and that the Friedman rule still holds in the presence of distortionary taxation.

17. This characteristic of the inflation tax corresponds to the well-known Laffer curve effect.

18. In both cases, Manikow includes a time trend as an additional explanatory variable.

19. Kenny and Toma (1993) argue that empirical tests of optimal seigniorage assume that relative collection costs and tax bases have not changed significantly over time. By directly controlling for variations in these variables (although only through questionable proxies), they find substantial support for the theory in the United States.

5

Political Capacity and Private Investment[1]

Yi Feng and Baizhu Chen

INTRODUCTION

This chapter investigates the effects on private investment of macropolitical uncertainty characterized by the level of change in relative political capacity (*RPC*). We suggest that an increase in the variance of a government's political capacity contributes to political uncertainty, thereby reducing economic activities including private investment. This hypothesis is statistically tested on the aggregate data of forty developing countries from 1978 through 1988. The empirical results indicate that, as expected, private investment decreases as the variance of relative political extraction increases.

In recent years, the relationship between domestic politics and economic performance in developing countries has been the subject of research in both political science and economics. In this context, the present chapter studies changes in aggregate private investment over time. The issue of private investment is important for developing and former communist countries interested in activating the private sector (Haggard and Kaufman 1992; Riker and Weimer 1993), because as recent research suggests, private investment in developing countries is essential to aggregate economic growth (Khan and Reinhart 1990; Firebaugh 1992).

In this chapter, we deal with the relationship between private investment and macropolitical uncertainty. Specifically, our focus is on the political control exercised by an elite as expressed by variations in government capacity. Historically, there have been two opposing views regarding the relationship between private investment and a strong autocratic government. While one group tends to argue that among developing countries an authoritarian system is more likely to attract private investment (e.g., O'Donnell 1978; O'Donnell and Schmitter 1986), the other group concludes that democracy, political freedom, and civil liberties promote private investment while autocracy discourages it (e.g., Kormendi and Meguire 1985; Pastor and Hilt 1993).

The beginning chapters of this book have developed and operationalized the concept of relative political capacity. Organski and Kugler define political capacity as "the ability of government to effectively carry out tasks imposed on it by its own political elite, by other important national actors, or by the pressures of the international environment" (Organski and Kugler, 1980, 72). While Organski and Kugler (1980) and Kugler (1994) focus on the capabilities of the government to extract national resources, Arbetman (1990, 1995) theorizes about the capacity of the government to penetrate the economy. As found in Chapter 1 of this book, *RPC* is independent from political freedom and from the nature of a polity. Therefore, political capacity may offer new insights into many problems which remain unexplained by other political or economic variables.

This chapter shows that political uncertainty resulting from the variance of *RPE* adversely affects private investment, confirming numerous studies that show that uncertainty causes a decrease in private investment (Grier and Tullock 1989; Rodrik 1991; Aizenman and Marion 1993). Thus, a high level of variability in political capacity increases macropolitical uncertainty, which in turn decreases private investment in the same way that macroeconomic uncertainty does. This suggests that a lack of consistency in a government's capacity to rule the nation or to organize the society will generate political uncertainty in the marketplace. As one businessman says, "[One] can make money under any policy situation as long as it does not change every fifteen minutes" (Rodrik 1991). Although this may be an overstatement reflecting the sentiment of an avid entrepreneur, it is nevertheless generally true that investors are deterred from making long-term investments if the political capacity of the government changes frequently. The emphasis in this chapter is therefore on the variances, rather than the levels, of relative political capacity.

BACKGROUND

Investors are typically faced at the outset of a business formation with certain initial costs of investing. These costs make investors especially sensitive to uncertain changes in the policy and competency of the government. We propose that, whatever the level of political capacity achieved, governments that increase or reduce political competency, or that continually vacillate between being a strong and a weak government, induce economic uncertainty, compared to governments whose political capacity is stable and consistent. Consequently, whether weak or strong there is less political uncertainty with a government of stable political capacity than with a government whose political capacity varies. Such variation affects investment. Typically, an individual's decision to invest is based on two concerns: expected returns and variance of returns. If the level of returns is kept constant, an increase in the level of the variance of returns will decrease the expected utility of the investment, assuming the commonality of risk-aversion among investors. Political uncertainty, caused by the high variability of political capacity, increases the variance of the returns and thereby decreases the value of the investment.

Many studies (e.g., Pindyck 1988; Dixit 1989; Rodrik 1991) suggest that uncertainty generates an option value of waiting when investment is subject to sunk costs, which tends to reduce private investment. Uncertainty about a government's capability to control the nation or to deal with special interest groups weighs heavily on the private investor's decision to enter the market. As the rational investor takes into account the entry and exit costs of investment under political uncertainty, the flow of private investment decreases.

This chapter is organized as follows. First, we propose a simple model to illustrate the effect of macropolitical uncertainty on private investment. Second, we discuss specification and data. Third, we present results. Finally, we detail the impact on investment of political and economic considerations.

THE BASIC MODEL

This section presents a basic model which examines the effect on private investment of the changeability of government political capacity. Two investment activities are assumed. One involves investing in a market under government influence, and the other, investing in a market not under government influence. In the former market, the investment return is a random variable due to the random effect of government politics and policy. This return is given as

$$R^* = (1-\tau)r \tag{1}$$

where r is the certain return without government influence and τ is the cost of the government policy on investment; τ is normally distributed with an expected value τ and a variance σ_τ^2, i.e. $\tau \propto N(\bar{\tau}, \sigma_\tau^2)$. When the government policy has a positive effect on investment returns, τ is less than zero, and when it produces a negative effect, τ is greater than zero. Note that τ here has to be interpreted broadly, and somewhat metaphorically. It stands for politics that affect private investment. Among negative examples of this variable are infringement on property rights, lack of patent legislation, abuse or misuse of resources to satisfy special interest groups, and violations of human rights. Examples of positive externalities include public goods such as infrastructure, schools, a framework for property rights, and other institutions which facilitate private investment.

The market not subject to government influence offers a certain return

$$r^* = r. \tag{2}$$

In equation (2), the investor invests his or her money in a capital market where government policy does not have an effect on capital return. This hypothetical market is exemplified in cases of capital flight where, fearful of the negative consequences of government intervention at home, investors send their money abroad, where the domestic government will have little influence on the return on invested capital.

It is assumed that there are initially N investors in the first investment activity given by equation (1); each of them is endowed with one unit of capital. They make the decision whether to switch to the alternative market, given considerations reflected by equation (2). It is further assumed that to undertake an investment, investors have to bear an entry or exit cost: ($\varepsilon \in [0,\infty)$). Without such cost, all investments would occur in the market with a certain return, given $\bar{\tau} > 0$. The investors differ in their entry cost ε, which is distributed according to the probability distribution function $f(\varepsilon)$. Consequently, the value of switching to the certain investment activity with the entry cost ε is

$$V_c = r/\delta - \varepsilon \tag{3}$$

where δ is the discount factor.[2]

If the investors decide to stay in the uncertain market, the value of their investment is

$$V_u = (r - \bar{\tau} r)/\delta - v(\sigma_\tau^2),$$

because the high variance of government politics reduces the value of the investment for a risk-averse investor.

The investor will stay in the uncertain market if $V_c < V_u$, i.e., specifically,

$$V_c = r/\delta - \varepsilon < V_u = (r - \bar{\tau} r)/\delta - v(\sigma_\tau^2), \tag{4}$$

which leads to

$$\varepsilon > \bar{\tau} \, r/\delta + v \, (\sigma_\tau^2) = \varepsilon_0 , \tag{5}$$

where ε_0 may be considered the critical value of the entry cost. Thus, the investors with $\varepsilon > \varepsilon_0$ will stay in the uncertain market.

From equations (4) and (5), the total amount of the investments that remain in the uncertain market is

$$I = N \int_{\varepsilon_0}^{\infty} f(\varepsilon) d \, \varepsilon . \tag{6}$$

From equation (6) we derive the effect of government politics on investment

$$dI / d\bar{\tau} = -N \, f(\varepsilon_0) \, d \, \varepsilon_0 / d\bar{\tau} = -N \, f(\varepsilon_0) \, r/\delta < 0 \tag{7}$$

and

$$dI / d \, \sigma_\tau^2 = -N \, f(\varepsilon_0) \, d \, \varepsilon_0 / d \, \sigma_\tau^2 = -N \, f(\varepsilon_0) \, v'(\sigma_\tau^2) < 0. \tag{8}$$

Although equation (7) confirms the intuitive reasoning that an increase in the expected economic cost resulting from government politics will cause a decrease in private investment, our central theoretical interest is expressed by equation (8), which states that the variance of government politics on investment causes a decrease in the amount of investment. In the context of relative political capacity, a change in the level of the government's effective control creates macropolitical uncertainty, which in turn leads to a decline in private investment. Under similar circumstances, there are two extreme prototypes of government: the government whose political capacity remains nearly constant over time, and the government whose political capacity fluctuates. We posit that the absence of variability in political capacity produces consistency of policy outcomes. The government whose capacity fluctuates gives rise to unexpected policy changes to which the investors and the market as a whole have to adjust. Therefore, given a certain level of entry cost, investment in a market will decrease as the result of an increase in the inconsistency of that government's relative political capacity.[3]

SPECIFICATION AND DATA

This section presents a preliminary empirical look at some political determinants of private investment. As it stands, the approach here does not constitute a direct test of the model described in the preceding section. Instead, we focus on the broad implications of the approach exemplified by the model. One major implication is that political uncertainty caused by changes in government political capacity deters investors from investing. In particular, the model suggests that when a government cannot keep its political capacity relatively constant, private investment decreases.

A statistical model is specified to test the effect on private investment of macropolitical uncertainty as shown by the variability of relative political capacity:

$$PRIVATE = \alpha+\beta X+\gamma Y+\mu \tag{9}$$

where:

PRIVATE	= private investment as a percentage of GDP,
X	= the changeability of government political capacity,
Y	= a set of relevant economic and political variables,
μ	= the error term.

Unless otherwise noted, all data are averages for the years 1978-1988 because long-term changes are being examined without focusing on cyclical variation in investment or changes related to business cycles.

To assess private investment we use the investment data for forty countries compiled by Pfeffermann and Madarassy (1991) and combine them with political variables (Taylor 1985; Gastil 1978-1988; Arbetman 1990, 1995) and economic variables (Summers and Heston 1991; Barro 1991; Pfeffermann and Madarassy 1991). All countries are less developed countries (LDCs), except Turkey and Portugal, which may be categorized as OECD countries.

Macropolitical uncertainty is reflected by the concept of changeability in government political capacity. It is measured by the standard deviation of relative political extraction (*RPE*) for each country over the period 1977 through 1987. Organski and Kugler suggest that "political capacity consists of three interrelated elements: the level of penetration of government power into national society, the capacity of the governmental system to extract resources from its national society, and finally, the performance of government in delivering such resources to their intended ends" (Organski and Kugler 1980, 208). We consider the second element the most critical for phenomenon that deal with economic issues such as inflation, trade, growth, and investment. For this reason the standard deviation of relative political extraction (*RPESTD*) is used as a proxy for the changeability of government political capacity.

We postulate that higher standard deviation of *RPE* indicates a higher level of uncertainty about government control and competency. The sign on the parameter estimate of this variable should be negative, for when the investor perceives a high propensity for change in the level of government control, he or she will be uncertain about the direction the market is likely to take, and will decrease investment accordingly.

Barro (1991) and Grier and Tullock (1988) find that political and social uncertainties manifested by revolutions, assassinations, and coups d'état discourage private investment. Schneider and Frey (1985) conclude that riots and strikes have a negative impact on foreign direct investment. In this study, the number of deaths from political violence per 10,000 of the population (*DEATH*) is included to take into account the additional uncertainty created by political and social violence on private investment, for it is a better indicator of the severity of political turbulence than merely the number of revolutions, coups d'état, strikes, or riots. This variable differentiates the *degree* of violence both across different types of political violence and within the same type of political violence (Taylor and Jodice 1983). One would expect a negative sign on the parameter estimate of this variable.

Investment responds to economic as well as political considerations. While the Tobin-Mundell hypothesis states that anticipated inflation causes portfolio adjustments that lower the real rate of interest and raise the level of investment, Stockman (1981) finds that higher anticipated inflation reduces economic activities in general, thereby lowering investment. Gregorio (1993) suggests that the effect of the level of inflation on investment is negligible if the elasticity of intertemporal substitution is sufficiently small. Kormendi and Meguire (1985) find a negative impact of inflation on growth, and Schneider and Frey (1985) find a negative impact of inflation on foreign direct investment. Levine and Renelt (1992), however, in their study of a large sample, find that inflation is not robustly correlated with either growth or investment share. Consequently, for this study, the expected sign of inflation (*INF*) remains indeterminate.

The standard deviation of inflation is a measurement of the variability of inflation. Hayek (1944) and Friedman (1977) both argue that the variability of inflation causes uncertainty in the market information about prices, and therefore reduces overall economic activity. The variance of inflation may be considered a proxy for macroeconomic uncertainty (Gregorio 1993). Capital flight, pessimistic perceptions, and delays in investment decisions can all result from uncertainty. Grier and Tullock (1989) state that the standard deviation of inflation is negatively related to growth. This chapter involves mostly developing countries, and since in these cases changes in inflation are likely to be caused by political crises that reduce economic activity, one expects the sign on the standard deviation of inflation (*INFSTD*) to be negative.

Human capital accumulation is regarded as the most important factor in economic growth by some scholars (e.g., Lucas 1986; Romer 1986; Young 1992). According to them, knowledge-driven growth can lead to a constant or even an increasing rate of return. Empirical evidence has revealed a positive relationship between education and growth (Barro 1991; Levine and Renelt 1992; Young 1992). Education both increases and improves human capital, which raises the efficiency of physical capital; more and better human capital will make physical capital more productive and more profitable. The elementary school enrollment rate in 1960 (*PRIM60*) is therefore included as an indicator of the initial accumulation of human capital and is expected to have a positive impact on private investment.

Public investment (*PUBINV*) is viewed either as having a crowding-out effect on private investment (Pastor and Hilt 1993), or as enhancing private investors' expectations by providing infrastructure and a more buoyant aggregate market (Taylor 1988; Greene and Villanueva 1990).[4] In our view, governments may either provide public goods which promote private investment or divert resources to projects that do not encourage private investment. Accordingly, the sign on this variable is held as indeterminate.

Finally, expected growth is measured by the average growth rate of real *GDP* per capita for the period 1968-78 (*EXPGRO*). Its sign is expected to be positive, as investors have a tendency to invest when they anticipate sustained economic growth based upon their assessment of past economic performance. Our data for education is drawn from Barro (1991), for investment, from Pfeffermann and Madarassy (1991), and for expected growth and inflation, Summers and Heston (1991).

EMPIRICAL EVIDENCE

In Table 5.1, using OLS regression methods, we tested two models containing political and economic variables.[5] Because heteroskedasticity could be important across countries, standard errors for the coefficients are based on White's (1980) heteroskedasticity-consistent covariance matrix. The adjusted R^2 is reported at the bottom of the table.

Results focusing on economic variables show that the expected growth rate and level of education have a strong positive and statistically very significant effect on private investment. The higher the expected growth rate and the more students enrolled in school in their age groups, the larger the private investment as a percentage of *GDP*. The standard deviation of inflation (*INFSTD*) is found to have an adverse influence on

TABLE 5.1 Political and Economic Determinants of Private Investments: Aggregate Data for Forty Developing Countries: 1978-1988

Variables	Economic Model			Political Economic Model		
	Coefficient	Std. Error	T-value	Coefficient	Std. Error	T-value
PRIVATE INVESTMENTS						
EXPGRO	1.023	0.238	4.30*	1.413	0.216	6.54**
PRIM60	0.075	0.018	4.17**	0.061	0.016	3.78**
INF	0.138	0.306	0.45	-0.083	0.247	0.34
INFSTD	-0.200	0.107	-1.87*	0.018	0.098	0.19
PUBINV	0.009	0.182	0.05	0.031	0.145	0.22
RPESTD				-0.160	0.046	-3.46**
DEATH				-0.001	0.000	-3.00**
CONSTANT	0.046	0.026	1.77*	0.052	0.021	2.44*
R²	0.645			0.778		
Number of Observ.	40			40		

* Significant at 10 percent level, two tails.
** Significant at 1 percent level, two tails.

private investment, and its parameter estimate is statistically significant at the 10% level. Macroeconomic uncertainty, as indicated by this variable, stands out as a negative factor for private investment. Theoretically, public investment may complement or replace private investment, and inflation may either increase or decrease investment in general. Empirically, both variables have a positive sign in our sample, though neither is statistically significant.

Results for the political-economic model in Table 5.1 show that the combination of the two sets of variables improves the estimates by the criteria of both adjusted R^2 and the standard error of the regressions. The standard deviation of relative political extraction that captures political uncertainty passes the strict test of significance and bears the expected negative sign. Macropolitical uncertainty, as characterized by the changeability of government relative capacity, has a negative impact on investment. The implication of the theoretical model in this chapter is thus strongly supported by this result.

The number of deaths from political violence that implies the intensification of political uncertainty is highly significant and holds the sign expected. Among these developing countries an increase in the number of political deaths indicates an increase in the level of political polarization and the degree of political violence. These political and social upheavals add to the uncertainty of the political environment for the marketplace, and thereby reduce economic activity, including private investment. The parameter estimates and levels of significance for the standard deviations of political extraction, expected growth, primary school enrollment, and number of deaths from political violence are very robust and exhibit little change under alternative specifications.

The main surprise is that the standard deviation of inflation becomes insignificant when used together with political variables, while expected growth and education remain significant. This indicates that a change in government political capacity may be a better indicator of the level of private investment than some of the variables used in the economics literature to indicate macroeconomic uncertainty (for instance, Grier and Tullock 1989; Aizenman and Marion 1993). Perhaps the level of change in RPE dominates the effect of change in inflation on investment, as the latter is very often the result of macropolitical uncertainty. Yet, compared with macroeconomic uncertainty, macropolitical uncertainty exerts a fundamental effect on private investment. Macropolitical uncertainty may have two effects on private investment: an indirect effect through the channel of inflation, and a direct effect. The test result in this section shows that the direct effect dominates the indirect effect.

CONCLUDING REMARKS

We have examined the effect of macropolitical uncertainty on private investment and have shown that such uncertainty, as measured by the change in the level of government political capacity, causes private investment to decrease. The empirical evidence is based on forty less developed countries (LDCs). Thus, to activate and maintain an inflow of private investment into their economies, LDCs should emphasize both policy consistency and political stability. From the economic perspective, it is also essential that developing countries enhance the education of their populations, as the accumulation of human capital plays a pivotal role in the acquisition and use of private capital. Finally, the developing economies that grew rapidly in recent years will be more capable of engaging private investment than those which have grown gradually. Presumably a history of high rates of growth engenders the rosy expectation in the minds of investors that rates will remain high in the future.

Because countries can do little to change their past, they should concentrate on improving their present. To attract private investment, governments can enhance national education and reduce macropolitical uncertainty. While it is relatively easy and straightforward for a country to set an educational policy goal, implementing the policy is not simple. Also, it is more difficult for it to curtail political uncertainty, since changes in the level of the government's political extraction create such uncertainty. In particular, in market economies that allow private incentive, variability of government control serves as a signal that the parameters circumscribing economic activities may be about to be altered. Because economic agents pay entry and exit costs whenever they invest, changes or anticipated changes in government control of financial and economic markets force them to decrease their investment in order to minimize these costs. From the foregoing, it can be concluded that for the government of a developing country to attract private money and continue such investments in the future, it must first set in motion consistent economic policies with regard to education, taxation, redistribution, property rights, and public investment, and must insure an acceptable level of political certainty.

NOTES

1. We thank Marina Arbetman, Bruce Bueno de Mesquita, Jacek Kugler, and Thomas D. Willett for their helpful comments.
2. For the sake of simplicity, it is assumed that once the investor has made his

or her move, he or she will stay in the chosen market and not change again (Rodrik 1991).

3. The investor may substitute consumption for investment when investment loses its allure due to an increase in the uncertainty of the market. Then the rational choice of the investor will be based on a comparison of the value of investment with the utility of consumption. For the sake of simplification, only the investments in equations (1) and (2) are compared here.

4. A detailed theoretical and empirical study of the relationship between private investment and public investment in developing countries was undertaken by Chen and Feng (1994).

5. The Pearson correlation coefficients are examined for all the variables discussed in the preceding section. There are several conclusions. First, a significant negative relationship between government political extraction and political deaths is identified. This result confirms our understanding of relative political extraction. When the government is strong, political violence, such as revolutions and coups d'etat, which cause political deaths, are unlikely to occur. Second, the aggregate level of change in inflation level is positively related to the aggregate level of change in government capacity. The connection between the two levels of variability implies that macroeconomic uncertainty and macropolitical uncertainty can go hand in hand. Third, there is a positive correlation between relative political extraction and public investment; this may indicate government intervention into the economy through public investment, a process which requires relatively high political capacity on the part of government.

6

Political Capacity and
Economic Growth[1]

David A. Leblang

INTRODUCTION

Growth rates across the nations of the world exhibit tremendous variance. A simple illustration demonstrates this point: Between 1960 and 1985, the average growth rate of per capita gross domestic product for the nations of the world was approximately 2%. Chad was the slowest grower—actually exhibiting a negative growth rate of 2.8%—while Singapore was on the other extreme—growing at the remarkable rate of 7.5% per year (computed from Summers and Heston 1991).

How can this variance be explained? For the most part, political science literature has been split between international and domestic explanations for economic growth. Studies that use the international system as the appropriate level of analysis look at fluctuations in the world economy and/or at power disparities between countries as explanations for national economic growth. National level explanations look at the ideology of the regime and/or the distribution of bargaining power between groups in society as explanations for growth. Similarly, the economics literature can be broken into micro- and macrolevel theories of growth. Microlevel theories focus on individual preferences and saving or consuming behavior, while macrolevel explanations tend to correlate aggregate economic trends (e.g., trade, productivity, exchange rates) with economic growth.

What remains is an assortment of theories as diverse as the phenomena they attempt to explain. What, then, is the relationship between political development and economic growth? Rather than examining particular policies or ideologies in the aggregate, this chapter examines what the political system actually does. Therefore, the question can be posed as follows: Is the government able to provide an environment that is conducive to economic growth? Approached in this way, variations in economic growth can be traced to the capacity of the political system. It is the government that establishes the institutional framework within which economic inputs are translated into economic growth.

The approach used in this chapter follows work in the fields of political development, political demography, and international relations. That work conceives of political capacity as the ability of a government to mobilize human and material resources for its own ends (Organski and Kugler 1980). This notion of political capacity is attractive for two reasons. First, it directs our attention away from labeling governments in terms of their ideologies. An approach emphasizing political capacity sees no a priori reason why, for example, a democratic political system should be more successful than an authoritarian regime when it comes to "making a market." It is fairly clear that differences in ideology alone do not and cannot explain differences in economic growth rates across countries (Przeworski and Limongi, 1993; Leblang 1996). Given that there is strong interest in understanding the political economy of economic growth, it is important to know how capable the government is in providing or maintaining a market.

Second, political capacity has been conceptualized in terms of the government's ability to reach society (Arbetman 1990, 1995) and to extract revenue (Organski and Kugler 1980). This approach provides a quantitative measure of political capacity that separates political from economic development and measures the performance of nations at similar levels of development across time and space. Consequently, the theoretical and empirical implementations of political capacity allow us to model the effects of political change on the rate of economic growth.

The central argument of this paper is that the effect of political capacity on economic growth is conditioned by the level of economic development of the nation. Thus, the extent to which a politically capable government is able to provide a market conducive to economic growth depends on the level of wealth in a country. Further, the interactive relationship between political development, economic development, and economic growth is nonlinear. Political factors matter the most when a country is very poor, but as an economy becomes wealthier, the effect of political factors on the growth rate diminishes (Organski, et al. 1984). In practical terms, the richer a country, the more important are economic factors in explaining economic growth; the poorer a country, the more important are political factors.

I will elaborate this argument by examining the importance of political capacity in the growth process and integrating political capacity with an endogenous growth model, spelling out the nonlinear relationship among political capacity, economic wealth, and economic growth. Then I test the propositions developed previously via a pooled cross-sectional and time-series analysis on 85 countries over a period of 25 years. The final section discusses the results.

POLITICAL CAPACITY AND ECONOMIC GROWTH

In order to include political capacity in a model reflecting the process of economic growth, it is essential to understand what it means to say that a government is capable. State capacity has been defined as anything from the cohesiveness of governmental decision-making structures (Haggard 1990) to the ideology of the decision makers (Adler 1987), to the techno-cratic competence of the decision makers (Becker 1983), to the relative autonomy of decision makers (Evans, et al. 1985). A notion of capacity has been a recurrent theme in the literature on political development and state building. This literature has shed some light on the problems and causes of political development (e.g., Huntington 1968; Tilly 1975; and Jackman 1993), but is weak in the identification of the central elements of political development. Rather than defining capacity in loose, qualitative terms, the term political capacity in the present context refers to the ability or effectiveness of a political system to advance its chosen goals (Arbetman 1990, 1995; Kugler and Domke 1986; Organski 1958; Organski and Kugler 1980; Organski, et al. 1984). This definition says nothing about the norma-tive value of the chosen goals. It simply states that a government is effec-tive to the extent that it can achieve its desired ends, regardless of what those ends may be.

In asking these questions about the interaction between politics and economic growth, the present chapter makes an explicit break with the prevalent convention in the political development field that economic and political progress go hand in hand. According to this view, if a nation possesses a high level of wealth, then it will also be capable of performing efficiently in the political realm. The view is based on observations of the developmental history of the West. Countries in Western Europe, parts of North America, and Japan have industrialized and established efficient bureaucratic structures. The error in this approach lies in the fact that it does not permit the economic and political structures of a country to be analyzed separately. Indeed, by equivocating economic and political development, this approach sidesteps the need to construct a separate indicator of political capacity. However, as nations undergo the transition from preindustrial to industrial development, it is readily observable that the independence of the political and the economic sectors becomes more profound. In preindustrial societies a change in the social, economic, or political sector did not cause a change in the other sectors. By contrast, in industrial societies even casual observation suggests that a change in the structure of the economy has direct consequences for the way in which political power is exercised, and vice-versa.

Before measuring political capacity, we must first define it as the ability of the political system to carry out its basic functions and implement desired policies. These functions include provision of law and order, protection of public and private property rights, and enforcement of other formal rules. The focus of state action may change over time and across countries, but in order to implement its own objectives, the state must overcome the potential resistance of various groups both inside and outside its national boundaries. State capacity, then, should indicate the power of government vis-à-vis these forces. In the economic sphere as well, the government must be able to create and enforce property rights structures, measure and monitor exchange, and provide monetary stability. The idea that fiscal activity is linked to political performance has a long history. Scholars in international relations, political development, economic history, and sociology have all adhered to the view that regardless of what the state wishes to do, it must have resources (see, e.g., Organski et al. 1984 and Levi 1988). Without question, the building of armies, the waging of war, the provision and enforcement of social rules, and the formulation and implementation of policy require revenue. The connection between rule and revenue cannot be exaggerated. Revenue is an absolute requirement for effective rule.

As the size and complexity of the market increase, so does the government's requirement for revenue.[2] The shift from personalistic exchange relationships to scale economies and highly interdependent, specialized production enlarges the potential for opportunistic behavior. Institutions for monitoring exchange and enforcing agreements now become necessary. As the market becomes more and more complex, the revenue requirements for "market maintenance" become greater and greater. For the government to be able to capture additional taxes, it must have the resources to enable it to measure exchange. The government's ability to perform the functions of measurement, monitoring, and enforcement depend on its ability to generate revenue. Governments can increase their portion of social wealth by expanding the sources of their revenue, increasing the tax rate, or a combination of both. The coordination of economic activity, reduction of transaction costs, and enforcement of property rights all require a government that is able to make its power known and implement its policies. It is difficult to conceive of any other type of government operation that depends so much on public compliance. It follows, then, that a capable political system will be able to provide the political foundations required by the complexities of the modern economy.

As governments mature, they seek to expand their control over their populations and obtain ever larger portions of resources from them. To extract revenue, government must make its presence felt throughout society. Establishing the capacity to extract is in the interests of the government, for the more effective the government is at raising revenue, the more it can attempt to extend its reach to previously untouched sectors (Organski and Arbetman 1993).

Although there may be other dimensions of political performance, writers on state building, economic history, and political development have recognized that extraction is the most costly, complicated, and dangerous function. This is because populations usually resist this type of interference with their lives more than any other type of government action (Ardant 1975; Tilly 1975; Organski and Kugler 1980; North and Weingast 1989). The process of extraction "involves deeply intrusive state interventions in civil society, especially when revenue creation takes the form of income taxation. And indeed, we are likely to find developed organizational capacity of the state, if at all, in this area" (Evans et al. 1985, 54). We can observe the process of institutional development and redefinition by looking at the bargains struck by government in order to prevent political upheaval. The line to be drawn here is so important that Ardant has characterized the fiscal system as the "transformer" of the economic infrastructure into the political structure (1975, 220).[3]

One should ascertain how much government revenue is attributable to political as opposed to economic factors. The specifics of this *RPE* measure, the data to construct it, and the way it is developed are discussed by Kugler and Arbetman (Chapter 1).

NONLINEARITIES, RELATIVE POLITICAL EXTRACTION, AND ECONOMIC GROWTH

The traditional expectation from the political science and economic literature is that a nation's level of socioeconomic development is linearly related to its level of political development. In explaining variations in economic growth, the present study breaks with tradition in two significant ways. First, it is posited that the effect of political capacity on a nation's growth rate depends on the level of wealth of the nation; that is, there is an interaction between political and economic development. Second, this interactive effect is not constant—the effect diminishes as a nation grows wealthier.

At the initial stage of socioeconomic development, the effect of political institutions on economic growth is the strongest. In this environment, economic markets are imperfect, if they exist at all. Governments must step in and fill the "economic vacuum." The argument is that governments can help prevent or overcome problems of market failure. Anne Krueger (1990) suggested that like markets, governments can also fail. In addition to failures of commission (e.g., state marketing boards, public sector deficits, etc.), there can also be failures of omission. Kruger argues that some of these failures of omission were the "deterioration of transport and communications facilities, which raised costs for many private and public sector activities; maintenance of fixed nominal exchange rates in the face of rapid domestic inflation, buttressed by exchange controls and import licensing; insistence upon nominal rates of interest well below the rate of inflation with credit rationing so that governments could supervise credit allocation among competing claimants; and failure to maintain existing infrastructure facilities" (1990, 10).

These failures of omission may not be a result of purposeful behavior, but rather occur because a government lacks the ability to act otherwise. Stated differently, politically capable governments in the poorest of developing nations will generate tremendous benefits at the margin, because economic activity is generally at subsistence levels and the portion of income able to be saved and invested is small. If private revenue for investment does exist, incentives are low because returns from investment are uncertain (see Chapter 5). At the lowest levels of economic development, then, initial changes in the market can have the largest and most profound effect on growth.

As a nation develops economically and becomes wealthier, political change has a diminishing effect on economic growth. A wealthier economy becomes a better integrated economy, and the enforcement of rules and contracts consumes a larger and larger portion of the available political resources. The subsequent addition to social wealth gives the government a larger pool of resources (not to mention an increase in potential tax bases), which it can extract and redirect. These actions, however, require the government to increase its administrative presence and provide the political infrastructure necessary for sustained growth. The result is an increasingly complex political environment where more specialized rules, more complicated monitoring, more agency problems, and more demands from the population translate into diminishing returns to political inputs. Thus, increases in political capacity at this stage of a nation's development should not generate the tremendous spillover associated with similar changes that occurred when economic development was just beginning. Consequently, political capacity will continue to have a positive effect on economic growth, but its impact will become weaker as the nation grows wealthier.

Finally, as nations continue along this path and become wealthy, changes in political capacity should have a negative effect on economic growth. First, the costs of marginal increases in political performance become prohibitive relative to their expected benefits. The more the government attempts to establish additional economic rights and responsibilities, implement redistributive policies, and manipulate the economy for political purposes, the greater the cost relative to the payoff. Moreover, at this stage of economic development governments usually provide a host of public goods including welfare, health care, and education, that once in place must be continuously maintained. Frequently, however, expenditures rise faster than revenues, and governments begin to face fiscal crises. This situation arises because governments at this level of economic development are already generating tremendous amounts of revenue through taxation, and therefore even marginal changes in fiscal policy generate resistance. At this level of development, then, our expectation is that the performance of the political system should have a marginally negative effect on the growth rate of the economy.

THE POLITICS OF ECONOMIC GROWTH

The growth rate of a nation ($GROWTH$) is influenced by the interaction between political extraction (RPE) and economic development (GDP). This statement is modeled via simple regression with an interactive term:

$$GROWTH = \alpha - \delta_1 GDP + \delta_2 RPE + \delta_3 (GDP \times RPE). \qquad (1)$$

Second, to determine the effect of a change in RPE on a change in $GROWTH$ for a given level of GDP, we differentiate $GROWTH$ with respect to RPE. The line determined by this relationship is named D:

$$D = \frac{\partial GROWTH}{\partial RPE} = \delta_2 + \delta_3 GDP. \qquad (2)$$

The interpretation of D is straightforward: As GDP increases, the effect that RPE has on $GROWTH$ changes by δ_3, with the ordinate intercept given by δ_2. The theoretical expectation is that this interaction will be negative: at lower levels of GDP, the effect of RPE on $GROWTH$ will be the greatest. As GDP increases, the effect of RPE on $GROWTH$ will decrease.

At this point, the slope of the line D does not change; it is constant for all levels of GDP:

$$D' = \frac{d(D)}{D(GDP)} = -\delta_3. \qquad (3)$$

The second part of the argument advanced requires that the effect of *RPE* on *GROWTH* changes as *GDP* increases, but it changes at a nonconstant rate. What needs to be shown is that the slope, F, of the line decreases at a diminishing rate as *GDP* increases. In other words, the effect of a change in *RPE* on *GROWTH* is expected to matter less (in absolute value) as *GDP* increases. To provide this nonlinear relationship, a term is added to the original interactive model in equation (1). Growth now is modeled as follows:

$$GROWTH = \alpha + \delta_1 GDP + \delta_2 RPC + \delta_3(GDP \times RPC) + \delta_4(GDP^2 \times RPE). \quad (4)$$

Again, the effect of political capacity on a nation's growth rate for a given level of wealth is found by differentiating *GROWTH* with respect to *RPE*. This produces a line that can be called *F* (see figure 6.1).

$$F = \frac{\partial\, GROWTH}{\partial\, RPE} = \delta_2 + \delta_3\, GDP + \delta_4 GDP^2. \quad (5)$$

The slope of *F* is found by differentiating *F* with respect to *GDP*:

$$F' = \frac{d(D)}{D\,(GDP)} = \delta_3 + 2\delta_4 GDP. \quad (6)$$

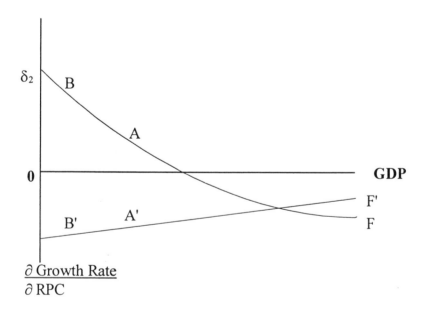

∂ Growth Rate
∂ RPC

FIGURE 6.1 Relationship among *RPE*, *GDP*, and Growth Rate

The slope of F (given by F') is not constant; it depends on the level of *GDP*. As Figure 6.1 shows, the points A and B on F tell the effect of *RPE* on *GROWTH* for a given level of *GDP*. If the tangents were drawn at these points, their slopes would be given by the vertical coordinates of A' and B' on F' that the slope of F at every level of *GDP* is given by the vertical coordinate of F'. It could be said that A is smaller in absolute value than B; that is, F is falling more rapidly at B than it is at A.

The nonlinearity presented in Figure 6.1 can be summarized as follows: At lower levels of *GDP*, the effect of *RPE* on *GROWTH* is the greatest and positive. As a country becomes richer, the effect of *RPE* on *GROWTH* diminishes and eventually becomes negative. The slope of the line relating a change in *GROWTH* to a change in *RPE* for a given level of *GDP* changes; it diminishes as the country grows richer in a non-linear pattern.

Now that the nature of the relationship among relative political extraction, economic development, and economic growth has been specified, the economic portion of the model can be discussed.

SPECIFICATION OF THE BASELINE ECONOMIC MODEL

One of the major challenges of this study is the specification of the economic portion of the model. An improper specification of the relationship between economic factors and growth will lead to spurious conclusions about the importance and effect of political capacity on economic growth. The variety of growth theories and the assortment of models derived from them are enormous (Levine and Renelt 1991), and I must try to be consistent with the latest generation of economic growth theories as well as test the effect of political intervention on the largest possible sample of countries.

Specification of the base-line model of economic growth begins with the initial level of development—the country's "starting point"—and takes into account the "convergence" hypothesis of neoclassical economics. As De Long put it:

Economists have always expected the "convergence" of national productivity levels. The theoretical logic behind this belief is quite powerful. The per capita income edge of the West is based on its application of the storehouse of industrial and administrative technology of the Industrial Revolution. This storehouse is open: modern technology is a public good. The benefits of tapping this storehouse are great, and so nations will strain every nerve to assimilate modern technology and their incomes will converge to those of industrial nations (1988, 1138).

To use this technology productively, nations must have a sufficiently developed population. This premise is at the heart of the endogenous growth literature exemplified by Barro (1990, 1991), Lucas (1988), and Romer (1986, 1990). This literature breaks with neoclassical growth models, which argue that reproducible capital produces diminishing returns to scale.[4] Endogenous growth theories assume that there are constant returns to a broad range of reproducible inputs, including human capital. Romer (1986), for example, has argued that human capital is the key to new technological developments which result in increasing social returns to knowledge. Expansion of human capital in terms of both education and learning-by-doing also plays a pivotal role in Lucas's (1988) examination of economic development. In Barro's empirical model, school-enrollment rates are used as proxies for the initial level of human capital. This approach is consistent with both neoclassical theory and the expectations of the endogenous growth literature. Barro explains:

> For a given starting value of per capita GDP, a country's subsequent growth rate is positively related to these measures of initial human capital. Moreover, given the human-capital variables, subsequent growth is substantially negatively related to the initial level of per capita GDP. Thus, in this modified sense, the data support the convergence hypothesis of neoclassical growth models. A poor country tends to grow faster than a rich country, but only for a given quantity of human capital...(1991, 409).

Therefore, the economic model will consist of indicators for the initial level of wealth of a nation (*GDP*), the initial level of human capital investment (*PRIM & SEC*), and the level of physical capital investment as a percentage of *GDP (INV)*. In addition, a variable to control for government expenditures (*GOV*) will also be included. This variable is the focus of many studies of "rent-seeking" behavior (e.g., Weede 1984) and is used as a control variable in both Barro (1990) and the present study. The expectation that *GOV* will be negative is based on the arguments that public spending crowds out private spending, that public sector expenditures are inefficient and wasteful, and that "the substitution in consumption of politically-priced public goods for market-priced public goods reduces the incentives of economic actors" (Scully 1992).

$$GROWTH = \alpha - \beta_1 GDP + \beta_2 PRIM + \beta_3 SEC + \beta_4 INV - \beta_5 GOV \qquad (7)$$

Combining the baseline model equation (7) with the interactive, nonlinear specification of the relationship among political capacity, economic development, and economic growth in equation (3) yields the following model to be tested:

$$GROWTH = \alpha - \beta_1 GDP_{it} + \beta_2 PRIM_{it} + \beta_3 SEC_{it} + \beta_4 INV_{it} - \beta_5 GOV_{it}$$
$$+\delta_2 RPE_{it} + \delta_3 (GDP_{it} \times RPE_{it}) + \delta_4 (GDP_{it}^2 \times RPE_{it}) \qquad (8)$$

EMPIRICAL ANALYSIS: TEMPORAL AGGREGATION AND METHODOLOGY

The sample covers the years 1960—1985. For the pooled cross-section and time-series case, the time domain of each observation is not the traditional unit of one year. To control for contractions in the world economy, changes in the business cycle and other shocks, the variables in the time-series equations are grouped in five-year time blocks. In other words, each country has five observations: 1960—1964, 1965—1969, 1970—1974, 1975—1979, and 1980—1984.

Economic theory necessitates that the initial conditions for income level and education be specified. If this analysis were strictly cross-sectional, these conditions would be satisfied by regression of the growth rate from 1960 through 1985 on the initial stock of human capital and *GDP* per capita in 1960. In the pooled case, however, the specification of initial conditions becomes more difficult, as the initial values must be simulated. In order to achieve this simulation, ten-year moving averages were used that required the collection of data from 1951 through 1985 for the three variables. The initial value of *GDP* in 1960, for example, is the average value of *GDP* for the years 1951—1960. This average was obtained for every year during 1960—1985 before the five-year averages were computed.

The regression analysis utilizes a pooled cross-sectional time series design. Pooling the data allows examination of the effects of both economic and political variables on economic growth as these values change over time and across countries. In addition, because smaller units of time have been included in the analysis, both the empirical results and the theoretical conclusions derived from the analysis will better reflect reality.[5]

EMPIRICAL RESULTS

Table 6.1 presents estimates for the baseline model equation (7) in column 1. The results confirm expectations. Attention is focused first on the endogenous growth portion of the model. With the proxies for human

TABLE 6.1 A Politico-Economic Model of Economic Growth. Pooled Cross-Section and Time Series Analysis.

Variables	Baseline Model			Interactive Model		
	Coefficient	Std. Error	T-value	Coefficient	Std. Error	T-value
ECONOMIC GROWTH						
PRIMARY#	0.018	0.045	0.40	0.053	0.042	1.26*
SECONDARY#	0.020	0.006	3.33**	0.020	0.006	9.23**
INV (% GDP)	0.160	0.015	10.67**	0.120	0.013	9.23**
GOV (%GDP)	-0.090	0.020	-4.50**	0.090	0.013	-6.92**
GDP#	-0.270	0.060	-4.50**	-0.220	0.100	2.20*
RPE				2.580	0.600	4.30**
(GDP*RPE)				-0.630	0.140	-4.50**
(GDP2*RPE)				0.017	0.008	2.13**
CONSTANT	1.78	0.500	3.56**	1.640	0.050	3.00**
R^2	0.38			0.70		
Number of Observ.	425			425		
SEE	0.998			0.981		
Prob F	0.0000			0.0000		
Log Likelihood	-894.97			-859.56		
F-test Interaction						
$F_{(3,419)}$				51.04		
Prob F				0.0000		

* Significant at 10 percent level, two tails.
** Significant at 1 percent level, two tails.
# Initial Level

capital, investment, and government consumption held constant, a country's initial level of per capita *GDP* has a significant negative effect on its subsequent rate of economic growth. This result is consistent with the convergence hypothesis that countries lagging behind in their economic development will, because of diminishing returns to scale, grow faster relative to more developed countries. Quantitatively, the coefficient indicates that a $1,000 increase in the initial level of *GDP* of a country will decrease its subsequent average rate of growth by approximately one-quarter of one percent.

The results also support the endogenous growth hypothesis that countries with higher initial levels of human capital should experience higher rates of per capita economic growth. The coefficient on secondary school enrollment is positive and significant, supporting the claim that an increase in secondary school enrollment as a percentage of the population has the long-term effect of increasing the rate of economic growth. Endogenous growth theories that stress increasing returns to physical capital investment are also supported. Romer's (1990) claim pertaining to the importance of human capital is based on the argument that it is the key input in the research sector that provides the new ideas that underlie technological progress.

Both control variables are significant and have the expected signs. Capital investment (*INV*) as a percentage of gross domestic product is very significant (t=10.7) and positive. This supports the proposition that investment is instrumental in the growth process. Additionally, the variable for government consumption share of *GDP* [GOV(%GDP)]is significant and negative, indicating that government consumption can squeeze out private consumption and distort the economy. As a whole, the model is statistically significant and explains almost 40% of the variation in economic growth rates across countries and over time.

Table 6.1 also contains the fully specified nonlinear relationship among economic development, political development, and economic growth (column 2). Overall, the interactive model is a good representation of the growth process. Taken as a whole, the model is statistically significant and a substantial improvement over the baseline model. There are three different indicators that show that this is the case. First, adding the interactive and nonlinear political components increases the R^2 term by 84% over the baseline specification. The interactive model explains 70% of the variation in economic growth rates over time and across countries, with the political components alone explaining 32% of that variation. The decrease in standard error of the estimate (SEE) and the log of the likelihood function also indicate that the interactive model is superior to the baseline model.

Taken together, the interactive and nonlinear components of the model are significant, but because it is argued that *RPE* does not have an independent, but rather an interactive, effect on a nation's growth rate, it is important to ascertain whether the coefficients for *RPE, GDPxRPE,* and *GDP²xRPE* are jointly significant.[6] Individual standard errors were computed from the variance-covariance matrix of coefficients and indicate that each of the variables is significantly different from zero (For details, see Judge et al. 1988). Thus, the interactive components that specify nonlinearity are also both jointly and individually significant.

In interpreting the coefficients of these variables, it should be noted that the endogenous growth and other control variables remain significant and continue to have the expected sign in the interactive model. Our theoretical expectation—the reason we added *RPE, GDPxRPE,* and *GDP²xRPE*—is that the effect of *RPE* on *GROWTH* will change as *GDP* increases. Political capacity should have a strong positive effect when a country is very poor, and this effect should diminish as a country becomes richer. This downward trend is supported by the coefficients. When everything else is held constant, the coefficient of *RPE* indicates the independent effect of political capacity on a country's growth rate when *GDP* is zero. This is not very meaningful; no country has zero wealth. Additionally, there is no theoretical interest in the independent effect of *RPE* on *GROWTH*; the interest is in the effect of *RPE* on *GROWTH* for a given level of *GDP*. It should be negative, as *GDP* increases, the magnitude of the effect of *RPE* on *GROWTH* decreases. Further, it is argued that this slope will diminish in absolute value as *GDP* increases. Recall that to ascertain whether this expectation is validated, in equation (5) we differentiate the interactive model with respect to *RPE*, and its parameter estimates are presented as equation (9):

$$F = \frac{\partial GROWTH}{\partial RPE} = 2.58 = 0.63 \, GDP + 0.017 GDP^2. \tag{9}$$

Differentiation of *F* with respect to *GDP* gives the slope of *F*:

$$F = \frac{d(F)}{d(GDP)} = -0.63 + 0.034 \, GDP. \tag{10}$$

Consistent with the proposition, the effect of *RPE* on *GROWTH* is positive until a country reaches a *GDP* per capita income of $4,710. For countries that have per capita incomes of more than $4,710, increases in political capacity have a negative effect on the national growth rate. However, initial expectations were that this value would be moderately higher, starting with the mean *GDP*, which in the sample is about $3,389, or $1,500 *below* the empirically determined inversion point. Despite this disparity we confirm the expectation that attempts to increase political capacity have undesired effects in the more economically developed countries. More importantly, the line F' confirms that politically strong governments matter the most in the poorest countries. Two items are of consequence here. First, this line always lies below zero, indicating that the curve F is downward sloping.[7] Second, the slope of F' is positive and decreasing in absolute value, indicating that the effect of a change in RPE on $GROWTH$ for a given level of GDP diminishes as GDP increases.

In substantive terms, the ability of the political system to effectively correct for market failure declines as the country grows richer. Further, small changes in the political capacity of a nation matter most when the country is very poor. As the economy becomes stronger, the effect of political capacity on the rate of economic growth—whether positive or negative—diminishes.

CONCLUSION

Variations in economic growth rate across countries and over time cannot be understood without taking into account both political and economic development. Political development, operationalized in terms of political capacity, affects the growth rates of poor and rich countries differently. In countries that are just beginning the process of economic development, politically capable governments are able to prevent or alleviate market failure. As an economy becomes richer, the political system's ability to affect growth diminishes, as does the magnitude of that effect. The findings are consistent not only with the theoretical structure developed in this work, but also with earlier theories of economic growth. In addition, they lend some empirical substance to many largely descriptive works in the field of political science.

The theoretical implications are interesting. First, evidence is provided that models of growth that are exclusively economic in character are incomplete. To specify an economy's production function accurately, it is necessary to make the environment within which exchange occurs an explicit part of the model. Countries in the developing world can grow if they possess the political will to design, implement, and enforce efficient political structures. As these countries grow in wealth, the effect on the economy of alterations in these political structures diminishes.

Second, the specification of a government's ability to generate revenue enhances our understanding of the political development of a nation better than does an examination of the state in traditional "regime type" terms. As Joan Nelson has argued, "A good deal of attention has been focused on regime type, but the contrasts between democratic and authoritarian regimes may be less important than some more precisely specified institutional variables that cut across types of regimes" (1991,

275). When it comes to the promotion of economic growth, governments of all ideologies are faced with similar choices, and we have shown that capable governments enhance growth in developing societies regardless of regime, suggesting that our focus could shift from regime type to performance of political systems.

NOTES

1. I would like to thank Diane Owen, L. Lynne Kiesling, and Art Denzau for very helpful suggestions on this paper. This paper also benefited from discussions with Marina Arbetman, Jacek Kugler, Bob Margo, Bob Archibald, and Donald Hancock. Marina Arbetman generously provided the data on relative political capacity and Taff Tschamler provided outstanding research assistance.

2. Tax revenues are an obvious indicator of the government's ability to influence individual behavior in the market. The questions of whom to tax, how to tax them, and what rate of taxation to employ are all significant political questions. The founder of fiscal sociology, Rudolf Goldscheid, argued that "the budget is the skeleton of the state stripped of all misleading ideologies" (quoted in Levi 1988, 6). If a government wishes to increase its tax revenue, it has four options: broaden the tax base; increase the rate of taxation; increase the productive capacity of the economy; or acquire additional territory. David Friedman (1977) has examined the interrelationship between taxation and nation building. The size and shape of a nation adjust over time to whatever size and shape maximize revenue for the state. When the state relies on tariffs on trade, it will generally expand up to the length of its major trade route. When the state relies on land taxes, territory will be smaller because no state administration can tax more than the full economic rent of the land. If taxes on labor are the key to revenue, then the state will attempt to maximize its size in order to increase the costs of migration or 'exit.' It is not certain that states in the modern world will follow this trend; however, historical precedent does seem to indicate that government will attempt to penetrate new areas under its jurisdiction in the quest for additional revenue.

3. The reasoning is well founded. The Magna Carta is an acknowledgment by a sovereign of the limits of his reach; however, it is not the only one. "The urban merchants and craftsmen in the rising towns of the Middle Ages were also able to secure rights and privileges for themselves in relation to the crown, in exchange for the financial assistance they were able to provide the monarchs in their struggles to pacify the unruly barons" (Findlay 1990, 196). Generally, the granting of certain rights by the state can help to fill the treasury's purse. In their study of seventeenth-century England, North and Weingast argue that "it is not always in the ruler's interest to use power arbitrarily or indiscriminately; by striking bargains with constituents that provide them some security, the state can often increase its revenue" (1989, 806).

4. Ehrlich (1990) and Verspagen (1992) provide useful surveys of this literature.

5. The pooled model creates some statistical problems (Sayrs 1989). This type of design makes it difficult to obtain parameter estimates that are efficient, unbiased, and easily interpretable (Judge, et al. 1988; Stimson 1985). In addition to

risking heteroskedastic disturbances, a pooled cross-section and time-series design usually also violates another assumption underlying ordinary least-squares estimation: that the error terms are not autocorrelated. These statistical problems are handled by means of Kmenta's Cross-Sectionally Heteroskedastic and Timewise Autoregressive Model (Kmenta 1986, 618-22). This procedure was adopted for two reasons. First, because of the small number of time increments for each cross section, estimation of a consistent autoregressive parameter was not a problem. Second, the assumption of cross-sectional independence is reasonable because the observational units are independent nation states. The Kmenta procedure is a two-stage least-squares application of OLS. The models were also estimated using fixed effects. Those results were not significantly different from the ones reported.

6. This is done by testing the null hypothesis that these coefficients are not significant. The test statistic is distributed as an F. The bottom two rows in Table 6.1 provide the F-statistic. Its magnitude is more than great enough to reject the null hypothesis. As a result, we can conclude that taken together, the interactive components have a significant effect on *GROWTH*.

7. This is confirmed by taking the second derivative of F. If the second derivative is positive, then the curve has a minimum.

7

Political Capacity, Macroeconomic Factors, and Capital Flows

S. S. Adji, Y. S. Ahn, C. M. Holsey, and T. D. Willett

INTRODUCTION

Numerous empirical studies have shown that there is a negative relationship between direct foreign investment and the political instability created by political strikes, demonstrations and riots, mass arrests, changes in the government, armed attacks, assassinations, guerrilla warfare, coups d'état, and civil wars.[1] Of course, these unstable political actions provide only a narrow measure of political environments. The study documented in this chapter employs a broader political economy analysis that concentrates on the role of political considerations in influencing economic policies. Therefore, in addition to the political instability created by political protests, demonstrations, and riots, it includes quantitative measures of relative political capacity (see Chapter 2). This approach more closely approximates the capable-incapable distinction that has been developed in the qualitative international political economy literature about economic policies in developing countries (see, for example, Kahler 1986; Haggard and Kaufman 1993; Nelson 1990; and Sachs 1989).

In addition to considering the influence of a broader range of political variables than has been customary, this study uses a pooled data set which includes cross-sectional as well as time-series data for the empirical work. Prior studies have predominantly concentrated on either time-series analysis of a single country or on cross-sectional analysis of a single time period. Consequently, their results are only applicable to the determinants of direct foreign investment in the particular country or time period utilized. The pooled data approach overcomes much of this country/time period specificity, and therefore permits more general statements to be made about the determinants of direct foreign investment in developing countries.

This study focuses on a set of twenty-three developing countries for the period 1970 to the onset of the international debt crisis in 1982 (see Appendix A), because the international debt crisis has altered investor responses to economic and political stimuli and therefore altered coefficient values on independent variables. Support is found for the view that political variables have an important influence on international capital flows and that both traditional measures of political instability and measures of relative political capacity have independent explanatory powers.

What follows is a brief review of measures of relative political influences and the empirical literature on direct investment flows to developing countries. Thereafter, the model and empirical results are discussed, as well as some difficulties in distinguishing the influences of economic factors on direct foreign investment from the influences of strictly political variables.

POLITICAL INFLUENCES ON DIRECT FOREIGN INVESTMENT

A number of studies have considered the effects of political and economic variables on direct foreign investment (see Appendix B for a summary). Here, a brief perspective on this literature is offered, with note taken that the typical political variable used is some form of political instability. Although early studies often had difficulty obtaining significant coefficients, most provided weak empirical support for the hypothesis that political instability affects direct investment flows negatively. Moreover, the vast majority of recent studies using more refined measures of political instability found relationships between political instability and direct investment flows that are not only negative but also significant. In most of these studies, relatively little attention is given to the channels through which political and economic variables influence direct investment. It seems understandable that authors would take it as self-evident that political instability would deter investment (see, for example, Edwards 1991b, and Woodward and Rolfe 1993). As has been emphasized recently in the literature on the political economy of macroeconomic policy, political instability has had different meanings to different authors (see Burdekin 1995). For example, at one extreme it is associated with political violence and coups, whereas at the other it may merely mean the frequency with which the party in power is voted out of office under democratic procedures. In either case, political instability is likely to reduce investment, but the channels through which these effects would operate would be quite different. This consideration becomes especially important when one is interested in the interactions among political and economic variables.

In structuring research design and interpreting empirical results, it is of fundamental importance to consider these interrelationships. The common tendency of empirical studies in this area has been to throw an array of economic and political variables into an equation and begin running regressions. This practice implicitly assumes that the effects of all of the right-hand-side variables included are independent of one another—that they are additive—but often this may not be the case. It is now widely recognized that economic policies are usually determined through the operation of the political process. For example, although it is generally acknowledged that inflation is primarily a monetary phenomena, political considerations often have a strong influence on monetary policies (see Chapter 4). Where political variables operate primarily through their influence on monetary policy, therefore, it would not be appropriate to include both the money supply and the political variables in a single equation explaining inflation. However, this is what often happens when political instability is measured by the frequency of changes in government. If administrative shifts occur through democratic processes, then their primary influence on investment operates through revised economic policies that alter the expected profitability and riskiness of investments. There is considerable theoretical and empirical support for the view that closely contested elections can generate pressure for governments to adopt policies which are politically popular in the short run but harmful to the economy in the long run. The political business cycle is an important example of this political pressure (see, for example, Willett 1988). Consequently, political instability even in "stable democracies" could harm the environment for investment through its effect on economic policies. Political instability as political violence, however, would likely have a direct adverse effect on foreign investment over and above any effect it might have on domestic economic policies, due simply to the increased danger to persons and property (see Chapter 5).

One major purpose of this study is to broaden the range of political variables used in empirical studies of direct investment flows to include the types of measures of political capacity developed by Organski and Kugler (1980) and extended by Arbetman (1990) and Snider (1986). With these types of measures, explicit consideration of the interrelationships among economic and political variables is especially important.

As detailed in Chapter 1, Organski and Kugler (1980) define political capacity as "the ability of government to effectively carry out tasks imposed on it by its own political elite, by other important national actors, or by the pressures of the international environment." Political capacity is expected to affect capital flows primarily through its effects on economic policy and, hence, on the economic variables in our model. Since political capacity is a proxy for the effectiveness and the strength of governments and their reach over populations, a country with low political capacity is more likely to have difficulty in promulgating appropriate macroeconomic policies than a country whose political capacity is high. Capacity has an economic component of extraction and a demographic component of reach. The lower the political extraction of a country, the less able is its government to extract revenues from the society and the more likely it becomes that it will have budget deficits that may result in future high inflation and, consequently, increase uncertainty. Because it has limited reach, such a country is also more likely to create new taxes or increase existing taxes on a small pool, thereby reducing the return on investment. Therefore, political capacity affects capital flows through its effect on economic policy. Because a country with high political capacity is expected to have more stable economic policies than a country with low political capacity, foreign investors are expected to invest more in the country with high political capacity.

As the preceding discussion indicates, there is a clear rationale for expecting measures of political capacity to influence foreign investment through channels that differ from those through which measures of political violence operate. However, the effects of both would run through economic policies, so a serious problem of interpretation may be generated when both political capacity and economic policy measures and outcomes are included in the same equation as right-hand-side variables. When both types of variable are included, the political capacity variable may to some degree take into account the effects of expectations about future economic policies. This issue will be discussed in detail later in this chapter.[3]

THE THEORETICAL FRAMEWORK

Interactions among economic and political variables vary according to the particular issues being investigated. Consequently, at the outset of an empirical study, it is essential to lay out the theoretical framework which motivates it. In the present case, the dependent variable is annual international flows of direct investment. Therefore, exogenous variables are assumed to operate through their effects on the expected rate of return and the riskiness of investment. Developments which raise the mean expected rate of return should increase investment, whereas factors which increase the dispersion of the probability distribution of expected outcomes around this mean—i.e., which increase expected risk—should decrease investment.

The following paragraphs give a brief discussion of the variables included in the study and their expected effects. The data sources and the construction of the variables are discussed in Appendix C.

1) The higher the real *GDP* per capita of a country, the better its economic performance, and the higher the purchasing power of the population. As a result, more foreign investors are willing to invest in that country. This suggests a positive correlation between real *GDP* per capita and foreign private capital flows.

2) The higher a country's level of real *GDP*, the larger the market size and, hence, the higher the probability that firms will be able to operate at an efficient level of output. Therefore, a positive relationship between real *GDP* and foreign investment flows is hypothesized.

3) A high real *GDP* growth rate indicates rapid economic progress and good prospects for future economic development. This suggests that the real *GDP* growth rate will be positively correlated with foreign private capital flows.

4) A high rate of inflation, because of its association with unevenly distributed changes in other economic variables, directly generates greater uncertainty. It also suggests the inability or unwillingness of the government to manage the economy. On both grounds, then, the higher the inflation rate, the less inclined foreign investors will be to risk investing in the country. A negative relationship is therefore hypothesized.

5) A large share of government expenditure in *GDP* may indicate excessive and unproductive government spending, which hinders economic performance and threatens higher taxes in the future. However, high government expenditures may also indicate the government's willingness to develop infrastructures that support the activities of private enterprise. Therefore, the expected correlation between the flow of foreign private capital and the share of government expenditure in *GDP* is not clear.

6) A large government budget deficit suggests an inability or unwillingness on the part of the government to manage its budget and the economy. Therefore, it is expected that the government budget deficit will be negatively correlated with foreign investment.

7) Trade policies may increase the incentives to invest in a country if these policies increase the profitability of investment. Foreign investors may be attracted to a country with an export oriented strategy if its government provides incentives to produce export

goods. On the other hand, foreign investors may likewise be drawn to invest in the country that adopts an import-substitution strategy if they can produce and sell their products in the domestic market under government protection. Therefore, it is not clear which industrialization policy will attract the greater amount of foreign investment.

8) A high debt service ratio is a sign that a country may have difficulty in servicing its foreign debt. If the debt service ratio is extremely high, there is a possibility that capital movements will be restricted, and, therefore, it will be more difficult to repatriate profits back to the investing country. On the other hand, a high debt service ratio may indicate expectations that the country has the ability to repay its debt. Therefore, the effect of a high debt service ratio on foreign private capital flows is not clear.

9) The devaluation or depreciation of a country's currency in real terms may increase the profitability of export- and import-competing industries; increase the wealth of foreign investors in terms of the domestic currency; reduce the price of domestic assets in terms of foreign currencies; decrease the cost of investment in terms of foreign currencies; and reduce uncertainty and the prospect of volatile exchange rate movements, which may cause capital losses to foreign investors. Therefore, it is expected that real devaluation or depreciation of a country's currency will have a positive influence on foreign investment.[4]

10) Overvaluation of a country's currency acts like a tax on export- and import-competing industries. It also increases uncertainty and the prospect of an exchange rate devaluation, which may cause capital loss on assets denominated in the domestic currency. Therefore it is expected that overvaluation will have a negative influence on foreign investment.

11) The IMF provides credit to countries which appear to be in temporary balance of payment difficulties. To obtain this credit, the country usually agrees to follow policy recommendations suggested by the IMF. A high value of IMF credit suggests that the country is a problem debtor to which private lenders are unwilling to lend. However, an increase in the value of IMF credit also shows that the country is willing to adhere to the IMF's adjustment program, which may ultimately correct the balance of payments and other economic problems. In this latter case, incentives for direct investment in the country increase. Therefore, the correlation between IMF credit and capital flows is not clear.

12) Domestic political instability in a country, such as political demonstrations, strikes, and riots, may disrupt the economy by increasing uncertainty about future economic policies, and thereby increasing

the risk associated with any expected future stream of profits. Domestic political instability may also adversely affect investment by generating concern about physical violence toward the foreign investor's property and employees. Therefore, one would expect political instability to be negatively correlated with foreign investment.

13) Relative political capacity reflects the strength of the government of a country. The higher the political capacity of a country, the stronger is its government, and the more stable its expected future economic policy. This consideration suggests that relative political capacity will be positively correlated with foreign private capital flows.

The predicted effects of the macroeconomic and political variables on the expected return on investment and degree of risk are summarized in Tables 7.1 and 7.2. In Table 7.1, real *GDP*, the real *GDP* growth rate, real *GDP* per capita, real exchange rate depreciation, exchange rate overvaluation, trade policy, the ratio of government expenditure to *GDP*, relative political capacity, and are categorized as variables that affect the return on investment. It can also be seen that the inflation rate, exchange rate overvaluation, real exchange rate depreciation, ratio of government expenditure to *GDP*, ratio of government budget deficit to *GDP*, political instability, relative political capacity, debt service ratio, and *IMF* credit are categorized as variables that affect the degree of risk.

Table 7.2 summarizes the effects of macroeconomic and political variables on the return on investment and degree of risk, and subsequently on direct foreign investment. Relative political capacity and real exchange rate depreciation have positive effects on foreign investment through their effects on both return and risk. Therefore, the net effect of these factors on foreign investment is positive. Real *GDP*, real *GDP* per capita, the real *GDP* growth rate, and trade policy also have an expected net positive effect on foreign investment. This result occurs because these variables have a positive effect on the return on investment. The debt service ratio and IMF credit may either increase or decrease the degree of risk. Therefore, the net effect of these factors is indeterminate. The net effect of the ratio of government expenditure to *GDP* on direct foreign investment is also indeterminate. This variable may have either a positive or a negative effect on the return on investment, and it may also increase the degree of risk. Because the ratio of the government deficit to *GDP*, the inflation rate, and political instability all have negative effects on foreign investment through their effects on risk, the net effect of these variables is negative. The net effect of exchange rate overvaluation is also negative, because overvaluation has a negative effect both on expected return and on risk.

134

Table 7.1 Summary of Macroeconomic and Political Variables that Affect Return on Investment and Degree of Risk

Determinants of Direct Foreign Investment	Variables Used in this Study	Effect on Return	Effect on Risk
1. Return on Investment			
Market Size	Real *GDP*	+	
Growth of Market	Real *GDP* Growth Rate	+	
Purchasing Power of Population	Real *GDP* per Capita	+	
Competitiveness of Domestic and Export Industry	Real Exchange Rate Depreciation	+	
	Exchange Rate Overvaluation	-	
	Trade Policy	+/-	
Government's Willingness to Develop Infrastructures	Ratio of Government Expenditure to *GDP*	+	
Effectiveness of the Government	Relative Political Capacity	+	
2. Degree of Risk			
Potential for Unexpected Exchange Rate Adjustment	Inflation Rate		+
	Exchange Rate Overvaluation		+
	Real Exchange Rate Depreciation		-
Lack of Good Economic Management	Ratio of Government Budget Deficit to GDP		+
Political Instability	Political Demonstrations, Riots, and Strikes		+
Ineffectiveness of the Government	Relative Political Capacity		-
Probability of Capital Controls that May Limit Profit Repatriation	Debt Service Ratio		+
	IMF Credit		+
Credit Worthiness	Debt Service Ratio		-/+
Excessive Government Spending	Ratio of Government Expenditure to *GDP*		+

Table 7.2 Summary of the Effects of Macroeconomics and Political Factors on
Direct Foreign Investment

Variables	Return on Investment	Effects of Direct Degree of Risk	Foreign Investment Net Effects
Real *GDP*	+	0	+
Real *GDP* per Capita	+	0	+
Real *GDP* Growth Rate	+	0	+
Ratio of Government Expenditure to *GDP*	+/-	+	?
Ratio of Government Budget Deficit to *GDP*	0	+	-
Debt Service Ratio	0	+/-	?
IMF Credit	0	+/-	?
Trade Policy	+/-	+/-	?
Inflation Rate	0	+	-
Real Exchange Rate Depreciation	+	-	+
Exchange Rate Overvaluation	-	+	-
Political Instability	0	+	-
Political Capacity	+	-	+

EMPIRICAL RESULTS

The effects of macroeconomic conditions and political environment on direct foreign investment are analyzed using pooled cross-sectional, time-series data for 23 developing countries over the years 1970—1981 (see Appendix A for a list of the countries). Pooling tests and the Hausman (1978) test indicate that the fixed effects model best fits the data.[5] Therefore, this model, which allows the intercept term to vary across cross-sectional units—countries in our case—is employed in the empirical analysis. The initial estimation regresses nominal direct foreign investment on the macroeconomic variables, previously discussed and listed in Table 7.3, as well as various measures of political influences which are described in more detail below. A second set of regressions undertakes the same analysis employing real rather than nominal direct foreign investment as the dependent variable.

Because the purpose of this study is to investigate the applicability of broader measures of the political environment than have been investigated to date, the empirical analysis includes several political variables. Following prior research, a standard measure of political instability as approximated by the total number of political protests, demonstrations, and riots is employed. To expand upon political measures, however, two different measures of relative political capacity (**RPC**) are included. The first is relative political extraction, which was developed by Organski and Kugler (1980). The second is the revised version of the measure for relative political capacity as formulated by Arbetman (1990) and Kugler, Arbetman, and Organski (1994 and this volume, Chapter 10) which consists of three variables: relative political extraction (**RPE**), relative political reach (**RPR**), and their interactive term, relative political extraction x relative political reach (**RPExRPR**).

To determine how individual measures affect direct foreign investment, several specifications have been estimated. The basic regression concentrates solely on macroeconomic variables. Then these results are compared to regressions incorporating macroeconomic variables in conjunction with different combinations of the political variables.

The regression results for direct foreign investment measured in nominal terms on macroeconomic variables only, presented in the second column in Table 7.3, show that the adjusted R^2 indicates that macroeconomic and political variables explain 86% of the variability of direct foreign investment. All variables except the ratio of the budget deficit to **GDP** have the expected signs, and all but real **GDP** growth rate, **IMF** credit rating, and inflation rate are significant with at least a 10% confidence level. Real **GDP**, real **GDP** per capita, ratio of government expenditure to **GDP**, and debt service ratio are, in fact, significant at the 1% level. The insignificance of the **IMF** variable does not conflict with the analysis because the theory presented predicts an indeterminate sign on this variable. Therefore, the only puzzling result is the significant positive coefficient on the ratio of the budget deficit to **GDP**, a point which will be discussed in the following section.

The role of political variables is examined by including political instability and relative political capacity as independent variables in the model. The regression results of direct foreign investment on macroeconomic and political variables, reported in column 3 in Table 7.3, show that the addition of the political variables has little effect on the adjusted R^2, but all of the various measures of political influence have the predicted sign and are significant at least at the 10% confidence level.[6]

In experiments dropping different political variables from the regression we found that the inclusion of the political capacity variables has little

Table 7.3 Effects on Nominal Foreign Direct Investments

Variables	Equation 1			Equation 2			Equation 3		
	Coeff.	Std. Error	T-value	Coeff.	Std. Error	T-value	Coeff.	Std. Error	T-value
NOMINAL FDI									
REAL GDP	0.039	0.0048	8.13**	0.039	0.0048	8.08**	0.035	0.0052	6.70**
R GDP/CAP	0.118	0.0043	2.74**	0.118	0.0429	2.76**	0.135	0.0467	2.88**
R GDP GRO WTH	-0.178	2.7430	-0.65	-0.570	2.7419	-0.21	-1.081	2.7570	-0.39
GOV.EXP/GDP	10.324	4.0102	2.57**	9.549	4.0201	2.37**	7.363	4.5666	1.61
DEFICT/GDP	6.831	4.7858	1.47*	6.570	4.7694	1.38	3.673	5.3276	0.69
DBT SV. RATIO	8.532	1.8216	4.68**	8.752	1.8190	4.81**	10.046	1.9624	5.12**
IMF CREDIT	-0.016	0.0564	-0.29	-0.016	0.0562	-0.28	-0.016	0.0563	-0.29
TRADE POLICY	137.3	43.5896	3.15**	135.74	3.1257	3.13**	108.09	45.787	3 2.36**
INFLATION	-0.266	0.2458	-1.08	-0.209	0.2470	-0.85	-0.15	0.2515	-0.56
RER DEPREC.	0.651	0.2570	2.53**	0.633	0.2562	2.47**	0.573	0.2585	2.22*
RER OVERVAL.	-0.102	0.0221	-4.58**	-0.098	0.0222	-4.40**	-0.099	0.0222	-4.47**
POL. INSTAB.				-2.065	1.2093	-1.71	-2.196	1.2080	-1.82*
RPE							890.25	538.384	1.65*
RPR							919.94	509.548	1.81*
RPE X RPR							-791.04	531.925	1.49
R²	0.86			0.862			0.863		
Number of Observ.	276			276			276		

*   Significant at 5 percent level.
** Significant at 1 percent level.

influence on the coefficients of the political instability variable, and vice versa. This suggests that they represent separate types of political influence.

The regressions in Table 7.3 follow most prior studies in that the dependent variable is specified in nominal terms. Given the substantial amount of inflation (and economic growth) which occurred over the period in question, however, it is doubtful that one should follow this practice. The same set of incentives should attract substantially greater capital flows in 1981 than in 1971. One approach which takes the effects of inflation and growth into account is to calculate the dependent variable in real terms.[7] This was done by deflating nominal capital flows according to the changes in the average price level of industrial countries.

Table 7.4 shows that the primary effect of defining foreign direct investment in real terms is on inflation and on the relative political capacity variables. The coefficients and statistical indicators of other macroeconomic variables and political instability remain qualitatively similar to those of the nominal specification. The coefficients on inflation rise substantially and become statistically significant. The relative political capacity variables (relative political extraction, relative political reach, and relative political reach x relative political extraction) retain coefficients of the predicted sign, but only relative political reach is significant. Again we found that political instability and the political capacity variables appear to be measuring different types of political influence. At first glance, the poor performance of the relative political capacity variables appears puzzling. As discussed in the following section, however, these results can be at least partly explained.

SEPARATING OUT POLITICAL AND ECONOMIC INFLUENCES

Given the range of variables commonly included in direct investment flow equations, it is difficult to draw a sharp distinction between economic and political variables. Inflation, for example, is clearly in one sense an economic variable which is explained in large measure by monetary developments. But these monetary developments are in turn heavily influenced by government actions which respond to political economy pressures. Conceptually, both the size of the government budget deficit and the rate of inflation may be considered alternative types of measures of the degree of a country's political capacity. Therefore, when the standard measures for political capacity are added to equations already including fiscal and/or inflation variables, it becomes highly inappropriate to consider the coefficients of these standard measures and their contributions to R^2 as measuring the total importance of political considerations. What one is really considering in such a case is the comparative

Table 7.4 Effects on Real Foreign Direct Investments

Variables	Equation 1			Equation 2			Equation 3		
	Coeff.	Std. Error	T-value	Coeff.	Std. Error	T-value	Coeff.	Std. Error	T-value
NOMINAL FDI									
REAL GDP	0.036	0.0096	3.71**	0.035	0.0095	3.65**	0.035	0.0104	3.41**
R GDP/CAP	0.162	0.0845	1.91*	0.162	0.0841	1.92*	0.120	0.0917	1.31
R GDP GRO WTH	2.972	5.3776	0.55	2.175	5.3729	0.41	2.015	5.3990	0.37
GOV.EXP/GDP	18.137	7.8618	2.31*	16.562	7.8778	2.10*	22.022	8.9624	22.02**
DEFICT/GDP	11.806	9.3823	1.26	11.277	9.3460	1.21	16.447	10.4559	1.57
DBT SV. RAT IO	12.588	3.5712	3.53**	13.035	3.5645	3.66**	12.328	3.8514	3.20**
IMF CREDIT	0.075	0.1106	0.68	0.076	0.1102	0.69	0.086	0.1106	0.78
TRADE POLICY	197.92	85.4557	2.32	194.70	85.0218	2.29*	205.88	89.8618	2.29*
INFLATION	-1.224	0.4819	-2.54**	-1.111	0.4841	-2.29*	-1.22	0.4936	-2.47**
RER DEPREC.	0.464	0.5038	0.92	0.429	0.5020	0.86	0.474	0.5074	0.93
RER OVERVAL.	-0.160	0.0434	-3.70**	-0.153	0.0435	-3.51**	-0.158	0.0435	-3.63**
POL. INSTAB.				-4.196	2.3698	1.77*	-4.485	2.3707	-1.89*
RPE							714.34	1056.63	0.68
RPR							1425.82	1000.03	1.43*
RPE X RPR							-890.50	1043.95	-0.85
R²	0.866			0.868			0.868		
Number of Observ.	276			276			276		

* Significant at 5 percent level.
** Significant at 1 percent level.

ability of various statistical measures to explain behavior of interest.

In interpreting statistical results in this area, it is also important to consider carefully the unexpected possible interrelationships which may exist among variables. For example, in the present study it was surprising to find that budget deficits consistently retained positive coefficients. High budget deficits would be expected to indicate lack of coherence in government policies, which should discourage investment. Furthermore, it is widely believed, with a good deal of empirical support (Burdekin 1995), that large budget deficits are a major source of inflationary pressure in developing countries. This specification includes the inflation rate as an independent variable. Therefore, although an increase in the budget deficit should have a negative effect on incentives for capital inflows, the expected sign on an increased budget deficit, when inflation is held constant, is indeterminate. On the one hand, a higher deficit might plausibly increase the expected future rate of inflation and therefore discourage capital inflows. On the other hand, where confidence in a government is high, it may be able to run a sizable temporary deficit without substantially affecting inflationary expectations. The finding of consistently positive coefficients on the budget deficit variable could be a reflection of such confidence factors, when the inflation rate does not change.

A further difficulty of interpretation concerns the extent to which variables reflect current economic developments versus expectations of future developments. As recent research has shown, at least partial use of adaptive expectations can at times be rational. Although the initial inclination in our study was to interpret the addition of political capacity variables to inflation in the equations as adding a substitute for expectations of future inflation, such a clear dichotomy of interpretation is not possible because current inflation is likely to be a partial influence on expected future inflation. The use of pooled time-series, cross-sectional data could also substantially influence the number of expectational elements included in estimated coefficients, as compared with the use of standard time-series data in the estimation of the same equations.

The combination of these considerations may help explain why the political capacity variables are not consistently significant in the equations and why the political instability variable, which is less closely related to the fiscal and inflation variables, is found to "work better" across equations than do the political capacity variables. In addition, such interrelationships may explain cross-equation variations in the size and statistical significance of the inflation and fiscal variable coefficients. In Table 7.3, the coefficients on the ratio of government expenditure to *GDP* fall when the political variables are included, while in Table 7.4 they follow a mixed pattern. Similarly, the positive coefficients on the budget deficit ratio decrease in Table 7.3 as the political variables are added, whereas in Table 7.4 they increase only when all of the political variables are included.

Furthermore, in Table 7.3 the coefficients on inflation are low and insignificant, and they vary little as the political variables are added. In Table 7.4, the coefficients on inflation are high and significant. These results are consistent with the initial argument that it would likely prove difficult to make a clear differentiation between economic and political influences. We interpret our statistical work as providing support for the usefulness of the Arbetman-Kugler-Organski political capacity project, and also as highlighting the need to consider a broader range of measures for political capacity and to pay careful attention to their potential interactions with variables traditionally used in purely economic explanations of behavior. Indeed we believe that inflation rates may be a useful alternative measure of political capacity for some purposes.

The measure of trade policy orientation used in this chapter further illustrates these basic points. Viewed purely as an economic variable, a high level of protection would have conflicting effects on the incentives for direct investment. For investment designed primarily to serve the domestic market, higher import barriers would increase the incentive to invest. On the other hand, an inward trade orientation makes it more difficult for a nation to export as well as to import. Therefore, investment intended primarily to generate production for export markets would be more readily attracted to countries with liberal trade policies. The findings in this chapter of consistently positive and statistically significant coefficients on the trade policy variable could therefore be taken as evidence that export platform investment dominates the flow of direct investment to the countries in the sample.

It is suspected, however, that there is an additional factor at work. An internal trade policy orientation may well be a good measure of a country's general economic policy orientation. In that case, the statistical relationship between trade policy and capital flows might be considerably stronger than would be implied by the direct economic effects alone of changes in trade policy on risk-return calculations of investing firms.

CONCLUSIONS

The results of this study provide support for the view that it is important to take political as well as economic considerations into account when looking at the incentives for international investment. They highlight the need to pay careful attention to the types of political variables included and to the nature of their interrelationships with economic variables. It is fundamentally wrong to think of political measures merely as variables to be added to equations containing relevant economic variables.

The results confirm that there may be important differences in the channels through which different types of political considerations operate. Furthermore, the nature of these different channels may vary from one area of application to another. A naive reading of the empirical results of the present study could suggest that the broadening of a traditional purely economic perspective to include political considerations would yield only a modest improvement in the understanding of the area of direct foreign investment flows, since there is little change in the adjusted R^2. However, such a cursory reading of the results would miss the crucial point, namely, that to a substantial degree, political considerations operate through their influences on economic policy behavior and the private sector's expectations about future policy actions. Consequently, there is no clear separation between economic and political variables. It is essential to recognize this fact both when designing models for empirical research and when interpreting the results derived therefrom.

APPENDIX A: COUNTRIES INCLUDED IN THE DIRECT FOREIGN INVESTMENT REGRESSION ANALYSIS

1. Argentina	9. Guatemala	17. Pakistan
2. Bolivia	10. Honduras	18. Philippines
3. Brazil	11. Mexico	19. Thailand
4. Chile	12. Peru	20. Ghana
5. Colombia	13. Sri Lanka	21. Kenya
6. Costa Rica	14. Indonesia	22. Zambia
7. Dominican Republic	15. Korea	23. Turkey
8. El Salvador	16. Malaysia	

APPENDIX B: REVIEW OF PREVIOUS EMPIRICAL STUDIES

Most survey studies have concluded that political instability in the host country has a negative effect on direct foreign investment. By contrast, the results of econometric studies have been mixed. Accordingly, the studies under review here will be divided into three groups: survey studies, early econometric studies, and more recent econometric studies.

The early survey studies conducted by Aharoni (1966), Basi (1963), Root (1968), and Schreiber (1970) reported that political instability in the host country deters direct foreign investment. These results were supported by the more recent survey studies of Bass, McGregor, and Walters (1977), Frank (1980), Buckley, Berkova and Newbould (1983), El Haddad (1988), and Yue (1993), who confirmed that political instability has a negative effect on the flow of direct foreign investment. These studies were conducted by asking foreign investors, through direct interviews or mailed questionnaires, whether political instability in a country would affect their decision to invest in that country.

Several early econometric studies criticized the early survey work. Green (1972), Bennett and Green (1972), and Green and Cunningham (1975) noted that Basi (1963) and Aharoni (1966) rely on investors' statements or micro-observations of investment decision makers rather than on actual investment behavior. They performed cross-country analyses of the determinants of direct foreign investment and found that political instability was not a significant determinant of direct foreign investment. In these papers, political instability was approximated by the Feierabend and Feierabend political instability index. Feierabend and Feierabend (1966) identified thirty types of politically destabilizing events and assigned each a weight from zero to six according to its level of intensity. The more destabilizing the event, the more weight it received. An election, for instance, was accorded a weight of zero. The resignation of a cabinet official received a weight of one; peaceful demonstrations, a weight of two; assassinations of a significant political figure, three; mass arrests, four; coups d'état, five; and civil wars, six.[8]

Levis (1979) also used the Feierabend and Feierabend political instability index in analyzing the effect of political instability on direct foreign investment in less developed countries. He found that the effect of political instability was significant in the short run, but not in the long run. Kobrin (1976) showed that government instability, subversion and rebellion did not affect the flow of direct foreign investment.[9] He argued that what was important was not political disruption and instability per se, but the ramifications that discontinuities in the political environment have for business operations.

More recent econometric studies have used different measures for political instability, but their results strongly support the hypothesis that political instability has a significant negative effect on flows of direct foreign investment. Root and Ahmed (1979) found that frequent executive transfer deters direct foreign investment. Schneider and Frey (1985) showed that political instability, measured as the total number of political strikes and riots, has a significant negative effect on the inflow of direct foreign investment. Nigh (1985) found that political instability in the host country, approximated by the index of conflictive intranation events, also has a negative significant effect on direct foreign investment.[10] Edwards (1991b) found that political instability and political violence in the host country deter the inflow of direct foreign investment. In Edwards's study, political instability was approximated by the political instability index and political violence was measured by the political violence index.[11] Both indexes were developed by Cukierman, Edwards, and Tabellini (1989). The United Nations Center on Transnational Corporations (1991) used the index of political stability developed by the Political Risk Service as a measure of political stability. The results of the United Nations study showed that political stability has a positive effect on direct foreign investment in newly industrialized countries and less developed nations.

Woodward and Rolfe (1993) also used the political stability index developed by the Political Risk Service. The results of their study also showed that political stability is positively correlated with direct foreign investment.

APPENDIX C: VARIABLE DEFINITIONS AND SOURCES

Dependent Variables

NOMINAL DIRECT FOREIGN INVESTMENT = Capital provided by foreign investors—either directly or through other enterprises connected to the investors—to a domestic enterprise or received by the investors from that enterprise. It includes equity capital supplied by the foreign investors and reinvested earnings controlled by them (IMF 1977). Because the data for gross direct foreign investment are not available, this study uses net direct foreign investment data, in millions of U.S. dollars. Source: International Monetary Fund, *International Financial Statistics,* magnetic tape, 1993.

REAL DIRECT FOREIGN INVESTMENT = Nominal direct foreign investment divided by the consumer price index (CPI) of developed countries. Source: International Monetary Fund 1993.

Independent Variables:

REAL GROSS DOMESTIC PRODUCT PER CAPITA =
Source: Summers and Heston (1991, 327-68).
REAL GDP = Real gross domestic product multiplied by population. Source: Summers and Heston (1991, 327-68).

REAL GDP GROWTH RATE = $(RGDP_t - RGDP_{t-1})/RGDP_{t-1}$
where:
$RGDP_t$ = Real *GDP* in year t. Source: Summers and Heston (1991, 327-68).

INFLATION RATE = $[(CPI_t - CPI_{t-1})/CPI_{t-1}]\ 100$
where:
CPI_t = consumer price index in year t. Source: International Monetary Fund 1993.

RATIO OF GOVERNMENT EXPENDITURE TO GDP = (Government Expenditure/*GDP*) (100). Source: International Monetary Fund, various issues.

RATIO OF GOVERNMENT BUDGET DEFICIT TO GDP = (Government Budget Deficit/*GDP*). Source: International Monetary Fund, various issues.

DEBT SERVICE RATIO = $[(P + i) / X]$
where:
P = principal repayment for foreign debt;
i = interest payment for foreign debt;
X = export value.
Source: World Bank Tables, various issues.

REAL EXCHANGE RATE DEPRECIATION = $[(RER_t - RER_{t-1}) / RER_{t-1}]$ 100
$RER_t = ER_t (CPI_t, USA / CPI_{t,j})$
where:
ER_t = nominal exchange rate in period t;
RER_t = real exchange rate in period t;
$CPI_{t,j}$ = consumer price index in country j in period t;
CPI_t,USA = consumer price index in the U.S. in period t.
Source: International Monetary Fund 1993.

EXCHANGE RATE OVERVALUATION = $[(ERBLACK - ER)/ER]$ 100
where:
ERBLACK = black market exchange rate;
ER = official exchange rate.
Source: International Currency Analysis Inc. 1993.

IMF CREDIT: The IMF-approved programs are of three types: (1) standby arrangements, (2) extended fund facilities designed to meet conditions synonymous with underdevelopment—i.e., economies suffering from serious balance of payments problems stemming from structural maladjustments in production and trade where prices and cost distortions have been widespread, and (3) compensatory financing facilities, designed for raw-material-exporting countries whose balance of payments difficulties are partly attributable to drops in export earnings for which they are not responsible. The IMF credit in this study includes the last two programs, EFF and CFF. Source: International Monetary Fund 1993.

TRADE POLICY: The trade policy variable is derived from Greenaway and Nam (1988). They categorize trade policies in forty-one developing countries as strongly outward oriented, moderately outward oriented, strongly inward oriented, and moderately inward oriented. Based on these categories, trade policies can be divided into two broader groups: outward oriented and inward oriented. A dummy variable is assigned a value of one if the country adopts an outward oriented trade policy and a value of zero if the country adopts an inward oriented trade policy.

POLITICAL INSTABILITY: Political instability is approximated by the total number of political demonstrations, strikes, and riots. Source: Taylor and Jodice (1988).

RELATIVE POLITICAL CAPACITY: Organski and Kugler (1980, 72) defined political capacity as "the ability of government to effectively carry out tasks imposed on it by its own political elite, by other important national actors, or by the pressures of the international environment." The higher the political capacity of a country, the more capable or stronger the government of that country is. Political capacity consists of three interrelated elements: the level of penetration of governmental power into national society, the capacity of the governmental system to extract resources from its national society, and, finally, the performance of the government in delivering such resources to their intended ends. Organski and Kugler proposed that the second element was the most critical one for the purpose of measuring political capacity, and they turned to government revenues as their measure of political capacity. Because absolute government revenue levels show the wealth of a society, but do not necessarily reflect political mobilization, Organski and Kugler measured political capacity in relative terms. They used relative political extraction (*RPE*) as a substitute for relative political capacity (*RPC*):

$$RPE = \text{ACTUAL TAX RATIO} / \text{TAXABLE CAPACITY},$$

where:
ACTUAL TAX RATIO = taxes collected / GDP = (T / GDP);
TAXABLE CAPACITY = (T / GDP) Predicted.

The taxable capacity for developing countries is estimated by employing pooled cross-countries time-series regression according to the following equation:

$$(T/GDP) = b0 + b1\ (TIME) + b2\ (MINERAL\ PRODUCTION/GDP)$$
$$+ b3\ (AGRICULTURE\ PRODUCTION/GDP) + b4$$
$$(EXPORTS/GDP).$$

Snider (1986) modified the measurement of Relative Political Capacity by considering the influence of structural differences between fuel mineral exporting countries and non-fuel mineral exporting countries; between low-income and other countries; and between high-income oil exporting countries and middle-income oil exporters. He took into account the influence of these differences by including dummy variables.

Arbetman (1990) and Kugler, Organski, and Arbetman (1993) revised the measurement of Relative Political Capacity by including the effects of Relative Political Reach (*RPR*). Relative Political Reach is constructed as the ratio of a country's active population to what one would expect the active population to be. They proposed the revised version of Relative Political Capacity as:

RPC = b0 + b1 Relative Political Extraction + b2 Relative Political
    Reach + b3 (Relative Political Extraction) (Relative Political Reach).

Source: The editors of this volume, Tulane University and Center for Politics and Policy, Claremont Graduate School.

NOTES

1. Although a few studies have produced signs opposite to those predicted by theory, the vast majority of previous empirical research has produced a negative (although not always significant) coefficient on the political instability variable.

2. An important exception is Schneider and Frey (1985).

3. Problems of interpretation are further increased by arguments that the structure of taxation, especially the use made of the inflation tax, can be used as a complement to the Organski-Kugler approach to representing political capacity as the ratio of actual to expected government tax revenue. In this view, for example, the political capacity calculations and the rate of inflation may be seen as alternative manifestations of political influences. Therefore, the adverse effects of inflation may reflect not only the direct effects of inflation on the profitability of investments, but also broader effects indicative of political weakness, which may in turn generate adverse effects in other policy areas. Such an interpretation of inflation as a signal of domestic economic tension and political weakness is given by Schneider and Frey (1985). See also Arbetman and Ghosh (Chapter 8, this volume).

4. It should be noted, however, that where devaluation is associated with an economic policy crisis, investment inflows may be discouraged in the short run.

5. F-tests were used to test overall homogeneity of intercepts and slopes across cross-sectional units. Although slope coefficients were found to be homogeneous, intercepts varied across cross-sectional units. The Hausman (1978) test was then employed to determine whether the fixed effects or random effects of differential intercepts best fit the data. The fixed-effects model was found to be a superior specification.

6. It is interesting to note that the interactive term ($RPE \times RPR$) has a sign opposite that of the RPE and RPR coefficient estimates. As Arbetman (1990, 1995) explains in greater detail, such estimates imply that marginal increases in either RPR or RPE have less effect when governments exhibit high levels of political capacity—that is, when governments have large values of RPE and RPR. To assess the marginal effects of RPE on FDI with this interaction term, one can differentiate the FDI equation with respect to RPE, obtaining

$$\frac{\delta FDI}{\delta RPE} = \delta RPE + \delta RPE.RPR$$

and indicating that the effect of RPE on FDI depends on the level of RPR, and vice versa. Based on our empirical results of equation 3 in Table 7.4, the estimated marginal effect of RPE on FDI is

$$\frac{\delta FDI}{\delta RPE} = 714.340 - 890.499 \; RPR.$$

This shows that marginal *FDI* to *RPE* decreases with increases in *RPR*. For example, marginal *FDI* to *RPE* is 447.2 at *RPR* = 0.3, but 90.1 at *RPR* = 0.7. If one sets the marginal effects of *RPE* on *FDI* equal to zero and solves for the *RPR* that maximizes *FDI*, one obtains *RPR* = 0.802 (= 714.34/890.45). Note that if *RPR* is greater than 0.802, then marginal *FDI* to *RPE* turns negative.

7. An alternative approach, albeit a crude one, is to take the effects of inflation and growth into account by including a time trend. When applied, however, this procedure did not substantially affect the results.

8. There were thirty types of events. They and their associated weights were used to place nations along a seven-point scale. Each nation was given a three-digit political instability index number. The first digit from the seven-point scale represents the weight attached to the most destabilizing event which occurred within the time period being studied. The second and third digits represent the sum of weights given to all national events during the period examined. These two digits were used to rank nations by their stability levels within each of the scalar positions.

9. Government instability was approximated by the weighted linear index of armed attacks and guerrilla warfare. Rebellion was approximated by the weighted linear index of regime type, general strikes, riots, purges, assassinations, coups d'etat, revolutions, and irregular executive changes.

10. The index of inter-nation events and the index of intranation events were developed by Azar (1980). He scaled internation events according to the Azar-Sloan fifteen-point scale and intranation events according to the Azar-Sloan nine-point scale. These scales assess the degrees of cooperation and conflict which characterize the event.

11. The index of political instability was computed by Cukierman, Edwards, and Tabellini (1989). They constructed their index of political instability by endogenously estimating from the data the probability of government change for a given year. This was done by fitting a probit equation on government change onto pooled time-series and cross-sectional data for 79 countries, over the years 1948—1982. The index of political instability was then constructed by averaging the estimated probabilities of government change over that time period. The index of political violence was constructed as the sum of the yearly frequency of political assassinations, violent riots, protests, political attacks, and politically motivated strikes.

8

Political Capacity and
Black Market Premiums[1]

Marina Arbetman and Dipak Ghosh

INTRODUCTION

Exchange rates are a recurrent policy theme in the political economy literature. In an open economy, finding the "equilibrium" exchange rate eases problems of long-term allocation of resources and capital flows. Policy makers have the choice of either allowing the market to determine the equilibrium rate or trying to determine the rate themselves by imposing on the market either fixed or flexible exchange rates. Government intervention in the exchange market has proven repeatedly to be economically inefficient (Greenwood and Kimbrough 1987). In spite of this fact, governments persist in imposing ceilings upon the official exchange rate in order to minimize shortages of foreign currency for economic reasons, or to alleviate political uncertainty.

It has also been shown that a devaluation follows when the divergence between the official exchange rate and the black market rate is large (Edwards 1991a). But to date, the premium has been modeled as exogenous, and very little emphasis has been placed on understanding the causes of premiums. It is proposed that the existence of premiums is an indicator of both economic and political problems; therefore, the research query is twofold. First, from an economic perspective, we propose to identify constraints on the supply of foreign exchange reserves, which governments use as reasons to intervene in foreign exchange markets. Second, from a political perspective, we propose to investigate the effect of politics on premiums. It is assumed that if governments were efficient, they could impose adequate macro-economic policies, provide an environment of political stability, and refrain from intervening in the market.

In this chapter, a model of black market premiums (defined as the ratio of the nominal black market exchange rate to the nominal official exchange rate) is developed. This model uses both political and economic variables, because neither can be isolated from the other. The evolution of this model is discussed in the next two sections, followed by an explanation of the econometric methodology. The results, presented in the last section, show that any corrective action by government is based on both political and economic factors, and that both thus play a role in determining black market premiums. In the concluding comments we assess the power of politics and economics to explain premiums when governments are effective and when they are ineffective.

MODELS OF EXCHANGE RATES

Most studies concentrate on the official exchange rate, because this is a key variable in understanding international flows of goods and capital (for a survey, see Baillie and McMahon 1989, Chapter 3). Yet the choice of which official rate to study poses a challenge, because in many countries a system of multiple exchange rates exists (financial, commercial, tourist, etc.). Governments establish these multiple exchange rate systems to impose taxes and subsidies or to maximize the supply of foreign currency, even if attempts to impose different prices for the same goods interfere with the smooth functioning of the market. Regardless of the presence of such distortions, however, increasing reserves is always a goal of government because increased reserves provide it with fiscal flexibility that it would not otherwise have. Thus, whenever a government feels that the shortage of foreign exchange has reached an alarming level, and that government is unable to pursue other policies, it will impose price ceilings and/or quantity controls. Such actions, in turn, create a black market for foreign exchange, where transactions occur in spite of government intervention.

The black market premium is a signal to the government that its policy of maintaining a price ceiling on foreign exchange has failed and that resources are being diverted. Black markets constitute a loss of international reserves to the government, because foreign exchange obtained in black markets does not go into the government treasury but remains, albeit illegally, in private hands. Moreover, exporters may choose not to exchange all their revenues at the official rate, which is always less than the black market rate—a circumstance which leads inevitably to under-invoicing of exports. Consequently, by controlling foreign exchange rates, the government not only loses foreign currency to black market dealers, but also loses revenues from existing export taxes.

For these reasons, the black market exchange rate is a barometer of government performance. Rapidly appreciating black markets indicate that despite government promises to the contrary, participants do not believe the government can sustain a stable rate and speculate against domestic currency by paying a premium for their foreign currency (Mussa 1982). This speculation arises because individuals faced with political uncertainty naturally seek strong, portable currencies that can protect their economic standing under any foreseeable circumstances. Therefore, in an uncertain political environment the effectiveness of monetary control will decrease as individuals cease to believe that the government is sincere in its efforts to stabilize the economy. Simultaneously, the demand for foreign currency will increase as people lose faith in their domestic currency and prefer to shift their portfolio holdings to foreign currencies to hedge against the risk of both political and economic instability (Frenkel 1976).

Attempts to model the nominal and real black market rates abound (Arbetman 1990, 1995; Greenwood and Kimbrough 1987; Gupta 1981; Pitt 1984), but none of these studies has attempted to model the black market premium. Most previous explanations of the black market exchange rate concentrate on the causes of a black market in foreign exchange, but they do not explain what factors cause the premium to increase or decrease.

From our perspective, the difference between official and black market rates is a matter of timing. The black market rate is the efficient processor of information, whereas the official rate is artificially depressed and will eventually converge toward the equilibrium dictated by market forces. An explanation of the divergence between official and black market rates is an essential preliminary to any determination of the policies necessary to correct the situation. The degree of overvaluation of the exchange rate, as indicated by the magnitude of the black market premium, gives a rough estimate of the eventual cost of adjustment necessary in the economy. In political terms, devaluations are considered by the ordinary people in most developing countries to be selling out to foreign powers, and therefore governments which devalue will lose political support at home and, in democracies, may not be re-elected.

EXISTING MODELS OF PREMIUMS

There have been relatively few attempts to model the black market premium. Two such studies were undertaken by Dornbusch et al. (1983) and Edwards (1991b). Dornbusch et al. model the premium in Brazil as a function of the existing stock of black market dollars, the nominal interest rate differential, the stock of cruzeiro assets, the commercial policy of the government, and the official real exchange rate. They show that "the central role of the portfolio decisions, in conjunction with rational expectations or perfect foresight, implies that changes in financial markets or in the capital market induce an immediate jump in the premium and a subsequent adjustment path for both the premium and the stock of dollars"(p. 39). They also show that a seasonally high stock of dollars will lead to a seasonally low level of the premium.

Edwards (1991b) uses a more elaborate model containing annual data for twelve developing countries for the period 1962—1984 to explain the premium. He models the premium as a function of the excess supply of domestic credit, the lagged value of the nominal exchange rate, the ratio of total government consumption over *GDP* as a proxy for government consumption of nontradeables, the rate of growth of real *GDP*, and the terms of trade. Holding all other factors constant, he shows that expansive macroeconomic policies will increase the premium, whereas nominal devaluations will reduce the premium.[2]

These two models of premiums base their explanations on domestic factors. However, for the large sample of countries with various degrees of dependence on the external sector, focusing on external causes is more appropriate. Two main points need to be argued. First, from an economic point of view, focusing on the external sector—especially the supply of and demand for exchange rates—should render a more comprehensive explanation. Expansive macroeconomic policies cause inflation and lead to a decline in the value of the domestic currency, thereby fostering disequilibrium in the balance of payments. However, if the government has an adequate supply of foreign currency, it will have no incentive to promulgate policies which will ultimately devalue its currency. Bottlenecks in the foreign sector are, either directly or indirectly, the main constraint in countries where black markets exist. A black market for foreign exchange emerges only when there is a shortage of foreign currency.

Second, neither of these models considers the effects of politics on the existence and levels of black market premiums. This omission constitutes an inappropriate restriction on the model. The role of politics in determining the spread cannot be ignored, for the decision to impose controls on the market (which leads to the creation of a black market) is not based solely on economic reasons, but also on political constraints. When a government lacks the political capacity to persuade the citizenry of the necessity for tough economic stabilization measures which will, in the short run, reduce the standard of living, then such a government has no choice but to resort to coercive measures to stabilize the economy. These measures include imposing strict quantity controls in the foreign exchange markets, which in turn lead to shortages in the foreign currency derived from official sources and ultimately to the creation of a black market for foreign exchange.

A POLITICAL ECONOMY MODEL OF PREMIUMS

The model discussed here assumes that the existence of black market premiums is related economically to the external sector and domestically to the political inefficiency of the government. To confront the shortage of foreign exchange, countries can choose one of two main policy approaches. The first is genuine and is derived from a positive balance of trade, capital flows, or reserves. The second is artificial, in that excess demand for foreign exchange is restricted not by market forces, but by the imposition of political controls. This second policy approach is often taken by governments that are unable to provide environments of political certainty wherein the market could work on its own. The demand for foreign currency, therefore, is very often inflated as a result of political decision making. For example, in an environment of political domestic uncertainty, the population feels compelled to buy foreign currency as a means of defending their well-being against the possibility of rapidly depreciating domestic assets.

Confronted with a shortage of foreign currency, governments attempt to increase its supply by fostering exports, and to constrain its demand by reducing imports. The healthiest way to build up the supply of foreign exchange is via a positive balance of trade. One alternative is to restrict import and exchange transactions. This alternative is politically more costly than increasing exports, because sectors of the economy dependent on imports have to carry the financial burden of these restrictions and will become alienated and withdraw their support from the government. A more lasting policy alternative is available for the government that is able to realign the exchange rate by reducing the demand for goods and services to a level consistent with the national income. Government can promote a shift in demand from tradeables to nontradeables and provide incentives for expansion within those sectors in which the country enjoys comparative advantages. This course is likely to be slow and politically difficult, especially if the short-term costs are high and the long-term benefits will not be enjoyed by the incumbent government. For this reason weak governments, which most frequently face this decision, do not adopt such policies.

The easiest political means of controlling exchange rates is to effect an improvement in the profitability of exports by means of devaluation. Under Marshall-Lerner conditions, devaluation renders exports cheaper and imports more expensive, thus reducing the gap between supply of and demand for foreign currency. Thus the degree of overvaluation of the domestic currency is a good indicator of how imminent a devaluation is. Once the devaluation has taken place, the premium decreases immediately as the official exchange rate closes the gap with the black market rate. This is the choice of weak governments, but their actions simply postpone the crisis and do not alleviate the structural conditions that motivated this action in the first place.

A government will be tempted to intervene in the foreign exchange market if it wishes to keep its exchange rate at a predetermined fixed level. But in order to do so, it has to have enough reserves to be credible in the exchange rate market.[3] For example, when the government decides to maintain a fixed exchange rate regime, its level of international reserves determines whether any quantity controls will be needed to maintain the fixed rate. If the international reserves are relatively high, then the government can maintain the fixed rate simply by buying and selling its domestic currency. The Argentine situation in 1995 provides a good illustration of this approach.[4] The government has liberalized the economy and begun privatizing many government-owned firms. Even foreign nationals have been allowed to purchase these firms. The foreign exchange proceeds from these sales have been used to sell dollars on the open market and keep the value of the Argentine currency at an artificially high level by holding the exchange rate for the Argentine currency against the dollar at an artificially low level. By avoiding quantity controls and supplying whatever the market demands at the fixed exchange rate, the government has managed to keep a black market in foreign exchange from developing. This is, however, a fragile equilibrium. The government can maintain this position only so long as it has sufficient dollar reserves, whether from the privatization proceeds or from any other sources. The only long-term solution to the black market problem is for government to have a current account surplus, which will build up international reserves so that it will have the necessary funds to intervene in the foreign exchange market on a regular basis. Any short-term solution, such as borrowing reserves to prop up the currency or depending on temporary sources of foreign exchange like the selling off of public enterprises will eventually lead to the government's running out of reserves and force it to return to quantity controls, thereby leading to the re-emergence of the black market. In sum, any variable that affects international reserves will affect the premium as well.

The capital account also provides a means of covering shortages of foreign currency. Governments find it difficult to proclaim that difficulties with the balance of payments are caused by fundamental disequilibrium, because they would then have to adopt stringent macroeconomic policies in order to correct this imbalance. In turn, those groups affected by a fall in their real incomes might threaten the survival of the government. Instead, it is politically easier to adopt policies that respond to disequilibrium in a temporary manner, such as foreign loans. But a permanent need for hard currency cannot be satisfied by means of a constant flow of loans because, under the condition of an uncorrected fundamental disequilibrium, the flow will eventually stop. Therefore, high levels of external debt might be an indication of future problems in the country's balance of payments position when the loans become due. To deal with the expected higher future requirement for foreign exchange, the government will therefore restrict the supply of foreign exchange to the general public (e.g., by imposing controls) in order to maximize the supply of scarce foreign exchange for itself. The more severe these restrictions, the greater will be the premium. The higher the level of external debt, the greater the restrictions placed by the government on free operation of the foreign exchange markets, and the greater the black market premium.

OPERATIONAL CONTROLS OF EXCHANGE RATE POLICIES

Governments might need to impose controls as an artificial way of constraining the public's demand for currency. In theory, the more rigid the controls, the harsher the punishment for defying the rules of the government. But even this high risk does not deter consumers from buying foreign currency; it just makes it more expensive. Therefore, the existence of controls does not indicate that the government is achieving its objective of maximizing its share of foreign exchange. If the government is willing (and has the resources) to supply the market with whatever quantity of foreign currency is demanded at the fixed exchange rate, then there is no incentive for the development of a black market. It is only the existence of a fixed exchange rate system in conjunction with quantity controls that gives rise to the black market.

Domestic political efforts to control exchange systems can be classified according to the degree of effort used to enforce penalties on black market foreign currency transactions. *Pick's Currency Yearbook* and the *World Currency Yearbook* define four types of average yearly controls which countries impose on their currency exchanges. The following definitions, paraphrased from these sources, reflect policies used to control domestic exchange rate policies:

1) **Free Currencies** are monetary units whose financial transfer to other countries is, in general, not bound by licenses or official permission. Their value is not the object of black market transactions, but many free currencies are still subject to commercial controls based on bilateral trade agreements.

2) **Liberal Control Currencies** are currencies whose free market value

differs, often substantially, from official parity. Ownership of foreign banknotes, of bank balances abroad, or of gold is either legal or tolerated. Infractions of currency legislation are not punishable by jail sentences.

3) **Strict Control Currencies** are the objects of active black market transactions. Foreign banknotes have multiple official values, are surrounded by voluminous protective legislation, and cannot be transferred abroad without special permits or licenses. Ownership of foreign banknotes or foreign bank currencies is illegal and punishable by confiscation, heavy fines, or prison sentences. Financial censorship prevents publication of black market values of hard currencies in local newspapers.

4) **Dictatorial Control Currencies** are currencies whose official values are very high and enforced by severe penalties. Foreign currencies without exception are the object of black market transactions, which list hard currencies at premiums varying between 200% and 1500% of their official value. Ownership of anything other than national units is punishable by long prison sentences. Sometimes even the death sentence is imposed for crimes against the national currency.

As regards the black market, a politically imposed "penalty structure" should depress the economic demand for foreign currency when the costs of not abiding by the law are high (Krueger 1993; Gupta 1981). Governments that choose to intervene to prevent black marketeers from buying or selling foreign currency must threaten them with costly consequences, including confiscation, fines, and prison sentences. An ineffective government in this situation can therefore make the situation even worse because it lacks the political strength to maintain exchange rate controls. This implies that the more rigid the controls, the higher will be the premium.

The growth rate of real *GDP* is used to take into account the effect of domestic economic variables that will influence expectations of future developments in the balance of payments. The higher the growth rate of real *GDP* in a country, the greater the country's ability to improve its balance of payments position. This is because the increased domestic production provides the government with an excess supply of goods, which can then be exported. In an open economy, domestic industry would concentrate on the production of those goods in which that country possesses a comparative market advantage; with economic growth, the supply of these goods would eventually exceed their domestic consumption and thus lead to increased exports. Thereafter, with an improved balance of payments position, the government could reduce controls on exchange rates, thereby enabling them to approach the black market rates and, as a result, reduce black market premiums.

Finally, it is hypothesized that political variables have a strong effect on the level of the black market premium. After economic constraints have been taken into consideration, trust in the government's policy will discount the need to hedge against domestic currency. Relative political capacity (*RPC*) is used as a proxy for government efficiency. *RPC* has two main components: relative political reach (*RPR*) and relative political extraction (*RPE*). *RPR*, which refers to the government's capacity to reach the population, means that government elites can obtain their people's active support or at least their consent for policies they intend to pursue. *RPE* refers to the government's capacity to gather material resources to advance their chosen policies. A strong government is able to collect revenues above the average established by all other governments with similar economic characteristics. Conversely, a weak government will extract below the norm (see Chapter 1). The higher the value of *RPE*, the higher will be the political capacity of the government and the lower will be the premium.

MODEL OF BLACK MARKET PREMIUMS

A simple model is proposed that focuses on external factors and is based on the assumption that an "unrestricted" supply of foreign currency will be a deterrent to the formation of a black market. The supply will enable the government to intervene directly in the market and maintain the value of the domestic currency at any level it chooses, by buying and selling the domestic currency instead of resorting to strict controls. Ceteris paribus, the black market premium will be high when the currency is overvalued, when controls are severe, when reserves are low, and when external debt is high. The premium will also be high when government is inefficient and when trust in the government's capacity to deliver on promised policies is low. These elements can be simply expressed as follows:

$$PREMIUM = a_0 - a_1 \text{ } Real \text{ } Official \text{ } Exchange \text{ } Rate + a_2 \text{ } External \text{ } Debt - a_3$$
$$Current \text{ } Account \text{ } Balance + a_4 \text{ } Reserves - a_5 \text{ } GDP \text{ } Growth - $$
$$a_6 \text{ } RPR - a_7 \text{ } RPE + a_8 \text{ } Controls \quad (1)$$

Following are the definitions of the variables. The data are from World Currency Yearbook, International Financial Statistics Yearbook (IFSY), World Tables (WT), and Yearbook of International Trade Statistics (YITS).

All variables that are in current U.S. dollars were converted to constant 1985 dollars.

PREMIUM: Black market premium defined as the ratio of the nominal black market rate to the nominal official rate.[5]

REAL OFFICIAL EXCHANGE RATE: Calculated as follows:

Real Official Rate = $\dfrac{E\ P^*_t}{P_t}$

where:
P^* = a weighted average of wholesale prices and exchange rates of the three main trading partners and oil for each country,
E = the nominal official exchange rate, and
P = the domestic consumer price index.

With the real official rate defined in this way, an appreciation of the exchange rate will show up as a decline in the index.[6]

EXTERNAL DEBT: Includes short- and long-term debt in millions of U.S. dollars.[7]

CURRENT ACCOUNT BALANCE: The current account balance.[8]

RESERVES: Total foreign exchange reserves.[9]

GROWTH: The growth rate of real *GDP*.[10]

RGDPTT: Real *GDP* adjusted by terms of trade.

RPR: Relative Political Reach.[11]

RPE: Relative Political Extraction.[12]

CONTROLS: Degree of quantitative restriction placed on foreign exchange markets by governments.[13]

In general, both strong and weak governments need to put their political houses in order before implementing economic policies. Effective governments might find the costs of increasing their already relatively high political capacity very high indeed, so they may be better off leaving the foreign exchange markets to their own devices. It is anticipated that politics will serve as the better explanation for high black market premiums when governments are ineffective. Conversely, economic variables will have the stronger effect when governments are efficient. Therefore, our model will be analyzed separately for efficient and inefficient governments.

THE RESEARCH APPROACH

The data set represents 92 countries for the years 1960 to 1988. Annual data are used for all variables. Equation (1) is estimated with a random effects model using the Generalized Least Squares estimate as described in Hsiao (1986: Chapter 3). This is appropriate because we assume that there will be omitted variables. Some of these omitted variables reflect factors peculiar to both individual cross sections and time durations for which the data are obtained; other variables reflect individual differences that affect the observations for a given cross section in more or less the same way over time; and still other variables are specific to time durations but affect individual units more or less equally. This assumption is reasonable because we are using a panel data set consisting of 92 cross sections and 29 time intervals. In addition, there is reason to believe that some of the explanatory variables like balance of trade, external debt, and real official exchange rate are correlated. This leads to multicollinearity, in the presence of which a GLS estimation is appropriate.[14]

The use of annual data makes the model insensitive to short-term changes. Because the numbers for the premium are annual averages, much of the variation in the exchange rates is lost. Therefore, log levels are used rather than changes in the variables in order to retain maximum sensitivity in the data. Changes (first differences) in annual data would result in the partial loss of whatever information the data contains.[15]

RESULTS

The main hypothesis of the present study is that political variables are a strong, thus far neglected determinant of black market premiums. It has been argued that the government's economic resources must be built up first, because without a certain level of resources the government has no tools at its disposal with which to undertake any political or economic measures for development. Moreover, if the government is unsuccessful in providing basic amenities to its citizens, it will hardly be able to persuade them of its sincere efforts to increase its international reserves and thereby reduce the black market premium.

The effect of balance of payments and political capacity on the level of

TABLE 8.1 Political and Economic Determinants of Premiums, 1970-1989

Variables	Coefficient	Std. Error	T-value
PREMIUM			
REAL OFFICIAL RATE	-0.421	0.039	-10.73[**]
CURRENT ACCOUNT	0.170	0.205	0.83
EXTERNAL DEBT	0.060	0.016	3.76[*]
RESERVES	-0.029	0.001	-2.11[*]
GDP GROWTH	-0.728	0.164	-4.44[**]
CONTROLS	0.238	0.256	9.31[**]
RPR	-0.539	0.255	-2.11[*]
RPE	-0.309	0.047	-6.54[**]
CONSTANT	0.67	0.016	4.25[**]
R^2	0.31		
Number of Observ.	804		

[*] Significant at 10 percent level.
[**] Significant at 1 percent level.

the premium was investigated directly. The model for all the countries in the sample was estimated, using primarily the time span 1970—1989 due to lack of data on external debt previous to 1970. The overall results show an R^2 of 0.31. The economic variables show the expected behavior: The less the constraint on the supply of foreign currency, the lower is the premium. The political variables also have the expected effect that the more efficient the government, the more likely it is to avoid high premiums. Each of the explanatory variables of the model will now be analyzed in greater detail.

The real official exchange rate plays an important role in determining the premium. This is not surprising as the real official exchange rate, to a large extent, determines the level of international reserves, which has already been shown to affect the premium. In general, the more devalued the currency, the higher the premium. Table 8.1 shows that when the real exchange rate is overvalued and expectations of a major devaluation increase, the premium tends to be large. Indeed, once a devaluation takes place, the premium declines as the official exchange rate then approaches market value.

As expected, the coefficient on external debt is positive and significant. Maintaining a high level of external debt is an easy way, in the short term, for a government to encourage an expanded use of credit or to promote a continuous flow of foreign exchange. At the same time, a high level of external debt causes the population to assume that the supply of foreign exchange will decline as future loans fall due. Moreover, continued international borrowing sends a signal to lenders that there are macroeconomic misalignments in the economy that the government either has not controlled or is not making an effort to control. This uneasiness on the part of lenders ultimately causes the supply of loans to dry up, thereby destroying the government's ability to intervene in the foreign exchange markets to hold the price of its currency constant. The result will be a rise in the premium, as the public's expectation of an imminent rise in the exchange rate increases the demand for foreign exchange. Thus, in the long run, external debt actually depletes the government's reserves and hampers its efforts to intervene in foreign exchange markets.

A sound method for holding the exchange rate fixed requires the government to use its foreign exchange reserves to intervene directly in the market by buying and selling its own currency, instead of imposing controls that cause a black market to develop. The level of reserves and the black market premium should be inversely related, for direct intervention will be easier and maintainable over a longer period if the level of reserves is high. In Table 8.1, this is exactly what the negative and significant coefficient on reserves indicates. The balance of trade also is expected to have a negative coefficient, because a government whose country enjoys a positive balance of trade will have credibility in the eyes of the public that its efforts to control the black market are sincere. The population knows that the government has the resources to maintain whatever level of foreign exchange rate is established. However, that coefficient is insignificant, probably because governments that choose to intervene in foreign exchange markets finance this intervention by borrowing funds instead of by building up reserves or maintaining a positive balance of trade. Indeed, in the presence of a positive balance of trade, black market premiums would either disappear or at least would be greatly reduced, and therefore balance of trade should not play a significant role in determining the level of premiums. Only debt financing of market intervention could explain the continued existence of premiums. This conclusion is borne out by the results of the study.

The control for economic growth also is significant and has the expected negative sign. In countries that experience positive economic growth, populations are optimistic about their economic future, which includes a steady supply of foreign currency. Conversely, when the expected growth is negative, populations are pessimistic about the future and their governments will attempt to preserve reserves by implementing the types of coercive policies that foster black markets.

The significant control variable implies that, in the absence of any political credibility, the government will resort to increasingly stricter controls on foreign exchange markets to improve its level of international reserves, thereby pushing up the premium as more and more people look toward the black market to satisfy their demands for foreign currency. Moreover, once the economy has deteriorated sufficiently, people lose all faith in their domestic currency and begin to hoard foreign currency, most often U.S. dollars, which then becomes the preferred medium of exchange for all transactions.

Table 8.1 shows that political capacity of governments is important in determining the black market premium. Both variables, *RPE* and *RPR*, are significant and have the expected signs, for the higher the efficiency of government, the lower the premium. The market for foreign exchange reflects not only the economic condition, but also the political climate of a country, as it mirrors expectations about future performance. Government performance can be viewed from two perspectives, one being the resources it can extract from the population, and the other its capacity to convince the population to abide by its rules. In the case of premiums, a government's capacity to reach the population has a stronger impact than the government's capacity to extract (b = -0.539 for *RPR* and b = -0.309 for *RPE*). As expected, the black market premium is a good barometer of government performance, and shows that, along with main-taining a certain level of resources, governments also need to build up the trust of the population.

Once it has been established that politics lie at the core of the explanation of black market premiums, the next step in our analysis is to consider levels of political capacity. The expectation is that at low levels of political capacity, the economic variables will not play a significant role, but the political variables will, because, at low levels of political capacity, marginal increases in government capacity provide a sense of reassurance to the public with regard to policy implementation. Governments that can show that they will carry out their announced policies to control the premium will be rewarded. Conversely, lack of government credibility will lead to higher premiums as people, lacking faith in the government's policies and consequently in the domestic currency, turn more and more to the black market to satisfy their requirements for foreign currency. Improvements in the weak government's political capacity should, therefore, play a major role in reducing the premium. Once the government has become efficient, however, the economic variables in the model should start to play a significant role. The costs of increasing an efficient government's capacity are too high to be practical, as at this point the population may feel that the unaccustomed government intervention is intrusive and confiscatory. Therefore, the efficient government's ability to control the premium will be a function of how well it uses the economic resources at its disposal. Its best option may well be to leave the market alone. In sum, once a government has attained a certain degree of credibility and has persuaded its people of the necessity for specific yet unpopular economic measures to control the premium, further changes in its political capacity should not have a significant effect on its credibility, and therefore should not have a significant effect on the premium, either.

The model was estimated at low levels of political capacity ($RPR<1$ or $RPE<1$) with the expectation that political variables would take the lead among the explanatory variables; it was estimated at high levels of political capacity ($RPR>1$ or $RPE>1$) with the expectation that economic variables would be the major weighting factors. The results for the cases when $RPE<1$ and $RPE>1$ are similar, as shown in Table 8.2.

In general, the results are as expected. The explanatory power of the model is higher for efficient governments ($R^2 = 0.43$) than for inefficient governments ($R^2 = 0.32$). The degree of overvaluation is a significant predictor of premiums. Currencies tend to be more overvalued in the case of inefficient governments ($b = -0.63$) than in the case of efficient governments ($b = -0.13$). The control for economic growth is significant in both cases, although it is marginally significant at the 5% level and becomes insignificant at the 1% level when governments are inefficient. The coefficient is also higher ($b = -0.69$) for efficient governments. As in the general case, current account balance is still insignificant in both cases. As expected, the level of reserves is significant when governments are efficient—but not when they are inefficient.

The interpretation of external debt is not as straightforward. In the case of inefficient governments, the external debt has a substantial positive effect on the premium. This could be because at low levels of political capacity, the government lacks the ability to implement domestic policies to control premiums and has to borrow money from foreign creditors to finance intervention in exchange markets. Yet, contrary to expectations, external debt has a significant negative effect on the premium when governments are efficient. This could be because for a government with a high level of political capacity, an increase in the level of its external debt is seen as a temporary measure taken by the government to control the black market. Indeed, because the government has a high level of credibility, people may believe that this debt-financed market intervention will be temporary and that the government will implement the necessary macro-economic policies to correct the imbalances in the economy responsible for the premium in the first place.

Political controls are significant in both cases, showing that, whatever the level of capacity, the stronger the controls imposed on the foreign exchange market, the higher will be the level of the premium. But overall, this suggests that inefficient governments should concentrate efforts on improving the political system in order to deliver sound macroeconomic policy. Economic bonanzas have only temporary effects on their economic

TABLE 8.2 Political and Economic Determinants of Premiums in Efficient and Inefficient Governments, 1970-1989

Variables	Inefficient Governments			Efficient Governments		
	Coefficient	Std. Error	T-value	Coefficient	Std. Error	T-value
PREMIUM						
REAL OFFICIAL RATE	-0.63	0.046	-13.66**	-0.13	0.060	-2.18**
CURRENT ACCOUNT	0.55	0.842	0.65	-0.37	1.709	-0.22
EXTERNAL DEBT	0.14	0.019	6.94**	-0.08	0.026	-2.98**
RESERVES	0.01	0.017	0.41	-0.10	0.021	-4.80**
GDP GROWTH	-0.39	0.189	-2.03*	-0.69	0.253	-2.73**
CONTROLS	0.22	0.026	8.36**	0.49	0.059	8.22**
RPR	-0.95	0.337	2.80**	-1.72	0.417	-4.12**
RPE	-0.30	0.057	-5.32**	-0.12	0.076	-1.67*
CONSTANT	0.06	0.050	1.21	-0.07	0.026	-2.53*
R^2	0.43			0.32		
Number of Observ.	496			299		
Prob F	0.0000			0.0000		

* Significant at 10 percent level.
** Significant at 1 percent level.

outlook, unless their political systems are conducive to delivering long-lasting and stable results. Also as expected, political extraction is not a significant predictor of premiums when governments are efficient. In such cases the market seems to take over and marginal changes in the level of extraction produce no effect on the levels of premiums. Also, when governments are efficient, increases in political extraction (*RPE*) are not significant, although the level of reach (*RPR*) is significant even at high levels of government efficiency. One possible explanation is that if premiums (and therefore black markets) exist under governments with high levels of political efficiency, they do so because of the relatively low levels of credibility and trust that these governments enjoy vis-à-vis their populations. Increasing the credibility of the government and the public's trust in its policies will then be the only means of effecting a decrease in the premium. The mere existence of premiums means that politics is part of the game, although for efficient governments the market regains an importance that is overshadowed by politics among less capable governments.

CONCLUSIONS

We have tested a simple model of premiums, based on political and economic explanations, that describes the problem of black markets for foreign currencies, which is still widespread in developing countries. The issue of premiums is clearly important, not only because the premium is a barometer of political performance, but also because exchange rates are the link to the external world in an increasingly interdependent international environment. Unfortunately, little research has been done in this area, and almost all is concentrated on a few specific countries and on domestic economic variables. The effects of politics are ignored completely. In economic terms, the supply of foreign exchange determines the flexibility a government has to manipulate the foreign exchange market. In political terms, as we argue, an efficient government fosters an environment of certainty and trust in its ability to implement the necessary macroeconomic adjustments in the economy to preclude the rise of a black market in hard currency.

The results obtained show that both economic and political factors affect the level of the premium. The supply of foreign currency was approximated by the level of reserves, the balance of trade, and the external debt. Premiums decrease at high levels of reserves and increase when external debt is high, showing that the public's expectation about expansive domestic policies provides it with incentives to hedge against the domestic currency. Unexpectedly, the balance of trade is not significant, even though improving it is the healthiest way of providing foreign currency. Perhaps the effect of the balance of trade is subsumed in the level of reserves. But economic growth is an important control. When the economy provides an optimistic outlook, premiums decrease. Politics, the expressed concern of this study, are also important. As anticipated, governments that are efficient and rank high in both reach and extraction can control black markets and therefore experience lower levels of premiums. It has also been shown that political controls on foreign exchange transactions are counterproductive.

The analysis was extended to determine whether the effects of economic and political actions differed in the case of a capable versus an incapable government. We found that when a government is inefficient, a marginal increase in political capacity makes a real difference in the premium, and that the economic variables are not as important as the political ones. In the case of an effective government, however, politics loses its edge. These results have important implications for policy. The degree of trust in the government and the credibility of the government's policies are good across-the-board predictors of black markets. An inefficient government must first persuade the population that it will take the necessary steps to render a stable and productive economic environment.

In sum, this analysis of the determinants of premiums indicates that efficient governments should rely on the market to control premiums, and that inefficient governments should direct their efforts toward the political system rather than toward attracting an expansive supply of foreign currency to solve the problem of black markets in foreign exchange.

APPENDIX: ESTIMATION OF THE EDWARDS MODEL

Edwards estimates the following equation:

$$Premium_t = a_0 + a_1 Excre_t + a_2 E_{t-1} + a_3 GCGDP_t + a_4 Growth_t + a_5 TOT,$$

where:
EXCRE = excess supply of domestic credit;
E = nominal exchange rate;
GCGDP = ratio of government consumption over *GDP*;
GROWTH = growth rate of real *GDP*;
TOT = Terms of Trade (Edwards 1991, 146).
We use ratio of government tax revenues over *GDP* as a proxy for GCGDP, and we use the lagged value of the real exchange rate instead of the nominal. Our results using the same sample as in Table 8.1 are given in Table 8.3.

TABLE 8A.1 Estimation of Edwards Model

Variables	Coefficient	Std. Error	T-value
PREMIUM			
REAL OFFICIAL RATE	-0.05	0.012	-3.86**
EXCESS CREDIT	0.18	0.065	2.72**
GOV.REV/GDP	0.62	0.113	5.51**
GROWTH	-0.42	0.119	-3.57**
TOT	0.11	0.034	3.13**
CONSTANT	0.001	0.006	0.18
R^2	0.07		
Number of Observ.	1037		

* Significant at 5 percent level, two tails.
** Significant at 1 percent level, two tails.

NOTES

1. We thank Insan Tunali, Tom Willett, and Jacek Kugler for helpful suggestions. The responsibility for all remaining errors is entirely ours.

2 To establish a base line, Edwards's model was estimated using our sample (see Appendix) and, although the predictors are significant, the explanatory power of the model is relatively low ($R^2 = 0.07$).

3. How this fixed level is arrived at, or even the pros and cons of a fixed exchange rate regime, is not the concern of this chapter. Instead, the factors which affect the black market premium, given the exchange rate regime of the country, will be analyzed.

4. An interesting exception to this general rule is India. Prior to 1991, the Indian government maintained fixed exchange rates and strict quantity controls. This led to the establishment of a thriving black market. However, in 1991, controls were relaxed, various economic liberalization measures were instituted, and the Indian rupee was devalued by about 26%. Since then, there has been strong market pressure on the rupee to appreciate against the dollar, as demand for the rupee has been high due to booming exports and the inflow of direct foreign investment in Indian capital markets. Since 1992, the Indian government has held the value of the rupee constant at approximately 31.4 rupees to the dollar, instead of allowing it to appreciate to the free market value. This is an example of a government keeping its currency at an artificially low level.

5. Sources: Black market rate: PICKS and WCY (several issues) and Adrian Woods (1988). Official rate: IFSY, line af (average), units of national currency per dollar.

6. Sources: Official exchange rate: IFSY, line af. CPI: IFSY, line 64. WPI: IFSY, line 63 (for the cases of Kenya, Malaysia, Nigeria, Senegal, and Singapore the wholesale prices are not available, and the consumer price index was used instead). Trading partners: YITS   Oil price: YITS.

7. Source: WT, Country pages (several issues).

8. Source: IFSY, line 77ad, in current U.S. dollars.

9. Source: IFSY, line 11d, in current U.S. dollars.

10. Source: *Penn World Tables* (Summers and Heston).

11. Source: Arbetman (1995).

12. Source: Arbetman (1990); Kugler (1994).

13. Source: PICKS and WCY, several issues.

14. Because the data set extends from the years 1960 to 1988, it might seem that the first obvious hypothesis test would be a Chow test for the stability of the parameters of the model during pre-1974 and post-1974 periods (to correspond to the breakup of the Bretton Woods system). This test was not performed for two reasons: (i) The effective duration of the model is actually from the years 1970 to 1988 because the figures for the debt are available only for this period. With just a maximum of three observations per country for the pre-Bretton Woods period, it was felt that the results of a Chow test would not reveal very much; (ii) The breakup of the Bretton Woods system primarily affected the developed countries, who chose to move to a system of floating exchange rates, and not the developing countries, who continued to maintain fixed exchange rates even after 1974. Because the existence of black markets can be explained only by the existence of fixed exchange rates, and the countries which followed such policies were not affected by the breakup of the Bretton Woods system, there is no economic reason to expect that the model would not be stable across the entire sample period.

15. The Phillips-Perron unit root test was performed on the premium series, and the results were a mixture of stationary, unit, and explosive roots (see Perron 1988 for a description of these tests). Moreover, as stated by Perron (1988), the power of the unit root tests will be a function of the span of the data and the number of observations. Because annual data for 29 years (the whole sample) were used, the power of the tests will be limited and little can be concluded from them.

PART THREE

Political Applications

9

Political Capacity and Government Resource Transfers

Daniel E. Ponder

INTRODUCTION

For all its messiness, federalism is widely seen as having been a successful experiment in government for the American political system.[1] But what form of government is it? Whether by design or serendipity, what values emerge from its practice? It is almost definitionally true that federalism consists of a mixed regime. It seeks to combine the best of disparate systems while avoiding their shortcomings. Scholarly considerations of the practice of federalism converge on some aspects, and then part ways again without achieving consensus.

This chapter does not settle the issue. Rather, it engages in exploratory analysis which tests some of the notions held by scholars. Specifically, it uses a theoretical and methodological approach borrowed from international politics that emphasizes the political capacity of governments to study one important facet of intergovernmental relations: the distribution of federal monies to state governments. The results indicate that although the federal government exerts considerable discretion in deciding which states will receive federal funds, states exert a fair amount of control over their fiscal destinies, both internally and with respect to the federal government, when they are politically capable of responding to federal opportunities. Politically capable states can secure an advantaged position in the increasingly competitive market for federal funds vis-à-vis other states. Somewhat surprisingly, the emergent distributional patterns reported in this chapter show no egalitarian strand that would narrow the gap between needy states and their richer counterparts. Instead, a pattern in the distribution of federal resources emerges where states that have greater relative political extraction are at an advantage in the race for money, and in fact manage to receive amounts over and above what they might otherwise get if monies were parceled out solely on the basis of egalitarian principles.

BACKGROUND

The ability of state governments to obtain federal money and the central government's decisions that determine where and how much money will be allocated, have received a fair amount of theoretical and empirical attention over the last twenty-five years. In particular, studies have asked how allocation decisions made by Congress, the president, and the bureaucracy apportion national resources among state and local governments and individual citizens. Examples of these resources are provisions for programs such as food stamps, housing vouchers, income supplements, or other supports for the poor, as well as tax credits for businesses willing to invest in depressed areas such as state-delegated enterprise zones. Other examples are health care programs such as Medicare and Medicaid, employment programs, highway construction, and various other programs implementing federal policy. Several studies have sought to explain the origins and maintenance of distribution programs and the equity with which they are applied (Arnold 1979; Dye and Hunley 1978; Friedland and Wong 1983; Owens and Wade 1984; Saltzstein 1977; Sharkansky 1968).

The present study concerns the questions raised in previous research, and derives its theoretical and historical roots from the familiar Lasswellian definition of politics as "who gets what, how, and when" (Lasswell 1958). The question is a deceptively simple one, especially when couched in terms of the "what" and "when" components. It is tempting to believe that all the researcher has to do is study the actual allocation of resources and the temporal space within which money is distributed to gain a sense of these two dimensions. However, when the "how" component is considered, the question becomes more complicated and needs to be recast: To what extent are resources supplied to states that need them most? Put another way, what is the nature of the tension between the fiscal conditions of a state and the ability of that state to secure federal funds?

Studies of distributional equity are especially important in light of the different patterns in the growth rate of federal money allocated to state and local governments that have emerged in the last half century. Figure 9.1 demonstrates the various trends which have occurred in the intergovernmental realm over the last forty years. For example, aggregate intergovernmental funds totaled only $2.3 billion in 1950, and represented 5.3% of all federal expenditures and 11.6% of gross domestic outlays. By

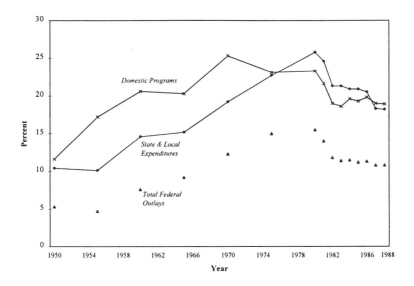

FIGURE 9.1 Federal Grants as a Percentage of Total Federal Outlays, 1950—1988

Notes
Data reflect federal grants as a percentage of total federal outlays, domestic programs, and state and local expenditures. All years reported are fiscal years. Data have been smoothed to reflect continuous trends. Source: Adapted from data reported in Office of Management and Budget, *Budget of the United States Government, Fiscal Year 1992* (Washington, D.C.: U.S. Government Printing Office, 1991), 132-133,166. Reported in Stanley and Niemi (1992, 321).

1988, they had grown to $115.4 billion, or about 19 percent of federal expenditures, and roughly one-fifth of state and local expenditures. These outlays increased mostly in response to the New Federalism initiatives of the Johnson administration, in which federal categorical programs nearly replaced block grants to state and local governments (Pressman 1975, 13). Richard Nixon subsequently revised and aggregated many of these programs under the rubric of revenue sharing. Additional differentiation materialized under the auspices of the community and urban revitalization programs during the Ford and Carter years. These programs were eventually curtailed under New Federalism II, or the "Reagan Revolution," in which real domestic outlays to state and local governments as a percentage of federal expenditures declined precipitously.

States increased their fiscal dependence on the federal government during the 1950s, 1960s, and early 1970s. However, state access to federal

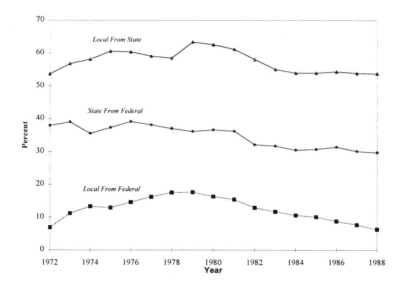

FIGURE 9.2 Fiscal Dependency of Lower Levels of Government on Higher Levels

Notes
Data reflect intergovernmental revenue as a percentage of general revenue from a government's own sources. Source: Adapted from data reported in U.S. Advisory Commission on Intergovernmental Relations, *Significant Features of Fiscal Federalism, 1990*, Volume 2 (Washington, D.C.: Advisory Commission on Intergovernmental Relations, 1990), 64, 92, 94. Reported in Stanley and Niemi (1992, 322).

dollars became more restricted as funding levels dropped almost 10 percentage points in the decade between 1978 and 1988. As Figure 9.2 illustrates, this dependent relationship flourished throughout the 1970s and early 1980s, but declined substantially during the 1980s Reagan period, when revenue sharing was phased out. Taken together, these trends indicate that competition for federal aid became extremely keen as the intergovernmental market for federal funds was tightening. As in most markets with scarce resources, information costs and exogenous forces outside of the direct control of players dominated, and intergovernmental transfers from the central government to subsidiary governments became increasingly coveted prizes for states and localities.

It is against this background of increasing demand for federal intervention and decreasing federal capability or willingness to supply aid that some studies add one or more theoretical components to Lasswell's definition of politics. When we concentrate exclusively on specific grants or intergovernmental projects, the most provocative of these components are "why" and "where" (Arnold 1979; Rich 1989). Why are allocation decisions made as they are, and where are they distributed or concentrated? "Why" resources are distributed as they are will be addressed this chapter. Much of the conventional wisdom states that political or economic indicators (e.g., partisan affiliation of legislators and the president, state or district representation in Congress, per capita income, unemployment levels) are fundamental factors in determining monetary flow patterns. The research described in this chapter examines the effect of an often cited but little studied variable that may substantially affect these decisions: the influence of political extraction on the effectiveness of the state in attracting aggregate-level federal funds.

THEORY AND HYPOTHESIS

Many of the explanations of intergovernmental fiscal relations cited in Appendix 1 are similar to Arnold's (1979) theory of reciprocity. To build on these studies, an exploratory research design that examines another factor is put forth to explain some of the fundamental structural differences between these studies and to test the importance of partisan political variables. The important factor to be explored is administrative efficiency, operationalized as the ability of state government to extract economic resources in the form of taxes from its population.

Measures of political extraction are examined within and across states in order to explain both a state's relative success in extracting funds to adequately finance governmental programs, and the relative fiscal need of a state vis-à-vis other states in the federal system. One way to measure the efficiency of a state is to measure the extraction of its resources, i.e., the relative success it enjoys in tapping the resources of the society. Relative political extraction (*RPE*) provides an estimate of the success of a government in carrying out the goals that it has set for itself using the resources with which it has to work. A problem arises, however, because divergent theoretical strands could easily lead to at least three plausible scenarios. First, relative political extraction could have *positive* effects on federal transfers. Second, relative political extraction could have *negative* effects on federal transfers. Finally, there could be *no* relationship between political extraction and federal transfers. The last of these possibilities is self-explanatory. The first two will be discussed in detail.

Following Organski and Kugler's formulation, detailed in Chapter 1, the index of political extraction indicates the degree of both governmental effort and governmental performance in tax collection and is, therefore, a prime indicator of government performance in the extraction of resources.

Tax capacity is estimated by examining the taxable resources of a state, which are defined by the state's economic structure—for example, whether the state employs a sales tax or an income tax and how much revenue could be extracted from one or the other. Therefore, tax capacity is the amount of resources within a state that could *potentially* be tapped. Tax effort reflects the willingness of the state to collect those resources.

RPE can be considered an alternative measure to Rich's (1989) political variable measuring the administrative capacity of states to coordinate efforts to win funds for project grants. It also sheds light on Sharkansky's (1968, 1969) work.[2] In his study of state economic growth, Brace (1991) measures state institutional capacity as legislative capability (i.e., the amount spent on internal control by legislatures [per legislator]), and formal gubernatorial powers as measured by the Schlesinger Index.

The analysis in this chapter differs from that of other studies by considering the factors cited above as endogenous and employing *RPE* as a measure of governmental presence instead. *RPE* reflects exogenous factors by taking into account the relative performance of state governments, and illuminates endogenously driven circumstances among the states which are subsumed under and standardized by the *RPE* index. Therefore, the first hypothesis is that the greater the political extraction of a government's administrative apparatus, the greater the relative flow of federal funds to that state will be. A higher level of *RPE* is related to a state's employment of superior mechanisms for seeking grants-in-aid, project grants, loans, matching funds, payments to federal workers (all of which effectively increase the tax base of the state), and for carrying out programs which are required as pre-conditions for receiving federal funds. In short, as a state's political extraction increases, the transaction costs associated with securing federal funds decrease.

Whichever way the findings point, it is important to avoid equating efficiency with magnitude of extraction. Simply because a state is able to extract a large amount of resources from its population does not necessarily mean that it is administratively efficient. At a certain level of extraction, there may be adverse political consequences that will affect the government's autonomy to implement alternative taxation policies. A convenient example is the state of Missouri. After a period of essentially unchecked increases in local taxes, state voters passed the Hancock Amendment. This initiative prohibited local governments in Missouri from increasing taxes for more than four years without submitting the proposed increase to the voters and having it ratified by a two-thirds majority. The result in this case is that local government independence in raising revenue is now restricted.[3] It is also possible that, at a certain level of extraction relative to population, increased funds obtained from within the state may cause the forfeiture of federal monies, for the more money a state or local government is able to raise on its own, the less it may be eligible to receive from the federal government. Conversely, some programs are based on a matching grant system. Under this system, the more a state or local government is able to contribute to the program, the more it is eligible to receive from federal sources. The point is that efficiency and extraction are *similar* but not *identical* characteristics of government, and thus incentives may exist for a state or local government to strike a balance between the two. Consequently, there may exist some definite interactive effect between political capacity and the level of fiscal need exhibited by states.

THEORETICAL RELATIONSHIPS

The relationship between states' political efficiency and their ability to obtain funding is depicted in Figure 9.3. States in quadrant 1 are inefficient poor states that attract a great deal of federal funds relative to their tax base simply because they are poor and automatically eligible for formula grants. States in quadrant 2 are the most efficient states. They have high political capacities but do not extract so much in taxes that they disqualify themselves from receiving a substantial amount in federal funds, regardless of the form those transfers take. These states would be more likely to employ highly efficient administrative systems that excel at

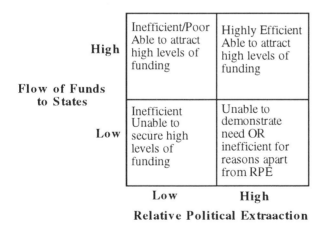

FIGURE 9.3 Theoretical Relationship of State Efficiency Levels to Ability to Attract Federal Funds

attracting federal dollars. States in quadrant 3 are either unable to demonstrate need or are inefficient for reasons other than political extraction (e.g., executive level decisions *not* to apply for certain federal funds, lack of grantsmanship skills, and so on). Finally, those in quadrant 4 are highly inefficient and unable to attract federal funds primarily because of their lack of administrative ability to win grants in a competitive environment for scarce resources.

Even if a state is very low on the efficiency scale, it may still be able to attract nondiscretionary funds from the federal government. However, such a state will be unable to attract as much as it might have if it had a more efficient administrative capacity. Thus, a state that is both efficient and poor will be able to attract a relatively large share of federal funds. If it is both inefficient and poor, it will attract a smaller share. Finally, if a state is both rich and efficient, it will garner a larger proportion of funds relative to less wealthy states operating at the same or similar levels of efficiency.

Other political control variables postulated in the literature are tested. One factor that is expected to be related to the ability of a state to attract federal funds is the level of federal government employment located within the state. Many federal programs within states are national programs run by federal employees. Considered in this light, employment opportunities exist at all levels of government and attract federal resources, which in turn draw additional employment to the state for the supervision and allocation of these expanded resource bases.

In short, the hypotheses may be stated as follows: First, the greater the level of political extraction of a state, the higher the probability that it will receive a larger proportion of federal funds relative to those states with lesser political capacities. Second, when measures of state efficiency are introduced into the model, levels of governmental employment and traditional partisan political factors should exhibit diminished explanatory power, reflecting the reciprocal logrolling relationships found in Arnold (1979). Third, there may be an interactive effect between the the political efficiency of a state and its ability to exhibit a need for federal funds. Thus, the flow of federal funds is directly related to the political capability of the state to attract such funds.

DATA AND METHODS

In the analysis the dependent variable is the flow of federal funds to states. It is a dollar amount that is adjusted proportionally to reflect the amount of money returned to the state in the form of federal aid for each dollar extracted. Because this research is exploratory in nature, *all* federal funds flowing into a state are considered, regardless of the nature of such funds. The only criterion is that the funds must originate within the federal government. The data for 1967—1988 were aggregated into blocks to form a three-year moving average so that abnormally high or low years would not distort the average estimates of funding flows under more normal conditions (Stanley and Niemi 1992, 320). For example, if a state sustained a massive natural disaster (such as the midwestern floods in the summer of 1993 and spring of 1995) and consequently received an inordinate amount of federal relief in any particular year, this sharp increase in funding would be diluted in the process of averaging over time. The analysis also provides a mechanism for controlling previous trends in budgeting and therefore explains antecedent inertia in monetary flow estimates.

The data used to estimate state $RPE^{\#}$ is derived from political capacity for four years: 1967, 1975, 1982, and 1988 (Stanley and Niemi 1992, 316-317).[4]

A state's relative need is a continuous variable reflecting whether the state's per capita personal income was below or above the national per capita personal income. In essence, it is the ratio of a state's per capita income to the national average. Because, in theoretical terms, "need" alone might not prove sufficient to attract maximum levels of federal aid in the absence of administrative efficiency, an interactive term, $RPE^{\#}NEED$, was created to capture the simultaneous effects of $RPE^{\#}$ and need. A negative coefficient for this variable indicates that $RPE^{\#}$ is more important to needy than to non-needy states; a positive coefficient would indicate the opposite. In order to test these conceptualizations, an independent estimate was made of each, along with an independent estimate of their interaction.

Much of the literature (Arnold 1979; Owens and Wade 1984; Reid 1981) questions the conventional wisdom that partisan political variables are of primary importance in explaining distributional patterns. Despite the fact that legislators and executives influence the allocation of moneys, these studies have found that partisanship *per se* has relatively little influence overall, given the norm of universalism that exists in Congress and in state legislatures. To ensure that the present model remained consistent with these studies and to test the effect of partisanship on distributional patterns in the presence of political efficiency, data were collected on the partisan distribution of Congress, the partisan affiliation of governors,[5] and the partisan affiliation of the president in each of the one-year periods examined. Moreover, some of the literature on comparative policy analysis indicates that left-wing parties are important explanatory variables, since they influence government expenditures on social programs (e.g., Heidenheimer, Heclo, and Adams 1990; Arbetman, Adams, and Hancock 1990). To extend this thesis in a somewhat different fashion, data on the percentage of Democrats in state legislatures were collected. The theory is that leftist parties may also tax more than other parties, and thus increase the level of political extraction. Otherwise, a state legislature has little effect on a state's decision to seek aid (an external condition). However, once federal money has been awarded to the state (an internal condition), the legislature has a strong effect on economic growth and distribution decisions. Because this study focuses on the importance of external factors, coalition effects are expected to be weak, but are included in order to produce as complete a picture as possible. Extending this effort somewhat further, all states were coded "1" if they were southern, and "0" otherwise. This variable taps the liberalism dimension, because for most southern states the term "Democrat" cannot be considered equal to "liberal," at least for most of the years of this study.

One factor that has been underexamined in the literature is government employment in the states. Levels of federal, state, and local employment may affect the political capacity of the state and through it the level of funding received. To control for this possibility, data were collected on the number of federal government employees concentrated in the states, standardized by 10,000 population.[6] Also included were variables measuring the per capita farm employment and per capita defense dollars entering the states. These variables may systematically influence government subsidies, and so are included as control variables.

Finally, a dummy variable was constructed that divided all of the preceding variables into segments. This was done for pooling purposes, as well as to enable separate regressions to be tested on the different years to determine the level of variation between years and the relative rank ordering of each variable. This procedure was used to ascertain whether the relative importance of the variables changed from time duration to time duration.

A pooled cross-sectional design was employed in order to highlight the independent effect of political factors on the distribution of federal moneys to the states over a number of years when the effect of other variables is held constant. A simple least-squares fit to the data was not appropriate because the right-hand endogenous variable ($RPE^{\#}$) is a non-linear function of the left-hand endogenous variable. $RPE^{\#}$ is a function of all exogenous variables in the model, and of squared and cubed functions of these variables as well. After these additional terms were included in the model, the equation was identified and two-stage least squares were employed for all estimations of the model.

MODEL SPECIFICATION

A complex model was set up that included the main elements of the theory. Those elements were political extraction, structural variables (i.e., employment), economic variables (i.e., need), and political variables. This relationship is described in equation 1:

$$FFF = b_0 + b_1RPE + b_2RPE^*NEED + b_3NEED + b_4FEMP + \\ b_5PCTAGEMP + b_6DEFPRCAP + b_7DEMOCRAT + \\ b_8GOVERNOR + b_9HOUSE + b_{10}SENATE + b_{11}REGION + e \quad (1)$$

where:

FFF (Federal Flow of Funds): These numbers are the estimated amount of federal expenditures in each state for each $100 of federal taxes paid by the residents of the state. They include all federal expenditures, allocated by state. All numbers are adjusted so that overall there is $1.00 of revenue for each $1.00 of expenditure. Source: Stanley and Niemi (1992, 319-20).

TAX EFFORT = the ratio of the state's actual collection to its tax capacity. The relative index of tax effort is created by dividing each state's tax effort by the average for all states. The index for the U.S. average is 100. This follows the procedure used in Organski and Kugler (1980).

TAX CAPACITY = the amount that each state would raise if it applied a national average set of tax rates for twenty-six commonly used tax bases. The index is the per capita tax capacity divided by per capita averages for all states, with the index for the average equal to 100. Source: Stanley and Niemi (1992, 316-17); *Significant Features of Fiscal Federalism, 1990* (1990, 186-187).

$RPE^{\#}$: Tax Effort/Tax Capacity. (See Appendix B)

NEED: determined by a two-step operationalization procedure. First, the ratio between each state's personal income per capita and the national personal income per capita was computed. This computation yielded a coefficient which was then subtracted from 1. Source:

Statistical Abstract of the United States, various editions.

FEMP: This is the number of paid civilian employees in the federal government, by state, as of December 31 of each year studied. It excludes members and employees of Congress, the Central Intelligence Agency, National Security Agency, and the Defense Intelligence Agency, as well as employees overseas, temporary census enumerators, seasonal and on-call employees, and temporary Christmas help of the U.S. Postal Service. Standardized by 10,000 population. Source: *Statistical Abstract of the United States,* various editions.

GOVERNOR: In each of the periods examined, it was determined whether the governor was of the same party as the president (coded 1 if "yes", 0 if "no"). Source: *Congressional Quarterly Almanac,* various editions.

SENATE: The number of senators in each state who are of the president's party (0, 1, or 2). Source: *Ibid.*

HOUSE: The proportion of the state delegation to the House of Representatives that is of the president's party. Computed as a percentage of the total state delegation. Source: *Ibid.*

DEMOCRAT: The percentage of Democrats in state legislatures, calculated by state. Source: *The Book of States,* various editions.

PCTAGEMP: The percentage of employees in each state who are employed in the agricultural sector. Source: *Statistical Abstract of the United States,* various editions.

DEFPRCAP: The dollar amount spent in defense and military related endeavors. Source: *Statistical Abstract of the United States,* various editions.

REGION: Each state was coded 1 if it was part of the south (i.e., Alabama, Arkansas, Florida, Georgia, Kentucky, Louisiana, Maryland, Mississippi, North Carolina, South Carolina, Tennessee, Texas, and Virginia) and 0 otherwise.

TIME: The year variables periodized (1967 = 0, 1975 = 1, 1982 = 2, and 1988 = 3).

TABLE 9.1 Effects of Explanatory Variables on the Flow of U.S. Federal Funds to the States: 2SLS

Variables	Full Model			Truncated Model		
	Coefficient	Std. Error	T-value	Coefficient	Std. Error	T-value
FLOW OF FEDERAL FUNDS						
Institutional:						
RPE	188.06	49.04	3.84**	186.26	47.78	3.90**
RPE*NEED	-0.02	0.005	-3.70**	-0.02	0.005	-3.73**
Fiscal:						
NEED	-0.87	0.51	-1.72	-0.82	0.50	-1.62
Structural:						
FEMP	0.20	0.03	6.89**	0.21	0.03	7.18**
PCTAGEMP	0.15	0.09	1.58			
DEFPRCAP	0.02	0.008	2.43*	0.02	0.008	2.54*
Structural:						
DEMOCRAT	0.03	0.09	0.33			
GOVERNOR	-4.64	2.77	-1.67			
HOUSE	-0.02	0.05	-.36			
SENATE	0.48	1.89	0.25			
REGION	1.07	4.26	0.25			
CONSTANT	64.88	8.66	7.49**	66.89	6.95	9.21**
R^2	0.60			0.59		
Number of Observ.	96			196		

* Significant at 5 percent level.
** Significant at 1 percent level.

RESULTS AND DISCUSSION

The results of the full model expressed in equation (1) are presented in Table 9.1.[7] They offer overwhelming support for the proposition that $RPE^{\#}$ is a strong and positive predictor of distribution patterns. As expected, influence peddling does not distort patterns of federal transfers of resources. This finding is consistent with the expectation that universalism is a dominant force at the federal level. The result is also consistent with Arnold's (1979) contention that targeted reciprocity operates between members of Congress and bureaucrats, it being given that the relationship is blind to questions of party. However, a more refined operationalization of political variables would be needed to support this contention further. There is stronger support for Arnold's argument that grants are not allocated on the basis of partisanship.

The results are different from expectations raised by Holcombe and Zardkoohi (1981), and Friedland and Wong (1983). It is possible that individual senators, representatives, and even presidents sometimes manage to acquire particular resources for their constituencies in excess of resources acquired by others. However, such distortions in distribution do not affect the overall federal transfer of resources to any significant degree. Surprisingly, there is support for Saltzstein's (1977) argument that the distribution of aid to states is *negatively* related to the state's level of need. In light of these clear results, all political variables and other insignificant variables were dropped from further analysis.[8]

In the second test, all insignificant variables were removed. As a result, the model was truncated into a more precise expression of the hypothesized relationships. Recall that the theoretical discussion leads to the expectation that $b_1, b_3, b_4, b_5 > 0$. The truncated model allows for a more exact estimate of the effect of these variables on federal flow of funds to the states. The truncated model shows that institutional variables reflecting the capacity of states to perform their jobs, along with fiscal and structural variables, are important determinants of the flow of government transfers. In order to clarify their impact, they now will be a nalyzed separately.

Most of the signs are in the anticipated direction. The truncated equation ($R^2 = .59$) shows the same amount of variance as the more complex model. The amount of variance explained is now almost equally divided between the structural and institutional/fiscal variables. As anticipated, relative political extraction is positively related to transfers in resources. State governments that extract support from their own populations for their programs more effectively than other states are capable of taking advantage of the opportunities presented by the federal government. Indeed, a one-unit increase in $RPE^{\#}$ is associated with an increase greater than \$186 per \$100 extracted by the federal government. This result seems rather high; however, it must be remembered that $RPE^{\#}$ increments are small, and no state came close to attaining a "2".

Now, let us consider the implications. If a state can move from, say, an $RPE^{\#}$ equal to approximately 1.0 to an $RPE^{\#}$ of 1.1 (a realistic expectation), then that state will increase its federal transfers by about \$18 per \$100 collected. When this is considered in the context of aggregate tax levels, it accounts for an astounding increase in the level of federal funds flowing into a state.

Clearly these results show that federal aid is systematically allocated to those states that have already succeeded, relative to their competitors, in the local environment. These states can accelerate the programs they *already have in place* by taking advantage of resources denied to those who are less effective, even if equally needy. Clearly, these transfers should have the effects that would be anticipated by a Keynesian model: As the government becomes more effective in allocating resources to its own programs, it also becomes better able to tap into a larger pool of resources from the federal government. The overall effect is that those states that have initiated programs with local funding can further expedite their efforts with federal funding, whereas those that have failed to implement programs congruent with federal guidelines have no opportunity for programmatic expansion, and so fall behind.

NEED is again negatively related to funding levels, though it barely fails to achieve statistical significance. It is certainly true that needy states that receive money from the federal government simply because they automatically qualify for formula grants. However, when analyzed in the presence of the interaction with political effectiveness, such differences are *less* significant for states with relatively greater political capacities, because they are able to garner additional funds by means of programs, matching funds, and competitive grants. Therefore, Saltztein's (1977) conclusion of a negative relationship between the need of the state and the level of federal funds flowing into that state is supported here.

This work provides insights into the normative questions of distributional equity raised in studies such as Page (1984), and provides preliminary support for the notion of hierarchical federalism wherein the federal government directs money to those states that are able to absorb such funds. Also supported is the notion of a concomitant regime within which the hierarchical relationships are somewhat countered by a strong individualistic strand, where states exert a large influence on their allocation of federal monies over and above the level of any expectation based on need.

As regards the interactive effects, the results indicate that the interaction between $RPE^{\#}$ and a state's fiscal need is significant but negligible. This finding adduces evidence that the relative effect of political extraction is approximately the same for all states, with the effect for needier states being only slightly greater than the effect for richer states. The intercept for needy states is higher across the board than it is for non-needy states. In general, however, the interactive effect of $RPE^{\#}$ and *NEED* remains more or less constant.

Of the structural results, *FEMP* is significant and positive. This is not surprising, because federal employment provides both programmatic policies and salaries paid to employees. *DEFPRCAP* is also significant and positive, though its magnitude is not great. This finding reflects competition for defense contracts and the efforts of state governments to attract those projects. Contrary to theoretical expectations, there does not appear to be a curvilinear relationship between $RPE^{\#}$ and the ability of states to attract federal funds. Seemingly, the more extractive a state is in absolute terms, the less it will be able to attract funds from the federal government because of its decreasing ability to adduce need. Several functional forms were estimated to capture this ineffectiveness, but no significantly different patterns emerged.[9]

Finally, I tested for the existence of underlying structural breaks. An obvious break occurred when Nixon implemented revenue sharing in the form of grants that bypassed states in favor of local governments. Another break might have occurred during the Reagan administration when revenue sharing was eliminated. To test for these breaks, the regressions for each year were rerun. No major differences were found outside of the variation that would normally be expected in a pooled cross-section design. More importantly, the rank orderings of the variables and the strength or weakness of the coefficients remain constant across all years.

CONCLUSION

This chapter examines theoretically and empirically the relationship between a state's political extraction and its ability to attract federal money. All money flowing to a state from federal sources was examined, regardless of the classification of those resources. A model was developed to compare the effects of a series of structural, fiscal, partisan, and institutional variables on the inflow of federal funds to states. The results indicate that the federal government is successful in its attempt to redistribute resources by means of transfers. However, states with relatively higher levels of political extraction are able to attract relatively greater shares of federal resources than are ineffective states. The reason for this is that these relatively efficient governments incur fewer transaction costs in both attracting and absorbing federal funds than do states that have not been able to cultivate strong extractive capabilities.

These findings add fuel to the debate about the sources of federal allocations. They show that partisanship does not play a consistently systematic role in decision-making, supporting the "universalism" argument put forth in many studies of congressional decision-making, but this does not shed much light on decisions that remain within the discretion of bureaucratic agencies.

What kind of regime the federal system is has also been the subject of much debate. This chapter offers preliminary support for the notion that American federalism combines strands of hierarchy and individualism. It is hierarchical in the sense that the federal government directs funds to states based on a number of programmatic and policy criteria. It is individualistic in the sense that the individual states have a great deal of discretion in securing funds over and above what they would receive based on need alone. This discretion is maximized for those states that can optimize their level of relative political extraction.

One weakness of this study is that it does not distinguish between grants, direct payments to individuals, and procurement projects. All funds were studied collectively. Because there is strong evidence that $RPE^{\#}$ affects monetary flow patterns in a systematic way, the findings should be tested against data that partitions funding flows into congressional districts, and a search should be undertaken for a discernible difference between the effect of $RPE^{\#}$ on discretionary and non-discretionary funds.

Nearly forty years ago, Harold Lasswell defined politics as who gets what, how, and when. This research has examined "why" resources are distributed as they are, and shows that the flow of federal funds to states is directly related to the political capacity of the state to absorb such funds. This conclusion bodes well for states that can increase and sustain their political capacity vis-à-vis other states.

APPENDIX A: ALTERNATE PERSPECTIVES ON WHY AND WHERE FEDERAL RESOURCES ARE TRANSFERRED

Studies of distributional equity and the dissemination of federal moneys to states have offered a number of causal explanations for the patterns they have discovered. These studies can be partitioned into those that focus on national-level factors and those that concern themselves with state- or local-level factors. Also, some studies add an explicit normative component grounded in the tenets of democratic theory. Whatever the level at which they make their arguments, they agree on the framework within which the "why" and "where" components fit. Theoretically, the "why" component emerges from these studies as an objective function of the federal government, or, in the specific case of grants-in-aid, of the granting agency. The "where," on the other hand, appears as twofold: It is dependent on input values at the funding source, and it is affected by the type and extent of political, social, or economic influence brought to bear upon the governmental decision (congressional, bureaucratic, or otherwise).

National-Level Explanations

National-level explanations have traditionally stressed the influence of institutional actors (e.g., Congress, the bureaucracy, and, occasionally, the president) on allocation patterns. Among the more influential of these explanations has been R. Douglas Arnold's (1979) study of the reciprocal influence relations existing between Congress and the bureaucracy. Arnold's theory proposes the existence of a mutual agreement between congressional committee members and bureaucrats in agencies and departments. According to his thesis, bureaucrats allocate increased shares of benefits to members of Congress (especially those who hold seats on key oversight or appropriations committees) who have voted, or may be persuaded to vote, for continuing or increasing funding levels to their agencies. By doing so, bureaucrats maximize legislative coalitions in support of their particular programs of interest. In return, members of Congress vote for continued funding of agencies in order to repay those agencies for past allocations to their home districts, and to increase the probability that they will continue to receive allocations favorable to their districts and/or their objectives in the future.

The dominant finding of these national-level studies is that political variables matter. There is something less than a consensus, however, on the relative influence of these variables on distributional decisions. Several studies of distributive policymaking have centered on the degree to which political factors influence distributive decisions (Copeland and Meir 1984; Friedland and Wong 1983; Hooton 1993; Holcombe and Zardkoohi 1981; Ray 1980; Reid 1980; Saltzstein 1977). The puzzling thing is that much of this literature is contradictory in its findings. For example, Holcombe and Zardkoohi (1981) state that political considerations, such as seniority in the Senate, larger percentage of majority membership in the House of Representatives, and membership on influential committees in both houses, help to explain the allocation of grants. On the other hand, Copeland and Meir (1984) note that although logrolling functions in Congress certainly have some marginal effect on the apportionment of funds, money is distributed almost completely on the basis of population.[10]

State and Local Explanations

An alternative explanation of distributive politics and allocation decisions is advanced by Michael Rich (1989). After studying six programs, Rich concludes that local and state governments exert a strong influence on federal decision patterns. Factors such as previous experience with federal programs, population, and especially the structural characteristics of individual programs are taken into account in the awarding of grant money. Reciprocal bargaining processes inherent in the political process are still important in the allocation of project grants, but are less important in the case of formula grants, where "universalism" is the observed norm in congressional vote patterns (Gilmour 1988; Mayhew 1974; Miller and Oppenheimer 1982). In concluding his study, Rich calls for a micropolitical approach to understanding distributional dynamics.[11] Similarly, Saltzstein (1977, 382) observes that political and organizational indicators are related to a state's ability to acquire federal moneys. However, at the level of local government, politics, rather than the "intent of federal legislation," is the determining factor in securing funds.

A topic related to state ability to attract federal money is the activity of state governments directed toward promoting economic growth. Although several studies focus on the role of state governments in researching and implementing policies to stimulate the economy (Brace 1991; Eisinger 1988; Jackson 1988, 101; Osbourne 1988), a largely overlooked but related theoretical question is the degree to which economic growth correlates with the ability of states to extract money from the federal government in the first place. Because many funding programs are related to the ability of states to provide a certain level of funding in order to obtain matching funds, economic growth may play a part in the ability of a state to secure federal resources.[12]

On the practical side, decisions of state and local agencies to apply or not to apply for federal moneys are influenced by whether or not their agencies will face prohibitive opportunity costs as part of the process of applying for federal aid, especially project grants (Reid 1980; Rich 1989; Stein 1979). State and local governments have limited worker time to devote to the application process, and they often operate under imperfect conditions in making their grant requests, even to the point of not knowing about the availability of funds.

These studies do much to elucidate the nature of grant life cycles, and are especially important now that the national government has decreased the number of formula grants available to states and communities and has moved toward project grants, attached to which are various sacrifices, including information costs and resource expenditures involved in constructing successful grant applications in a highly competitive environment.

Equity Expectations

A third strand of research focuses heavily on the equity (i.e., fairness in considering a state's fiscal need) with which funding programs are carried out. The literature in this area scrutinizes the success with which governments direct resources to those constituencies most in need of financial assistance (Holcombe and Zardkoohi 1981; Page 1984; Saltzstein 1977). Normative arguments in favor of promoting equality permeate Page's otherwise empirical analysis of several components of governmental action, which run the gamut between those states that bear the bulk of the tax burden and those that receive governmental welfare benefits. In a similar study, Saltzstein (1977) is more pessimistic about the ability of higher levels of governmental aid to reach those states whose economic need is greater than that of other states. Indeed, he finds that "some of the relationships are opposite in direction to the 'greater need, greater aid' hypothesis" and that "[no] support was presented for the frequently stated assumption that federal aid is supplied to people and communities that are socially or economically deprived"

(381-382). Finally, Wildavsky's (1984) provocative essay addresses the market-oriented approach to federalism and the question of which political cultures are most likely to value what types of aid. He analyzes various conceptual frameworks, including hierarchies, centralization, noncentralization, individualism, and egalitarianism, but he offers no empirical conclusions about the specific nature of the tradeoffs manifest in the federal system.

APPENDIX B

Table 9A.1 Coefficients of State RPEs, 1967-1988

STATE	1967	1975	1982	1988
Alabama	1.27	1.03	1.17	1.11
Alaska	1.05	.49	.58	.40
Arizona	1.15	1.17	.96	.97
Arkansas	1.08	1.00	1.03	1.14
California	.87	1.08	.85	.81
Colorado	1.02	.85	.67	.83
Connecticut	.79	.90	.85	.63
Delaware	.73	.68	.73	.68
Florida	.81	.73	.69	.79
Georgia	1.15	1.03	1.14	.95
Hawaii	1.36	1.09	.90	.98
Idaho	1.15	1.01	.99	1.22
Illinois	.74	.88	1.08	1.03
Indiana	.96	.94	.99	1.07
Iowa	1.00	.88	1.09	1.36
Kansas	.91	.78	.83	1.14
Kentucky	1.06	.99	1.07	1.09
Louisiana	.96	.90	.73	1.08
Maine	1.30	1.24	.27	1.07
Maryland	1.02	1.05	1.06	.99
Massachusetts	1.23	1.32	1.18	.73
Michigan	.96	1.05	1.29	1.17
Minnesota	1.25	1.21	1.12	1.08
Mississippi	1.53	1.37	1.30	1.45
Missouri	.89	.88	.90	.96
Montana	.89	.89	.88	1.20
Nebraska	.71	.80	.96	1.09
Nevada	.42	.48	.42	.51
New Hampshire	.74	.74	.75	.52
New Jersey	.91	.94	1.06	.81
New Mexico	.98	.88	.71	1.19
New York	1.28	1.63	1.85	1.39
North Carolina	1.23	1.01	1.15	1.02

North Dakota	1.05	.81	.72	1.06
Ohio	.82	.77	1.02	1.07
Oklahoma	.78	.74	.62	1.00
Oregon	.95	.96	.96	1.09
Pennsylvania	1.09	.95	1.19	1.03
Rhode Island	1.15	1.27	1.64	1.05
South Carolina	1.52	1.10	1.30	1.22
South Dakota	1.18	.93	1.05	1.22
Tennessee	1.12	.94	1.12	.99
Texas	.77	.61	.51	.92
Utah	1.28	1.03	1.13	1.36
Vermont	1.35	1.15	1.15	.95
Virginia	1.05	.94	.96	.88
Washington	.95	1.03	.91	1.04
West Virginia	1.28	.96	.93	1.13
Wisconsin	1.32	1.17	1.47	1.32
Wyoming	.56	.45	.52	.76

Standard Deviation = 0.234

NOTES

1. See, for example, the various perspectives of the authors in Golembiewski and Wildavsky, eds., (1984). For an analysis of the origins of federalism as a less than benevolent structural arrangement, i.e. as a mechanism for perpetuating the institution of slavery while minimizing the level of conflict on this issue between states and the federal government, see Riker (1964).

2. Sharkansky (1968, 146-147) examined the relationships between governmental processes and the larger political system of the state. He found that expenditure levels respond to certain economic, political, and governmental phenomenon within each state. It might be suggested that administrative primacy in expenditure is more likely to occur at the state level, rather than the federal. He finds that previous expenditures correlate highly with current expenditures, as well as with a high proportion of state revenues received as federal aid. Also, the larger a state's bureaucratic apparatus relative to its population, the greater the chance that the bureaucracy will have an effect on federal funding decisions.

Sharkansky also sees taxes as concrete indicators of governmental presence, often expressed in terms of growth, levels of employment, and stability (Sharkansky 1969, 7). Most states now have balanced budget requirements, which render resources increasingly scarce due to the limitations imposed upon their disbursement. These budget restrictions increase incentives to attract a greater than "sufficient" level of federal aid, defined as the ability of a government to fulfill its implicit and explicit obligations to its citizens through governmental programs. This aid may take the form of direct payment transfers to individuals, state-level aid to local governments, or federal aid to state and local governments. Although one must notice that these latter funds have been seriously curtailed by the decision of the Reagan administration to repeal Special and General Revenue

Sharing programs, they remain coveted objectives for localities.

3. For more on the Hancock Amendment and its consequences for Missouri's largest cities, see Sharp and Elkins (1987).

4. The empirical estimation of $RPE^{\#}$ for this chapter differs slightly from the specification of Kugler and Arbetman, Chapter 1 of this volume, therefore the notation $RPE^{\#}$.

5. The Schlesinger Index of Gubernatorial Power was not employed because it focuses on formal constitutional powers and thus points inward to the circumstances existent within the state. Partisan affiliation taps a dimension that reflects the degree of influence a governor can have merely by representing a certain state of affairs that, theoretically, funnels money from one level to another based on the predisposition of the federal government and the executive establishment of a state to agree on programmatic goals.

6. Data for state and local government employment also were collected. However, they were not included in the analysis presented here for two reasons. First, there is little theoretical reason to expect these variables to affect distributional decisions in any systematic way. Second and more important, when they were included in the model, they had no explanatory power whatsoever. Because they were of no use in the model, they were excluded from the analysis presented here.

7. In all of the tests, the state of Alaska was eliminated from the analysis because Alaska represented a consistent outlier. This is most likely a result of the unusually high amounts of aid received by Alaskan citizens and the state's abnormally high tax capacity caused almost entirely by the presence of oil. Both of these factors distorted the estimates. There were also huge amounts of federal aid to state agencies in the form of oil development, pipeline maintenance, and the like.

8. Though *GOVERNOR* was significant, it was not included in further analysis. This omission was made for two reasons: First, all other elements related to *GOVERNOR* (i.e., partisan political forces) had been eliminated as insignificant; second, when included in the truncated model, the variable is not significant at any conventional levels. Therefore, to analyze more clearly the effect of the institutional, structural, and fiscal components that were important predictors of flow patterns, *GOVERNOR* was dropped from the analysis.

9. Because of space limitations, those results are not presented here.

10. The model in the present study differs from Copeland and Meir's in that in the former, population is already accounted for in the calculation of the indices that reflect the flow of federal funds to states. Population is accepted as a given and disparities are searched for in the consequent distribution patterns.

11. This research strategy focuses on state and local governments as prominent decision makers because they are the ones who choose to apply for formula grants, how often to apply, how much to apply for, and so on.

12. Although this analysis does not make explicit use of economic growth, the relative economic conditions of each state are included in the operationalization of two explanatory variables: relative political extraction, and economic needs of states relative to other states.

10

Political Capacity and Demographic Change

Marina Arbetman, Jacek Kugler, and A. F. K. Organski

BACKGROUND

This chapter posits that strong governments create structural conditions that lead to declines in general fertility and mortality rates, and accelerate the transition from expanding to stationary populations. It starts with the structural perspective provided by the demographic transition model originally proposed by Thompson (1929) and Notestein (1945), which stipulates that societies that have increasing socio-economic development will experience declines in death rates followed by a lagged reduction in birth rates. Following this structural framework, economists and demographers routinely relate changes in per capita income and improvements in socio-economic development to declines in vital rates. Cross-sectional and historical evaluations show that vital rates decline in patterns consistent with those anticipated by the demographic transition model (Coale 1975; Demeny 1989; Bongaarts 1992). However, serious challenges to the classic model deal with the timing of changes and the specification of factors in societies undergoing demographic change (Cowgill 1949; Freedman 1994; Kirk 1971; Nam and Philliber 1984; Bongaarts 1992; Organski et al. 1984, Chapter 1). For instance, although observation suggests that political structures are responsible for unexpected declines in fertility and mortality rates in China, economic productivity or socio-economic development suggests this society should be undergoing serious population expansion instead of easing the imbalance between fertility and mortality. Such concerns are reflected by demographers, who study policies designed to manipulate fertility and mortality rates and explore the effects of family planning, health, education, and, more recently, empowerment of women (Sinding, Ross, and Rosenfeld 1994; Freedman 1994; Camp 1993; Bongaarts, Mauldin, and Phillips 1990). Socio-economic structures are frequently introduced in such evaluations. Bongaarts (1992), for example, observes that as income rises, the number of births per women drops consistently, but the unmet demand for population planning remains constant. He concludes that declines in fertility rates across levels of development can be achieved by meeting the demand for effective birth control policies. Similar connections between structural changes and the unmet demand for health, education, and empowerment are translated into policy alternatives that could lead to declines in fertility rates in developing nations (Sinding, Ross, and Rosenfield 1994; Camp 1993; Bongaarts, Mauldin, and Phillips 1990; Watson 1977). Inexplicably, in most studies the impact of government structure is disregarded.

The objective of this chapter is to change the focus of political analysis from policy to structural determinants of fertility and mortality rates. Greenhalgh's (1990) extensive review identifies isolated works, such as those of Ness and Ando (1984) and Migdal (1988), that argue persuasively that structural links exist between strong societies and declines in populations. However, unlike economists and demographers, political analysts seldom explore the state-society links to demographic changes. There are two important exceptions particularly relevant for this work. Organski et al. (1984) show that, regardless of policy preference, substantial and unintended reductions in fertility and mortality rates take place in societies where political costs are low. Rouyer's (1987) detailed study of India's population planning programs shows that equivalent population planning policies will reduce fertility rates when strong political systems are in place, and that such policies are less effective under weak governments.

This chapter extends these investigations in political demography. It is theorized that in addition to improvements in economic well-being, strong political systems, capable of reaching the desired targets in their populations and extracting resources effectively from the available pool, will close the gap between falling mortality rates and lagging reductions in fertility. The argument that is being made should be clear. Countries undergoing rapid demographic transformations will experience reductions in fertility and mortality— in part, because of policy planning programs, and in part indirectly, because of the unintended consequences of other governmental policies. Fundamental to this claim is the notion that stronger governments are the more likely to affect indirectly the demographic patterns of their nation. For example, vital rates change as a byproduct of increased internal security, expanded transportation networks that ease migration and urbanization, advancement of public health coverage, and the implementation of laws that open employment and educational opportunities to women. These changes, individually and combined, lead to indirect reductions in fertility and mortality. Therefore, it is suggested that governmental actions that impose effective regulations and laws that fundamentally restructure opportunities in societies affect both population patterns and socio-economic well-being in a cumulative manner.

This argument has important implications for developing nations. It will be shown that political strength does not require previous or concurrent economic productivity spurts or improvements in social development, but depends instead on the ability of the domestic elite to mobilize populations and obtain resources for governmental goals. Consequently, it is proposed that political strength leads to population decline above and beyond the effects of economic productivity. If this insight is correct, the path to stable populations is open even to the least affluent and least developed members of the international system.

The analysis of how changes in political structures affect demographic change is presented in four parts. First, the demographic transition model is sketched to establish the broad dynamics that connect structural economic changes to vital rates and to establish a base model. Second, details of the components of political strength and expected interactions among these components are provided. Third, results of the combined model are presented and evaluated. Fourth, the implications of the interaction between politics and demography are detailed.

THE DEMOGRAPHIC TRANSITION IN VITAL RATES

Thompson (1929) and Notestein (1945) outlined the classical demographic transition model. Figure 10.1 presents the central dynamics and expected variations in vital rates associated with socio-economic growth.

The demographic transition model proposes that massive declines in birth and death rates, from the high rates that characterize developing societies to the low birth and death rates found in developed societies, are primarily caused by the economic changes that spur socio-economic development. The high birth and death rates during the first stage, aptly labeled the stage of high potential growth, are a function of uncertainties about survival generated by poor nutrition, unsanitary conditions, and a lack of knowledge about population planning in subsistence economies. These factors lead households to place a high value on producing large families in order to ensure continuity. In the stage of high potential growth, populations are stable because high fertility is nullified by high infant mortality and relatively short life spans. These conditions characterized most populations in the past, but only a few societies still face such high mortality rates today.

As a country improves its economic well-being and enters the stage of

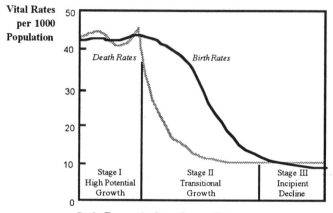

FIGURE 10.1 Idealized Demographic Transition

transitional growth, the mortality rate drops. That this decrease in mortality rate precedes changes in birth patterns is a function of higher economic productivity, which translates into a more abundant and reliable food supply, improved sanitary and health conditions, and consequently, lower mortality rates. Yet, despite a considerable decline in mortality, birth rates remain high. The reason for this lag is that the conditions that contribute to lower mortality rates also contribute to high birth rates. Indeed, the dynamic process represented by the demographic transition is the anticipated population increase resulting from the lag that occurs between the decline in death rates and the decline in birth rates. This stage characterizes population patterns in the developing world today, where population imbalance has produced conditions best characterized as "population explosions" (Coale 1975; Demeny 1989; Organski et al. 1984; Tsui and Bogue 1978).

As economic well-being and social development improve further, nations reach the stage of incipient decline, when birth rates decrease and ultimately match the already lower mortality levels attained during the stage of transitional growth. The shift from large to small families is induced partly by transformations in the social values driven by considerations of economic well-being, and partly by demands imposed on the household by the economic life of advanced societies. Factors that contribute to the decline of fertility rates are improved public health, which diminishes child mortality and extends life spans, and extended educational opportunities, which delay family choices and provide access to a wide array of population planning alternatives. At this stage, population expansions cease and stable populations emerge once more. Decreased birth rates may even fall below death rates, resulting in an overall population decline (Van de Kaa 1987).

The demographic transition model provides a persuasive, idealized summary of demographic change driven largely by improvements in economic and social conditions. Yet, as indicated, this parsimonious representation of a more complex reality is not completely congruent with the historical record. Nam and Philliber (1984) report that European pre-industrial fertility rates were not universally high but instead differed across and within nations and were also highly volatile. In the developed world, mortality and fertility have also behaved differently than originally expected. Therefore, although the overall pattern represented in the demographic transition is consistent with the gross record, the structural interactions are underspecified. A major omission is the disregard for the role that political structures play during the demographic transition.

RELATIONSHIP BETWEEN POLITICAL STRUCTURES
AND VITAL RATES

The classic demographic transition model suggests that structural changes associated with modernization determine the behavior of vital rates. The task of this chapter is to specify the political aspects of this structural change so that they can be effectively explored. To accomplish this, we offer cross-national measures of political structures and then a specification of the demographic transition model that includes such political structures. Jackman's (1993) excellent and exhaustive treatment of political capacity details the development of alternate definitions and concentrates on institutional age and legitimacy to measure this concept. His work details an emerging consensus in the discipline that state strength can be conceptualized as political capacity, but indicates at the same time that the empirical measurement of this concept remains in dispute.

Political capacity is conceptualized here as the ability of government to carry out the task chosen by its political elite and other national actors (Organski and Kugler 1980; Organski et al. 1984; Organski and Arbetman 1993; Arbetman 1990, 1995; Chapter 1 of this volume). From this perspective, one polity is more capable than another when its government can generate more human and material resources to attain the goals its elite has chosen. Two different but related components are used to estimate the concept of political capacity: (1) the ability of the government to effectively extract resources from the pool produced by a society, and (2) the ability of the government to reach and mobilize its population.

Reach and extraction behave autonomously but are nevertheless closely intertwined aspects of governmental capacity. The buildup of political structures with relation to population changes takes place sequentially. Governments first increase political capacity by mobilizing populations. Only then do they expand their capacity by extracting resources from the material pool produced by society. Reach, therefore, precedes extraction because only after the government has mobilized human resources and created the sense of a national whole, can significant fiscal extraction be sustained. Political capacity then, begins with governing elites reaching into the population, and extraction consolidates and deepens that reach.

In the context of demographic change, the sequence of political change suggests that nonlinear patterns characterize relations between political change and vital rates. A political sequence is also reflected in the dynamics that lead to reductions of mortality and then fertility. It is suggested that from a political perspective, reducing mortality is far easier than preventing fertility because extending life spans is congruent with population preferences, while altering family size requires revamping long-held habits and expectations. Therefore, governments that penetrate society even minimally can generate large mortality reductions simply by the introduction of public water purification and sewage control, the provision of basic public medical facilities and, most importantly, by the guarantee of increased public safety. Such actions produce dramatic declines in mortality rates as infants survive the first years of life and the average life span of the population is extended. Both effects are eagerly welcomed by populations.

Governments face a much more difficult task when they attempt to change fertility patterns. To produce substantive reductions in fertility, populations must reduce their expectations of family size. Policy work shows that this response can be generated in the population by expanded access to population planning programs, by increased universal education and employment opportunities for women, and by urbanization and migration from the countryside (Bongaarts, Mauldin, and Phillips 1990; Camp 1993). Governments that penetrate their populations will induce some reduction in fertility, but only strong governments with the fiscal base and means to build educational facilities, improve health, provide effective population planning, and institute laws that increase economic opportunities for women will substantially deflate fertility patterns. Control of fertility patterns may not be on the agenda in countries with strong governments, but the indirect effects of governmental intervention will nevertheless alter basic fertility patterns in such societies. This reasoning leads to the proposition that the pattern anticipated in the demographic transition model reflects expectations derived from political structures. Reach should first profoundly affect mortality, and fertility should lag and respond only to eventual increases in extraction. Consequently, the measure of political reach should be more effective than the measure of extraction in explaining the initial drop in mortality and early changes in fertility. Extraction, however, should facilitate more effective assessment of the changes in fertility that end the demographic transition by re-establishing stable populations.

BACKGROUND: THE CASE OF CHINA

China's birth rate has received much attention in the press since the 1979 implementation of the policy which set a limit of one child per family. This case, in fact, prompted the initial study of the links between structural economic changes and vital rates. To determine what the likely cause of

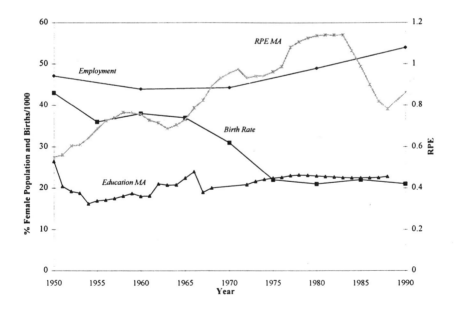

FIGURE 10.2 Female Employment, Female Education, Birth Rate, and RPE in China, 1950-1990.[1]

the rapid fertility decline might be, several traditional demographic variables were considered. The results of the findings are illustrated in Figure 10.2.[1]

Figure 10.2 clearly shows that the birth rates of China have been declining since the 1950s, decreased at an even more rapid rate in the mid-1960s, and began to level out in the mid-1970s. The continuous decline of this series illustrates that the strict birth control policy implemented in 1979 by the Chinese government had negligible effects on birth rate levels. Furthermore, female education and employment in China, which did not experience dramatic changes during the 1950—1990 period, bear little relation to declining birth statistics. The only variable that has a strong relationship with the birth rate is relative political extraction. The directly inverse relationship between *RPE* and birth rate between 1950 and 1984 suggests that gains in political capacity lead to a decline in levels of birth. The collapse between 1984 and 1988 shows that fertility trends will not resume previous patterns. These findings are supported by a growing body of literature within the field of political and economic demography, which has developed as a response to the "absence of clear-cut theoretical pro-positions concerning the demographic transition" (Richards 1977, 537-553). Moreover, demographers such as Ansley Coale's Princeton-based group, Rudolph Andorka, John Cleland, Christopher Wilson, and, independently, Charles Tilly, have become "increasingly dubious about any general statements concerning the social determinants of fertility decline" (Tilly 1986, 323-328). Therefore, studies such as this, which work from the top down, suggest that unspecified level forces are instigators of fertility change (Greenhalgh 1990). We propose that political structures are such forces.

CONCEPTS AND MEASURES

Demographic Variables: Crude Birth and Death Rates

Crude Birth Rates (*CBR*) for populations are estimates of the number of births in a given year divided by the total mid-year population per thousand. Crude Death Rates (*CDR*) are estimates of the number of deaths in a given year divided by the total mid-year population per thousand. The United Nations (1978, 1990) provides generally agreed upon crude rates which are used as the standard base for estimates of demographic change. These base crude rates are adjusted to remove large distortions that emanate from differences in age structures of populations. Consequently, fertility rates are overestimated in nations with relatively young populations, because of the large proportion of women of reproductive age, while death rates are underestimated in countries with expanding populations. In the following example, the standard procedures for minimizing distortions caused by age structures were followed to discover the age-adjusted base, using the population of England and Wales at five-year intervals. The following calculation is made:

$$SDA_{jt} = ASMR_{jt} * ASP \tag{1}$$
$$ACDR = \Sigma_k SDA_{jt} / \Sigma_k ASP \tag{2}$$

where:
$ACDR$ = adjusted crude death rate
CDR = crude death rates
k = age
j = nation
t = time
SDA = standardized number of deaths by age
$ASMR$ = age-specific mortality rate (when unavailable, calculated using model life tables)
ASP = age-specific standard population (England and Wales, 1960)

For some developing nations where age-specific data about mortality were not available, sporadic estimates were derived for age-standardized mortality rates using male life expectancy at birth in conjunction with the Western family of the Coale-Demoeny life tables. These rates in turn were used to obtain estimates of mortality rates (for details, see Organski et al. 1984, 79-83). The $ACDR$ reduces variations caused by population structure and can be used to contrast rates of decline across countries.

To reduce the differences in the proportion of couples of childbearing age in a given population, the ratio at five-year intervals of the number of women ages fifteen to forty-four in each nation to the number of women in the same age group in the standard population was established. The adjusted crude birthrate was then obtained by the following simple procedure (for details, see Organski et al. 1984, 83-84 and Appendix):

$$ACBR_{jt} = (PWP_{jt} / PWSP)\ CBR_{jt} \tag{3}$$

where:
$ACBR$ = adjusted crude birth rate
CBR = crude birth rate
PWP = percentage women 15-44 in national population
$PWSP$ = percentage women 15-44 in the standard population (England and Wales, 1960)
The adjusted crude birth rate takes into account actual fertility

declines and controls for a larger or smaller proportion of fertile females. Therefore, one can compare comparatively young populations, where a large proportion of fertile women unduly increases the birth rate, with relatively old populations, where a small proportion of fertile women artificially depresses the fertility rate.

SAMPLE AND CONTROLS TO MODEL THE DEMOGRAPHIC TRANSITION

To reflect the three stages of socio-economic development—high potential growth, transitional growth, and incipient decline—that are postulated in the demographic transition model, countries have been classified into the sets of less developed, developing, and developed. The less developed nations represent the poorest countries in the world with per capita products in the first through the fiftieth percentile during any one year in a five-year period starting with 1960. The set of developing countries consists of nations with per capita products above the less developed nations but not in the top first percentile, and who are not members of the OECD. The developed group consists of all OECD members and nations with income in the top first percentile. All OECD nations are classified as developed because in the first decade of this study some very advanced societies still exhibited the devastation induced by World War II and would, despite strong showings on alternate indicators of socio-economic development, otherwise be classified as developing due to a temporary and artificially low per capita product. The standing of each nation is updated every five years, allowing changes in category to reflect growth or decline in economic performance (see Appendix A for sample).

The analysis presented here is for the years 1960—1985. All nations of more than one million inhabitants were originally selected. Explicitly excluded were Lilliputian city-states such as Hong Kong, Liechtenstein, and Monaco, whose political and demographic structures are seriously affected by migration. Nations with centralized economies in Eastern Europe and the former Soviet Union are not included, because the available time series on estimated political structures are not long enough (Arbetman and Kugler 1995). This exclusion is regrettable, as major changes in the demographic patterns of these societies are underway. However, in another way, the exclusion was fortunate since certain subtle implications of the rapid declines in fertility and major increases in mortality that followed the political collapse of the former Soviet Union now allow exploration of the validity of the model presented here. Finally, developing nations are excluded for periods when data are insufficient to estimate either their socio-economic, demographic, or political performance. These exclusions, concentrated among the poorest nations in Latin America, Asia, and Africa, probably bias results in areas where rapid changes in mortality may still be taking place. Further, the unintended exclusion of the less developed nations acts against the thesis because it is among these nations that political reach should affect mortality most dramatically.

THE SOCIO-ECONOMIC VARIABLE: GROSS DOMESTIC PRODUCT PER CAPITA

Many ways to estimate socio-economic factors have been proposed. In cross-national works, two major alternatives are: (1) use of gross output per capita to take into account economic productivity in society, and (2) use of the UN Development Index, which provides a complex set of highly correlated socio-economic elements. Gross domestic product is used in the present study because it is highly correlated with the UN Development Index, it shows in a single comprehensive measure multiple levels of economic development, and it is not implicitly contaminated with the political variables that are provided. Data in constant equivalents from the *World Bank Socio-Economic Data Bank.* Kravis, Heston, and Summers (1979); and Beckerman (1966) clearly outline the problems created by conversion of currency into a common denominator and the further standardization into constant values over time. They argue, however, that no readily available nonmonetary substitute for productivity is less flawed (see also Organski et al. 1984, 79-82).

POLITICAL VARIABLES: POLITICAL CAPACITY

The political capacity variable used in this model is defined in Chapter 1. Changes in the political capacity of states are fueled by a government's capacity to achieve stated goals. To do so, governments must improve their ability to penetrate their society and reach their human assets and thereafter enhance their ability to extract resources from the pool of material assets produced by the society. Concurrently improving both reach and extraction should further enhance capacity. In the political domain, development begins with political reach. We posit that, in the early stages, changes in reach dictate changes in political capacity. But as governments become stronger, extraction adds to political reach and eventually dominates changes in political capacity. At critical points in the development cycle, political reach and extraction are highly correlated.

Organski et al. (1984) show that over the modernization trajectory, the highest political costs of building up the political system are at two extremes: in the initial period of development, and once the society has become fully developed. There is an intuitive explanation for these patterns. In the less developed societies, the organization of political structures is difficult because so few in the population are already organized for political purposes and there is so little material wealth to spare for the effort of becoming organized on a larger scale. Massive efforts are needed simply to gain access to households. In developed societies, on the other hand, governments have already achieved high levels of political reach and a large share of the population is mobilized. Therefore, when governments increase extraction to enhance the effectiveness of their established goals, they encounter organized opposition to new policy initiatives which they must overcome in order to proceed.

MODELING THE EFFECTS OF POLITICS ON
DEMOGRAPHIC TRANSITIONS

The demographic transition model (see Figure 10.1) anticipates that the largest reductions in fertility occur in developing countries during the stage of transitional growth when such societies face a potential population explosion. On the other hand, only moderate decreases in fertility are expected during the stages of high potential growth and incipient decline. Given these conditions, each stage is considered as a self-contained entity within a larger process of demographic change. Recall that governmental capacity to reach its population should be a more important determinant of fertility decline than extraction during the first two stages because the political elite must first mobilize the potential in the society, before it can effectively extract resources from the overall product of that society. Indeed, in developed societies that have attained the stage of incipient decline, the political flexibility of governments is vast, but their ability to improve their level of extraction is reduced because human and material resources have already been tapped effectively. For this reason, developing societies have the largest political potential and the lowest political flexibility (Chapter 1). Political capacity in these societies, therefore, should have only a limited effect on demographic change.

The structural relationship between political and demographic behavior is complex but as a first approximation, it is proposed that at each stage of the demographic transition improvements in political capacity and economic productivity will depress vital rates. This relationship can be stated as follows:

$$Vital\ Rates_k = \alpha_0 - \alpha_1 RPC_k - \alpha_2 GNP/CAPITA_k \qquad (4)$$

where:

k = Stage.

Because relative political capacity is a compounded variable combining both governmental reach and extraction, the extended postulated relationship for each stage is:

$$Vital\ Rates_k = \alpha_0 - \alpha_1 RPE_k - \alpha_2 RPR_k + \alpha_3 (RPRxRPE)_k - \alpha_4 GNP/CAPITA_k. \quad (5)$$

We postulate that governmental reach, extraction, and per capita income depress vital rates independently. This specification can effectively provide for variations in vital rates at each stage in the demographic transition. Therefore, one can detect whether at defined socio-economic stages governmental reach prompts more important demographic changes than extraction. Consideration is given to the nonlinear relationship between reach and extraction to detect whether changes in reach for a given level of achieved governmental extraction, or vice versa, induce additional declines in vital rates. Similar effects between the socio-economic and political factors are not considered because they are independent in theory and indeed prove to be so in practice.[2]

To take into account the nonlinear patterns in the demographic transition model, the data are partitioned into sets of less developed, developing, and developed countries. The coefficients in the stage of *high potential growth* should show that political capacity increases lead to dramatic drops in mortality, but that birth rates remain relatively high. In the stage of *transitional growth*, improved political capacity in developing nations should lead to declines in both vital rates, but birth rates are expected to be more affected than mortality rates. Finally, in the stage of *incipient decline*, demographic structures in developed societies have undergone major changes, and variations in political factors should therefore be greatly attenuated. To provide for these changing effects, a pooled cross section is used wherein economic, political, and interactive coefficients are estimated separately for each stage (Friedrich 1982; Kmenta 1986; Amemiya 1985; Jaccard, Turrisi, and Wan 1990).

TABLE 10.1 Decomposed Effects of Political Capacity & Economic Productivity on Birth Rates at Each Stage of the Demographic Transition, 1960-1985
(*For Details on Base Estimation see Appendix B*)

ADJUSTED BIRTH RATES (ABR)

	Estimated Coefficient	Nonlinear Estimated Coefficients		
		RPE=0.5	RPE=1.0	RPE=1.5
DEPENDENT VARIABLE				
Stage of High Potential Growth				
LESS DEVELOPED	63.23	58.60	54.01	49.42
GDP LESS DEVELOPED	-.0075	-.0075	-.0075	-.0075
RPE LESS DEVELOPED	-9.23			
RPR LESS DEVELOPED	-11.94	-9.34	-6.06	-3.91
INTER LESS DEVELOPED	5.34			
Stage of Transitional Growth				
DEVELOPING	98.27	84.3	70.4	56.4
GDP DEVELOPING	.0002	.0002	.0002	.0002
RPE DEVELOPING	-27.91			
RPR DEVELOPING	-68.39	-54.01	-39.60	25.23
INTER DEVELOPING	28.77			
Stage of Incipient Decline				
DEVELOPED	112.96	84.4	51.7	21.1
GDP DEVELOPED	-.0015	-.0015	-.0015	-.0015
RPE DEVELOPED	-61.22			
RPR DEVELOPED	-85.56	-55.12	-24.62	5.81
INTER DEVELOPED	60.91			

N = 2185 OBSERVATIONS
R-SQUARE BETWEEN OBSERVED AND PREDICTED = 0.72 R-SQUARE ADJUSTED = 0.72
R-SQUARE ADJUSTED EXCLUDING POLITICAL CAPACITY (RPP,RPE AND INTER) = 0.58

RESULTS

The Politics of Birth

The effect of politics and economics on fertility rates during the three stages of the demographic transition is reported in Table 10.1 and Figures 10.2 through 10.4. A pooled-cross-sectional regression used to estimate the coefficients for *GDP* per capita, governmental reach (*RPR*), extraction (*RPE*), and the interaction (*INTER*) concurrently distinguishes the less developed, developing and developed nations undergoing the three stages of the demographic transition process (Appendix B presents detailed coefficients as relative deviations from the base estimate established for developed nations.) In Table 10.1, the first column shows the estimated co-efficients for each stage computed at the mean. The next three columns show the interaction between political reach and political extraction holding *RPE* constant. In the case of fertility, variations in reach are preserved because declines in birth rates should occur early in the developmental process.

To illustrate the nonlinear effects of politics on fertility, estimates of the interaction effects of *RPR* and *RPE* are calculated setting *RPE* at 0.5, 1.0, and 1.5. This range was chosen because 90% of developing nations in the data set fall within this interval. For developed nations, however, this range is too wide. The point estimates of nonlinear effects in Table 10.1 are extended in Figures 10.3, 10.4, and 10.5 and directly show the effects on fertility at each stage of the demographic transition. The effects of *GDP* per capita within each stage cannot be represented in a three-dimensional graph, but they are fixed for each stage. Consider now the results (See also Appendix B for details).

The patterns anticipated by the classic demographic transition emerge in the pooled-cross-sectional analysis. Across the stages of development, economic performance is strongly associated with marked declines in birth rate. Controlling only for the three stages of the demographic transition and economic performance already accounts for approximately 58% of the decline in fertility. The addition of political factors adds slightly over 20% to that accounting. Therefore, from a static perspective, it is concluded that declines in fertility are caused in large measure by the socio-economic stage a country has attained.

The dynamics of the demographic transition are, however, illustrated by changes within each stage, not by the pattern left after the process has been completed. The test in this chapter, therefore, is designed to take into account the effects of changes of economic productivity and political capacity on fertility within each stage. In other words, these effects should provide for strengthened political structures which may have effects on fertility rates within each stage of the demographic transition allowing variation in socio-economic effects, but controlling for the long-term structure of economic development in the international system.

This investigation is important because economic development alone may not be sufficient to re-establish stable populations in the developing world. Indeed, as Myrdal (1968) and Gershenkron (1962) argued and Kuznets (1971) was among the first to show, after calculating the tradeoff between population and economic growth the pace of economic growth in the forseeable future would be insufficient to dramatically alter existing population distributions. They concluded that without major, unanticipated acceleration of economic growth in the developing world or the massive transfer of resources between developed and developing societies, populations in the developing world would continue to expand rapidly, thus preserving the vicious circle of poverty in developing societies and allowing the gap between rich and poor to widen. The relatively slow growth of individual output and meager improvement in social indicators in the developing world over the last three decades support this bleak forecast (World Bank 1989, 1992).

Contrary to the expectations of the past three decades, nations like China, Sri Lanka, and most recently Bangladesh have experienced large declines in fertility without concurrent improvements in their economic

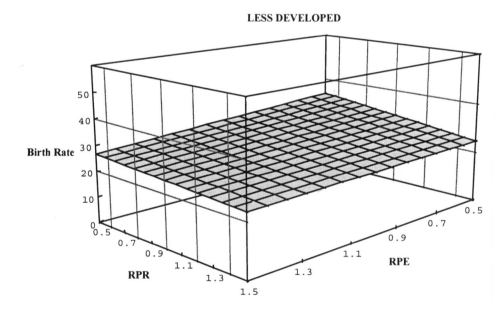

FIGURE 10.3 Impact of Political Capacity on Birth Rates during the Stage of High Potential Growth: Less Developed Countries

well being. Such declines can be traced to increases in the political capacity of their governments within each of the three stages of the demographic transition, which may set the stage for the economic improvements that propel nations from one stage to the next.

Consider the effect of politics on fertility rates in the stage of *high potential growth*. Table 10.1 shows that improvements in *GDP* per capita reduce fertility levels. Likewise, as expected, increased political reach and extraction substantively depress birth rates. In addition, decreases in fertility result from interactive increases in extraction and reach. Figure 10.3 shows, moreover, that during the stage of potential growth, nations that manage to increase the reach of the government from 0.5 to 1.5 would reduce the birth rate by 14 births per thousand.

The contribution of political reach dominates that of extraction. Increasing governmental reach, as anticipated, generates large declines in fertility. Increases in political extraction and joint increases in governmental reach reduce fertility only at the margin (see also Table 10.1). Therefore, during the stage of high potential growth, congruent with expectations, governmental reach is responsible for substantive changes in the birth rate when economic productivity and political extraction are held constant. However, the interaction between reach and extraction have

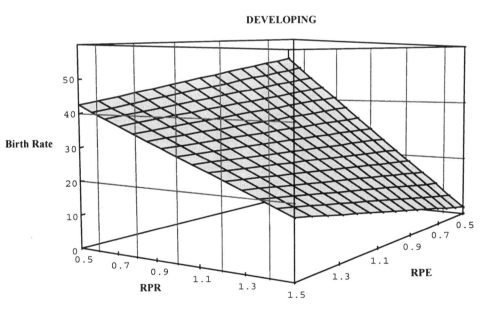

FIGURE 10.4 Impact of Political Capacity on Birth Rates during the Stage of Transitional Growth: Developing Countries

few effects.

Let us now turn to developing nations. The results in Table 10.1 and Figure 10.4 show that political factors are overwhelmingly responsible for reductions in fertility within the stage of transitional growth. Note that although changes in productivity produce unexpected but very slight increases in fertility, declines at this stage are caused by political reach and extraction. At this critical middle stage of transitional growth, when populations can literally explode, the effect of reach and extraction is more balanced. Governments able to penetrate and extract resources from the population will dramatically reduce fertility in their societies. For the first time, strong nonlinear patterns emerge. Figure 10.4 illustrates that as reach increases from 0.5 to 1.5, fertility rates fall from over 40 births per thousand to fewer than 20 when extraction is high, and to fewer than 10 when extraction is low. The low end of the scale suggests the low birth rates that characterize societies with stable populations, which were anticipated only in developed societies with high productivity per capita.

These results support the proposition that political improvements can end the threat of a population explosion. However, the full picture is not congruent with early expectations. For instance, unexpectedly, in societies where both governmental extraction and reach increase concurrently, the decline in fertility is less pronounced than when extraction remains low. One would anticipate that as extraction rises, so will the availability of transportation, health, education, and working opportunities for women. Perhaps the reason that this does not occur is that in some traditional, authoritarian societies, such as Iran, a strong pro-natalist policy associated with increased extraction wards off long-term declines in fertility. Policy analysis at this level may therefore unravel the reasons for such discrepancies.

Despite this drawback, however, one cannot lose sight of the enormous overall reductions in fertility rates reported here. Massive changes in populations within the stage of transitional growth are linked directly to governmental capacity to reach the population. Developing societies that improve their political reach can create the conditions for stable populations without concurrently improving individual productivity. Indeed, the massive reductions in fertility rate, as in the case of China, that preceded improvements in economic productivity, may have been caused by the strengthening of political structures in that society (Greenhalgh 1990). These results imply that the process of demographic change is not driven solely or even mainly by socio-economic improvements as originally anticipated. Rather, it is driven in large part by prior strengthening of political capacity.

The implications are far-reaching and recast population problems in a new perspective. If population explosions can be prevented by increases in

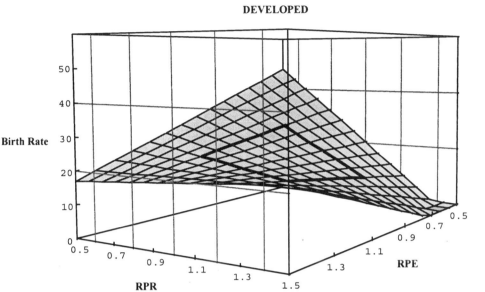

DEVELOPED

FIGURE 10.5 Impact of Political Capacity on Birth Rates during the Stage of Incipient Decline: Developed Countries

the capacity of governments to mobilize human resources to advance their goals, and substantial improvements in economic productivity are not a pre-condition to the attainment of stable populations, then the prospects for global development are far less bleak than has been predicted by exclusive analysis of socio-economic structures.

With regard to the stage of incipient decline, the results for developed societies must be viewed with some care. In Figure 10.5, the small core area represents 90% of the sample and is equivalent to the total range for developing societies, where variations in reach and extraction are far wider. Table 10.1 shows that improvements in economic productivity now are associated with steady declines in birth rates. The political results are complex and unexpected. Table 10.1 and the core area in Figure 10.5 show that births remain under 20 per thousand, and changes in fertility are limited even in developed nations that enhance political capacity above the norm. Extensions outside of this range, on the other hand, suggest massive changes in fertility.

When *RPE* drops to 0.5, high levels of governmental reach generate massive decreases in birth rates, while a concurrent drop in reach results in massive increases in fertility. These effects were originally attributed to unstable estimates extrapolated beyond the range where dense informa-

TABLE 10.2 Decomposed Effects of Political Capacity & Economic Productivity on Death Rates at Each Stage of the Demographic Transition: 1960-1985
(*For Details on Base Estimation see Appendix C*)

ADJUSTED DEATH RATES (ADR)

	Estimated Coefficient	Nonlinear Estimated Coefficients		
		RPE=0.5	RPE=1.0	RPE=1.5
DEPENDENT VARIABLE				
Stage of High Potential Growth				
LESS DEVELOPED	28.28	30.6	32.9	35.2
GDP LESS DEVELOPED	-.0091	-.0091	-.0091	-.0091
RPE LESS DEVELOPED	-2.09	-2.43	2.76	-3.09
RPR LESS DEVELOPED	4.65	.	.	.
INTER LESS DEVELOPED	-.67	.	.	.
Stage of Transitional Growth				
DEVELOPING	31.0	23.9	16.9	9.8
GDP DEVELOPING	-.00018	-.00018	-.00018	-.00018
RPE DEVELOPING	-3.01	-1.57	-.14	1.30
RPR DEVELOPING	-14.14	.	.	.
INTER DEVELOPING	2.87	.	.	.
Stage of Incipient Decline				
DEVELOPED	37.87	26.0	14.2	2.4
GDP DEVELOPED	-.00048	-.00048	-.00048	-.00048
RPE DEVELOPED	-20.27	-10.32	-.38	9.56
RPR DEVELOPED	-23.66	.	.	.
INTER DEVELOPED	19.89	.	.	.

N = 2217 OBSERVATIONS
R-SQUARE BETWEEN OBSERVED AND PREDICTED = 0.70 R-SQUARE ADJUSTED = 0.70
R-SQUARE ADJUSTED EXCLUDING POLITICAL CAPACITY (RPR,RPE AND INTER) = 0.65

tion on political performance was empirically registered. Following the collapse of the Soviet Union, however, there is room for informed speculation. These results suggest that governments that lose the ability to extract, but maintain a strong hold on the population, will face sharp fertility declines. Surprisingly, this is the pattern reported in Russia and East Germany after the collapse of their respective Communist regimes (*The Economist* 1994). Likewise, the anticipated increases in birth rates that should follow rapid declines in reach and extraction may represent the phenomenon of the "baby boom" that follows major wars, particularly in devastated societies that were on the losing side. It can be speculated that the loss of national political organization temporarily forces upon developed societies the fertility patterns characteristic of developing societies.

The main result obtained is, however, that improvements in the political performance of developed societies will have limited effects on further reducing the fertility rate in those societies.

The Politics of Mortality

The effects of political capacity on death rates are more consistent but much weaker than similar patterns for birth rates. Table 10.2 is similar to Table 10.1, but in this case when governmental reach is held constant and extraction allowed to vary, drastic declines in mortality will occur in the first stage only (See Appendix C). Further declines should respond to increased governmental organization and public expenditures.

Table 10.2 shows that mortality rates respond mainly to economic changes and are less affected by politics. Improvements in political capacity add 5% to the overall variance across the three stages of the demographic transition. The effects of politics on mortality rates within each stage are also less dramatic than the effects of politics on birth rates. Comparing similar coefficients in Tables 10.1 and 10.2 reveals that in the case of mortality, the relationships are consistent with the theory of the demographic transition, but are much attenuated. This may be partly because of the timing of changes. The largest declines in mortality should take place during the stage of incipient growth, while in the next two stages only minor adjustments should occur. The evaluation in Figure 10.6 shows that most societies have already undergone the early transformation from death rates in excess of 40 per thousand to 30 per thousand. During the stage of high potential growth, improvements in economic productivity and reach will further reduce the mortality rate to slightly over 20 per thousand. Consequently, political and socio-economic factors in both subsequent stages can only reduce mortality below an already low base.

A brief analysis of mortality changes within each stage will now be discussed. The results in Table 10.2 and Figure 10.6 show that among

LESS DEVELOPED

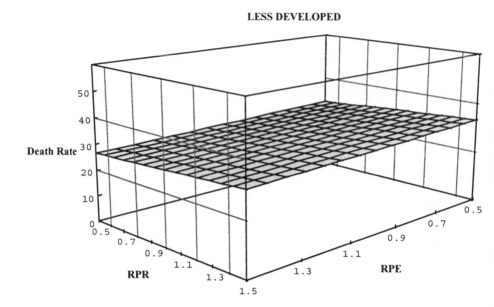

FIGURE 10.6 Impact of Political Capacity on Death Rates during the Stage of High Potential Growth: Less Developed Countries

less developed societies, increasing governmental reach substantially reduces mortality, while increasing extraction reduces mortality by only a small amount.

Unlike birth rates, reductions in death rates follow increases only in governmental extraction. Increases in *RPR* have an unintended effect. As postulated, the higher the political capacity, the larger the reduction in mortality. A comparison between Figure 10.4, which documents fertility rates above 40 per thousand, and Figure 10.6, which indicates average death rates of 30 per thousand, confirms the suspicion that this analysis explores only the very end of the stage of high potential decline. Very few societies in our data set endure mortality rates above 40 per thousand and have unstable populations because of high infant mortality and short life spans.

Now the stage of transitional growth will be described. The results in Table 10.2 again show that the political coefficients are consistent with expectations, but the aggregate effects on death rates remain relatively weak. Figure 10.7 reinforces these conclusions.

During the stage of transitional growth, increasing governmental reach and extraction has a consistent effect on death rates, which decline steadily from 30 to 20 per thousand. Interactions between governmental

215

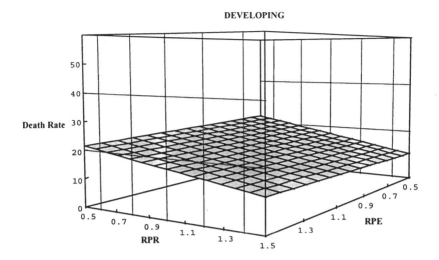

DEVELOPING

FIGURE 10.7 Impact of Political Capacity on Death Rates during the Stage of Transitional Growth: Developed Countries

extraction and reach accelerate this process slightly. In developing nations, governments that improve their political capacity will reduce mortality rates. Improvements in economic productivity will also steadily decrease mortality. As anticipated by the demographic transition model, life spans cannot be extended easily after relatively low mortality levels have been achieved during the latter part of the stage of high potential growth. Table 10.2 also shows the slight increases in mortality resulting from high levels of reach and extraction. This result suggests that the stress encountered in more competitive urban environments may marginally shorten life spans despite improvements in productivity.

Finally, we turn to the issue of mortality at the stage of incipient decline. Table 10.2 and Figure 10.8 illustrate the effects of politics on death rates in developed societies. As expected, changes in political structures have almost no effect on mortality rates within the 90% range of normal variation. Life spans achieved in most developed nations could initially decline, but they would eventually reach a natural plateau close to 10 per thousand. Interesting results occur in the area where the data are extended. Figure 10.8 suggests that if developed societies failed to maintain normal levels of both extraction and political reach, their death rates would double, but a loss of either extraction or reach would not

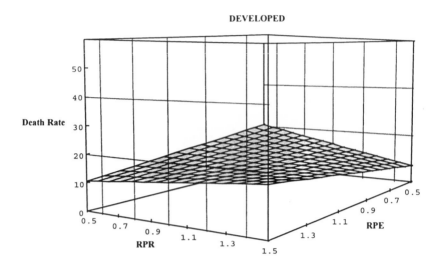

FIGURE 10.8 Impact of Political Capacity on Death Rates during the Stage of Incipient Decline: Developing Countries

affect mortality rates substantially. Faced with domestic instability or external war, developed societies could revert to the mortality patterns observed in developing nations. The patterns found in East Germany and Russia are consistent with these insights (*The Economist* 1994).

CONCLUSION

The main result of this analysis is that, in developing nations during transitional growth, government's capacity to reach their populations is the central factor that can induce dramatic declines in fertility. This result has several important implications. Stable populations can be attained in developing societies by improving political capacity without first achieving major gains in productivity. On the mortality side of the ledger, improvements in economic productivity explain most of the decline. Economic advancement creates the conditions for transitional growth and unstable populations; improvements in political capacity provide an environment conducive to the reestablishment of the lost stability.

These are sobering results. Most developing nations have already reduced their mortality rates and are undergoing population expansions.

By developing their political systems, these societies could reduce the population burden that inhibits their ability to improve their economic performance. Specifically, the elites of the society can substantially reduce fertility rates by increasing governmental reach and, to a lesser extent, by extracting additional resources from the society's pool. Consistent with previous work, this study has shown that economic growth is responsible for declines in mortality. But economic growth is not, as the common wisdom maintains, the main avenue towards reduced fertility. Rather, improvement in political capacity is chiefly responsible for massive changes in demographic patterns.

We have established the link between political capacity and population changes. This analysis implies that the debate about policy choices that dominates the literature in political demography may be misleading. If the results in this chapter are supported by further analysis, the fertility declines required to complete the demographic transition of developing societies are driven not by population policies, or by productivity gains, but are fundamentally determined by transformations in the political structures of those societies. Capable governments create the conditions for stable populations, and these in turn set the stage for further transformations in socio-economic structures.

This analysis also suggests that developing nations can stabilize their populations without first undergoing an economic growth spurt. Indeed, it appears that nations with politically capable governments can foster stable populations and thus create the primary precondition for economic growth and, eventually, economic convergence. The future of less developed and developing societies is therefore in the hands of their local elite.

It now may be concluded from the analysis that, if politics drives fundamental changes in population structures, these changes, in turn, set the preconditions for economic growth, equality, and modernity. The specter of quasi-permanent inequality between rich and poor has perhaps been overstated, and the economic convergence of the developed and developing world is in fact plausible. Political demography, then, is one key to the developmental process.

APPENDIX A: Table 10A.1 Relationship between Birth Rates, Political Capacity, & Economic Productivity at Each Stage of the Demographic Transition, 1960-1985*

OLS ESTIMATION USING HETEROSKEDASTICITY-CONSISTENT COVARIANCE MATRIX AND AUTOCORRELATION-CONSISTENT MATRIX WITH ORDER=1 BY NEWEY-WEST CORRECTION METHOD

ADJUSTED BIRTH RATES (ABR)

Variable Name	Estimated Coefficient	Standard Error	T-Ratio	P-Value
DEPENDENT VARIABLE				
LESS DEVELOPED	-49.73	12.87	-3.86	.001
DEVELOPING	-14.69	13.43	-1.09	.274
DEVELOPED (BASE)	112.96	12.04	9.38	.001
GDP LESS DEVELOPED	.0060	.0008	-6.96	.001
GDP DEVELOPING	.0017	.0001	8.94	.001
GDP DEVELOPED (BASE)	-.0015	.0001	-9.00	.001
RPE LESS DEVELOPED	51.99	12.28	4.23	.001
RPE DEVELOPING	33.31	13.10	2.54	.011
RPE DEVELOPED (BASE)	-61.22	11.22	-5.45	.001
RPR LESS DEVELOPED	73.62	12.13	6.06	.001
RPR DEVELOPING	17.17	13.29	1.29	.196
RPR DEVELOPED(BASE)	-85.56	11.57	-7.39	.001
INTER LESS DEVELOPED	-55.57	11.43	-4.86	.001
INTER DEVELOPING	-32.14	13.11	-2.45	.014
INTER DEVELOPED (BASE)	60.91	10.68	5.70	.001

N = 2185 OBSERVATIONS
DURBIN-WATSON = 0.15   RHO = 0.92
R-SQUARE BETWEEN OBSERVED AND PREDICTED = 0.72
R-SQUARE ADJUSTED = 0.72
RUNS TEST: 151 RUNS, 1127 POSITIVE, 1058 NEGATIVE

APPENDIX B: Table 10A.2 Relationship between Death Rates, Political Capacity, & Economic Productivity at Each Stage of the Demographic Transition 1960-1985*

OLS ESTIMATION USING HETEROSKEDASTICITY-CONSISTENT COVARIANCE MATRIX AND AUTOCORRELATION-CONSISTENT MATRIX WITH ORDER=1 BY NEWEY-WEST CORRECTION METHOD

ADJUSTED DEATH RATES (ADR)

Variable Name	Estimated Coefficient	Standard Error	T-Ratio	P-Value
DEPENDENT VARIABLE				
LESS DEVELOPED	-9.59	5.61	-1.71	.08
DEVELOPING	-6.87	6.03	-1.13	.25
DEVELOPED (BASE)	37.87	4.74	7.97	.001
GDP LESS DEVELOPED	-.0087	.00057	-15.20	.001
GDP DEVELOPING	.00031	.00009	3.34	.001
GDP DEVELOPED (BASE)	-.00048	.00007	-6.55	.001
RPE LESS DEVELOPED	18.18	5.56	3.26	.001
RPE DEVELOPING	17.26	6.22	2.77	.006
RPE DEVELOPED(BASE)	-20.27	4.68	-4.33	.001
RPR LESS DEVELOPED	28.31	5.07	5.57	.001
RPR DEVELOPING	9.53	6.09	1.56	.118
RPR DEVELOPED (BASE)	-23.66	4.47	-5.29	.001
INT LESS DEVELOPED	-20.56	5.14	-4.0	.001
INT DEVELOPING	-17.03	6.43	-2.64	.008
INTER DEVELOPED (BASE)	19.89	4.47	4.44	.001

N = 2217 OBSERVATIONS
DURBIN-WATSON = 0.1836   RHO = 0.90791
R-SQUARE BETWEEN OBSERVED AND PREDICTED = 0.70
R-SQUARE ADJUSTED = 0.70
RUNS TEST: 151 RUNS, 1004 POSITIVE, 1213 NEGATIVE
*Description of this procedure can be found in White H. (1980), and Newy, W and K. West,(1987).

APPENDIX C: COUNTRY SAMPLE (1960-1985)

Algeria, Angola, Argentina, Australia*, Austria*, Bangladesh, Belgium*, Bolivia, Brazil, Burma, Cameroon, Canada*, Central African Empire, Chad, Chile, Colombia, Costa Rica, Denmark*, Dominican Republic, Ecuador, Egypt, El Salvador, Ethiopia, Finland*, France, Germany, Ghana, Greece, Guatemala, Haiti, Honduras, Hong Kong, India, Indonesia, Iran, Iraq, Ireland*, Israel, Italy*, Jamaica, Japan*, Jordan, Kenya, Republic of Korea, Kuwait, Libya, Malaysia, Mexico, Morocco, Mozambique, Nepal, The Netherlands*, New Zealand*, Nicaragua, Niger, Nigeria, Norway*, Pakistan, Panama, Paraguay, Peru, Philippines, Portugal, Saudi Arabia, Senegal, Singapore, South Africa, Spain, Sri Lanka, Sudan, Sweden*, Switzerland, Syria, Tanzania, Thailand, Togo, Trinidad & Tobago, Tunisia, Turkey, Uganda, United Kingdom*, United States*, Uruguay, Venezuela, Zaire, Zambia, Zimbabwe.

* = OECD countries

NOTES

1. Data for the chart were obtained from the following sources: Gail P. Kelly. 1989. *International Handbook of Women's Education*. New York: Greenwood Press, 109-133. International Labour Office. *Economically active population: 1950-2025*. 1986. Geneva: International Labour Office, 25. Wolfgang Lutz. 1994. *Population Bulletin: The Future of World Population*. Population Reference Bureau, Inc. 49, (1): 11. Missing values for 1950-60 were obtained from Lewis Snider's data set.

2. The correlation between *GNP.CAP* and *RPE, RPR,* and *RPR*RPE* for all levels of development are: .27, -.10, .20. For less developed countries: .12, .30, and -.09. For developing countries: .31, .08, and .35. For developed nations: .14, .42, and .27.

11

Political Capacity and Violence[1]

J. Kugler, M. Benson, A. Hira, D. Panasevich

INTRODUCTION

Systematic analysis of international affairs suggests that international conflict is rare but crises can lead to severe confrontations. Among the small set of political disagreements that lead to crisis, only a few escalate into violent conflicts, and of these an even smaller fraction result in all-out war (Singer and Small 1972; Organski and Kugler 1980; Bueno de Mesquita and Lalman 1986; Houweling and Siccama 1988). Similar patterns characterize domestic competition. Of the very large number of political contests over domestic priorities, only a small fraction erupt into serious political disputes and an even smaller fraction produce violent domestic confrontations. Furthermore, within this small set of violent confrontations, the vast majority is resolved at very low levels of violence, while a minuscule minority escalates to severe violent conflict (Taylor and Jodice 1983).

This exploration of domestic instability is inspired partly by work in international politics, which shows that dynamic transitions rather than levels of national power hold the key to understanding the preconditions for war and peace in world politics (Organski and Kugler 1980; Kugler and Organski 1989; Houweling and Siccama 1988). A similar dynamic process may be at work in the domestic environment. To elucidate the relationship between domestic political violence and political structures, the levels and changes in the political extraction of both domestic elites and their opponents are explored. Therefore, the focus will be on political interactions between the government and its challengers. The levels and changes in the relative political extraction of a government should indicate whether the government is effective, but it cannot take into account whether the political opposition is able to mobilize political resources to take advantage of this opportunity to advance its own competitive policy options. For this reason, the concern of this study is with the relative control of political resources by the government and its political opposition. In this interactive context, policies advanced by the government are threatened with domestic political violence when the opposition is able to match closely the political resources at the disposal of the ruling elite, and the opposition concurrently rejects the existing status quo. Transitions in power at the domestic level are, therefore, a prelude to political violence and dissent.

In short, violent power transitions may be analyzed at the domestic as well as the international level. When the government's political capacity declines and the opposition gains strength at the expense of the government, or from a previously untapped resource, then opponents may be willing to risk conflict because they hope to replace the existing government. As at the international level (Organski and Kugler 1980; Gilpin 1981; Lemke and Kugler 1996), such conditions should bring forth the threat of violent conflict for dominance within the system.

RELATIONSHIP BETWEEN POLITICAL STRUCTURES AND DOMESTIC POLITICAL VIOLENCE

It is proposed that domestic political violence has explicit political underpinnings, which can be traced back to the structural characteristics of governments. These structural characteristics take into account the political capacity of government to extract resources from the society and to allocate such resources to the goals defined by the ruling elite (Organski and Kugler 1980). From this perspective, violence is a byproduct of the incapacity of governments to impose or gain acceptance of their goals. Political opponents choose violence as a viable means of political reform when the government is weak and support for options advanced by the government is weakening. Thus, in societies where political support shifts away from the policies advanced by the government toward those proposed by the opposition, policy issues remain unresolved and political contestants emerge that aim to replace the government. For this reason, the level of change in the political capacity of government and the government's relative strength against the opposition are signals that anticipate domestic political violence.

A weak government faced with serious political disputes is seldom able to act decisively. This inability to resolve policy disputes leads to a further decline in extractive capacity and to increasingly serious political contests that are eventually resolved by violent means. On the other hand, a government with high and rising levels of political extraction can defuse opposition by imposing policy reforms or, in the absence of a common solution, can crush the opposition. Therefore, strong governments avoid or minimize domestic political violence because they persuade or coerce their opposition to accept government policies. Weak governments procrastinate and allow disputes to fester, thereby allowing their opponents to grow in strength and create the conditions for domestic instability to arise. Political violence emerges when the government is unable to impose or advance its goals in the face of an equally powerful organized opposition.

The link between domestic instability and political extraction is not a direct one. Violence does not follow simply because governments are inept, nor can it be totally avoided by governments which are capable. Domestic political violence results from a complex relationship between the strength of a government vis-à-vis the opposition and the increase or decrease in relative capacity among these parties. For this reason, the strength of the government alone is insufficient to insure domestic stability. Indeed, weak governments may survive for protracted periods when a viable opposition has not materialized, whereas relatively strong governments may face violent opposition if the opposition is organized and rejects attempts by the government to govern.[2]

We are not concerned here with the type of political regime that emerges as a stable successor. Political violence is not seen as the result of competition among authoritarian, totalitarian, and democratic regimes. Rather, it is conceptualized as a competition among weak governments with strong oppositions which may be challenged by a host of potential successors. Seen from this vantage point, a weak authoritarian regime may be replaced by a democratic system—e.g., Argentina after the Falklands War or Peru after the reformist military regime. A weak democratic system may fall to a military challenge—Brazil after Goulart or Chile after Allende. A weak authoritarian government such as in Turkmenistan and Uzbekistan is replaced by a strong authoritarian government, whereas the incapable Soviet government of Latvia gave in to a democratic government.

Indeed, such changes in Eastern Europe and Latin America are not a move from centralized, noncompetitive regimes to open, competitive regimes, but rather a move from politically ineffective regimes to those that are more effective. We agree with Huntington's insight (1968, 1) on political development that "[t]he most important political distinction among countries concerns not their form of government but their degree of government."

Consider now the general structure that describes the relationship of domestic political violence to the distribution of capabilities between the government and the opposition. Figure 11.1 shows the dynamic process that underlies changes from accommodation to violence. The area at the lower left (2, 25, 1) indicates the conditions for domestic stability. Where political extraction is already high, the government increases its political control over the available resource pool and the weak political competitors avoid open policy confrontations and resolve political disputes through bargaining. For this reason, domestic political violence is seldom the vehicle of choice in societies such as the United States, the United Kingdom, or Japan, where political structures are institutionalized and supported by the consent of the masses. Violence is also rare, as in the Soviet Union from 1960 through 1989 and in China after the 1960s, where repression was pervasive and ruthlessly imposed.

The area at the lower right side of the graph (-2, 25, 3) defines the first preconditions for potential violence. The government's political resources are declining, indicating that the government is weakening. Under circumstances like those of South Africa prior to Mandela, political opponents openly challenge the policy preferences of the governing elite while the government thwarts their efforts. Political violence should rise if these challenges are not resolved by bargaining, and the relative political extraction of the government continues to fall.

Organized violence should rise sharply when the opposition is gaining ground on an already increasingly ineffective government (at the upper right of the graph, coordinates [-2, 75, 5]). A case in point is the regime of the Shah of Iran. In this example, the government lost its grip on political resources during the last years prior to the Islamic revolution despite an absolute rise in basic resources caused by the strong price of oil exports (Kugler and Arbetman 1989). Hence, a rapid decline in political extraction combined with an already low performance sets the conditions for serious revolutions.

The preconditions for a return to stability are shown at the upper left of the graph at coordinates (2, 75, 2). Governments whose political extraction is low now manage to increase political extraction at the expense of the opposition. As the political pendulum swings toward the government, bargaining should replace violent confrontation as a means of resolving disputes. In Iran, the successor government of the Ayatollah Khomeini arrested the precipitous political decline of the Shah's regime and re-established a modicum of political control. Despite economic losses, the political extraction lost during the revolution was recovered and even exceeded. A similar phenomenon is found in the major wars of the twentieth century, suggesting that patterns of domestic conflict may be similar to those found in international confrontations (Kugler and Domke 1986; Kugler and Arbetman 1989).

In sum, Figure 11.1 suggests that the relationship between domestic political violence and political extraction undergoes a specific sequence of

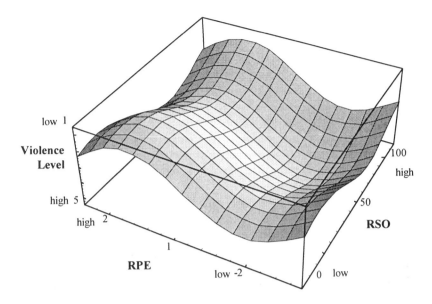

FIGURE 11.1 Domestic Political Violence Given Changes in Political Stability and Relative Strength of the Opposition Over Time.

phases. The inception of domestic political violence starts as one moves in a clockwise direction from region (2, 25, 1) to (-2, 25, 3) because the decline in political extraction of a government encourages political opponents to resolve disputes by violent means. If the government continues to decline, there is movement from (-2, 25, 3) to (-2, 75, 5). Then domestic violence enters a second phase wherein it is both severe and frequent. Under these conditions, true revolutions that change the type of regime are waged. Violent competition forces a further decline. Eventually, violence stops when governments in beleaguered societies reverse their political decline and move back to coordinates (2, 25, 1). Stability is re-established when bargaining replaces violent confrontation to resolve policy disputes as weak governments are replaced, or as governments become stronger and the strength of their political opposition declines. Paradoxically, therefore, the political conditions that generate conflict set the stage for weak political systems to become stronger.

CONCEPTS AND MEASUREMENT

The Political Extraction of Governments

Political extraction is the government's ability to extract human and material resources from the available pool to implement the policy chosen by the political elite and respond to pressures of the international and domestic environment. It has been operationalized in the manner stated in Chapter 1.

Political Strength of the Opposition

The political strength of the opposition gauges the competitive environment in each country. The political effort that opponents make cannot be measured directly because consistent public records of resources gathered by the opposition do not exist. Instead, expert judgments are used to measure the approximate relationship between government extraction and the strength of the main opposition by setting the government's extraction at one hundred and then evaluating the relative strength of the opposition against that of the government. When the relative strength of the opposition approaches one hundred, both sides are evenly matched. When it falls below that number, the opposition is politically weak in relation to the government. Instances of the political extraction of the government falling below that of the political opposition are not expected short of foreign intervention, and in such a case the government should have fallen. None of these cases were found in our sample.

This one-sided indicator of political opposition reflects research on war, and suggests that domestic political violence emerges when competitors control equivalent amounts of the national resources. Consequently, in a domestic political competition when power parity is approached, one expects that each side will anticipate marginal gains from a political confrontation. Violent disputes over policy should materialize when they are not resolved by a mutually accepted bargaining process.

Several Latin American and Eastern European experts were asked to assess the political resources available to the government and its opponents in Latin American countries from 1950 through 1993 and former Eastern Bloc countries from 1985 through 1993. To avoid the possibility of contaminating estimates by an indirect connection between political extraction and instability, these judges were not told that their evaluations would be used to anticipate violence. The accuracy of these judgments was assessed by contrasting the evaluations provided by the experts with detailed reports for specific Latin American and former Eastern Bloc nations. The match for a number of cases surveyed was over 95% (Kugler 1977).

In Latin America the reported political opposition was usually very weak relative to the government. This may perhaps be a general phenomenon. In most nations the government extracts most of the resources available to all political groups and uses those resources to implement policy choices without violent conflict. In rare cases the opposition and the government have access to equivalent resources, and when these rare conditions are met, violent conflict may emerge. This is consistent with the empirical observation that domestic competitions seldom escalate to violent confrontations, and only a small fraction of these rare conflicts escalates to high levels (Taylor and Jodice 1983).

Political Violence

Measures of domestic political violence attempt to take into account the level of open dissension over policy choices. Frequently used measures of political instability based on event data were explored but proved inadequate for this purpose because existing collections did not provide consistent data from 1950 through 1993, many observations were unavailable, and, most importantly, existing event data files do not adequately reflect the severity of violent domestic events of critical interest to this study.[3]

Domestic political violence is a very visible expression of domestic competition among political factions. These events are reported fairly accurately in standard event collections. To produce a standard series for the present study, chronologies were constructed for each event reflecting levels of political violence and mass opposition. From these chronologies the incidence and severity of events were coded. To maintain continuity, all reported incidents of political confrontations for the years 1950—1993 were taken from *Keesing's Contemporary Archives, Current History,* and RFE/RL daily reports and were coded. A single event, such as a strike, was counted as an incident regardless of its duration. Then each event was associated with political violence, if any, to create the following five-point scale:

1) **None:** Absence of reported opposition activities.
2) **Low:** Sporadic opposition actions with little or no violence. Attempted invasion or coup.
3) **Moderate:** Sustained opposition activities with two or more related incidents resulting in injuries and/or deaths perpetrated by organized groups such as unions or guerrilla organizations. Nonviolent coups and invasions.
4) **Severe:** High level of sustained opposition activity with violence by organized groups involving at least 0.01 percent of the urban population. Violent changes of government.
5) **Very Severe:** Virtual or actual civil war. High level of sustained opposition activity with violence by organized groups involving more than 0.01 percent of the urban population. United, organized opposition activity aimed at changing the government.[4]

As in the case of major international wars, rare but extremely serious events will substantially affect the results of this analysis. Yet, there is even less agreement on what constitutes a serious domestic conflict than on what constitutes a major war. For example, the Sandinista revolution changed the political environment in Nicaragua with much bloodshed, yet the Ayatollah Khomeini and Ms. Aquino led movements that equally transformed their respective domestic regimes with little initial violence. Moreover, domestic political violence continued once the Sandinista regime gained power, and Iran's peaceful revolution became violent during the process of consolidation, but the Philippine revolution remained relatively free of violent activity. To avoid bias, all coding was done prior to the analysis and such judgments were not revised.[5]

Relation Between Political Extraction and Domestic Political Violence

A short review of the anticipated relation between domestic political violence and various elements of political extraction is useful before the results are presented. Recall that the level of political extraction is expected to be negatively related to domestic political violence because a government that achieves high levels of relative extraction will be difficult to challenge. When a government's political extraction declines, the level of violence in a society will increase, particularly if the opposition gains ground by absorbing some of the resources lost by the government. An accelerated transfer of political resources is expected to be positively related to political violence because fast change is frequently associated with the decline rather than the rebuilding of new coalitions. Finally, as the opposition approaches parity with the government, political bargaining will be replaced by violent competition when serious political disputes emerge.

Several cuts are presented below to assess the validity of these inferences. The model was estimated using both an OLS and an ordered Probit estimation technique. The empirical findings for the two techniques were very similar. For reasons of interpretation, however, OLS was used as the primary estimation technique for this chapter. The first evaluation of domestic political violence provides a general overview (see linear model in Table 11.1).

The model accounts for slightly more than one quarter of the variation in the domestic political violence observed across Latin American and former Eastern Bloc countries.[6] The variables in the equation are significant and have signs consistent with the theory presented. When the government's political performance is low and the government is losing strength, politically motivated violence is high. When the opposition's

TABLE 11.1 Relation of Domestic Violence to Political Extraction, 1950-1993

Variables	Linear Model		
	Coefficient	Std. Error	T-value
VIOLENCE			
TIME	0.22	0.002	7.49**
RPE	-0.42	0.104	-3.99**
C. RPE	-0.59	0.234	-2.52*
RSO	0.024	0.002	13.35**
CONSTANT	0.73	0.172	4.25**
R^2	0.27		
Number of Observ.	753		
Prob F	0.0000		

* Significant at 10 percent level.
** Significant at 1 percent level.

political extraction is high relative to that of the government, political violence rises. The time trend is also an important determinant associated with the increase in violence. In part, this may be caused by an overall improvement in communication and information technologies that allow more accurate reports from around the world.
where:
VIOLENCE = yearly level of internal violence.
TIME = each year under analysis.
RPE = relative political extraction of the government at a given year.
C.RPE = the change in the relative political extraction of the government per year.
RSO = relative political strength of the opposition at a given year.

Regional Differences

To ensure that our model is generalizable across the world, we have controlled for regional differences. Recall that the observations used in this study are pooled from different countries and even different continents. Empirical assessments based on this type of data are vulnerable to various combinations of misspecification, since it is a pool of countries from two entirely different regions that experience dissimilar trends in their economic and political developments. (Violation of the classical assumption of homoskedastic variance is also a common problem with

TABLE 11.2   Relation of Domestic Violence to RPE Structures, Controlling for Regional
Differences in the Intercept, 1950-1993

Variables	Coefficient	Std. Error	T-value
VIOLENCE			
TIME	0.015	0.003	5.00**
RPE	-0.376	0.103	-3.65**
C. RPE	-0.551	0.232	-2.37*
RSO	0.027	0.001	27.00**
REG	-0.67	0.150	4.30**
CONSTANT	0.741	0.169	4.38**
R^2	0.285		
Number of Observ.	753		
Prob F	0.0000		

* Significant at 10 percent level.
** Significant at 1 percent level.

this type of data.)

Tests were performed for differences in the intercepts and slopes between Latin America and Eastern Europe to see whether regional factors make a difference in explaining domestic political violence.[7] The logic of these tests follows a typical panel data assessment that tests whether the intercepts and/or slopes differ across the countries belonging to different regions. For purposes of hypothesis testing, a dummy variable for the region (REG) is included. The variable takes on the value of '0' if a country is in Latin America and '1' if the observation comes from Eastern Europe. Also, a set of interactive elements between REG and four major variables from the list of proxies was generated. Table 11.2 presents the results of estimation with the control for region-specific intercept.

The F-test employed to test for their joined significance was insignificant at the 5% level, indicating that there is insufficient evidence to reject the null hypothesis that the marginal effects produced by the independent variables differ in Latin America and Eastern Europe. Therefore, despite differences in history, culture, and autonomous levels of domestic violence country to country, the theory linking domestic political violence to the extraction of the government and the opposition shows generally positive results.

TABLE 11.3 Relation of Domestic Violence to RPE Structures when Opponents are Close to Political Parity with the Government, 1950-1993

Variables	Coefficient	Std. Error	T-value
VIOLENCE			
TIME	0.03	0.011	3.02**
RPE	-10.37	2.390	-4.31**
C. RPE	-1.86	0.692	-2.69*
*RSO*RPE*	0.11	0.028	3.75**
CONSTANT	-4.06	0.520	7.81**
R^2	0.401		
Number of Observ.	60		
Prob F	0.0000		

* Significant at 10 percent level.
** Significant at 1 percent level.

Parity and Power

We have also explored the specific structural conditions that lead to the most pronounced conflicts in the domestic arena. Research on international conflict suggests that serious wars are waged when both parties approach power parity and both view the potential outcome of such confrontations favorably (Organski and Kugler 1980; Houweling and Siccama 1988). Recall from Figure 11.1 that applying the same logic to domestic instability, one expects that when domestic competitors have a realistic chance to succeed, they turn to violence in order to resolve serious political disputes. For this reason, severe domestic political violence should emerge when the political extraction of the government and of the opposition are approximately equal. To test this proposition, the next analysis incorporates only the subset of cases wherein the political resources held by domestic opponents is at least 75 percent of those held by the government (Table 11.3).[8] Under such conditions, the political opposition should have a reasonable expectation of success in direct confrontation with the government, and organized violence may be expected to follow if the two parties cannot reconcile their conflicts by bargaining. Moreover, because of the relative parity in political capability, sporadic violence prompted by a weak or disorganized opposition is unlikely. Furthermore, the interactive term of RSO*RPE is added to the analysis. By incorporating such a term, the simultaneous variation of both the strength of the government and of the opposition may be studied. The results obtained for this subset are encouraging.

The connection between political structures and violent domestic activity is strong and congruent with the theoretical expectations advanced at the outset. When the political opposition has a chance to succeed, the explanatory power of this model rises by more than 10% of the variance despite a much smaller number of cases. This suggests that when the government and the opposition are at conditions of parity, the crucial factor is how they vary together rather than how they vary independently.

This result adds further support to the power parity model applied at the domestic level in that, at conditions of parity, the power of the state and the opposition are only relevant in relation to their interaction with each other. The marginal effects produced by the independent variables are also consistent with the theory advocated. The magnitude increases enormously for *RPE*, doubles for its change, and increases five times for *RSO*. Therefore, the model discriminates more effectively among the cases of highest severity. The dynamics of domestic political conflict start to emerge: The likely victims of severe political challenges are politically inept governments that allow their political extraction to decay and concurrently face a competitive political opponent. Analysis of residuals shows there is some overprediction of levels of political violence. Instances of severe violence are effectively accounted for and this accounting extends for the first time as well to instances of lower severity, but the classification of intermediate levels of political violence is inadequate.

With such a small sample, it is difficult to generalize the effects of political extraction on political violence. However, the results are consistent with theoretical expectations, and the explanatory power of the model improves greatly despite depletion in the sample size. These tentative results warrant further, more extended and careful investigation.

CONCLUSIONS AND IMPLICATIONS

The study of the political extraction of government and its political opponents provides a means of accounting for the development of serious domestic violence to resolve political disputes. Domestic political violence reaches severe levels when the political extraction of the government is low, when the opposition approaches political parity, and, to a lesser degree, when the government loses its strength.

The dynamics of domestic conflict correspond closely to those observed in international confrontations. As in international competition, political groups resort to serious violence to resolve policy issues when the government and its political opposition approach a transition and each side can expect marginal gains from the use of violence to resolve domestic disputes. Political bargaining is the rule when the government dominates the political arena, and violent competition is therefore not feasible. Indeed, only one instance of severe domestic political violence is lost when the sample is reduced to cases where the opposition achieves political parity with the government, despite a dramatic reduction in the number of observations. Moreover, under political parity the model accounts strongly and accurately for all levels of political disputes. Extensions of the current model promise that political extraction could be used in conjunction with socio-economic factors to create a reliable early warning indicator of political violence.

NOTES

1. Thank you to Professor Mark Lichback for making us aware of important data issues within the domestic conflict literature.

2. This insight is suggested by the empirical analysis of war that shows that when major competitors or regimes acquire equivalent capabilities, the anticipation of marginal gains leads to major war (Organski and Kugler 1980; Kugler and Zagare 1987; Kugler and Organski 1989; Bueno de Mesquita and Lalman 1986; Bueno de Mesquita et al. 1985).

3. Event data available for the period under analysis provide counts of the incidence of protests, riots, strikes, and political demonstrations. No corresponding indication of violence resulting from such events is consistently coded because the two potential indicators of the severity of violent activity—political assassinations and deaths due to political activity—are not systematically related to protests, strikes or demonstrations. A domestic scale of political violence can be created only by arbitrary links between recorded incidents and aggregate severity. Experiments with weighting procedures adopted in previous research produced seemingly useful cross-sectional evaluations that proved to be unstable over time. Moreover, the lack of consistent temporal coverage vitiated any possibility of independently verifying the validity of such constructs (Taylor and Jodice 1983; Taylor 1985. For a discussion of index aggregation, see Jackman and Boyd 1979; Hazlewood 1973; Hibbs 1973).

4. Incidents of political violence were coded first by Andy Hira and Dmitry Panasevich from detailed chronologies constructed from *Keesing's Contemporary Archives*, 1950-1993, *Current History*, 1950- 1993 (vol. 18-84), and *RFE/RL Daily News Report*, 1990-1993. For each country a detailed summary description of events and its code is available. Judgments on the accuracy of the political capacity of the opposition were based on the aforementioned chronologies.

5. See note 3.

6. An interactive model was also estimated with the term *RPExRSO* added to represent more accurately the importance of the interplay between the strength of the government (*RPE*) and the strength of the opposition (*RSO*) rather than just looking at how these two terms vary separately. All of the coefficients had the predicted signs and were statistically significant. However, the addition of the new,

highly significant interactive term increased the variance marginally, indicating the lack of nonlinear components.

7. The idea of controlling for each cross-sectional unit was discarded because some of the countries have too few observations to contribute to the dataset.

8. In international politics, 80% is a typical cut-off point. However, the number of observations in the dataset requires that the boundary be lower.

12

Political Capacity, Growth, and Distributive Commitments

Lewis W. Snider

INTRODUCTION[1]

The question this chapter addresses is whether government capacity is strongly associated with policy effectiveness and the flexibility of governments to act. The more options available to a state, the more it should be able to manage the economy and promote sustained economic growth even in times of crisis or rapid change.

Regarding government capacity, much of the literature on the politics of external debt service and economic adjustment in the developing world has sought to catalog the political forces that explain "successful" adjustment (Nelson et al. 1989; Kaufman and Stallings 1989; Nelson 1990; and Haggard and Kaufman 1992). Implicit in many of these writings is the idea that policy insularity is more widespread in advanced industrial societies than in the developing world. In fact, quite the opposite is true. As economies develop and become more complex, the number of mobilized pressure groups in society with whom any government must negotiate in implementing policy also expands. Consequently, the proliferation of the distributive commitments governments make to an expanding number of constituencies undermines their ability to act flexibly in times of crisis.

GOVERNMENT CAPACITY AND DECISION AUTONOMY: EMPIRICAL ANALYSIS

The extractive capability of a government may be the foundation of its political capacity. However, this capacity is either constrained or enhanced by the degree to which a government enjoys decision autonomy in the presence of pressures from private interests, rent-seeking coalitions, and previous distributive commitments, and does not assume more tasks for itself than it can effectively carry out. When government capacity is "adjusted" or "weighted" for these constraints, it more accurately reflects the government's ability to promote sustained economic growth.

DEVELOPING VERSUS INDUSTRIALIZED GOVERNMENTS

The tasks and challenges confronting the governments of industrializing societies are different from those facing the governments of the OECD states. This is to be expected, since the policy instruments available to governments in developed industrial societies are much different from those available to governments in developing countries. For governments in many developing countries, alternative sources of fiscal revenue are limited by inefficient tax systems, weak or non-existent government bond markets, and limited access (if any) to foreign capital markets. Therefore, such countries would be expected to finance their fiscal deficits—and their growth—in large part by seigniorage (see Chapter 4).

If government capacity is truly a dynamic phenomenon, it is reasonable to expect that the political capacities of developing and OECD countries may affect their economic growths differently. Governments in developing societies do not have the same problems that governments in developed societies have in raising *new* resources to meet national objectives. Advanced industrial societies achieve absolute levels of extraction that are much higher than those of developing countries, but the marginal costs of achieving *additional* increases in extraction become progressively greater once such high levels have been realized (Organski et al. 1984). Therefore, although governments in advanced industrial countries have mobilized a larger share of society's resources, the government's political flexibility to further increase extraction at the margin is reduced relative to what is still available for mobilization (Kugler and Domke 1986, 52). The results of prior empirical research strongly indicate that the growth of extractive capabilities realized by the economically less developed nations is generally higher than that attained by the richer, more economically advanced countries, even though the latter extract a higher absolute share of *GDP* (Organski et al. 1984, 76-78). The least complex economies often show the greatest proportional growth in extraction and in relative political capacity. [2]

GOVERNMENT CAPACITY AND ECONOMIC GROWTH

If the difficulty governments have in raising new resources varies according to their level of development, the effect of political capacity on economic growth also varies (see Chapter 6). The diminishing marginal growth of extractive capabilities and political capacity observed as a country becomes more developed and more structurally complex illustrates the limits to which governments can continue to extract additional increments of society's wealth and so imposes a ceiling on the extent to which additional extraction can contribute positively to economic growth. One of these limits is the political price that must be paid to impose additional taxation as countries become developed. Political costs of extracting resources vary at the margins, not only across the development process, but across economic structure as well (Organski et al. 1984, 78). The crucial political costs are those that government leaders must pay to win over powerful elites and interest groups who, supported by constituencies in the mass population, resist contributing to state revenues and thus make the extraction of such resources more difficult (Organski et al. 1984, 49-50).

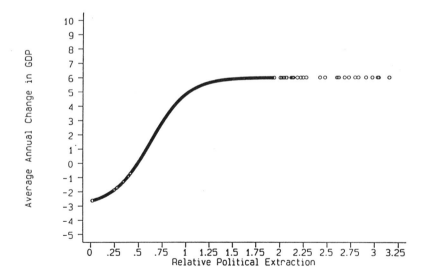

FIGURE 12.1 Expected Relationship between *RPE** and Growth

The hypothesized relationship between relative political capacity and economic growth is summarized in Figure 12.1 and is empirically validated in Snider (1996, Chapters 1, 6).

Countries that are still in the beginning phases of developing an industrial infrastructure have not yet fully established the institutional machinery needed to preserve national security (external defense and internal order), marshal resources to meet collective needs, and mobilize the population in support of national objectives. Consequently, the state's ability to penetrate and centrally coordinate the activities of civil society through its own infrastructure is limited. Empirically, this suggests that for the less developed countries, the *level* of political capacity may not affect economic growth strongly, but *the rate of increase* in political capacity is decisive.

Ease of collection is another reason many developing countries depend heavily on trade taxes as a percentage of total revenue. Many of them have yet to accumulate, centralize, and concentrate the resources necessary for effective control of the territory under their nominal jurisdiction. Indeed, the very act of expanding the state's authority and extractive capabilities is often associated with increased frequencies of collective violence, as agents of the state are pitted against various local and regional adversaries (Cohen, Brown, and Organski 1981, 901-910; Tilly 1975, 632-633; and Migdal 1988, 23-24).

Extractive capabilities continue to grow rapidly as states become semi-industrialized. Such states have largely succeeded in penetrating and coordinating the activities of society through their own civil and military infrastructures. Nevertheless, as increasingly larger segments of the population become enmeshed in the economic and military apparatus of the state, as productivity increases, and as the available pool of resources grows through expanded industrialization, one pattern remains: More taxes are needed to pay for expanding government services. However, the expansion of social tasks for which the government assumes direct responsibility is growing more slowly than its capacity to extract new resources from an expanding economy. It is at this point where the growth in political capacity should once again show a strong positive effect on economic growth.

As a state becomes fully industrialized, the growth in extractive capability and political capacity slows down. Economically, the marginal costs of welfare, health care, old-age benefits, education, and the support of mass armies level off. Political institutions have become well-established. Consequently, the political power of the state may recede into the background of economic activity. Empirically this means that variables representing state capacity should account for a smaller share of the variance in economic growth than variables representing different policy instruments for directing the economy. The growth in extraction cannot reach the point where it absorbs the resources needed to sustain the economic productivity and well-being of society that enable it to increase production. Any further increases in extractive capacity would dampen growth, not accelerate it. When the state becomes fully industrialized, it becomes more all-embracing, expanding its operations to cover more and more of the activities of civil society. This is where the political costs of increasing extraction at the margin begin to take off. As the state increases its social control and as increasingly larger segments of the mass population become caught up in the economic and military machinery of the state, the government must address a growing multiplicity of organized group interests, which have to be placated. Therefore, even though industrial states extract a larger absolute share of society's product, they experience the lowest average rate of growth in extractive capabilities and *RPE**. This also explains why the relationship between political capacity and economic growth might be weaker for the OECD countries as a group than for the developing countries.

Table 12.1 supports this general assessment and shows the means and standard deviations for the dependent variable's annual average economic growth; tax revenues as a percentage of *GDP*, a raw indicator of extraction; the raw political extraction variables; and those variables weighted for insularity against pressures from rent-seeking coalitions—across the levels of economic development just described. These summary data provide prima facie evidence that the effect of political capacity on growth does vary in a nonlinear manner with level of economic development. The average rate of growth of the advanced developing countries is noticeably higher than that of the less developed countries, even though their average political capacities are about the same.

A comparison of the means of tax revenues as a percentage of *GDP* clearly indicates that the advanced industrialized economies are extracting twice as much of their national resource base (28.4% of *GDP*) as are the least developed countries (about 14.6% of *GDP*). The higher the level of economic development, the higher is the average level of tax revenues collected. Yet, with the exception of the advanced developing countries, the mean *RPE** value is close to one. However, the average rate of growth for the least developed countries is noticeably (more than 2%) lower than that of the advanced developing economies.

The summary statistics for *RPE** and raw extraction also provide prima facie support for the propositions advanced by Callaghy (1989, 117) and Rueschemeyer and Evans (1985, 71). That is, the more social relations approach contractual market exchange conditions and bureaucratic organization, the higher is the probability of effective state intervention. It is the increasing penetration of civil society by market exchange and bureaucratic organization that helps to explain the greatly increased

Table 12.1 Summary of Differentials in Economic Growth, Extractive Capability, and Political Capacity across Levels of Economic Development

Variable	Number of Observations	Mean	Standard Deviation
LESS DEVELOPED COUNTRIES			
AVERAGE GROWTH	225	3.059	5.404
TAX REV % GDP	193	14.623	6.069
*RPE**	240	1.013	.3523
*WRPE**	181	.9123	.5568
*% Δ RPE**	230	.0123	.2993
*% Δ WRPE**	169	.1146	1.079
INFLATION	212	37.676	149.952
DEVELOPING COUNTRIES			
AVERAGE GROWTH	574	5.431	8.611
TAX REV % GDP	597	16.476	5.652
*RPE**	597	1.030	.3388
*WRPE**	537	.9406	.3521
*% Δ RPE**	573	.0275	.4995
*% Δ WRPE**	509	.0162	.2195
INFLATION	570	98.836	639.865

Variable	Number of Observations	Mean	Standard Deviation
ADVANCED DEVELOPING COUNTRIES			
AVERAGE GROWTH	134	6.593	4.263
TAX REV % GDP	137	23.826	9.656
*RPE**	144	1.342	.5533
*WRPE**	143	1.221	.3566
*% Δ RPE**	138	.0100	.1267
*% Δ WRPE**	127	.0154	.1782
INFLATION	138	21.172	45.160
ADVANCED INDUSTRIALIZED COUNTRIES			
AVERAGE GROWTH	420	3.514	3.410
TAX REV % GDP	420	28.765	8.653
*RPE**	420	1.006	.3033
*WRPE**	408	.9537	.2682
*% Δ RPE**	420	.0148	.1332
*% Δ WRPE**	406	.0098	.1294
INFLATION	420	7.685	4.542

Note: *RPE** has been calculated using a different equation than *RPE*.

transformative capacity of the modern state over that of largely agrarian societies. Therefore, indicators of direct state intervention in the economy should be more likely to promote growth in the advanced industrial economies than in the developing economies, where market exchange and bureaucratic organization have not become as well-established. What is unexpected is that the annual average growth rate for the unconstrained *RPE** variable is greatest for the middle income developing countries, not the least developed countries.

The advanced developing countries are distinguished by the highest average *RPE** scores[3] and the highest average rates of economic growth of any group in the sample. Their average raw extraction is substantially higher than that of other developing countries, but not nearly as high as that of the advanced industrialized economies. More important is that the annual average growth rate of the constrained *RPE** variable is higher than the annual average growth rate of the unconstrained *RPE** variables. The fact that the former is growing faster than the latter is an indication that as a group, these countries are not seriously constrained by rent-seeking coalitions. Nor is their flexibility reduced because their governments assumed direct responsibility for more tasks than they could effectively manage since this group includes Korea, Singapore, and Taiwan, the noticeable difference of these means from those of other groups suggests that the achievement of high rates of growth, economic liberalization, or export-oriented development requires a strong, capable state (see Appendix A).

Apart from comparisons of differentials in political and extractive capacities across levels of economic growth, the average rate of inflation varies substantially across levels of development. These summary statistics illuminate two important characteristics concerning the relationship between rate of inflation and level of development. First, the ability of the state to control inflation depends not only upon its political capacity, but also upon the degree to which market exchange and bureaucratic organization dominate social relations. Second, the rate of inflation that is *politically* tolerable varies with the level of economic development.

POLITICAL EXTRACTION VS. POLICY INSTRUMENTS: SPECIFICATION OF A BASELINE MODEL

The curve in Figure 12.1 suggests that relative political capacity may account for a significant share of the variation in economic growth within the range of -10 to +20%. Beyond that range, increases in *RPE** or the rate of growth in *RPE** would not be expected to have any explanatory value when other factors are taken into account. To unearth this relationship, economic controls must be added. For example, as an economy becomes more industrialized and complex, and as political institutions become better established, most governments have a wider array of policy instruments available to them with which to manage the economy and pursue other national objectives. Therefore, there should be a declining need to rely on the direct effects of state power as the government becomes more adept at using other instruments of economic management.

The objective of this chapter is not to explain economic growth, but to demonstrate how political constraints on state capacity affect a government's political performance with respect to critical economic outcomes, one of which is growth. Nevertheless, a baseline model of the relationship between certain economic factors and growth is essential to understand the effect of political capacity—constrained and unconstrained—on growth.

Four variables are used to represent various policy instruments. One, seigniorage, has already been mentioned. Developing countries may use seigniorage, but the result is likely to be pedal-to-the-metal inflation. Because seigniorage amounts to the net return on the extra assets that a country acquires from external holdings of its currency, it is an instrument that favors countries whose currencies are held by foreigners for trading or reserve purposes. These are generally the more industrialized countries. Seigniorage is also a relatively inexpensive source of government revenue if there is widespread tax evasion or if the costs of tax collection are high. Consequently, countries with more polarized or unstable political systems and thus more inefficient tax structures will have more incentive to rely on seigniorage as a source of revenue (Cukierman, Edwards, and Tabellini 1992). These would be the developing countries. The fact that a country has incentives to use seigniorage, however, does not mean the revenues extracted in this manner will be used to promote economic growth. Ironically, the OECD countries, the group with the least incentive to resort to persistent seigniorage, are the only group with sufficiently developed fiscal and monetary systems to effectively use seigniorage as an alternative extractive method to promote growth.

Inflation, the second instrument, may be thought of as a mechanism available to the developing countries for intervening in the economy, particularly for the purpose of transferring assets from one group to another. It is no accident that the middle-income developing countries exhibit the largest mean inflation rate in Table 12.1. This is the level of development at which public resistance to expanded government activity is the most intense. It is often at this stage of development that monetary, fiscal, and exchange rate policies are used to accommodate deficit finance, permit money creation, and provide windfalls, all to assist private entrepreneurs by creating profits on their behalf. Under these conditions, price inflation can be depended upon to lighten the repayment burden of entrepreneurs and force the public to save (Ranis 1990, 220).

Inflation is the end-product of existing monetary policy. The management or manipulation of monetary policy, however, ultimately rests on social and economic forces that in turn underlie political decisions or restrict them within a certain range. Economic factors alone can explain *how* inflation occurs, but economic factors alone cannot explain *why*. Additionally, because the outcome variable is the average annual percentage growth in nominal *GDP*, the rate of inflation is included as a control variable. If *RPE** has a decisive and positive effect on economic growth, it does so in spite of the inflationary effects of monetary policy or alternative revenue sources.[4]

The third instrument is direct state intervention in the economy. An indicator of the degree of such intervention is the type of control a state exercises over its currency. All the countries used in this study were classified according to the following currency control categories provided by the *World Currency Yearbook* (1988-89, 18): free, liberal controls, and strict controls (see Chapter 8 of this volume for a detailed explanation).

The introduction of currency controls permits the testing of some of the implications of Callaghy's concept of embedded liberalism. Presumably, the more direct control the state attempts to exert over society and the economy, the less efficient it becomes over time in generating the social energy and resources needed to promote public goals. The same dynamic may be at work in managing the economy where promoting economic growth is concerned. Countries classified as having strict currency controls are the comparison group against which states with less rigorous forms of currency regulation are compared.

The fourth instrument is investment in human capital. Without a skilled population, nations cannot use technology productively. Barro argues, for example, that a poor country grows faster than a rich country, but only for a given quantity of its human capital (Barro 1991, 409). The primary and secondary school enrollment ratios serve as measures for the level of human capital in an economy. At any given year, however, school enrollment ratios require a lengthy gestation period before the education being acquired can be translated into productive technological expertise. Consequently, in the developing countries current investment in human capital could produce a negative effect on growth, while, building on Barro's argument, the rate of increase in human capital should be positively linked to growth. In the developed countries, the relationship between human capital and growth should be the opposite: The current level of investment in human capital (school enrollment ratio) should be positively related to growth, and the rate of increase in that investment should not add substantially to growth.

Initial levels of wealth are another critical component in most growth models. However, because one of the assumptions underlying this study is that the effect of political capacity on economic growth varies with the level of economic development, the 61-country sample was divided into four groups based on per capita GNP in 1990 dollars:

1) *Least Developed Economies*: Countries with a per capita GNP of less than $630.00 in 1990.
2) *Developing Economies*: Countries with a per capita GNP of at least $630.00 and less than $3,900 per year; or whose exports of manufactures accounted for over 50% of total exports in 1984-1986.
3) *Advanced Developing Economies*: Non-OECD countries with a per capita GNP of at least $3,900 and less than $11,500. For the purposes of this analysis, Greece and Portugal are included in this category as their per capita income is far lower than the other OECD countries along with the newly industrialized countries Hong Kong, Israel, Singapore, and Taiwan.
4) *Industrial Market Economies*: All OECD countries with the exceptions of Greece, Portugal, Turkey, and Yugoslavia.

This division also provides for the notion of differences in initial levels of wealth without having to add an additional variable to represent it.

ESTIMATION

An estimate of relative political extraction is generated by an econometric model using weighted least squares regression that incorporates the economic controls previously described plus controls for trend. The model parallels those used by political scientists and applied to other policy domains (Kugler and Domke 1986; Kugler, Organski, Johnson, and Cohen 1983; Organski and Kugler 1980). The principal difference is that this model includes explicit controls for the extreme differences in taxable resources and tax structures found in high-income oil-exporting countries, and in the way taxable capacity is estimated for the developed countries (see Appendix B). Relative political extraction is the ratio of observed tax revenues (less social security contributions) as a percentage of *GDP* to predicted tax revenues adjusted for differentials in resource endowments and economic conditions. When a government is performing close to the norm compared to other governments with similar resource bases, this ratio will be close to one. When it is extracting below this norm, the ratio will be considerably less than one. Governments with an extractive capacity that is considerably higher than what would be expected given their resource base will exhibit ratios substantially higher than one.

MEASURING GOVERNMENT CAPACITY AS "FLEXIBILITY"

Just as the political factors that determine levels of political capacity cannot be specified directly, neither can the ability to act flexibly. However, the indirect byproducts of this ability can be observed. The ability to act flexibly—to intervene, withdraw, reform, or abstain—requires sufficient decision-making autonomy from private interests to deflect pervasive rent-seeking and to avoid becoming locked into previous distributive commitments. One sign that a state either has assumed responsibility for more social tasks than it is capable of managing effectively or lacks the minimum autonomy to keep rent-seeking within manageable boundaries is that government expenditures consistently exceed revenues. The shortfall might be compensated for in part by resorting to seigniorage as an alternative to higher ordinary taxation or interest-bearing public debt, but only for relatively small amounts. The continued imbalance between expenditures and revenues is an indication that the government has assumed responsibility for more tasks than it can manage capably, or that it cannot effectively limit the claims of private interests on public resources. Either way, the state's political capacity is growing more slowly than the expansion of tasks that the government has assumed. Therefore, the government's *effective* political capacity is reduced by the amount by which expenditures exceed revenues. It is operationalized by multiplying RPE^* by the ratio of government revenues to expenditures. This "constrained" political capacity score should be a more accurate indicator of the ability of the government to manage the economy and promote economic growth than the original "raw" score, particularly if the former is substantially lower than the latter.

The ratio of social security tax revenues to social security benefits paid out is another way to measure the effects of past distributive commitments on the government's ability to act autonomously in the present. Social security taxes can only be used for specific purposes defined by law. Therefore, the government has no real latitude in determining how such revenues are spent. Social security benefits represent the government's commitment to guarantee eligible members of society a minimum level of real income. If the value of the social security expenditures paid out exceeds the amount of social security taxes collected each year, "real" state capacity in any given year will be reduced by the degree of the imbalance. The second estimate of "constrained" political capacity consists of multiplying RPE^* by the ratio of social security to social security benefits paid out. However, because many developing countries do not have social security systems, this measure does not permit any strong inferences to be made regarding countries outside of the OECD states.

The research design is a cross-section pooled time-series design. The data set consists of 61 developed and developing countries, collected over a twenty-one year period (1970—1990)—for a total of 1,220 observations (see Appendix A). Not all of the countries are included in all the regressions, because of missing data on revenues, expenditures, or social security taxes and payments. Missing data on the social security variables for the developing countries may have introduced systematic bias into some of the results.

The pooled time-series structure, however, raises statistical problems arising from the possibility of autocorrelated error terms within each country and heteroskedastic disturbances (unequal variances) across a group of countries at any one point in time.[5] Ordinary least squares regression is not suited to a pooled time-series data set because it cannot simultaneously control for heteroskedastic disturbances in the cross-sectional analysis and autocorrelation in the error terms in the time series. Consequently, tests for serial correlation, such as the Durbin-Watson statistic, often yield unreliable results. In addition, the D-W statistic is not appropriate when lagged values of the dependent variable are included as an independent variable (as is the case here). The most serious problem concerns the ambiguous definition of "degrees of freedom" in the cross-sectional pooled time-series structure.[6] The possible confounding effects of serial correlation (trend) on economic growth can be isolated by including time (year of observation) as a variable. However, this does not address the problem of multicollinearity and heteroskedastic disturbances in the cross-sectional analysis. The regression analysis uses a two-stage weighted least squares (2SWLS) procedure to compensate for the systematic extraneous variance within countries. A two-stage estimation technique is necessary because the discussion of the control variables implies that seigniorage, inflation, and the investment in human capital may be partly a function of a government's political capacity, and thus cannot be considered entirely exogenous.

The primary question raised is whether the extractive capacity of the state that is adjusted for the differential flexibility of governments to act in times of crisis or rapid change provides a better understanding of the relationship between state capacity and economic growth than an unadjusted measure of this capability does. Decision autonomy is defined as the ability to maintain a minimal insularity against rent-seeking and the ability to remain unconstrained by past distributional commitments. Insularity against rent-seeking is defined as the ratio of central government revenues to central government expenditures. Most countries occasionally spend more revenue than they collect. Doing this repeatedly over a period of years suggests that the underlying problem is political, not fiscal. In this case more claims are being made on public resources than the government can satisfy—unless it can extract more revenue.

If a country has minimal autonomy on this measure, the ratio should be close to one. Therefore, multiplying the ratio by the raw RPE^* scores will not raise or lower the RPE^* values significantly. If the ratio is far less than one, multiplying it by the raw RPE^* values will yield an adjusted RPE^* value that is much lower than the original. This is an indication that the government's flexibility—its ability to remain unconstrained by past distributional commitments—has been degraded. If a country is strong on this measure of state capability, the ratio will be noticeably greater than one and its original RPE^* values will be increased. The litmus test is which measure of government capacity has the strongest effect on increasing economic growth. Consequently, the data analysis involves a two-step sequence: (1) using the original RPE^* score (both the level and the percentage change) as a causal variable, and (2) substituting RPE^* multiplied by the ratio of government revenues to government expenditures. Because the relationship between political capacity and economic growth is hypothesized to be nonlinear (see Figure 12.1), RPE^* is expressed in four different transformations within each level of development:

1) The inverse ($INVERSE\ RPE^*$) captures observations of low RPE^* and low average economic growth. These are countries in which agricultural production is the dominant sector of gross domestic product (GDP).
2) The level ($log\ RPE^*$) isolates RPE^* and average rates of growth.
3) The percentage change in RPE^* (% $\Delta\ RPE^*$) distinguishes rapidly growing state capacity and rapid growth rates. This variable should capture most of the observations for the least developed economies, but have a null impact on the growth of the OECD countries.
4) RPE^{*2} captures observations of average to above-average RPE^* and moderate economic growth.

The less-developed countries should not exhibit a strong relationship between their *levels* of political capacity and their economic growth. However, the *rate of increase* in their political capacity should have a strong positive influence on growth. The inflection point on the curve beyond which additional increments of political capacity are likely to dampen economic growth should not affect growth for the less developed economies, if for no other reason than that their governments have not yet succeeded in establishing the unchallenged authority of the state throughout the country. One of the few effective ways these states can intervene in the economy is through currency controls. To the extent that this intervention ultimately increases domestic investment in productive activities rather than encouraging speculation, the net effect of such intervention could be strong and positive. One way this could occur is if the currency controls were successful in preventing capital flight. Further, if currencies are internally convertible, domestic holders of liquid assets may convert these assets into a foreign currency and invest that money in the nontradeable goods sector to avoid the seigniorage tax. This is another reason why seigniorage is not expected to have any strong positive effect on growth in the less-developed countries, in addition to reasons noted earlier.

The levels of political capacity should show a strong effect on the growth of developing countries, but the rate at which political capacity increases should not affect growth appreciably. That is, government capacity is expanding, but not as rapidly as social tasks that governments have assumed. In addition, for some developing countries there remains the lingering problem of overcoming popular resistance to the extension of state authority at a time when an increasingly complex economy may be less responsive to state direction. The maintenance of currency controls may not be as effective in less developed countries if high rates of inflation and other government policies are providing strong incentives for capital flight instead of domestic investment. Seigniorage should remain an ineffective and unwieldy policy instrument.

In the advanced developing countries, extractive capabilities should be growing rapidly because these governments have largely succeeded in penetrating and coordinating the activities of society through the state's civil and military infrastructures. Productivity has grown by means of expanded industrialization, but expanded industrialization in turn amplifies the range of activities that government must coordinate. Nevertheless, the political capacity of these countries is growing faster than the rate at which the governments assume new social tasks. Because the economies of these countries are generally outwardly oriented, they are in a position to extract revenue from seigniorage. Because many of them pursue an export-oriented industrialization strategy, reliance on the type of government intervention represented by currency controls to direct the economy should not exert a strong effect on promoting growth. In fact, if the net effects of this sort of intervention exert a strong effect on growth, that effect should be negative. This is what sets the advanced developing countries apart from other developing countries. What separates those countries from the advanced industrialized states is that more revenues are needed to pay for expanding government activities; whereas in fully industrialized societies the need to further penetrate society and extract more resources has diminished. Therefore, the rate of increase in political capacity should exhibit a strong influence on economic growth in the advanced developing countries, but have no appreciable effect on growth in the OECD countries.

Precisely because there is a diminishing need to further penetrate society, the levels of political extraction in the advanced industrialized OECD countries would not be expected to affect economic growth significantly. In fact, for these countries, high levels of political capacity may be associated with negative growth. Governments in industrialized states usually face exorbitant political costs if they achieve additional increases in extraction (i.e., the rate of change [% Δ RPE^*] in political capacity). However, to the extent that the political costs of extracting additional resources are not prohibitive, success in extracting additional resources should translate into higher growth rates. Apart from the influence upon it of % Δ RPE^*, economic growth should not be very responsive to state capacity. As political institutions have become better established and governments have a wider array of policy instruments available to them with which to manage the economy, the direct effects of political capacity on economic growth should diminish and become indirectly mediated through other policy instruments.

But how is it known that the analysis using the constrained political capacity variables provides the most accurate description of the relationship between political capacity and economic growth? The following criteria are used to evaluate the performance of the models. For the least developed and middle-income developing economies, the "constrained" model should provide for at least an equal but preferably a greater proportionate reduction of error than the unconstrained model for two reasons. First, in these economies there are fewer organized pressure groups with which governments must negotiate to implement a given policy. Second, because market exchange mechanisms and bureaucratic organizations have not yet taken root, these governments have few alternative instruments to rely on in implementing policy. Consequently, the direction and intensity of the relationships between the political capacity variables and economic growth in the constrained model should exhibit greater consistency with theoretical expectations than the direction and intensity of the same relationships containing the equivalent variables in the unconstrained models.

If political constraints increase with higher levels of economic development, the unconstrained models should take into account a larger share of the explained variance for the advanced developing and advanced industrialized economies than the constrained models. At these more advanced levels of development, there is a diminishing need for the state to penetrate society. This diminishing need is accompanied by a diminishing marginal growth of extractive capabilities as countries become more structurally complex, and the state has more opportunities for indirect intervention in the economy via market exchange mechanisms and bureaucratic organizations than the governments of less industrialized countries have. Consequently, the constrained models should yield a lower proportionate reduction of error in economic growth than the unconstrained models. Similarly, the political capacity variables in the unconstrained models should show a closer correspondence to theoretical expectations than they do in the constrained models.

RESULTS OF THE DATA ANALYSIS

Each of the regression tables (Tables 12.2, 12.3, and 12.4) displays the results of the weighted least squares estimates for the baseline model and the weighted two-stage least squares estimates for the political capacity models using *RPE** scores adjusted for the government's ability to insulate itself from the pressures of rent-seeking coalitions. These results reflect the "true" capacity of the government to affect economic growth, no matter what the level of economic development may be. The regressions control for differences in inflation rates and for the degree of direct intervention in the economy as indicated by the category of currency controls. The natural logarithm of average economic growth is used because the original data are skewed. Log transformations compress the extreme ends of highly skewed variables closer to their means. The variables representing inflation rates and the degree of government intervention in the economy (via currency controls) are the same for both runs. Therefore, the magnitude and sign of the coefficients for these control variables along with their t-ratios should not vary significantly between the analyses of adjusted and unadjusted *RPE** scores within a given level of development.

THE LESS DEVELOPED COUNTRIES

Table 12.2 summarizes the results of regressing economic growth on the unadjusted levels of relative political extraction, as well as on political extraction weighted for the government's ability to insulate itself from rent-seeking pressures and the effects of assuming more social tasks than the state apparatus can manage. These two regressions can be compared to the baseline model to determine the improvement in the proportionate reduction of error that results from adding the political capacity variables. The results converge closely with the theoretical expectations discussed earlier.

The regression constant represents the average value of the dependent

TABLE 12.2 Estimating the Effects of Extractive Government Capacity on Economic Growth in Less Developed Countries, 1970-1990

Variables	Baseline Model			Unweighted Model			RPE* Weighted by Political Constraints		
	Coeff.	Std. Error	T-value	Coeff.	Std. Error	T-value	Coeff.	Std. Error	T-value
LOG AVERAGE GROWTH									
INVERSE RPE*				0.055 (0.154)	0.098	0.56	0.014 (0.169)	0.006	2.49*
RPE*				0.015 (0.023)	0.287	0.05	0.254 (0.611)	0.080	3.18**
%ΔRPE*				0.099 (0.141)	0.043	2.28*	0.033 (0.159)	0.015	2.23*
LOG RPE*²				-0.022 (-0.072)	0.024	0.91	0.072 (-0.927)	0.149	4.82**
PRIMARY SCH	-0.004 (-0.36)	0.0008	-4.72**	-0.003 (-0.33)	0.0007	-4.26**	-0.004 (-0.395)	0.0008	-4.98**
%ΔPRIM SCH	0.039 (0.134)	0.183	2.16*	0.035 (0.126)	0.017	2.05*	0.037 (0.138)	0.016	2.28*
LOG INFLAT	-0.050 (-0.203)	0.017	-2.96**	-0.003 (-0.358)	0.0006	-4.53**	-0.002 (-0.216)	0.0007	-2.74**
SEIGNIORAGE	-0.001 (-0.034)	0.003	-0.53	-0.001 (-0.022)	0.003	-0.35	-0.003 (-0.050)	0.004	-0.77
LIBERAL CONTR	0.604 (0.813)	0.084	7.17**	0.567 (0.798)	0.769	7.37**	0.598 (0.863)	0.0761	7.88**
STRICT CONTROL	0.333 (0.528)	0.067	4.95**	0.335 (0.566)	0.582	5.75**	0.342 (0.583)	0.580	5.89**
CONSTANT	2.967	0.759	3.91**	2.803	0.211	13.28**	2.713	0.871	3.11**
R²	0.28			0.37			0.48		
Number of Observ.	186			180			150		

* Significant at 5 percent level.
** Significant at 1 percent level.
Beta Coefficients between brackets

variable, economic growth, when the values of the causal variables are zero. Without the influence of the causal variables, economic growth for the less developed countries would have been running at an annual average between 2.7 and 2.97%. This compares to the actual mean growth rate of 3.1% for the less developed country subset.

The strength and direction of the coefficients for the currency control categories are interpreted with respect to countries that maintain no currency controls (*Free*). The coefficient for the *Free* comparison group is the value of the regression constant itself. The strong positive influence of the degree of direct state intervention in the economy, represented by categories of currency controls on economic growth, is also in line with expectations. Notwithstanding the economic distortions that direct government intervention can spawn in economies wherein market exchange and bureaucratic organization are not well established, less developed economies that do not maintain freely transferable currencies exhibit considerably higher growth rates than countries that maintain no exchange controls at all.

Inflation rates perform as expected. The higher the rate of inflation, the lower the rate of average economic growth. This result is consistent across all levels of economic development for both the adjusted and unadjusted *RPE** variables. As expected, seigniorage shows no strong influence on economic growth.

Regarding the WLS analysis using *RPE**adjusted for the degree of government insularity, adding these *RPE** variables accounts for an additional 20% of the variance in growth over the baseline model. All the political capacity variables exert a strong influence on economic growth in the anticipated direction. The results suggest that the ability to maintain a minimum of policy insulary from rent-seeking coalitions and a modicum of selectivity as to what tasks the state takes upon itself enhances the government's political capacity to promote economic growth. This conclusion is suggested not only by the increase in the adjusted R^2, but also by the strong effect that all the *RPE** variables have on growth, as predicted. This supports the proposition that states must maintain a minimum of policy insularity from rent-seeking pressures, and that the reach of the state should not exceed its grasp.

THE DEVELOPING COUNTRIES

The results for the developing countries (see Table 12.3) are generally consistent with theoretical expectations, except that the addition of the political capacity variables does not increase the adjusted R^2 over the baseline model nearly as much as in the previous analysis. However, it is the *RPE** variables, unweighted for political constraints, that improve the proportionate reduction in error the most. The levels of *RPE*^{*2}, both constrained and unconstrained, strongly affect economic growth in the expected directions. Also as expected, the rate of increase in weighted *RPE** does not. What is unexpected is that the *RPE** variables in the unweighted model provide the strongest empirical support for the curvilinear relationship between *RPE** and economic performance along the entire range of the curve. Some of the developing countries have expanded their political capacity to a point beyond which further levels of extraction run counter to promoting economic growth. This fact is suggested by the magnitude of the coefficient for the squared term (*Log RPE*^{*2}).

Government intervention in the economy, represented by the degree of currency controls, exerts no discernible influence on growth compared to the effect of this sort of intervention in less developed economies. Neither does seigniorage.[7] What is interesting is that while the relationship between development of human capital and growth remains the same, it is the investment in human capital at the secondary-school, not the primary-school level that contributes a truly strong effect.

THE ADVANCED DEVELOPING COUNTRIES

In the advanced developing countries, governments have largely succeeded in penetrating and coordinating the activities of society through the state's civil and military infrastructures (see Table 12.4). One of the most noticeable differences between this group and those already reviewed is that the model accounts for a much higher percentage of the variance for this group of countries than it does for countries in less advanced stages of development. This includes the baseline model. Another difference is that in the analysis using the constrained *RPE** variables, the upper inflection point, represented by *Log RPE*^{*2}, does not show the restraining effects of higher levels of *RPE* on higher rates of growth that were evident for the developing countries in Table 12.3. This null relationship suggests that the political capacity of the advanced developing countries can continue to expand without retarding economic growth. Why this is so is a matter of fascinating speculation. The explanation consistent with theoretical expectations is that these states exercised considerable selectivity in the tasks they undertook.[8] Their strategies of promoting industry used market mechanisms in order to conserve administrative resources. The model using the unconstrained *RPE** variables indicates that these countries as a group are adept at extracting revenues from seigniorage in ways that enhance economic

TABLE 12.3 Estimating the Effects of Extractive Government Capacity on Economic Growth in Developing Countries, 1970-1990

Variables	Baseline Model			Unweighted Model			RPE* Weighted by Political Constraints		
	Coeff.	Std. Error	T-value	Coeff.	Std. Error	T-value	Coeff.	Std. Error	T-value
LOG AVERAGE GROWTH									
INVERSE RPE*				0.637 (2.036)	0.098	6.52**	-0.001 (-0.02)	0.002	-0.43
RPE*				0.569 (0.942)	0.093	6.13**	0.250 (0.479)	0.076	3.29**
%ΔRPE*2				0.063 (0.169)	0.015	4.24**	-0.007 (-0.008)	0.039	-0.17
LOG RPE*				-0.862 (-1.469)	0.135	-6.41**	-0.092 (-0.395)	0.033	-2.77**
SECONDARY SCH	-0.0009 (-0.07)	0.0004	-1.66	0.0009 (-0.07)	0.0005	-1.66	0.002 (-0.16)	0.0005	-3.37**
%ΔSEC. SCH	0.022 (0.087)	0.011	2.01**	0.020 (0.072)	0.011	1.81	0.040 (0.138)	0.012	3.21**
LOG INFLAT	-0.045 (-0.321)	0.006	-7.17**	-0.050 (-0.326)	0.007	-7.11**	-0.038 (-0.305)	0.007	-6.10**
SEIGNIORAGE	-0.0004 (-0.029)	0.1008	-0.50	-0.0007 (-0.042)	0.0007	-1.03	-0.0004 (-0.028)	0.0007	-0.62
LIBERAL CONTR	-0.009 (0.035)	0.127	-0.71	-0.014 (0.047)	0.014	-1.00	-0.018 (0.067)	0.0136	-1.32
STRICT CONTROL	-0.003 (0.009)	0.0167	-0.18	-0.008 (0.02)	0.0178	-0.45	-0.012 (0.030)	0.0207	-0.58
CONSTANT	3.147	0.253	13.51**	1.963	0.190	10.36**	3.009	0.459	5.74**
R²	0.17			0.24			0.22		
Number of Observ.	503			495			450		

* Significant at 5 percent level.
** Significant at 1 percent level.
Beta Coefficients between brackets

TABLE 12.4 Estimating the Effects of Extractive Government Capacity on Economic Growth in Advanced Developing Countries, 1970-1990

Variables	Baseline Model Coeff.	Std. Error	T-value	Unweighted Model Coeff.	Std. Error	T-value	RPE* Weighted by Political Constraints Coeff.	Std. Error	T-value
LOG AVERAGE GROWTH									
INVERSE RPES				-0.759 (-1.36)	0.473	-1.60	0.197 (0.37)	0.228	0.86
RPE*				0.620 (2.28)	0.297	2.09*	0.161 (0.415)	0.186	0.28
%^RPE*				0.245 (0.179)	0.079	3.07**	0.260 (0.258)	0.071	3.67**
LOG RPE*				-0.904 (-4.17)	0.409	-2.21*	-0.070 (-0.518)	0.145	-0.48
PRIMARY SCH	-0.002 (-0.089)	0.0019	-1.05	-0.0009 (-0.03)	0.0019	-0.37	-0.0004 (-0.18)	0.0003	-1.19
%^PRIM. SCH	1.318 (0.125)	0.734	1.79	0.998 (0.101)	0.588	1.69	1.546 (0.706)	0.706	2.19*
LOG INFLAT	-0.084 (-0.571)	0.012	-6.97**	-0.033 (-0.524)	0.016	-2.09*	-0.054 (-0.373)	0.015	-3.51**
SEIGNIORAGE	-0.00004 (-0.096)	0.00003	-1.33	-0.00009 (0.266)	0.00002	-3.89**	-0.00003 (-0.070)	0.00003	-1.03
LIBERAL CONTR	-0.125 (0.039)	0390	-3.20**	-0.099 (0.269)	0.039	-2.51*	-0.249 (0.680)	0.061	-4.07**
STRICT CONTROL	0.072 (0.200)	0.043	1.68	0.078 (0.02)	0.251	1.98*	0.032 (0.088)	0.046	0.69
CONSTANT	3.056	0.072	3.92**	2.803	0.211	13.28**	2.713	0.871	3.11**
R²	0.54			0.68			0.60		
Number of Observ.	100			100			100		

* Significant at 5 percent level.
** Significant at 1 percent level.
Beta Coefficients between brackets

growth. Other direct forms of economic intervention via currency controls either produce no effect on growth or, as anticipated, exert a dampening effect.

As expected, expanded industrialization along with prior success in penetrating society extends the range of activities that government must coordinate. Therefore, more revenues are needed to pay for expanding government activities. The weighted model suggests that it is not the levels of RPE^* that are important in accounting for the variance in growth, but that the rate of increase in political capacity has the most direct impact. The inverse of RPE^* was not expected to account for a significant variance in growth because there should be few cases of low RPE^* and low growth for this category of countries. This expectation is supported by the results. It is the rate of change (% Δ RPE^*) in variables that contributes to growth. The advanced developing countries need more revenues to pay for more government activities, which, in turn, help to promote higher rates of economic growth. This finding strongly suggests that the ability of the advanced developing countries to keep the pressures of rent-seeking coalitions at bay and to avoid assuming direct responsibility for more tasks than they can handle is fairly robust. It is possible that this ability may exert an upward movement of the negative inflection point at which higher levels of political capacity begin to dampen economic growth rates.

Nevertheless, the analyses for this group of countries indicate some inconsistencies across the three models that require further discussion. Contrary to theoretical expectations, the model using the unconstrained political capacity variables yields more satisfactory results than the model using the RPE^* variables weighted for political constraints. Not only does the unconstrained model produce a higher proportionate reduction of error, but also the strength and direction of the political capacity variables are more consistent with theoretical expectations than are those of the constrained variant. Expanded industrialization may have amplified the range of activities that these governments must coordinate, but their political capacity is growing faster than the rate at which they assume new social tasks. The summary statistics in Table 12.1 show that the mean rate of change in these countries' unweighted RPE^* is the highest of the four development groups. They are in a much better position to extract revenue from seigniorage than other developing countries; and seigniorage shows a strong positive effect on growth using unconstrained political capacity, but exhibits no significant effect in the constrained model. Cumulatively these data suggest that the unconstrained model is the more accurate representation for the middle-income developing and the advanced developing countries precisely because they appear to be unfettered by the kinds of political constraints that are so prevalent in the least developed countries. The constrained model represents how the performance of these countries would diminish if they were less selective in the tasks for which their governments assumed direct responsibility; or if they were as susceptible to rent-seeking pressures as the less industrialized developing countries.

THE ADVANCED INDUSTRIALIZED COUNTRIES

Cumulatively the results in Table 12.5 illustrate the superior transformative capacity of fully industrialized societies over partially industrialized or agrarian ones. Table 12.1 showed that the advanced industrialized countries extract substantially higher average shares of national product, even though their average unweighted RPE^* is not different from that of the less developed or developing countries. The average political capacity levels of most fully industrialized states mask the fact that their average levels of extraction (*Tax Rev % GDP*) are close to the threshold where they may no longer contribute significantly to additional increments of economic growth. With a diminishing need to further penetrate society and the increased penetration of civil society by market exchange and bureaucratic organizations, the levels and the rates of increase in political capacity are not expected to affect economic growth significantly in advanced industrialized countries. Indeed, for these countries, high levels of political capacity may be *negatively* associated with growth.

Equally contrary to theoretical expectations, the unconstrained RPE^* model yields a better fit than the constrained state capacity model does. It provides for three times as much variance in growth as the baseline model, and twice as much variance as the model of constrained RPE^*. What the unconstrained model reveals is the transformative potential of an industrialized state despite the extreme difficulty of extracting additional increments of new resources.

The other results are consistent with theoretical expectations. The level of investment in human capital (as indicated by the school enrollment ratio) exerts a strong positive effect on growth, whereas the rate of increase in investment in this sector exerts a net negative effect on growth. This suggests that there is an inflection point in investment in human capital similar to the one identified in RPE^*. Additional increments of investment in human capital yield no short-term payoffs in terms of economic growth. That is not to say that new increments of investment in human capital might not exert a strong positive effect at some subsequent time.

Another important difference is that the industrialized countries can stimulate growth by means of a wider array of instruments than the developing countries can. This is suggested by the strong positive effect that seigniorage and currency controls have on growth. In the aggregate, the increased penetration of civil society by market exchange and bureaucratic organization in advanced industrialized countries means that

TABLE 12.5 Estimating the Effects of Extractive Government Capacity on Economic Growth in Advanced Industrialized Countries (OECD), 1970-1990

Variables	Baseline Model			Unweighted Model			RPE* Weighted by Political Constraints		
	Coeff.	Std. Error	T-value	Coeff.	Std. Error	T-value	Coeff.	Std. Error	T-value
LOG AVERAGE GROWTH									
INVERSE RPES				-0.364 (-1.13)	0.090	-4.06**	-0.803 (2.52)	0.319	-2.52*
RPE*				0.119 (0.35)	0.040	2.95*	0.847 (2.04)	0.396	2.13*
%ΔRPE*				0.016 (0.018)	0.041	0.39	0.058 (0.063)	0.447	1.29
LOG RPE*²				-0.322 (-1.61)	0.061	-5.32**	-0.896 (-4.65)	0.366	-2.45*
PRIMARY SCH	0.003 (0.16)	0.0009	3.28**	0.002 (0.09)	0.001	1.82	0.002 (0.11)	0.0009	2.13*
%ΔPRIM. SCH	-0.966 (-0.116)	0.397	-2.43*	-1.079 (-0.13)	0.373	-2.89**	-1.111 (-0.13)	0.390	-2.85**
LOG INFLAT	-0.035 (-0.21)	0.009	-3.96**	-0.009 (0.334)	0.001	-6.79**	-0.009 (-0.35)	0.001	-6.89**
SEIGNIORAGE	0.003 (0.18)	0.0008	3.77**	0.003 (0.184)	0.0008	3.96**	0.004 (0.243)	0.0008	4.89**
LIBERAL CONTR	0.013 (0.050)	.0134	0.97	0.053 (.217)	0.0137	3.87**	0.039 (0.16)	0.014	2.84**
STRICT CONTROL	0.090 (0.162)	0.275	3.27**	0.106 (0.19)	0.267	3.98*	0.110 (0.020)	0.027	4.05**
CONSTANT	2.606	0.101	25.77**	3.109	0.175	17.79**	2.643	0.152	17.43**
R²	0.08			0.17			0.32		
Number of Observ.	411			414			395		

* Significant at 5 percent level.
** Significant at 1 percent level.
Beta Coefficients between brackets

political capacity has a diminished direct effect on economic growth. However, where the state decides to intervene in the economy directly, that intervention is more likely to promote growth in industrialized societies than in the developing economies, where market exchange and bureaucratic organization have not become as well-established in ways that the state can utilize.

SUMMARY AND CONCLUSIONS

The flexibility of the government to respond effectively in times of crisis or abrupt and rapid change has been subjected to empirical testing. At a minimum, this sort of strategic flexibility requires some degree of insularity against political pressures from rent-seeking coalitions, and the ability to keep current policy options from being severely constrained by past distributive commitments. The assumption guiding the analysis was that the constrained political capacity variables were the more accurate reflection of real government capacity to act in moments of crisis or to respond to rapid change. Although constrained models performed better for the least developed countries than the unconstrained models (in terms of variance explained and consistency with the hypothesized curvilinear relationship between government capacity and economic growth), the opposite occurred for the middle income developing, the advanced developing, and the industrialized (OECD) countries. For these groups the unconstrained model yielded the best empirical fit. This is one indication that the political constraints faced by leaders in the less-developed group are of an entirely different nature from those faced by the governments of the more advanced developing countries, the newly industrialized, and the OECD countries.

Cumulatively, the results suggest that neither government capacity nor level of economic development is a static concept. The characteristics and activities of governments that promote larger social goals change over time and across national experiences. The noticeable differences in the magnitudes of the regression coefficients for the political capacity variables are a strong indication that social goals themselves do not remain static. They change over time and vary with national circumstances. The empirical findings strongly support the proposition that the ability to generate independent goals and the ability to extract resources from society are both integral to understanding the capacity of the government to respond to crises and successfully implement structural change. Yet the different results for the industrialized and the developing countries underscore the point that a definitive conception of what constitutes government capacity remains elusive, because these components of government capacity appear to be changing over time in response to changing social imperatives, levels of economic development, and national experiences.

Consequently, the empirical findings lead to a paradoxical conclusion. Governments in the less developed countries extract smaller shares of society's resources, and they have fewer policy instruments at their disposal than those of the more advanced developing countries and the advanced industrial countries. Yet the ability of the developing economies to act flexibly in moments of crisis and to change in the face of rent-seeking pressures is greater than that of the more advanced economies if for no other reason than that the former may be less limited by distributive commitments than the latter. Therefore, the political leaderships of the developing countries exercise more discretion than the elites of more industrialized societies over the smaller share of society's product available to them. But they do not exert more social control. "Social control" here refers to the ability of the state to use bureaucratic organization to provide contractual market exchange mechanisms for state purposes of intervention in the economy. This ability is an advantage enjoyed by the advanced industrialized countries, as indicated by the strong positive effect of seigniorage and currency controls on economic growth in these countries.

We know very little about the concept of government selectivity in choosing which tasks to undertake by direct action and which ones to accomplish by coordinating the energies of other social institutions. To date it has been too closely associated with the Asian success stories. Yet Turkey began the same strategy in the early 1980s and Mexico followed suit in 1989.

The notion of embeddedness is an exciting concept which demands much more investigation. If it can be demonstrated empirically that governments can increase their capacity by sharing power in order to maximize the amount of social energy they can direct in pursuit of national objectives, it would be a signal breakthrough in political economic theory that connects the logic of politics with the logic of economics.

APPENDIX A: LISTING OF CASES BY LEVEL OF ECONOMIC DEVELOPMENT

Less Developed Countries
Ghana, Indonesia, Liberia, Nigeria, Pakistan, Sudan, Tanzania, Uganda, Zaire, Zambia

Developing Countries
Algeria, Argentina, Bolivia, Brazil, Chile, P.R. China, Colombia, Costa Rica, Côte d'Ivoire, Egypt, Ecuador, India, Jamaica, Malaysia, Mexico, Morocco, Peru, Philippines, South Africa, Thailand, Turkey, Uruguay, Venezuela, Yugoslavia

Advanced Developing Countries
Greece, Israel, Korea, Portugal, Singapore, Taiwan

Advanced Industrialized Countries
Australia, Austria, Belgium, Canada, Denmark, Finland, France, Germany, Iceland, Ireland, Italy, Japan, Luxembourg, Netherlands, New Zealand, Norway, Spain, Sweden, Switzerland, United Kingdom, United States

APPENDIX B: Table 12A.1 Estimating Taxable Capacity for 81 Developing Countries, 1950-1990

Variables	Regular Coefficient	Beta Coefficient	Standard Error	T-Ratio
ADJUSTED TAX REVENUE AS A % OF GDP				
EXPORTS AS A % OF GNP	0.201	.080	0.041	4.955**
MINERAL PRODUCTION AS A % OF GDP	2.905	.768	0.176	16.477**
HIGH INCOME OIL EXPORTERS (HIOILEX)	-4.204	-.132	1.082	-3.886**
MINERAL PRODUCTION AS A % OF GDP*HIOILEX	1.612	.267	0.220	7.342**
HIGH INC./LOW TAX OIL EXPORTERS (HIOILOWT)	-7.062	.181	1.242	-5.684**
MINERAL PRODUCTION AS A % OF GDP*HIOILOWT	-4.302	-.670	0.243	-17.652**
NET OIL EXPORTING COUNTRIES (NETOILEX)	1.048	.070	0.304	3.453**
MINERAL PRODUCTION AS A % OF GDP*NETOILEX	-2.311	-.419	0.201	-11.524**
NON-FUEL MINERAL EXPORTERS (NFMINEX)	1.643	.181		5.511**
MINERAL PRODUCTION AS A % OF GDP*NFMINEX	-2.203	-.247	0.246	-8.967**
AGRICULTURAL PRODUCTION AS A % OF GDP	-0.723	-.211	0.054	-13.348**
YEAR OF OBSERVATION	0.712	.137	0.071	9.976**
CONSTANT	-12.705		1.409	-9.020**

Number of Observations 2759

Adj. **R²** .54

* Significant at 5% level
** Significant at 1% level

APPENDIX B: Table 12A.2 Estimating Taxable Capacity for 23 Industrialized (OECD) Countries, 1950-1990

Variables	Regular Coefficient	Beta Coefficient	Standard Error	T-Ratio
ADJUSTED TAX REVENUE AS A % OF GDP				
EXPORTS AS A % OF GNP	0.180	.489	0.009	18.975**
MINERAL PRODUCTION AS A % OF GDP	-0.194	-.068	0.076	-2.553**
AGRICULTURAL PRODUCTION AS A % OF GDP	-0.091	-.100	0.028	-3.280**
SOCIAL SECURITY BENEFITS AS A % OF				
TOTAL TAX REVENUES	-1.863	-.497	0.115	-16.131*
YEAR OF OBSERVATION	0.117	.245	0.015	7.606**
CONSTANT	-20.825		3.015	-6.907**
Number of Observations	70			
Adj. R^2	.39			

*   Significant at 5% level
** Significant at 1% level

Notes to Appendix B:

VARIABLES	DEFINITIONS
Exports as a % of GNP	Exports as a percentage of gross national product (GNP).
Mineral Production as a % of GDP (GDP).	Mineral production as a percentage of gross domestic product.
High Income Oil Exporters (HIOILEX)	Dummy variable: 1 = high income oil-exportingcountry (petro-economy), 0 = other.
Mineral Prod. %GDP*HIOILEX	Mineral production as a percentage of GDP, high income oil-exporting countries (petro-economies).
High Inc./Low Tax Oil Exporters (HIIOLOWT	Dummy variable: 1 = high income oil-exporting/low tax country (petro-economy), 0 = other.
Mineral Production as a % of GDP*HIOILOWT	Mineral production as a percentage of GDP, high income/low tax oil-exporting countries (petro-economies).
Net Oil Exporting Countries (NETOILEX)	Dummy variable: 1 = middle income net oil-exporting country, 0 = other.
Mineral Production as a % of GDP*NETOILEX	Mineral production as a percentage of GDP, middleincome net oil-exporting countries (petro- economies)
Non-Fuel Mineral Exporters (NFMINEX)	Dummy variable: 1 = Non-fuel mineral-cexporting country, 0 = other.
Mineral Production as a % of GDP*NFMINEX	Mineral production as a percentage of GDP, non-fuel mineral-exporting countries.
Agricultural Production as a % of GDP.	Agricultural production as a percentage of GDP.
Social Security Benefits as a % of Total Tax Revenues	Social security benefits paid out as a percentage of total tax revenues collected each year. Source: GFSY World Tables.

NOTES

1. Special thanks to Carol Al-Sharabati and Peter Vasilovich for research assistance in connection with this paper and to Kathleen Gumbleton for a critique of the final draft; and to Brian Ward and David Hopson for stimulating the author's thinking on the subject of constraints on *RPE* and for their critiques of an earlier draft.

2. Economic complexity is indicated by the level of industrialization indexed by the manufacturing of *GDP* share multiplied by share of exports accounted for by manufactures exports, and by the stage of economic development as measured by per capita *GNP* circa 1992.

3. The surprisingly high mean *RPE** scores for the advanced developing countries are inflated by the mean *RPE** of one country, Israel. When Israel is removed from this group, the mean *RPE** is 1.139 and the mean "raw extraction" level is 20.8%.

4. Exploratory data analysis revealed that for the entire sample, economic growth has been declining over time and so is negatively correlated with trend (year of observation). Both the average economic growth rate and *RPE** are declining steadily in the industrialized countries. Consequently, the year of observation was included in the data analysis to capture the impact of these secular trend effects on the outcome variables. However, since secular trend did not exert any significant causal impact on the outcome variable once the complete model was tested, the trend variable was dropped from the equation.

5. Unequal variances across countries are an indication that the observations are not equally valid for every country in the sample. The same problem can arise within a country over time. It is a problem that is confronted when working with data on developing countries.

6. For example, the pooled time-series data set used in this study consists of a total of 1,220 observations, collected over 21 years for 61 countries. Strictly speaking, there are only 61 cases (countries) that are truly independent of one another. The 21 observations for each of these countries are independent of the 21 observations for any other country in the sample. Within each country, the 21 observations can exhibit serial correlation (the effects of trend) and multicolinearity. Consequently, tests for serial correlation such as the Durbin-Watson statistic often yield unreliable results because they are based on the assumption that the 1220 observations have the same independence from one another as the 61 countries have from one another.

7. Notice that the magnitude of the standardized regression (beta) coefficients in Table 12.3 is greater than one. Beta coefficients are adjusted partial slopes that indicate how much change in the dependent variable is produced by a standardized change in one of the casual variables when the effects of the other casual variables are held constant. They are obtained by the following equation: $\beta_{yx} = b_{yx} (S_y/S_x)$, where S_y is the standard deviation of Y and S_x is the standard deviation of X. Some authors treat standardized regression coefficients the same as correlation coefficients and imply that beta coefficients cannot be less than -1.0 or greater than 1.0. However, as the equation suggests, if the standard deviation of Y is much greater than the standard deviation of X, the resulting beta coefficient will be greater than one. These high magnitudes can also occur if the value of the

unstandardized regression coefficient (b_{yx}) is greater than one. The interpretation is also straightforward: A change of one standard deviation unit in X produces an average change in Y of 1.47 standard deviation units.

8. Only two countries in this group, Israel and Singapore, show *RPE** values that are consistently above the norm.

PART FOUR

Extending Political Capacity

13

Political Capacity and the Economic Frontier

John H. Y. Edwards[1]

THE CONCEPT OF REVENUE RAISING "CAPACITY"

The determinants of government capacity to raise revenue and the determinants of revenues actually raised have been focal issues in inter-governmental relations and constitute a natural bridge between the disciplines of economics and political science. Measures of average "tax-effort" have been used by applied public finance economists to guide intergovernmental transfer policy at both the sub-national and international levels. Political scientists developed the concepts of tax capacity and tax effort into models of "relative political extraction" (*RPE*) that seek to explain deviations between observed revenues and estimated capacity. This chapter explores the underpinnings of the *RPE* concept in economic theory and suggests some refinements for both theory and measurement technique.

WHAT ECONOMISTS HAVE DONE

The Theoretical Literature

A full review of the literature about the economics of taxation and government size is beyond the domain of this chapter. Yet it is critical to emphasize that the *RPE* literature differs from it both in the questions asked and in the methodological approach to those questions.

Whereas the *RPE* literature is primarily concerned with why govern-ments raise the revenues that they do, theoretical research on the economics of taxation has employed two frameworks which do not give voice to this concern. In the optimal private/public mix literature, typified by Samuelson (1954) and Tiebout (1956), the emphasis is on social welfare maximization, which involves describing the optimal-sized government rather than the maximum feasible government. The second related economic framework dates back at least to Ramsey (1927) and concentrates on optimal taxation. Here, the level of revenues ("size" of government) is usually assumed to be given, and the analytical spotlight is on developing rules for raising these revenues in the least distortionary manner. Consequently, the optimal private/public mix literature abstracts from the problems of feasibility (political and economic), whereas the optimal tax framework literature transforms the tax level-setting process into an immaterial issue by assumption.

Closest to the concept of *RPE* in spirit is the "predatory government" or "Leviathan" strand of the public choice literature, typified by Brennan and Buchanan (1977a, 1977b). They cast government as a principal/agent distortionary behemoth. Self-interest precludes interest in furthering the common weal. In fact, the monopoly power that government enjoys over taxation induces government to become parasitic unless Leviathan is duly constrained by a constitution that strictly delimits this power. This type of public choice literature differs most from the work on *RPE* in its form. It is almost entirely discourse and is not set up for empirical testing. As Oates (1985) has argued, the empirical tests that can be derived from the Leviathan model describe a unidimensional understanding of political power and apparently do not support the Leviathan hypothesis.

The Empirical Literature: Tax Capacity Models

The concept of tax capacity and attempts to measure it originate in the early applied local public finance literature. Efficiency criteria often dictate that some of the more lucrative taxes, like the income tax, should be collected by the national government. On the other hand, many high-cost government services, such as education, are more efficiently administered at the state or local level. Efficient taxation and efficient expenditure rules are therefore likely to cause a "fiscal mismatch," which will oblige the central government to send some revenues back to the lower levels of government. In distributing revenues back to the states, the central government should consider the needs of local government and also exert an equalizing force.[2] The problem, as Break (1980, 105) states, "is to distinguish fiscal disparities that exist independently of the subsidy recipients' behavior from those that do not." That is, local government officials may shirk their tax-raising role if they know that the central government will make up the difference in revenues. Tax capacity models were created to satisfy the central government's need for an independent monitoring tool that could determine whether local governments were making as much of a "tax effort" as other subnational governments with similar characteristics.

This literature never attempted to separate political from economic concepts of taxing capacity. Quite the contrary, public finance practitioners have been comfortable with the notion that economic optimization and political feasibility act in concert to define what is measured as the mean "established" or "accepted" practice.

The International Monetary Fund (IMF) extended the use of average tax capacity models to the international arena (Bahl 1971). It is understandable that the IMF would not dictate revenue targets purely on the basis of economic criteria, but instead opt for compromise targets based on the average observed practice of governments. IMF dicta on what should be the appropriate level of government revenue generation, even if they originate from state-of-the-art public finance modeling, are likely to meet with resistance if they are perceived as diverging significantly from average established practice.

The choice of the name "tax capacity" for these models is now unfortunate, because what they measure is average practice, which involves a mixture of technological and political constraints on raising revenue. The point is that these measures already incorporate a political distortion if they describe a consensus level of taxation.

WHAT ARE POLITICAL SCIENTISTS MEASURING? POLITICAL CAPACITY AND POLITICAL EXTRACTION

The empirical literature on political capacity, typified by Organski and Kugler (1980) and Arbetman (1990, 1995), has helped considerably in developing our understanding of why there are variations through time and across countries in the proportion of national resources that governments employ. However, in developing the literature beyond these seminal pieces, the definition of "capacity" needs to be addressed explicitly. The leading empirical works that follow the *RPE* approach accept the economic measures of capacity and treat proximity of actual resources produced to the estimated capacity as a sign of government control, and deviations from estimated capacity are interpreted as signs of weakness or strength.

The structure of arguments used by political scientists is different from that which the modeling economists use. Government objectives and constraints on realizing them are not described as explicitly. Yet it is safe to say that in the empirical specifications of political capacity there is the implicit assumption that government seeks to maximize its share of national income. *RPE* models also clearly imply that the constraints on revenue maximization are "technological" rather than microbehavioral.

There are, therefore, two issues that need to be clarified. The first issue is the current convention of employing "average practice" measurement techniques. Given the foregoing discussion, this convention now seems inappropriate and should be replaced by frontier estimation methods. The second issue concerns the theoretical underpinnings of these models. It will be argued that not only has an inappropriate measurement technique been employed, but the wrong concept might have been measured as well.

EMPIRICAL ISSUES: WE SHOULD ESTIMATE THE FRONTIER, NOT AVERAGE PRACTICE

The first issue to be addressed is the method of measurement. *RPE* theory is concerned with the possibility of gauging political power by measuring the deviation between maximum feasible revenues and revenues actually raised. Yet empirical implementations actually measure the deviation from *average* revenues raised. Frontier estimation techniques are more congruent with the theory. Beginning with Farrell (1957), frontier models were developed to address a mismatch between economic theory and empirical measurement.[3] Aigner, Lovell, and Schmidt (1977) state that most economic theory is formulated in terms of minimum or maximum extremes: efficiency loci and outer "efficiency" envelopes. In contrast, the most commonly employed econometric techniques were implicitly modelling *average* performance.

Typical empirical papers on production began by examining a theoretical model in which firms were assumed to operate in a competitive environment. In the long run, competition drives all firms in the industry to employ the same technology, reaching a zero profit equilibrium. In this equilibrium, economic survival dictates that each firm produce the greatest amount of output that is technologically feasible, given the inputs it employs. The empirical implementations of such models specify a functional form for the production function and employ data on input quantities and prices. Production or cost function parameters are estimated using standard statistical techniques as ordinary least squares (OLS). The inconsistency between theoretical and statistical models arises from the fact that commonly used estimation techniques actually measure "average" (mean) performance and not maximum feasible performance.[4] Firms that appear to be "outliers" on the upside, may actually be the more efficient producers. If this is true, then the real economic relation is described by maximum, or "frontier" performance, not by the average performance of firms.

Frontier estimation techniques were developed largely in the context of production frontier estimation. The technique has been extended to firm cost and profit functions (see Forsund et al. 1980) and also beyond firm performance to other areas, such as the estimation of earnings frontiers in the labor economics literature (Polachek and Yoon 1987, Daneshvary et al. 1992).

Like production theory, *RPE* should be measured in relation to maximum feasible, or "capacity" revenue, not in relation to average revenue. Recall that current estimates of political capacity are based on statistical models of the form

$$G_i/GNP_i = B'X_i + e_{i,}$$ (1)

where:

G = adjusted tax revenues,
B = a vector of coefficients to be estimated,
X = vector of predetermined and/or exogenous variables,
i = index of individual observations.

The set of predetermined variables used in these models varies quite a bit, but typically includes per capita *GNP* as well as the shares of trade, exports, oil, and mining revenues in *GNP*. It is typically assumed that e ~ $N(0,\sigma^2)$. That is, estimates of *B* obtained from standard statistical models assume a two-sided, symmetric error. This implicitly imposes the perplexing condition that, on average, one half of the countries will seem to be collecting more than their capacity.

Frontier estimation techniques are more congruent with the theory in that they permit the specification of a class of statistical models with one-sided errors. Those that have only a one-sided error are collectively known as "deterministic" frontier models. Models in the subclass that includes both a one-sided error and a two-sided error are known as "stochastic" frontier models. An example of the latter is

$$G_i/GNP_i = B'X_i + (u_i - v_i),$$ (2)

where:

B = a vector of coefficients to be estimated,
X = the matrix of variables that explain the ratio of government expenditures (*G*) to *GNP*, and the subscript,
i = index of individual observations.

The two-sided normally-distributed disturbance "u" represents errors caused by such things as fluctuations in natural resource prices and inclement weather. The second error term "v" represents the one-sided error that measures individual departures from the frontier, such as those that would be attributable to political factors.

The researcher has many "flavors" to choose from. One decision that must be made is whether to specify a more restrictive "deterministic" frontier model, which assumes that u=0 but allows the individual v_i to be identified, or a "stochastic" frontier model,[5] like the one in equation (1). Another choice involves the type of truncated distribution to assume for "v".[6]

WHAT IS BEING MEASURED?

By now, it should be clear that at the core of any refinement of empirical technique must lie a clear understanding of what is being measured. The meaning behind the concept of capacity can be clarified considerably by drawing a distinction between economic and political notions of the constraints on revenue.

The need to distinguish economic revenue-raising *capacity* from the purely political determinants of observed revenue-raising *practice* is at the very heart of the political capacity and *RPE* literature. As previously shown, the focus on this difference contrasts with the applied economists' goal of determining average accepted practice. If measures of political capacity are to have meaning, it is essential to first determine, for a given vector of relevant characteristics, how much revenue a country is capable of generating *without regard to the degree of political control*. In the *RPE* context, the purpose of determining revenue raising capacity is to measure political power as a residual. It is therefore essential that measures of capacity be made as free as possible from political considerations. Consequently, the concept of capacity is better represented by an economically and technologically determined frontier than by an average of established practice.

This is an important conceptual beacon: There are two sides to the problem. Irrespective of their political power, governments face an economic limit on the amount of revenue they can raise. Hence, current methods of measuring capacity also suffer from an identification problem, analogous to the one encountered when attempting to estimate price/quantity relationships in a single-equation framework. The observed share of government in *GNP* is the outcome of two separate forces, but it is being measured as though there were only one. The economic frontier that describes the maximum feasible government for any given sized private sector needs to be carefully delineated. This is the first force. The second force is the political process that establishes a preference-ranking on all public/private combinations. It is the *interaction* of economic and political forces that determines the outcomes that are actually observed.

ECONOMIC CONSTRAINTS ON EXTRACTION

Three types of constraints determine the economic frontier: endowments, production technology, and revenue raising technology. Endowments of labor, capital, and energy are the raw physical substances that exist without the complex web of human society. Production technology, which can be metaphorically referred to as engineering know-how, determines the rate at which this raw material can be transformed into things that human society values more. Therefore, the private economy, in its abstract "ideal-type," can be imagined without government—as the process which, founded upon initial ownership of endowments and guided by human preferences, uses engineering know-how to transform and distribute the raw materials.

Government intervenes in this process in two ways: It defines the rules the process must follow, and engages in direct production and distribution. It finances these activities by coercively diverting revenues from the private sector. The third type of economic constraint is, therefore, the revenue-raising technology. This revenue-raising, or extractive technology is constituted of the set of revenue-raising tools (such as tariffs, the draft, income tax, and seigniorage) and the efficiency with which these tools are used (reduction of avoidance and evasion). Consequently, when the term "economic frontier" is used in the current context, it should refer to a frontier that is defined by endowments, production technology, and extractive technology.

As previously seen, in the economics literature the shape and location of production frontiers are defined by an exogenously determined state of technology[7] available to all. Given that technology, input vectors determine the feasible placement of individuals along this outer envelope of, or limit to production possibilities. The shape and placement of the frontier are taken as exogenous, and economics enters the picture only when measuring and explaining efficiency, which is defined as the difference between production possibilities and observed outcomes.

Paradoxically, in extending this framework to the realm of political capacity, we observe that the economics of maximum feasible revenue collection plays the role of the exogenous "technological" frontier. Economics plays the role of engineering, economists the role of engineers. The capacity frontier becomes the economically determined maximum revenue that a government can collect, given the size of its private sector.

A SIMPLE MODEL

If taxation were not distortionary, the economic frontier could be visualized as a production possibilities frontier that describes the transformation of private into public goods. Consider a simple economic model, where there is one input "X" and two outputs, "P" (produced by the private sector) and "G" (produced by the government). The government consumes X_G and the private sector consumes X_P, which together must satisfy the constraint

$$X_G + X_P = X. \tag{3}$$

Furthermore, it is assumed that production functions are

$$G = G(X_G) = X_G \tag{4}$$

and

$$P = P(X_P, X_G). \tag{5}$$

Substituting equation (3) into equation (5) yields the production possibilities frontier (**PPF**),

$$P = [(X - X_G), X_G]. \tag{6}$$

Also, the marginal rate of transformation (**MRT**, or slope of the **PPF**) is given by

$$MRT = P_2 - P_1, \tag{7}$$

where the subscripts 1 and 2 indicate derivatives of equation (5) with respect to its first and second arguments.

This simple model makes it clear that, together with endowments, productive and extractive technologies determine not a level of extraction, but a frontier, or upper limit for the set of private/public mix options.

The **PPF** is shown in Figure 13.1 as the line **ab**. If government expenditures complement private expenditures, total output may rise, as over the range **ad**, defining the *GNP*-maximizing level of government expenditures of G_d. In practice, it is unlikely that any country would be found operating with $G < G_d$. This is a "non-economic" region because both government and the private sector benefit from larger government over this range. It is thus possible to understand why there are no countries completely devoid of government.[8]

Political conflict over the size of government surfaces only when a larger government arises at the cost of a smaller private sector, as is true over the range **db**. If governments are able to set a dichotomous political agenda wherein options are "take-it-or-leave-it," and "all-or-nothing", then **af** can still be considered a Pareto improvement over G=0, with all benefits conferred to government interests.[9]

The *PPF* is determined by production technology alone. The economic frontier discussed here is likely to lie within the *PPF* since Pigouvian distortions (Pigou 1947) inherent in the revenue collection mechanisms reduce total output below what would be feasible from a purely engineering standpoint. Line **ac** in Figure 13.1 thus becomes the feasible economic frontier.[10]

ECONOMIC EFFICIENCY VERSUS POLITICAL POWER

Another conceptual guide appears when the discussion of *RPC* measurement is shown in the familiar structure of Figure 13.1: TWO types of political efficiency must be measured, not one. To distinguish between them, the first kind will be referred to as "economic efficiency" in tax collection and the second as "political power." Consider point **e** in Figure 13.1. In relation to point **f**, **e** is clearly inefficient in that economic revenue collection technology makes it possible to have higher private sector expenditure, even while maintaining public expenditures at the level G_e. Similarly, for the same political cost, measured as the reduction in private expenditures given by the distance aP_e, it is possible to increase government expenditures to G_g. From either standpoint, **e** is administratively inefficient because either more government, or a larger private sector, or both can be obtained from the same resources simply by modifying revenue collection procedures.

In contrast, compare points **f** and **g**. Both points are economically efficient, but **g** involves a higher ratio of public to private expenditures. The aim of *RPE* measures should be first to establish that such differences exist and then to explain why they arise. If two nations, or one nation at two different periods in its history, face identical economic feasibility frontiers, and both are found on the frontier, why is one observed with a government of size G_g and the other with a smaller government G_e? Most economists would willingly bow out of the discussion at this point and turn it over to political scientists. But traditional measurement of political capacity confuses economic efficiency with purely political power or capacity. This can also be seen in Figure 13.1. The empirical *RPE* literature attempts to explain the ratio of government size to *GNP*. In the model and in Figure 13.1,

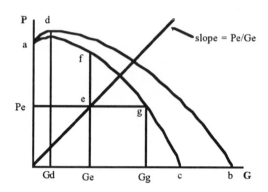

FIGURE 13.1: Political Capacity and the Economic Frontier

$$GNP = P + G \tag{8}$$

so the measure of political extraction "*PE*" becomes

$$PE = G/(P+G). \tag{9}$$

Dividing numerator and denominator by G yields

$$PE = 1/(1+P/G). \tag{10}$$

Equation (10) shows that all nations with the same P/G ratio will be measured as performing equally. However, it is clear that the ratio P/G simply describes the slope of rays going through the origin of the diagram in Figure 13.1. Traditional measures of RPE therefore do not distinguish between countries that lie inside the frontier and those that lie on the frontier.

Little confidence can be placed in the rankings that result from this method. A nation situated at point e would have political extraction measured as the ratio $PE_e = G_e/(P_e+G_e)$.[11] Political capacity for a country situated at f would be measured as $PE_f = G_f/(P_f+G_f)$. Notice that because $G_f = G_e$, $PE_f < Pe_e$, which is contrary to what seems intuitively desirable. In fact, all observations on the frontier to the northeast of the point where the ray from the origin going through e crosses the frontier would be classified as extracting less than e. All observations along that ray would be measured as equal.

Perhaps the empirical *RPE* literature has implicitly assumed that all countries function on the economic feasibility frontier. If this were so, it could be further argued that the P/G ratio fully describes location on the frontier and, in so doing, correctly ranks the political price being borne by governments at various points along the frontier. However, this line of argument does not work well either. First, it is not enough to assume that governments always operate on *the* frontier because there is more than one frontier. In fact there is an infinite number, a "map" of such frontiers: one for each resource endowment.

Second, for a literature whose theoretical insight is often empirically driven, it seems incongruent to assume away what might be tested. Would it be flying in the face of accepted political theory to argue that governments purposely operate inside the economic frontier? On the contrary, there are many examples of governments raising revenues in a manner that is known to be economically inefficient.[12]

Another interesting distinction is made apparent by this alternative theoretical perspective, namely the distinction between the *total* cost of government and the *marginal* cost of government. The total cost of government is the change in the private sector that would result from reducing G from its reference level to zero. The marginal cost of government is given by the slope of the economic frontier,[13] and this slope may be different on different frontiers, even along a given P/G ray. Consider two countries, one operating on the frontier at point **g** in Figure 13.1 and the other operating inside the frontier at point **e**. The total cost of government is the same for both countries, namely the distance between points **a** and P_e. The marginal cost of government is zero for the first country and is given by the slope of the frontier at point **g** for the economically efficient government. Which is more important, the marginal or the total cost of government?

If governments are assumed to be administratively efficient, then the emphasis is on marginal cost. The assertion that P/G fully captures the price of government, therefore, actually assumes two things: that all countries operate on the frontier and that the slopes of the frontiers are the same along any ray through the origin.[14]

In summary, it is necessary to distinguish measures of economic efficiency from measures of political power. Economic efficiency determines whether the public/private mix is on the economic frontier. Political power explains the relative placement of nations *along* the public/private frontier. Given the state of economic technology, the placement of individual nations along the frontier may depend on factors which vary nation to nation, such as type of political system, means of income distribution, degree of ethnic homogeneity, prevalence of military conflict, and size of natural resource endowment.[15] Placement within the frontier because of politically-induced administrative inefficiency is also possible, and measures of *RPE* should be careful to distinguish this possibility as well.

MEASURING THE FRONTIER: EMPIRICAL SPECIFICATION

The theoretical model developed here is relatively straightforward. Implementing it empirically will be somewhat more difficult. Consider the simplest sort of two-sector specification: an economy with two inputs, K and L, which are employed in producing private output, P and public output, G. The outputs are produced with Cobb-Douglas technology of the form

$$P = K^{\alpha} L^{\beta} \tag{11}$$

$$G = K^{\tau} L^{\Phi}. \tag{12}$$

Total output for the economy at any given point in time is given by $GNP = P + G$. The resource endowment constraints

$$K_p + K_g = \underline{K} \tag{13}$$

$$L_p + L_g = \underline{L} \tag{14}$$

imply an economic link between the private and public sectors, which defines the production possibilities frontier. In this example, the frontier can be shown to take on the shape given by

$$ln \, P = \alpha \cdot ln \, K^y + \beta \cdot ln \, \{\underline{L} - [G^{(1/\Phi)} \div K_g^{(\tau/\Phi)}]\}. \tag{15}$$

Equation (15) describes a function that assumes its maximum value when $G = 0$. Although this appears to violate the previous assertion that there may exist a range over which private output and public output are complementary, empirical implementations of equation (15) provide a reasonable approximation to the true functional form, as long as there are no observations in the noneconomic region.

The problem here is that the relation between G and P in equation (15) is highly nonlinear, which rules out the class of simpler estimators that have been employed to date. An alternative approach is to specify a translog (Berndt and Christensen 1972) or similar form that, although not derived directly from a fully specified model, can be assumed to approximate a general functional form.[16] Equation (15) then becomes

$$\ln P = \alpha_0 + \alpha_K \ln(K_p) + \alpha_L \ln(L_p p) + \alpha_g \ln(G) \qquad (16)$$
$$+ 1/2 \{\beta_{kk} [\ln(K_p)]^2 + \beta_{11} [\ln(L_p)]^2 + \beta_{gg} [\ln(G)]^2\}$$
$$+ \tau_{kl} [\ln(K_p)] [\ln(L_p)] + \tau_{kg} [\ln(K_p)] [\ln(G)]$$
$$+ \tau_{lg} [\ln(L_p)] [\ln(G)] + (u\text{-}v).$$

Here u and v are, respectively, the two and one-sided errors described in Equation (1). Equation (16) can and, if possible, should be modified to account for differences in human capital. Note that Equations (1) and (16) differ in substance as well as in form. For example, the latter equation depends only on the productive resources available to the private sector, including government output.

CONCLUDING COMMENTS

The conceptual underpinnings of *RPE* measurement have been explored. Two modifications are suggested. The first is that estimates of frontier be used rather than average revenue collections as the standard against which the relative political capacity of governments is measured (see Chapter 14). The second is that the *RPE* discussion be shaped so that the relation between economic efficiency and political power will be made clearer. This reshaping of the discussion will require estimating the economic frontier. The economic literature on tax capacity might also benefit from being recast in a manner that distinguishes movements along the frontier from movements toward the frontier. A host of statistical and theoretical issues await resolution in the refinement of this new approach to measuring political capacity.

NOTES

1. I am indebted to Marina Arbetman for her encouragement and guidance in writing this chapter.

2. See Musgrave (1961) and Oates (1972, 81-85) for early discussions of intergovernmental grants.

3. Forsund et al. (1980) provide an excellent survey and discussion of the literature.

4. For example, in a simple one-variable linear model, with a zero intercept, the OLS estimator collapses to the sample mean.

5. See van der Broek, et al. (1980). Battese and Coelli (1988) and Cornwell, et al. (1990) discuss approaches that employ panel data to identify individual deviations from the frontier.

6. See Bauer (1990) for a recent survey.

7. A state of techonoology such as might be given by established engineering practices.

8. It is also quite possible that the frontier is D-shaped, meaning that the maximum absolute size of government is reached at some $P^*>0$, well before the private sector shrinks to zero. In this case a second noneconomic region $P = \{P: P<P^*$ and $G<G_{max}\}$ would exist, over which self-interested government would seek a larger private sector. The current "economic liberalization" of China is an example of this concept.

9. G_f is similar to the "reversion" level described in the model developed in Romer and Rosenthal (1979).

10. Following traditional specifications, this lower frontier would also be determined by such technological constraints as the state of knowledge about tax system design, recordkeeping, compliance, monitoring, and enforcement.

11. Subscripts indicate levels of G or P associated with those points. To avoid cluttering the diagram, not all such levels are indicated in Figure 13.1.

12. For example, Latin American governments have often financed expenditures with inflation or trade taxes even though income and value added taxes are widely thought to be more economically efficient. Interesting discussions on this topic as it relates to Brazil are found in Edwards and Oliveira (1993).

13. The marginal rate of transformation of private into public goods.

14. The class of homothetic functions satisfies the second assumption. If outcomes are viewed as resulting from constrained optimization, then the objective functions would also have to be homothetic. The slope of the economic frontier at the observed outcomes could then be called "prices."

15. The size of the natural resource endowment will affect placement along the frontier to the extent that the public is myopic with regard to revenue extraction. That is, revenue exraction is less politically costly for government from one source (say oil revenues) than from another (say income taxes). A full inquiry into these issues is beyond the scope of this chapter (see Chapter 1 of this volume).

16. Another advantage of the translog specification is that it permits an easy test of the homotheticity assumption.

14

New Estimates of Political Capacity

Cheryl M. Holsey and Ling Cao[1]

INTRODUCTION

Over the past two decades an extensive literature has been developed based on Organski and Kugler's (1980) approach to measuring the political capacity of governments. This literature has progressed greatly, particularly in the area of identifying variables capable of determining *RPE* levels. However, in one important respect it remains lacking. As Edwards (Chapter 13) suggests, researchers have not taken advantage of relatively recent developments in econometric theory to further refine *RPE* estimates. Although prior research has constructed estimates using the ordinary least squares (OLS) estimating technique, the frontier estimation (FE) procedure provides an approach that is ideally suited to the construction of *RPE* estimates.

In this chapter, the advantages of employing the FE technique are explored. A detailed explanation of the manner in which such estimates can be obtained and an illustration based on these procedures are provided.[2] Initial analysis employs the FE-based measure of *RPE* as the independent variable, and these results are then compared to those obtained with OLS-based estimates of *RPE*. The next section describes the specific procedures employed to construct FE-based estimates within the context of pooled cross-sectional, time-series data sets, followed by the estimations and a brief comparison to OLS-based estimates. Concluding remarks are presented in the last section. Although the analysis does not provide strong support for the new empirical approach, it does reveal that there are important distinctions between empirical results when OLS-based estimates are replaced by the FE-based estimates of *RPE*.

A THEORETICAL COMPARISON OF FE AND OLS-BASED ESTIMATES

John Edwards (Chapter 13) discusses the limitations of OLS-based estimates of *RPE* and the advantages inherent in the FE technique. Here we revisit these issues. For example, the FE technique allows construction of the *RPE* variable concentrating on absolute (APC) rather than relative levels of political capacity. This concept of *APC* is superior to *RPE* because it allows for comparisons between countries regardless of levels of development. An appropriate measure of *APE* would be the proportion of potential resources that a particular government is able to collect through its political effectiveness. *APE* can be implemented empirically focusing on tax revenues as follows:

$$Y_i = \alpha + \beta X_i + v_i - \mu_i \tag{1}$$

where:
Y_i = the actual tax revenue for the ith country,
X_i = an economic variable (such as per capita income) that determines potential tax collections,[3]
v_i = the usual white noise disturbance term.[4]

The μ_i term is of special interest because it reflects the political capacity of the country in extracting private sector resources. This is a particularly convenient solution to the lack of directly observable measures of political capacity that take into account the effects of the unobservable, and therefore omitted, variables. In equation (1), μ_i is the lower bound and assumes a value of zero if the country's political machinery is perfectly effective, and it assumes a positive value as the country exhibits lower levels of political capacity. This interpretation of μ_i is fundamentally different from the usual white noise disturbance term v_i. In particular, μ_i cannot be assumed to have a mean value of zero because it is a positive-only disturbance term.

Within the context of equation (1), the political extraction variable (*PE*) can be stated as:

$$PE_i = \frac{\alpha + \beta X_i - \mu_{it}}{\alpha + \beta X_i} \tag{2}$$

where $\alpha + \beta X_i - \mu_i$ equals tax collections. Potential tax collections equal $\alpha + \beta X_i$ when governments are perfectly efficient, and since the political extraction variable is a ratio, its values are bounded by zero and one.[5]

Construction of the *PE* variables requires estimation of equation (1), since neither the numerator nor the denominator of equation (2) is observable. However, due to the presence of the additional disturbance term (μ_i), the parameters of interest cannot be estimated unless further restrictions are applied to the specification. Unfortunately, such restrictions do not allow construction of the absolute *PE* level, but rather allow only the construction of measures of political extraction relative (*RPE*) to the ability of other countries to extract taxes. *RPE* serves as an adequate substitute for the more desirable, but unavailable, *PE* variable.

Prior efforts to construct *RPE* measures have been based on the OLS estimating technique (see Chapter 1). The general procedure has been to combine the disturbance terms μ_i and v_i into a single (composite) disturbance term to estimate equation (1) using the OLS procedure, as follows:

$$\hat{RPE} = \frac{Y_i}{\hat{\alpha} + \hat{\beta} X_i} \tag{3}$$

where Y_i is actual tax revenues.

The denominator of equation (3) causes this ratio to be interpreted as relative rather than absolute political capacity. To obtain desirable estimator properties using OLS, one must assume that the composite disturbance term ($v_i - \mu_i$) has a zero mean (Kugler 1983). Therefore, the μ_i term can no longer be viewed as a one-sided disturbance term, where zero indicates 100% political capacity and positive values imply inefficiency. Instead, μ_i must be considered a two-sided error term with a mean value of zero, where positive values imply above average political capacity or effectiveness levels, and negative values imply below average political capacity levels. Moreover, $\alpha + \beta X_i$, the fitted value of Y_i from the regression procedure, must be reinterpreted as the (estimated) average value of Y_i relative to the average political extraction level of a government with this particular level of economic resources.[6]

The discussion of the OLS-based estimate illustrates that the denominator of equation (3) estimates average performance and does not estimate potential tax collections for a particular government, as called for in the original theory (Organski & Kugler 1980). Furthermore, Y_i, defined as ($\alpha + \beta X_i + v_i - \mu_i$) in the OLS specification, fails to measure taxes that a particular government is able to collect solely *through its political effectiveness* as called for in the original theory. Instead, the numerator of the OLS estimate provides for actual tax collections and includes increases or decreases because of random shocks to the economy and/or political system. Consequently, the OLS-based estimates of *RPE* fail to capture either the number or the denominator implied by the original theory. The FE technique for estimating *RPE* measures is introduced as an alternative closer to the original conception. Although the FE procedure is described in the next section, several points are pertinent to the current discussion. In finite sample sizes, the FE estimate of political extraction must be considered a relative rather than an absolute estimate, as is the case of OLS. However, the meaning of relative is fundamentally different across the two estimation procedures. Within the context of OLS, relative implies political extraction levels compared to the average political capacity of countries. In the context of FE procedure, comparisons are made relative to the level of *PE* attained by the most efficient country (or government) in the data set (Cornwell, Schmidt and Sickles 1990).

FE-based estimates of *RPE* can be illustrated by altering the equation for the PE variable (equation 2) as follows:

$$\hat{RPE_i} = \frac{\hat{\alpha} + \hat{\beta X_i} - \hat{\mu_i^*}}{\hat{\alpha} + \hat{\beta X_i}}.\tag{4}$$

Note that with the exception of μ_i^*, each parameter and coefficient is identical to that of equation (2). The residual term (μ_i^*) takes into account the political incapacity (or ineffectiveness) of the ith country relative to that of the most efficient country in the data set, rather than the absolute level as implied by equation (2).

However, the FE-based estimates can be considered absolute measures of political extraction levels in the limit. As sample size increases toward infinity, μ_i^* approaches μ_i, and the frontier-based *RPE* estimator converges to the estimate of PE as defined in equation (2), since the efficiency level of the most efficient observation approaches 100% efficiency (Schmidt and Sickles 1984).

THE FRONTIER ESTIMATION PROCEDURE

In this section, the specific procedures employed to construct FE-based estimates of *RPE* variables are described within the context of pooled cross-sectional, time-series data for N countries and T time periods. Although there are several ways to estimate stochastic frontier models, the analysis presented here is based on a technique developed by Schmidt and Sickles (1984) and extended by Cornwell, Schmidt, and Sickles (1990), Hausman and Taylor (1981) and Amemiya and McCurdy (1986). This methodology produces consistent estimates of the political incapacity term

(μ_i), and it achieves this goal without placing restrictive assumptions on the distribution of μ_i (see Jondrow et al. 1982).

Within the context of a pooled data set, the theoretical specification for actual tax collections (equation 1) can be restated as:

$$Y_{it} = \alpha + \beta X_{it} + v_{it} - \mu_{it},\qquad(5)$$

where:

Y_{it} = the actual tax revenue for the ith country in time period t,
X_{it} = an economic variable (such as per-capita income) which determines potential tax collections,[7]
v_{it} = the usual white-noise disturbance term.[8]

As in equation 1, the disturbance term μ_{it} reflects the level of political inefficiency or incapacity, and it is assumed to be a one-sided disturbance term that is greater than or equal to zero.

As specified above, the parameters of interest in equation (5) (α, β, and μ_{it}) cannot be estimated because the specification implies a different level of political inefficiency for each observation in the data set, unless additional assumptions concerning the behavior of the political incapacity variable are made. Following Cornwell et al. (1990), who assume that inefficiency is a quadratic function of time, equation (5) can be respecified by the following set of equations:

$$Y_{it} = \alpha_{it}^{*} + \beta X_{it} + v_{it},\qquad(6)$$

$$\alpha_{it}^{*} = \Theta_{i1} + \Theta_{i2}t + \Theta_{i3}t^2,\qquad(7)$$

$$\Theta_{i1} = \alpha - \mu_i.\qquad(8)$$

In equation (6), the political incapacity disturbance term (μ_{it}) has been incorporated into the intercept term, where individual country and time-specific intercepts are a function of a constant intercept (α), and the country and time-specific political incapacity disturbance term (μ_{it}). Consequently, the intercept term (α_{it}^{*}) varies across both time and cross-sectional units. Equation (6) cannot be estimated without the addition of further restrictions because it requires the estimation of a separate intercept term for each observation as well as an estimate of the common slope coefficient (β). Equations (7) and (8) introduce restrictions that enable the estimation of equation (6). Equation (7) states that for each country, the intercept varies over time (t) in a quadratic fashion. Because variations in the intercept are caused entirely by the disturbance term μ_{it}^{*}, political inefficiency for a particular country varies over time in the same quadratic fashion. If $\Theta_{i2} > 0$ and $\Theta_{i3} < 0$, for example, then political incapacity levels within a particular country follow an increasing path over time, but at a decreasing rate. Other trends are possible, depending on the signs of the theta parameters.[9] Equation (8) specifies that the country-specific intercept term (Θ_{i1}) is a function of the original intercept term (α), which is constant across both cross-sectional units and time periods, and a country-specific component (μ_i) that reflects each country's initial political incapacity level for the base time period (when t = 0).

To illustrate how equations (6) through (8) can be used to estimate β and μ_{it}, the Schmidt and Sickles (1984) simplified version of the model, in which inefficiency levels vary only across cross-sectional units, is first considered. Assuming time invariant political incapacity levels, Θ_{i2} and Θ_{i3} of equation (7) both equal zero, and the set of equations therefore reduces to:

$$Y_{it} = \hat{\alpha}_i^* + \hat{\beta}X_{it} + v_i, \tag{9}$$

$$\hat{\alpha}_i^* = \alpha - \mu_i. \tag{10}$$

Equation (9) is the well-known dummy variable or fixed effects model commonly employed for pooled cross-sectional, time-series data sets. To obtain estimates of β and $\hat{\alpha}_i^*$, Schmidt and Sickles employ the standard procedure of applying OLS to the equation. They then obtain estimates of μ_i by assuming that the most efficient cross-sectional unit in the data set, i.e., the country with the largest estimate of $\hat{\alpha}_i^*$, is 100% efficient, implying that the estimate of μ_i for this particular cross-sectional unit is zero. Estimates of political incapacity for other countries are subsequently calculated by subtracting individual intercept estimates from that of the most efficient cross-sectional unit. A geometrical representation of the Schmidt and Sickles technique for three countries is illustrated in Figure 14.1. An OLS estimation of equation (9) produces estimates of the country-specific intercept terms as well as an estimate of the common slope coefficient. Because the intercept term for country 1 has the highest estimated value, country 1 is designated as politically efficient and μ_1 is set equal to zero. Estimates of political incapacity for Countries 2 and 3 are then calculated by subtracting $\hat{\alpha}_2^*$ from $\hat{\alpha}_1^*$ and $\hat{\alpha}_3^*$ from $\hat{\alpha}_1^*$, respectively.

It is important to note that $(1 - \mu_i)$ is the estimate of RPE_i as defined in equation (4). Because μ_i is calculated as the estimate of μ_i relative to that of the most efficient country in the sample, it is obviously a measure of relative rather than absolute political incapacity. In addition, the procedure has the effect of normalizing μ_i so that this estimate reflects

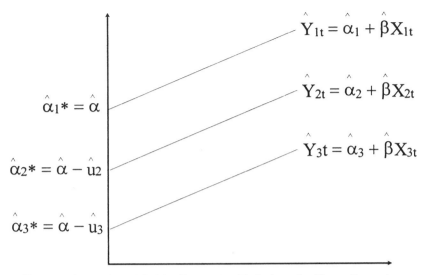

$$\hat{Y}_{1t} = \hat{\alpha}_1 + \hat{\beta} X_{1t}$$

$$\hat{Y}_{2t} = \hat{\alpha}_2 + \hat{\beta} X_{2t}$$

$$\hat{\alpha}_1{}^* = \hat{\alpha}$$

$$\hat{Y}_{3t} = \hat{\alpha}_3 + \hat{\beta} X_{3t}$$

$$\hat{\alpha}_2{}^* = \hat{\alpha} - \hat{u}_2$$

$$\hat{\alpha}_3{}^* = \hat{\alpha} - \hat{u}_3$$

FIGURE 14.1 Schmidt and Sickles Estimation Technique for These Countries

the proportion of political incapacity of the ith country, therefore $(1 - \mu_i)$ reflects the proportion of political incapacity of the ith country. If, for example, $(1 - \mu_i) = 0.80$ then the ith country is operating at 80% of its political capacity, i.e., it is collecting 80% of its potential tax collections ($RPE_i = .80$).

With this background, an estimation within the context of the more sophisticated model implied by equations (6) through (8) can be considered. The usual assumption in the RPE literature that μ_i and X_i are uncorrelated is given, and the FGLS procedure in the actual estimation of RPE_{it} variables is used. The discussion will focus on this process.

As opposed to the fixed effects model, which concentrates exclusively on equations (6) through (8), the first step of the FGLS procedure is to estimate equation (5).[10] The FGLS residuals are then regressed on a constant, time and time squared as implied by equation 7 using the OLS estimating technique.[11] Estimates of the country- and time-specific intercept terms ($\hat{\alpha}_{it}{}^*$) are then obtained by constructing the fitted values from this second regression procedure. Estimates of μ_{it} are obtained in a similar way to that described above in the simple case, except that a perfectly efficient country is designated for each time interval. As such, T observations are considered 100% efficient. Consequently, there are T observations where μ_i is set equal to zero. Estimates of political incapacity for other countries are then calculated by subtracting individual country- and time-specific intercepts from the intercept of the most efficient country for that particular time period.[12]

FE-BASED ESTIMATES OF *RPE*

The procedures described in the previous section enable construction of individual country- and time-specific FE-based estimates of *RPE* for 81 countries over a 32-year interval from 1960 through 1991. Since the ultimate purpose is to compare FE-based estimates of *RPE* against those using OLS-based estimates, the estimates are constructed in a manner consistent with assumptions and variables employed in developing OLS-based estimates of *RPE*. Within this context, the specification for actual tax collections can be restated (equation 1) following that of Kugler and Arbetman (Chapter 1), but adding some variables to control for possible intercept dummy variations across observations:

$$TAX.GDP = f(\alpha, AGR/GDP, EXP/GDP, MIN/GDP,$$
$$HEALTHEX, GDP, WAR, OIL, v, \mu) \tag{11}$$

where f is assumed to be a general linear function and each variable implies a vector of country- and time-specific values. The added variables *WAR* and *OIL* take on a value of 1 if the country is involved in an external war at time t, or if it is a major (non-OPEC member) oil exporter for the post-1972 years; v is the white noise disturbance term; and μ is the one-sided disturbance term reflecting political incapacity levels.[13]

Organski and Kugler's original specification has been expanded to include several additional variables. *GDP* controls for the effects of business cycles, and its expected sign is ambiguous. A recession, for example, negatively affects both the numerator and the denominator of *TAX/GDP*. Consequently, the overall effect of decreased *GDP* levels depends on which effect (if any) dominates. Positive signs are expected for the *OIL* and *WAR* coefficients, because tax collections increase in war periods and oil-based economies provide an exceptionally accessible tax base for suitably endowed countries.

FE-based estimates of *RPE* are constructed following the explained procedures. Therefore, the initial step is to perform this regression on equation (11) using FGLS. FGLS residuals are then regressed against a constant, time, and time squared as implied by equation (7). The estimates of country- and time-specific intercept terms ($\alpha_{it}*$) are obtained by calculating fitted values from this second OLS regression procedure.

The final step in constructing individual estimates of μ_{it} deviates slightly from that described. Rather than designate a single country as the most efficient in each time period, four separate countries are designated as 100% politically efficient. Therefore, each group has a different intercept for its frontier boundary. One reason for this deviation is that there are obvious differences in potential political capacity levels inherent in the data set, which includes countries spanning the spectrum from developing to industrialized nations. Therefore, estimates of the country- and time-specific intercept terms ($\alpha_{it}*$) are split into three developmental groups: Developed (OECD countries), Developing, and Least Developed.[14] A fourth category contains OPEC member countries, because their abundant oil resources provide a unique tax base, which implies a higher intercept term for a given level of political capacity. Within each of the four groups, estimates of political capacity for nonefficient countries are calculated by subtracting individual country- and time-specific intercepts from the intercept of the most efficient country for that particular time period in that particular group.

Results of the FGLS regression of equation (11) are presented in the first column of Table 14.1. Estimated coefficients for *AGR/GDP, EXP/GDP, HEALTHEX, GDP,* and *OIL* are of the expected sign and significant at the one percent level. Although the negative signs of the *RMIN* and *WAR* coefficient estimates are opposite to that predicted by theory, neither coefficient is significant, and the results are consistent with prior estimates.

Primary interest lies in the FE-based estimates of *RPE* and how they compare to OLS-based estimates (see Chapter 1 of this volume). Figure 14.2 illustrates both estimates of *RPE* for the United Kingdom. Perusal of this graph reveals that there is a marked difference in yearly variation: FE-based estimates follow fairly stable trend patterns, whereas OLS-based

TABLE 14.1 FGLS Regression Results for Equation (12)

Variables	Coefficient	Std. Error	T-value
TAX/GD			
AGR/GDP	-0.1744	0.0124	-14.09**
EXP/GDP	0.0835	0.0105	7.97**
MIN/GDP	-0.0041	0.0216	-0.19
HEALTHEX	0.7270	0.0609	11.93**
GDP	-0.218e-10	0.064e-10	-3.44
WAR	-0.0054	0.0044	-1.24
OIL	0.0411	0.0076	5.41**
R^2	0.23		
Number of Observ.	2510		

* Significant at 5 percent level.
** Significant at 1 percent level.

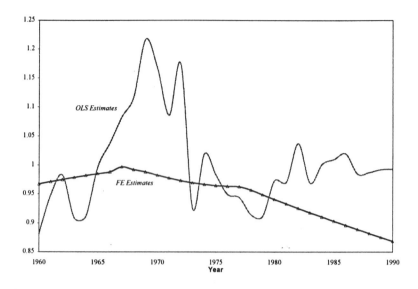

FIGURE 14.2 FE- and OLS-Based Estimates of *RPE* for United Kingdom

estimates vary widely. For the data set, average yearly variation in the FE-based estimate of *RPE* is only 0.53%, whereas the OLS-based estimate on average varies yearly by 4.68%.

The fact that the FE-based estimates are generally stable suggests the superiority of these estimates of political capacity. Consider the case of the United Kingdom from 1970 through 1974. OLS-based estimates show a decrease in *RPE* of approximately 7% from 1970 to 1971, followed by an increase of approximately 8% in 1972, a decrease of approximately 21% in 1973, and an increase of approximately 10% in 1974. These variations are simply counterintuitive: It is difficult to believe that governmental strength, particularly in a developed country, would follow such wide swings. The FE-based estimates, on the other hand, show consistent but minor decreases in political strength over this period: -0.51%, -0.44%, -0.37% and -0.29%, respectively. Therefore, they portray a more believable pattern of political power over time.

The technical reason for the variational difference across estimators is most likely caused by the numerator of the OLS-based estimator, which is defined by equation (3). Recall from the prior discussion that the OLS-based measure employs actual tax collections (Y_i) as its numerator, and that Y_i is equal to $\alpha + \beta X_i + v_i - \mu_i$. Consequently, it fails to match the original Kugler and Organski conception of *PE* (equation 2) because of the additional disturbance term, v_i. Furthermore, v_i follows the usual white noise pattern with a zero mean and with randomly distributed positive and negative values across observations. Therefore, it is likely that the oscillating pattern exhibited by the OLS-based estimates of *RPE* for the United Kingdom, as well as those of other countries, are caused by these random shock patterns. As such, the variational difference between FE- and OLS-based estimates is caused by the artificial variation in the OLS estimates, created by the erroneous inclusion of the random error term, v_i.

There are several empirical issues that need to be addressed by the *RPE* literature before definitive FE-based *RPE* estimates can be constructed. For example, prior research has tested for the presence of heteroskedasticity or serial correlation in pooled cross-sectional, time-series data sets, but has not tested for the validity of the common slope coefficient assumption, even though these countries exhibit a wide range of economic development (Organski and Kugler 1980: Appendix). In addition, treating certain regressors such as *GDP* and *HEALTHEX* as exogenous to the model is highly questionable, implying that two-stage least-squares estimation of equation (11) might be required to produce estimators with desirable properties.

In the FE estimate, the assumption that political inefficiency and independent variables are uncorrelated should be tested.[15] If this assumption is violated, then it is inappropriate to construct FE-based *RPE* estimates (as has been done) using the FGLS technique. A distinct advantage of the FE procedure over the OLS procedure, however, is that, although this assumption must hold under OLS, in the FE procedure it simply means that estimates must be obtained using the fixed effects (dummy variable) model as described.

CONCLUDING REMARKS

As noted at the outset of this chapter, the concept and operationalization of political capacity have produced a thriving and highly promising literature. Its progress, however, has been limited by a prior inability to develop estimates of *RPE* that are consistent with the original theory. The analysis addresses this issue by introducing the FE-based estimate of *RPE*. In addition, the econometric methodology required to construct such an estimate is described and illustrates that empirical analysis within the context of the FE-based estimate differs substantially from that employing the standard OLS-based measure of *RPE*. It should be stressed that the FE-based measure is not simply a refinement of current technique. Although the FE-based estimates of *RPE* have of necessity been quite preliminary, the analysis suggests that further refinement of these estimators is a fruitful avenue for future research.

NOTES

1. During the conference on Economic Behavior and Political Capacity at Claremont in 1993, John Edwards suggested this avenue of estimation as a theoretically superior approach.

2. *RPE* estimates are constructed within the context of assumptions currently used in OLS-based estimates to enable controlled comparisons between the two techniques.

3. For simplicity, the specification is limited to a single independent variable.

4. Note that the white noise disturbance term is denoted by v rather than by the more standard designation μ. This is done to conform with existing notation in the frontier estimation literature.

5. For example, for a government operating at 100% political capacity, μ_i equals zero and PE_i equals one. If a government is less than 100% effective, μ_i is positive and PE_i is a value between zero and one.

6. Note that the fitted value of Y_i is usually referred to as the estimated average value of Y_i for a given X_i.

7. For the sake of simplicity, the specification is limited to a single independent variable.

8. As Greene (1980) notes, the assumption that v_i is a two-sided disturbance term denotes a stochastic frontier model, whereas assuming v_i to be a one-sided disturbance term would imply a full frontier model.

9. The time path for political incapacity need not follow the quadratic assumption. It could also be assumed to be a simple linear function, a cubic function, or even a higher level function of time.

10. If α_M is denoted as the estimate of the intercept for the cross-sectional unit at 100% efficiency, and $\hat{\alpha}_j$ as the estimate for another cross-sectional unit, then:

$$\hat{\mu}_j = \hat{\alpha}_M - \hat{\alpha}_j = \alpha - \hat{\mu}_M - (\alpha - \hat{\mu}_j) = \hat{\mu}_j, \text{ since } \hat{\mu}_M = 0.$$

11. It is useful to note that estimates of RPE_i can also be obtained through a feasible generalized least squares procedure (FGLS), if it can be assumed that μ_i and X_i are uncorrelated. In this case, equations (9) and (10) are restated as:

$$Y_{it} = \alpha + \beta X_{it} + v_{it} - \mu_i$$

where μ_i has been restored to its original position as a component of the composite disturban¢e term. This equation is a version of the random effects model for pooled cross-sectional, time-series data sets, and estimates of the slope and intercept are obtained directly from FGLS estimation. As described by Schmidt and Sickles, estimates of α_i^* are retrieved by computing the average of the residual terms for each cross-sectional unit. Estimates of μ_i and RPE_i are then calculated following the procedures just described for the fixed effects model.

12. If α_{Mt} is denoted as the estimate of the intercept for the cross-sectional unit

at 100% efficiency at time t, and α_{jt} as the estimate for another cross-sectional unit at time t, then:

$$\hat{\mu}_{jt} = \hat{\alpha}_{Mt} - \hat{\alpha}\tau_j = \alpha - \hat{\mu}_{Mt} - (\alpha - \hat{\mu}_{jt}) = \hat{\mu}_{jt}, \; since \; \hat{\mu}_{Mt} = 0.$$

13. As is well-established in the economics literature, automatic stabilizers cause tax collections to increase during boom periods (when *GDP* is high) and to decrease during recessionary periods (when *GDP* is low). These effects must be controlled for in order to assume that the disturbance term μ_i reflects only political ineffectiveness.

14. The classification system roughly follows that of Kugler et al. (1994). OPEC countries are treated separately.

15. In fact, the analysis provides preliminary evidence of the invalidity of this assumption. Using the Hausman (1978) test, the null hypothesis that the disturbance term and the independent variables are uncorrelated was rejected.

15

Alternative Approaches to Estimating Political Capacity

Thomas D. Willett

INTRODUCTION

The concept of political capacity developed by Organski and Kugler "attempts to capture whether elites have the tools to tap into human and material resources in their societies ... and use them for national purposes" (1980, 69). It focuses on "the capacity of the political system to carry out the tasks chosen by the nation's government in the face of domestic and international groups with competing priorities" (Kugler 1994). In the terminology of the recent literature on international political economy, political capacity refers to a combination of the competence of the government and its degree of autonomy from domestic societal pressures.[1]

A major virtue of this concept is that it is not institution specific; instead, it can be applied equally to systems with varying degrees of democracy and authoritarian control. This is especially important in light of the recent political economy research that documents the excessively simplified attempts to explain the performance of countries in different economic policy areas as a simple function of whether they have democratic or authoritarian political structures.[2] There can be both strong and weak democratic systems and strong and weak authoritarian regimes (see Chapter 1 and 2).

Efforts to develop cross-country measures of political strength are of obvious importance, and in my judgment Organski, Kugler, and Arbetman made a wise decision in focusing on tax revenues and population reach as their metric for investigation. As they note in this volume: "Few operations of government depend so heavily on popular support—or on fear of punishment." They emphasize that one should not look at the magnitude of tax revenues alone. Their focus is on trying to capture "political efficiency" or the strength of governments, which they argue will be related to some type of concept of revenues relative to taxable capacity, i.e., some type of measure of tax effort.

Despite the substantial problems involved in implementing this approach, the empirical work produced by Organski, Kugler, Arbetman and their students and colleagues has clearly demonstrated that this has been a fruitful avenue of research. As the papers in this volume demonstrate, the explanatory power of this approach with respect to a wide range of policy areas is quite remarkable. This has been especially so with respect to developing countries. The application to high-income industrial countries is much more difficult, in large part, I believe, because the political assumptions underlying their approach are more questionable in that setting, as discussed in the next section. Next an analysis of the structure of taxation is discussed as an alternative type of measure that is not as subject to these problems. The issues raised focus on the measures of political extraction and do not apply to the useful extension of the analysis by Arbetman to consider political reach as a separate dimension of political capacity.

AMBIGUITIES IN THE CONCEPT OF POLITICAL CAPACITY

The concept of political capacity is frequently described in terms of the ability of elites to reach the population and extract resources from society. This can be read as a fundamentally different concept from the effectiveness of society in organizing itself to extract the resources necessary to achieve common purposes such as the provision of national defense and other public goods. Among the various descriptions of political capacity that have been offered, both concepts can be found. In many settings these two different concepts would not offer greatly different predictions. At relatively low levels of political development, if governments do not squander a huge proportion of the revenues raised, then one would expect increases in tax revenue relative to estimates of an economies' taxable capacity or measures of reach to be a reasonable proxy for increasing strength of government in either sense. Thus Organski-Kugler-Arbetman type measures of political capacity should work relatively well for many developing countries, and this does appear to be the case.

However, as incomes and the level of political development increase, the fit between political extraction and the measures proposed should decline. The proportion of government spending devoted to the most important common purposes, such as provision of basic infrastructures, seems likely to decline. Consider, for example, two pure or ideal types of government spending. One is for the provision of public goods, which provide general benefits such as national security, improving the performance of the economy, etc. The second type is special interest redistribution, with the redistribution going to rent-seeking groups and individuals—not broadly supported humanitarian aid for the poor. Of course, most policies will contain a combination of both elements, but the proportions are likely to vary greatly across different government expenditures.[3] The basic point is that in such a world the volume of a government's activity may not be a good indicator of its capacity. It takes a strong government to abstain from activity that may serve special interests but harm the overall operation of the economy. Miles Kahler has called this the "orthodox paradox." For example, the increased incidence of protectionist policies in the United States over the last several decades reflects primarily a weakening of the strength of the government to hold off the pressures from special interests, not the strong autonomous government manipulating the economy for strategic gains that is envisioned in the realist paradigm of international political economy (see Willett 1995).

For advanced economies, decisions to spend and tax less may reflect a government that is more responsive to the interests of the general public and less responsive to special interests. In such cases, fewer taxes would be a sign of a strong, not a weak government. In general, as the ratio of rent-seeking to efficiency-enhancing policies increases, the ratio of tax revenues raised relative to simple measures of taxable capacity should be less useful as a measure of political strength. Of course, conceptually one can attempt to make adjustments for this, but this involves a much greater order of difficulty than is involved in present estimates of taxable capacity.

Efforts to make such adjustments would also have to squarely confront the differences in the two different concepts of political capacity discussed above. Under the first concept, that of extracting resources from society, redistribution in favor of "the government" or "the elites" would represent an increase in political capacity, while redistribution to "domestic and international groups with competing priorities" would reflect a decline in political efficiency or capacity.

From the standpoint of the second concept, that of extraction only for social purposes, increases in either form of redistribution would represent a decline in "political efficiency."[4] Note that from the standpoint of the second concept, political efficiency and the strength of the state are no longer synonymous. While greater redistribution to government elites could still plausibly be associated with a stronger government, it would reflect a decline in political efficiency. Greater redistribution to other rent-seeking groups would be associated with both decreases in political efficiency and decreases in the "strength" of government. Thus while from this perspective the government could be too strong, even where this were the case a weakening of government strength would not automatically imply an increase in political efficiency. These are challenges for more elaborate estimates.

A TAX STRUCTURE APPROACH

Fortunately, Organski and Kugler's basic insight can be effectively applied by other approaches that are not subject to the types of conceptual difficulties just discussed—although, of course, they will have other difficulties of their own. One alternative is to focus on the structure of taxation as opposed to making adjustments to levels of taxation.[5] There is a well-developed literature in economics on the theory of optimal taxation. While the mathematics in much of this literature can get very complicated, the basic idea is quite simple. To minimize the aggregate efficiency cost of raising tax revenues, taxes should be selected so that the efficiency cost per marginal unit of revenue raised should be equalized across all forms of taxation used. For example, if the government has available two types of taxes, one that carries a marginal efficiency cost of 20 cents per dollar raised, and the other that has a marginal efficiency cost of 40 cents, then to maximize efficiency only the first type of tax should be used. The efficiency costs of taxation include not only collection costs but also the costs of the distorted economic incentives generated by the taxation. While the former costs may be relatively constant per unit of revenue raised, the latter tend to display increasing marginal costs. Thus in equilibrium it will typically be economically efficient for the government to use a variety of taxes.

There is still considerable controversy among experts about the economic costs of some types of taxation, but there is also considerable agreement about the relative costs of a number of forms of taxation. From the standpoint of optimal taxation, so-called high cost taxes shouldn't necessarily be avoided entirely—because it is marginal, not average, costs that should be equalized—but higher average cost taxes should be used proportionately less than lower cost taxes. Thus while there would be a number of gray areas, public finance experts should be able to rank the relative economic efficiency of the tax structures across many countries. Fine gradations would be more difficult to make. For example, although the modest use of import tariffs and seigniorage (inflation tax) would not necessarily suggest a particularly inefficient tax system, heavy use of either or both of these sources should suggest economic inefficiency.

From a political perspective, if such inefficiency simply reflected a lack of economic understanding by the governments in question, then the use of the structure of taxation as an indicator of political capacity would be problematical. Frequently, however, there is an inverse correlation between the economic efficiency cost of taxes and their visibility. As is discussed extensively in the literature on the political economy of trade policy, not only are special interests often able to successfully lobby for policies that benefit them at the expense of the general public, but often these favors take forms that are particularly costly to the national economy. For example, typically a direct subsidy has lower economic costs than a tariff, which in turn has lower costs than a quota or voluntary export restraint (Lindert 1991). Protected groups typically strongly favor receiving this benefit in higher cost forms, because they tend to be less visible and are less likely to fall victim to future budget cutting or other reform efforts. Thus, the use of high economic cost forms of taxation and redistribution often reflect well-informed political calculations by governments and special interests rather than an ignorance of economics.

The visibility of direct taxes also gives governments incentives to run budget deficits. While there are many sound economic reasons for governments to run budget deficits in particular circumstances, large sustained budget deficits are likely to be a sign of political weakness. This is especially true when such deficits are financed by rapid money expansion, which fuels inflation. Indeed, the so-called inflation tax is a prime example of hidden taxation (see Banaian, McClure and Willett 1994). Even when a government recognizes the substantial long-run costs of higher rates of inflation, adverse public reaction typically occurs, if at all, only after a lag. Where governments have a short time horizon, the dictates of short-run political efficiency may differ substantially from those of economic efficiency and of long-run political efficiency. A strong political system would give considerable weight to these latter considerations. A weak political system would be likely to put heavy weight on the former.

To the extent that the use of economically inefficient, i.e., particularly high cost forms of taxation reflect deliberate government decisions based on short-run political feasibility and response to political pressures, they should be potential indicators of political capacity that could be applied to industrial as well as to developing countries.[6] Thus, for example, in general I would expect both a high general level of a country's trade barriers (both tariff and nontariff) and high ratios of budget deficits, tariffs, and seigniorage revenues to total government revenues to be strong indicators of low levels of political capacity.

The chapters by Al-Marhubi and Alcazar in this volume find that political capacity is a significant determinant of budget deficits and seigniorage revenues. My argument is that to some degree these latter variables may be useful as indicators of the political capacity of countries.

CONCLUDING REMARKS

None of the alternative types of measures of political strength discussed here are free from substantial difficulties of implementation. Given the inherent difficulties involved in constructing any type of statistical proxy for political capacity, it seems extremely unlikely that any one approach would completely dominate all others. Thus I would not want to argue that focus on the structure of taxation is an unambiguously superior approach to proxying political capacity that should replace the tax effort approach developed by Organski, Kugler, and Arbetman. It does seem to me, however, that it is worthy of serious consideration as a complementary approach.[7]

NOTES

1. For overviews of the recent IPE literature see Crane and Amawi (1991), Frieden and Lake (1991), and Ikenberry, Lake, and Mastanduno (1988).

2. For recent analysis and references to the literature see the contributions in Haggard and Kaufman (1992).

3. Ideally, for these purposes one would also consider the implicit tax and expenditure "price" of other forms of government interventions such as import quotas, price controls, etc.

4. Differences in preferences are, of course, one of the many difficulties involved in attempting to vigorously define political efficiency. As a rough approximation, the reader could think of my use of political efficiency as the degree to which government decisions conform to the informed median voter model. For further discussion of these issues see Mueller (1979) and Mueller, Tollison, and Willett (1976).

5. On the optimal tax literature, see Chapter 4 by Alcazar in this volume.

6. For a fruitful empirical application of the tax structure approach, see Snider 1996.

7. One aspect of this suggested research program would be the use of different measures in combination. To what extent under different circumstances can each type of measure add to the explanatory power of the others? In undertaking such work it will be important to think carefully about the causal relationships among the dependent and independent variables.

16

The Unfinished Agenda

Jacek Kugler and Marina Arbetman

As we conclude this volume we cannot but think beyond what has been accomplished up to now, and focus on future improvements in the theory and measurement of political capacity. The development of a measure of political capacity has proven successful. The work that has been done should serve as the point of departure for its continuation. And although we are comfortable with the theoretical specification of political capacity and its two subcomponents, reach and extraction, we are certain that future extensions will refine this concept. Just like *GDP*, which has been revised and recomputed, *RPC* will no doubt be estimated more accurately in the future. Both indicators offer analysts the first set of consistent, cross-national and cross-temporal indicators of political capacity that can be applied generally across the international system. We hope that the empirical success of the studies in this volume will persuade the reader that this direction is worth pursuing. There is no greater measure of success than to establish items on the agenda of future research.

Beyond debates over estimates one can look at alternate specifications of political capacity. For policy purposes it is attractive to measure political capacity without having to detail the institutions, cultures, religions, and regimes that differentiate governments. Despite his criticisms, Thomas Willett (Chapter 16) summarizes our own thoughts when he argues that "[g]iven the inherent difficulties in constructing any type of statistical proxy for political capacity, it seems extremely unlikely that any approach would completely dominate all others." The approaches he proposes could be used to complement the *RPC* measure proposed elsewhere in this volume. These constructive criticisms should be considered very seriously. The specification of *RPE*, for example, could be refined by calculating supply and demand constraints, while the fiscal effort could be calculated simultaneously as a function of economic constraints and economic commitments. Alternatively, the model used now should be expanded to include variables from the monetary sector that are especially appropriate after 1973, when the international financial market expanded, and to incorporate the impact of inflation as a determinant of tax collection.

Discussion continues over the central issue of who is maximizing what for whom. We propose that a government maximizes the long-term economic growth of a nation and ensures its own permanence in power. But is this a sufficiently broad definition of the social function governments seek? Given a choice, will governments advance these goals, or will they maximize the provision of far more broadly defined functions? Recall that in times of conflict, the maximization of the long-term economic growth is superseded by the short-term maximization of political permanence. However, it can be argued that in peacetime the function maximized is not clearly specified. Indeed, leaders may want to maximize the redistribution of resources to their supporters, while minimizing redistribution to the rest of the population. Such a policy would ensure political stability without ensuring stable growth. We have postulated, for simplicity's sake, that such discriminating policies cannot be maintained in the long term. A final answer about the goals of government, however, requires a full specification of political priorities and the exploration of their maximization across countries. Clearly this is work yet to be done.

A second theoretical problem raisedby this work relates to the mix between the public and private sectors. John Edwards (chapter 13) argues that the *RPC* models are closer to the Leviathan view of govern-ment than the optimal mix would suggest, but he grants that *RPC*'s macro specifications are "set up for testing." In his view, "political power explains the placement of nations along the public/private frontier," but does not explain why each position was chosen. A more extended specification of the trade-off between outcomes that are optimal from an economic and political perspective, adding the effects of crowding out, would enhance estimates of political capacity.

A third concern deals with the problem raised by Bird (1992): Do governments that extract or reach the population at levels lower than average do so out of their own volition, or because they lack political capacity? Improved controls can bring us closer to an answer, but such controls cannot fully resolve this concern without a clear specification of the political means that governments employ to reach their policy choices. As the work in this volume shows, even without a complete specification it is evident that political capacity variations are not random, but contain a large component of politics.

As A. F. K. Organski has pointed out, in the present measures of extraction and reach the political components of the model are not specified but are contained in the residual. This approach is taken because the political components were not known and, had they been known, the data to construct the indicators were lacking, and still are. The use of residuals to index the levels of capacity of political systems applies a brilliant finesse to all these problems. Further research should fill this lacuna. Indeed, refinements in specification and improvements in empirical techniques already proposed improve on current estimates. One approach, extended by John Edwards in Chapter 13, was first proposed by Organski et al.(1984, 74-79), who argued that political costs can be estimated as the difference between an adjusted maximum extraction and the real extraction. These authors argued that the measure of political costs represents a shift from estimating the political capacity of the system as the deviation from the average performance shaped by economic factors to a deviation from the most efficient performers. The new measure suggests a far richer theoretical explanation for the effectiveness of the *RPC* index. The drawback to in obtaining all the resources one could theoretically obtain is that the government could not pay the political costs that would be incurred with such an increase in its collection of resources. This approach offers the possibility of developing measures of politics that capture directly the political costs that shape the decisions of the leading coalition.

Edwards (Chapter 13) bases a political capacity index on an economic frontier determined by endowments, production technology, and revenue-raising technology. This frontier would describe "the maximum feasible government for any given size [of the] private sector." Edwards stresses that *RPC* indicators theoretically provide the appropriate focus but fail to measure deviations from the maximum levels of extraction. He further argues that the "choice of the name 'tax capacity' for these models is unfortunate, because [the base should approximate the maximum effort and not the] average practice, which involves a mixture of technological and political constraints on raising revenue." To improve this specification, Edwards then proposes to center the analysis on the economic frontier, providing an opportunity to compare the capacity of nation states and local governments across time and space against the most efficient performers. Edwards' proposal, operationalized by Holsey and Cao (Chapter 14), is suggestive and should be pursued further.

The final and perhaps most pressing item on the agenda for the future is an explicit specification of the policy interactions that generate political capacity. We know that political capacity measures work. Repeated valida-tions in a whole series of applications presented in this volume and else-where leave little room for doubt that the measure has proven its utility, and will continue to be ever more widely used. What we do not know is why the measure works. What are the micro-political foundations that explain why the measure reflects behavior as well as it does? It is time to try to find out.

Bibliography

Adler, E. 1987. *The Power of Ideology: The Quest for Technological Autonomy in Argentina and Brazil*. Berkeley and Los Angeles: University of California Press.

Aharoni, Y. 1966. *The Foreign Investment Decision Process*. Boston: Harvard University Press.

Aigner, D., C. A. K. Lovell, and P. Schmidt. 1977. "Formulation and Estimation of Stochastic Frontier Production Function Models." *Journal of Econometrics* 6:21-37.

Aizenman, J. 1989. "The Competitive Externalities and the Optimal Seigniorage." *Working Paper No. 2937*, National Bureau of Economic Research.

Aizenman, J., and N. P. Marion. 1993. "Macroeconomic Uncertainty and Private Investment." *Economics Letters* 41:201-10.

Alesina, A., and A. Drazen. 1991. "Why are Stabilizations Delayed?" *American Economic Review* 81(5):1170-88.

Alesina, A., and G. Tabellini. 1990. "A Positive Theory of Fiscal Deficits and Government Debt." *Review of Economic Studies* 57:37-49.

_____ 1992. "Positive and Normative Theories of Public Debt and Inflation in Historical Perspective." *European Economic Review* 36:337-44.

Amemiya, T. 1981. "Qualitative Response Models: A Survey." *A Journal of Economic Literature* 19:1483-1536.

_____ 1985. *Advanced Econometrics*. Cambridge: Harvard University Press.

Amemiya, T., and T. Mc Curdy. 1986. "Instrumental Variables Estimation of an Error Components Model," *Econometrica* 54:869-80.

Ames, B. 1987. *Political Survival: Politicians and Public Policy in Latin America*. Berkeley and Los Angeles: University of California Press.

Andorka, R. 1986. "Review Symposium of The Decline of Fertility in Europe." *Population and Development Review* 12(2).

Arbetman, M. 1990. *The Political Economy of Exchange Rate Fluctuations*. Ph.D. diss., Vanderbilt University.

_____ 1994. "The Concept of Political Penetration." In *Proceedings of the Conference on Political Capacity and Economic Behavior*, organized by the Center for Politics and Economics. Claremont, Calif.: Claremont Graduate School.

_____ 1995. "The Politics of Exchange Rates Fluctuations: The Untold Story." *International Interactions* 21:127-53.

Arbetman, M., J. T. Adams, and M. D. Hancock. 1990. "A Theoretic Model: The Influence of Parties on Expenditure." Paper presented at the Conference on European Studies, Washington, D.C.

Arbetman, M., and J. Kugler. 1988. "Black Market Exchange Rates, Domestic Instability and Politics." Paper presented at the annual meeting of the *APSA*, Washington, D.C.

_____ 1989a. *Political Uncertainty and Exchange Rate Fluctuation.*" Paper presented at the annual meeting of the American Political Science Association, Washington, D.C.

_____ 1989b. *"The Effects of Political Intervention on Black Market Exchange Rate Premiums."* Paper presented at the annual meeting of the American Political Science Association, Atlanta.

_____ 1995. "The Politics of Inflation: An Empirical Assessment of the Emerging Market Economies." In *Establishing Monetary Stability in Emerging Market Economies,* ed. T. D. Willett et al. Boulder, Colo.: Westview Press.

Ardant, G. 1972. *Histoire de L'Impot, Livre I.* France: Fayard.

_____ 1975. "Financial Policy and Economic Infrastructure of Modern States and Nations." In *The Formation of National States in Western Europe,* ed. C. Tilly, . Princeton: Princeton University Press.

Arendt, H. 1963. *On Revolution.* London: Penguin Books.

Arnold, R. D. 1979. *Congress and the Bureaucracy: A Theory of Influence.* New Haven: Yale University Press.

Azar, E. E. 1980. "The Conflict and Peace Data Bank (COPDAB) Project." *The Journal of Conflict Resolution* 24:143–52.

Azar, E. E., and T. Sloan. *Dimensions of Interaction: A Source Book for the Study of Behavior of 31 Nations from 1948 through 1973.* Pittsburgh: International Studies Association.

Baer, W. 1991. "Social Aspects of Latin American Inflation." *Quarterly Review of Economics and Business* 31:45-57.

Bahl, R. 1971. "A Regression Approach to Tax Effort and Tax Ratio Analysis." *International Monetary Fund Staff Papers* 18.

Baillie, R. T., and P. C. McMahon. 1989. *The Foreign Exchange Market: Theory and Econometric Evidence.* Cambridge: Cambridge University Press.

Banaian, K., H. J. McLure, and T. D. Willett. 1994. "The Inflation Tax is Likely Inefficient at Any Level." *Kredit und Kapital.*

Banaian, K. 1995a. "Seigniorage, Tax Moving and Politics." Paper presented at the Public Choice meetings, March 25, Long Beach, Calif.

_____ 1995b. "Inflation and Optimal Seigniorage in the CIS and Eastern Europe." In *Establishing Monetary Stability in Emerging Market Economies,* ed. T. D. Willett et al. Boulder: Westview Press.

Banks, A. S. 1971. *Cross-Polity Time-Series Data.* Cambridge: The MIT Press.

Barro, R. J. and D. B. Gordon. 1983. "Rules, Discretion, and Reputation in a Model of Monetary Policy." *Journal of Monetary Economics* 12:101-22.

Barro, R. J. 1990. "Government Spending in a Simple Model of Endogenous Growth." *Journal of Political Economy* 98:s103-s125.

_____ 1991. "Economic Growth in a Cross-Section of Countries." *Quarterly Journal of Economics* 56:407-43.

Basi, R. S. 1963. *Determinants of United States Private Foreign Investments in Foreign Countries.* Kent, Ohio: Kent State University, Bureau of Economic and Business Research.

Bass, B. M., D. W. McGregor, and J. L. Walters. 1977. "Selecting Plant Sites: Economic, Social, and Political Considerations." *Academy of Management Journal* 20:535–51.

Battese, G. E., and T. J. Coelli. 1988. "Prediction of Firm-Level Technical Efficiencies with a Generalized Frontier Production Function and Panel Data." *Journal of Econometrics* 38:387-99.

Bauer, P. W. 1990. "Recent Developments in the Econometric Estimation of Frontiers." *Journal of Econometrics* 46:39-56.

Becker, D. 1983. *The New Bourgeoisie and the Limits of Dependency: Mining, Class, and Power in "Revolutionary" Peru.* Princeton: Princeton University Press.

Beckerman, W. 1966. *International Comparisons of Real Income.* Paris: OECD.

Bennett, P. D., and R. T. Green. 1972. "Political Instability as a Determinant of Direct Foreign Investment in Marketing." *Journal of Marketing Research* 9:182–86.

Berndt, E., and L. Christensen. 1972. "The Translog Function and the Substitution of Equipment, Structures, and Labor in U.S. Manufacturing, 1929-1968." *Journal of Econometrics* 1.

Berndt, E. R. 1991. *The Practice of Econometrics: Classic and Contemporary.* New York: Addison Wesley.

Binder, L., et al. 1971. *Crises and Sequences of Development.* Princeton: Princeton University Press.

Bird, R. 1992. *Tax Policy and Economic Development.* Baltimore: Johns Hopkins University Press.

Bjurek, H., and L. Hjalmarsson. 1990. "Deterministic Parametric and Nonparametric Estimation of Efficiency in Service Production: A Comparison." *Journal of Econometrics* 46:213-27.

Blanchard, O., and S. Fisher. 1989. *Lectures on Macroeconomics.* Cambridge: The MIT Press.

Bongaarts, J., W. P. Mauldin, and J. F. Phillips. 1990. "The Demographic Impact of Family Planning Programs." *Studies in Family Planning* 21:299-310.

Bongaarts J. 1992. "The Supply Demand Framework for the Determinants of Fertility." Research Division Working Paper No. 44, The Population Council, New York.

Brace, P. 1991. "The Changing Context of State Political Economy." *Journal of Politics* 53:297-317.

Break, G. F. 1980. *Financing Government in a Federal System.* Washington D.C.: Brookings Institute.

Brennan, G., and J. Buchanan. 1977a. "Towards a Tax Constitution for Leviathan." *Journal of Public Economics.* 8.

_____ 1977b. "Tax Instruments as Constraints on the Disposition of Public Revenues." *Journal of Public Economics* 9.

Bresser P. L., and Dall'Acqua. 1991. "Economic Populism versus Keynes: Reinterpreting Budget Deficits in Latin America." *Journal of Post Keynesian Economics* 14:29-38.

Buckley, P. J., Z. Berkova, and G. D. Newbould. 1983. *Direct Investment in the United Kingdom by Smaller European Firms.* London: Macmillan Press.

Bueno de Mesquita, B., and D. Lalman. 1986. "Reason and War." *American Political Science Review* 80:1113-31.

Bueno de Mesquita, B., A. Rabushka, and D. Newman. 1985. *How to Analyze Politics.* New Haven: Yale University Press.

Bueno de Mesquita, B., and R. Siverson. 1995. "War and the Survival of Political Leaders: A Comparative Study of Regime Types and Political Accountability." *American Political Science Review* 89.

Bueno de Mesquita, B. 1977. "Nasty or Nice? Political Systems, Endogenous Norms, and the Treatment of Adversaries." *Journal of Conflict Resolution* 41:175-99.
_____ 1980. *The War Trap.* New Haven: Yale University Press.

Burdekin, R. C. K. 1991. "Inflation and Taxation with Optimizing Governments: A Comment." *Journal of Money, Credit, and Banking* 23(2):267–69.
_____ 1995. "Budget Deficits and Inflation: The Importance of Budget Controls for Monetary Stability." In *Establishing Monetary Stability in Emerging Market Economies,* ed. T. D. Willett, R. C. K. Burdekin, R. J. Sweeney, and C. Wihlborg. Boulder: Westview Press.

Burdekin, R. C., and L. O. Laney. 1988. "Fiscal Policymaking and the Central Bank Institutional Constraint." *Kyklos* 41(4):647-62.

Callaghy, T. M. 1989. "Toward State Capability and Embedded Liberalism in the Third World: Lessons for Adjustment." In *Fragile Coalitions: The Politics of Economic Adjustment,* ed. J. Nelson. New Brunswick & London: Transaction Books.

Calvo. G. 1978. "On the Time Inconsistency of Optimal Policy in a Monetary Economy." *Econometrica* 46(6):1411-28.

Cameron, D. 1982. "On the Limits of the Public Economy." *The Annals* 459:46-62.

Camp, S. L. 1993. "Population: The Critical Debate." *Foreign Policy.* 90:126-44.

Campbell, A., P. E. Converse, W. E. Miller, and D. E. Stokes. 1960. *The American Voter.* New York: John Wiley & Sons.

Caporaso, J. A., and Levine, D. P. 1992. *Theories of Political Economy.* Cambridge, England: Cambridge University Press.

Cheibub, J. A. 1994. "Political Regimes, Taxation, and Economic Growth: A Comparative Analysis." Ph.D dissertation, University of Chicago.

Chelliah, R. 1971. "Trends in Taxation in Developing Countries." *IMF Staff Papers* 18.

Chelliah, R., H. Bass, and M. Kelly. 1975. "Tax Ratios and Tax Effort in Developing Countries, 1969-1971. "*International Monetary Fund Staff Papers* 22.

Chen, B., and Y. Feng. 1994. "Public Investment and Private Investment: A Cross-National Analysis." Working Paper, The Claremont Graduate School.

Cheng Hsiao. 1986. *Analysis of Panel Data. Econometric Society Monographs,* No.11. Cambridge: Cambridge University Press.

Chelliah, R., H. Baas, M. Kelly. 1974. "Tax Ratios and Tax Effort in Developing Countries, 1969-1971. "*International Monetary Fund Staff Papers,* May.

Cleland, J., and C. Wilson. 1987. "Demand Theories of the Fertility Transition: An Iconclastic View." *Population Studies* 41.

Coale, A. 1975. "The Demographic Transition." *The Population Debate: Dimensions and Perspectives,* Vol 1. New York: United Nations.

Coase, R. 1960. "The Problem of Social Cost." *Journal of Law and Economics* 3:1-44.

Cohen, Y. B., R. Brown, and A. F. K. Organski. 1981. "The Paradoxical Nature of State Making: The Violent Creation of Order." *American Political Science Review* 75(4):901-10.

Cole, G. D. H. 1961. *The British (Common) People, 1746-1946.* New York: Barnes and Noble University Paperbacks.

Computing Resources Center. 1992. *STATA Reference Manual: Release 3.* 5th ed. Santa Monica, California: Stata Press.

Contini, B. 1979. *Lo Sviluppo di Un'Economia Parallela.* Milan, Italy: Edizioni di Comunita.

_____ 1981a. "Labor Market Segmentation and the Development of the Parallel Economy-The Italian Experience." *Oxford Economic Papers* 33:401-12.

_____ 1981b. "The Second Economy of Italy." *Taxing and Spending* 3:18-24.

_____ 1982. "The Second Economy of Italy." In *The Underground Economy in the United States and Abroad.* ed. Vito Tanzi. Massachusetts: Lexington Books.

Copeland, G. W., and K. J. Meir. 1984. "Pass the Biscuits, Pappy: Congressional Decision Making and Federal Grants." *American Politics Quarterly* 12:3-21.

Corbae, D., and S. Ouiliaris. 1988. "Cointegration Tests of Purchasing Power Parity." *The Review of Economics and Statistics* 70:508-12.

Cornwell, C., P. Schmidt, and R. C. Sickles. 1990. "Production Frontiers with Cross-Sectional and Time-Series Variation in Efficiency Levels." *Journal of Econometrics* 46:185-200.

Council of State Governments. Various Years. *The Book of the States.* Chicago: Council of State Governments.

Cowgill, C. P. 1949. "The Theory of Population Growth Cycles." *American Journal of Sociology* 55(2)1:163-70.

Crane, G. T., and Amawi Abla, eds. 1991. *The Theoretical Evolution of International Political Economy.* Oxford University Press.

Cukierman, A., S. Edwards, and G. Tabellini. 1989. "Seigniorage and Political Instability." *Working Paper No. 3199,* National Bureau of Economic Research, Cambridge, Mass.

_____ 1992. "Seigniorage and Political Instability." *The American Economic Review* 82(3):537-55.

Daneshvary, N., H. W. Herzog, R. A. Hofler, and A. M. Schlottmann. 1992. "Job Search and Immigrant Assimilation: An Earnings Frontier Approach." *Review of Economics and Statistics* 74:482-92.

De Haan, J., and D. Zelhorst. 1990. "The Impact of Government Deficits on Money Growth in Developing Countries." *Journal of International Money and Finance* 9:455-69.

De Haan, J., D. Zelhorst and Roukens. 1993. "Seigniorage in Developing Countries." *Applied Financial Economics* 3:307-14.

De Long, J. B. 1988. "Productivity Growth, Convergence, and Welfare: Comment." *American Economic Review* 78:1138-54.

Demeny, P. 1989. "World Population Growth and Prospects." Working Paper #4, The Research Division of the Population Council, New York.

Demopoulos, G. D., G. M. Katsimbris, and S. M. Miller. 1987. "Monetary Policy and Central Bank Financing of Government Budget Deficits." *European Economic Review* 31:1023-50.

De Nardo, J. 1985. *Power in Numbers.* Princeton: Princeton University Press.

Deutsch, K. 1966. "Social Mobilization and Political Development." In *Political Development and Social Change,* ed. Jason Finkle and Richard Gable. New York: John Wiley and Sons.

Dillon Soares, G. A. 1986. "Elections and the Redemocratization of Brazil." In *Elections and Democratization in Latin America, 1980-85.* ed. Paul Drake and Eduardo Silva. San Diego: Center for Iberian and Latin American Studies, University of California.

Dixit, A. 1989. "Entry and Exit Decisions under Uncertainty." *Journal of Political Economy* 97:620-38.

Dornbusch, R., D. Valente, C. Pechman, R. Rochas, and D. Simoes. 1983. "The Black Market for Dollars in Brazil." *The Quarterly Journal of Economics* 97: 25-40.

Dornbusch, R. and S. Edwards, eds. 1991. *The Macroeconomics of Populism in Latin America*. Chicago: Chicago University Press.

Downs, A. 1957. *An Economic Theory of Democracy*. New York: Harper Press.

Duverger, M. 1951. *Political Parties*. London: Methuen Press.

Dye, T. R., and T. L. Hunley. 1978. "The Responsiveness of Federal and State Governments to Urban Problems." *Journal of Politics* 40:196-207.

The Economist 1994. "Living, and dying, in a barren land." April 23, p. 54.

Edwards, J. H. Y., and J. T. Oliveira, eds. 1993. *Brazilian Fiscal Reform*. Sao Paulo: FIPE.

Edwards, S. 1991a. *Real Exchange Rates, Devaluation, and Adjustment: Exchange Rate Policy in Developing Countries*. Cambridge: The MIT Press.

_____ 1991b. "Capital Flows, Foreign Direct Investment and Debt Equity Swaps in Developing Countries." *Working Paper No. 3497*, National Bureau of Economic Research.

Edwards, S., and G. Tabellini. 1991a. "Explaining Fiscal Policies and Inflation in Developing Countries." *Journal of International Money and Finance* 10:516-48.

_____ 1991b. "Political Instability, Political Weakness and Inflation: An Empirical Analysis." *Working Paper No. 3721*, National Bureau of Economic Research, Cambridge, Mass.

Ehrlich, I. 1990. "The Problem of Development." *Journal of Political Economy* 98:s1-s12.

Eisinger, P. K. 1988. *The Rise of the Entrepreneurial State*. Madison: University of Wisconsin Press.

El Haddad, A. B. 1988. "Determinants of Foreign Direct Investment in Developing Countries: The Egyptian Situation." *Egypte Cotemporaine* 77:65–93.

Evans, P., D. Rueschemeyer, and T. Skocpol. 1985. *Bringing the State Back In*. New York: Cambridge University Press.

Evans, P. 1992. "The State as Problem and Solution: Predation, Embedded Autonomy, and Structural Change." In *The Politics of Economic Adjustment*, ed. S. Hagard and R. R. Kaufman, 140-81. Princeton: Princeton University Press.

Faig, M. 1988. "Characterization of the Optimal Tax on Money When It Functions as a Medium of Exchange." *Journal of Monetary Economics* 22:137-48.

Farrell, M. J. 1957. "The Measurement of Productive Efficiency." *Journal of the Royal Statistical Society* A120(part 3):253-81.

Feierabend, I. K., and R. L. Feierabend. 1966. "Aggression Behavior in Politics, 1948–1962: A Cross-National Study." *Journal of Conflict Resolution* 10:248–71.

Feijo, C. A., and F. J. C. de Carvalho. 1992. "The Resilience of High Inflation: Recent Brazilian Failures with Stabilization Policies." *Journal of Post Keynesian Economics* 15:109-24.

Feng, Y. 1995. "Regime, Polity, and Economic Performance: The Latin American Experience." *Growth and Change* 26:77-104.

Findlay, R. 1990. "The New Political Economy: Its Explanatory Power for LDCs." In *Politics and Policy Making in Developing Countries: Perspectives on the New Political Economy*, ed. G. Meier. San Francisco: International Center for Economic Growth.

Fiorina, M. P. 1981. *Retrospective Voting in American National Elections*. New Haven: Yale University Press.

Firebaugh, G. 1992. "Growth Effects of Foreign and Domestic Investment." *American Journal of Sociology* 98(1):105-30.

Forsund, F. R., C. A. K. Lovell, and P. Schmidt. 1980. "A Survey of Frontier Production Functions and of their Relationship to Efficiency Measurement." *Journal of Econometrics* 13:5-25.

Fosler, R. S., ed. 1988. *The New Economic Role of American States*. New York: Oxford University Press.

Frank, I. 1980. *Foreign Enterprise in Developing Countries*. Baltimore: Johns Hopkins University Press.

Freedman, L. P. 1994. "Family Planning as an Instrument of Empowerment." *International Family Planning Perspective* 20:31-33.

Frenkel, J. A. 1976. "A Monetary Approach to the Exchange Rate: Doctrinal Aspects and Empirical Evidence." *Scandinavian Journal of Economics* 78:2.

Frieden, J. A. 1991. *Debt, Development, and Democracy: Modern Political Economy and Latin America, 1965-1988*. Princeton: Princeton University Press.

Frieden, J., and D. Lake, eds. 1991. *International Political Economy*. 2nd ed. New York: St. Martin's Press.

Friedland, R., and H. Wong. 1983. "Congressional Politics, Federal Grants, and Local Needs: Who Gets What and Why?" In *The Municipal Money Chase*, ed. A. M. Sibragia. Boulder, Colo.: Westview Press.

Friedman, D. 1977. "A Theory of the Size and Shape of Nations." *Journal of Political Economy* 85:59-78.

Friedman, M. 1968. "Inflation: Causes and Consequences." Reprinted in *Dollars and Deficits*. Englewood Cliffs, N.J.: Prentice-Hall.

_____ 1969. "The Optimum Quantity of Money." In *The Optimum Quantity of Money and Other Essays*. Chicago: Aldine Publishing Company.

_____ 1971. "Government Revenue from Inflation." *Journal of Political Economy* 79:846-56.

_____1977. "Inflation and Unemployment." *Journal of Political Economy* 85:451-72.

Friedrich, R. 1982. "In Defense of Multiplicative Terms of Multiple Regression Equations." *American Journal of Political Science* 26:797-833.

Fua, G. 1976. *Occupazione e capacita produttive: La realta Italiana*. Bologna: Il Mulino.

Gaetani-D'Aragona, G. 1981. "The Hidden Economy: Concealed Labor Markets in Italy." *Rivista Internazionale di Scienze Economiche e Commerciali* 3.

Gallant, A. R. 1987. *Nonlinear Statistical Models*. New York: John Wiley & Sons.

Gastil, R. 1977-1987. *Freedom in the World*. Westport, Conn.: Greenwood Press.

Geddes, B. 1991. "Paradigms and Sandcastles in Comparative Politics of Developing Areas." In *Political Science: Looking to the Future*, ed. William Crotty. Vol. 2: *Comparative Politics, Policy, and International Relations*, 45-75. Evanston: Northwestern University Press.

Gerschenkron, A. 1962. *Economic Backwardness in Historical Perspective*. Cambridge: Belknap Press.

Gerschenkron, A. 1966. *Economic Backwardness in Historical Perspective*. Cambridge: Belknap Press of Harvard University Press.

Gilmour, J. B. 1988. "Hardball and Softball Politics: A Theory of Coalition Size in Congress." Paper presented at the annual meeting of the American Political Science Association, Washington, D.C.

Gilpin, Robert. 1981. *War and Change in World Politics*. New York: Cambridge University Press.

Goldstone, J. A., T. R. Gurr, and F. Moshiri, eds. 1991. *Revolutions of the Late Twentieth Century*. Boulder: Westview Press.

Golembiewski, R. T., and A. Wildavsky, eds. 1984. *The Costs of Federalism*. New Brunswick: Transaction Books.

Green, R. T. 1972. *Political Instability as a Determinant of U.S. Foreign Investment*. Austin: University of Texas.

Green, R. T., and W. H. Cunningham. 1975. "The Determinants of United States Foreign Investment: An Empirical Estimation." *Management International Review* 19:113–20.

Greenaway, D., and C. H. Nam. 1988. "Industrialization and Macroeconomic Performance in Developing Countries under Alternative Trade Strategies." *Kyklos* 41:419–35.

Greene, J., and D. Villanueva. 1990. "Private Investment in Developing Countries: an Empirical Analysis." Working Paper, International Monetary Fund, Washington, DC.

Greene, W. H. 1980. "On the Estimation of a Flexible Frontier Production Model." *Journal of Econometrics* 13:101-15.

_____ 1990. "A Gamma-Distributed Stochastic Frontier Model." *Journal of Econometrics* 46:141-63.

_____ 1993. *Econometric Analysis*. 2nd ed. New York: Macmillan.

Greenhalgh, S. 1990a. *State Society Links: Political Dimensions of Population Policies and Programs, with Special Reference to China*. No. 18. New York: Research Division of the Population Council.

_____ 1990b. "Toward a Political Economy of Fertility: Anthropological Contributions." *Population and Development Review* 16(1).

Greenwood, J., and K. P. Kimbrough. 1987. "Foreign Exchange Controls in a Black Market Economy." *Journal of Development Economics* 26:129-43.

Gregorio, J. D. 1993. "Inflation, Taxation, and Long-Run Growth." *Journal of Monetary Economics* 31(3):271-98.

Grier, K. B., and H. E. Neiman. 1987. "Deficits, Politics, and Money Growth." *Economic Inquiry* 24:201-14.

Grier, K. B., and G. Tullock. 1989. "An Empirical Analysis of Cross-National Economic Growth: 1951-1980." *Journal of Monetary Economics* 24:259-76.

Grilli, V., D. Masciandaro, and G. Tabellini. 1991. "Political and Monetary Institutions and Public Financial Policies in the Industrial Countries." *Economic Policy* 13:341-92.

Gupta, S. 1981. "Black Market Exchange Rates." *Kieler Studien*. Tubingen, Germany: J. C. B. Mohr (Paul Siebeck).

Gurr, T. 1970. *Why Men Rebel*. Princeton: Princeton University Press.

Haggard, S. 1990. *Pathways from the Periphery: The Politics of Growth in the Newly Industrializing Countries*. Ithaca: Cornell University Press.

Haggard, S., and R. Kaufman, eds. 1992. *The Politics of Economic Adjustment.* Princeton: Princeton University Press.

Haggard, S. and R. Kaufman. 1992. "The Political Economy of New Democracies." Paper presented at the Southern California Workshop on Political and Economic Liberalization.

Hammel, E. A. 1990. "A Theory of Culture for Demography." *Population and Development Review* 16(3).

Hauser, John R. 1978. "Testing the Accuracy, Usefulness, and Significance of Probabilistic Choice Models: An Information Theoretic Approach." *Operations Research* 26: 406-21.

Hausman, J. 1978. "Specification Tests in Econometrics." *Econometrica* 46:1251–73.

Hausman, J., and W. Taylor. 1981. "Panel Data and Unobservable Individual Effects," *Econometrica.* 46:1377-99.

Hayek, F. A. 1944. *The Road to Serfdom.* Chicago: The University of Chicago Press.

Hazlewood, L. 1973. "Concepts and Measurement Stability in the Study of Conflict Behavior Within Nations." *Comparative Political Studies.* 6:171-98.

Heidenheimer, A. J., H. Heclo, and C. Adams. 1990. *Comparative Public Policy: The Politics of Social Choice in Europe and America.* 3rd ed. New York: St. Martin's Press.

Herzog, H., R. Hofler, and A. Schlottmann. 1985. "Life on the Frontier: Migrant Information, Earnings, and Past Mobility." *Review of Economics and Statistics* 67:373-82.

Hibbs, D. 1973. *Mass Political Violence.* New York: Wiley.

Holcombe, R. G., and A. Zardkoohi. 1981. "The Determinants of Federal Grants." *Southern Economic Journal* 48:393-99.

Holt, R. T., and J. E. Turner. 1966. *The Political Basis of Economic Development.* Princeton, N.J.: D. Van Nostrand.

Hooton, C. G. 1993. "Politics vs. Policy in Federal Agencies: Grants-in-Aid at the Economic Development Administration." Paper presented at the annual meeting of the American Political Science Association, Washington, D.C.

Hopkins, Michael. 1983. "Employment Trends in Developing Countries, 1960-1980 and Beyond." *International Labour Review* 122(4).

Houweling, H., and J. G. Siccama. 1988. "Power Transitions as a Cause of War." *Journal of Conflict resolution* 32(1).

Hsiao, C. 1986. *Analysis of Panel Data.* Cambridge: Cambridge University Press.

Huntington, S. 1968. *Political Order in Changing Societies.* New Haven: Yale University Press.

Ikenberry, G. J., D. Lake, and M. Mastanduno, eds. 1988. *The State and American Foreign Economic Policy.* Ithaca: Cornell University Press

International Currency Analysis, Inc. Various Years. *World Currency Yearbook,* Brooklyn: International Currency Analysis, Inc.

International Labor Office. 1986. *Economically Active Population: 1950-2025.* Geneva: International Labour Office.

International Monetary Fund. 1993,. *International Financial Statistics.* Washington, D.C. Magnetic tape.

Jaccard, J., R. Turrisi, and C. K. Wan. 1990. *Interaction Effects in Multiple Regression.* Beverly Hills: Sage Publications.

Jackman, R. 1993. *Power without Force: The Political Capacity of Nation-States*. Ann Arbor: University of Michigan Press.

Jackman, R., and W. Boyd. 1979. "Multiple Sources in the Collection of Data on Political Conflict." *American Journal of Political Science* May.

Jackson, J. E. 1988. "Michigan." In *The New Economic Role of American States*, ed. R. S. Fosler. New York: Oxford University Press.

Johnston, J. 1984. *Econometric Method*. New York: McGraw-Hill.

Joines, D. H. 1985. "Deficits and Money Growth in the United States: 1872-1983." *Journal of Monetary Economics* 16:329-51.

Jondrow, J., C. Lovell, I. S. Materov, and P. Schmidt. 1982. "On the Estimation of Technical Inefficiency in the Stochastic Frontier Production Function Model," *Journal of Econometrics*, 19:233-8.

Judge, G. G., R. C. Hill, W. E. Griffiths, H. Lutkepohl, and T. C. Lee. 1988. *Introduction to the Theory and Practice of Econometrics*. 2nd ed. New York: John Wiley & Sons.

Kahler, M., ed. 1986. *The Politics of International Debt*. Ithaca: Cornell University Press.

Kaufman, R., and B. Stallings. 1989. "Debt and Democracy in the 1980's: The Latin American Experience." In *Debt and Democracy in Latin America*, ed. B. Stallings and R. Kaufman. Boulder: Westview Press.

Kelly, G. P. 1989. *International Handbook of Women's Education*. New York: Greenwood Press.

Kennedy, P. 1992. *A Guide to Econometrics*. Cambridge: The MIT Press.

Kenny, L., and M. Toma. 1993. "The Role of Tax Bases and Collection Costs in the Determination of Income Tax Rates, Seigniorage, and Inflation." Working Paper, University of Florida.

Khan, M., and C. M. Reinhart. 1990. "Private Investment and Economic Growth in Developing Countries." *World Development* 18(1):19-27.

Kimbrough, K. 1986. "The Optimum Quantity of Money Rule in the Theory of Public Finance." *Journal of Monetary Economics* 18:277-84.

King, R. G., and C. I. Plosser. 1985. "Money, Deficits, and Inflation." *Carnegie-Rochester Conference Series on Public Policy* 22:147-96.

Kirk, D. 1971. "A New Demographic Transition?" In *Rapid Population Growth*. Washington D.C.: National Academy of Sciences.

Klein, E. 1984. *Gender Politics: From Consciousness to Mass Politics*. Cambridge: Harvard University Press.

Kmenta, J. 1986. *Elements of Econometrics*. 2nd ed. New York: Macmillan.

Knight, J. 1992. *Institutions and Social Conflict*. Cambridge: Cambridge University Press.

Kobrin, S. J. 1976. "The Environmental Determinants of Foreign Direct Manufacturing Investment: An Ex Post Empirical Analysis." *Journal of International Business Studies* 7:29–42.

Kormendi, R. C., and P. G. Meguire. 1985. "Macroeconomic Determinants of Growth: Cross-Country Evidence." *Journal of Monetary Economics* 16:141-63.

Kravis, I., W. Heston, and R. Summers. 1975. *A System of International Comparisons of Gross Product and Purchasing Power*. Baltimore: Johns Hopkins University Press.

_____ 1979. *International Comparisons of Real Product and Purchasing Power*. Baltimore: Johns Hopkins University Press.

Krueger, A. O. 1990. "Government Failures in Development." *Journal of Economic Perspectives* 4:9-23.

_____ 1993. *Political Economy of Policy Reform in Developing Countries*. Cambridge: The MIT Press.

Kugler, J. 1983. "Use of Residuals: An Option to Measure Concepts Indirectly." *Political Methodology* 9:1.

_____ 1987. "Anticipating Severe Domestic Violence with Measures of Political Capacity." Paper presented at the annual meeting of the American Political Science Association September 3-6, Chicago.

_____ 1994. "The Concept of Political Extraction." In *Proceedings of the Conference on Political Capacity and Economic Behavior*, organized by the Center for Politics and Economics. Claremont, Calif.: Claremont Graduate School.

Kugler, J., and M. Arbetman. 1987. "The 'Phoenix' Factor Revisited." Paper presented at the annual meeting of the International Studies Association, April 1987, Washington, D.C.

_____ 1989. "Choosing Among Measures of Power." In *Power in World Politics*, ed. R. J. Stoll and M. D. Ward. Boulder: Lynne Rienner.

Kugler, J., M. Arbetman, and A. F. K. Organski. 1994. *Resetting the Demographic Clock*. Unpublished manuscript. Claremont: Claremont Graduate School.

Kugler, J., and W. Domke. 1985. "The Strength of Nations." Unpublished typescript.

_____ 1986. "Comparing the Strength of Nations." *Comparative Political Studies*.

Kugler, J., and A. F. K. Organski. 1989. "The Power transition: A Retrospective and Prospective Evaluation." In *Handbook of War Studies*. Massachussets: Allen & Unwin.

Kugler, J., A. F. K. Organski, T. Johnson, and Y. Cohen. 1983. "Political Determinants of Population Dynamics." *Comparative Political Studies* 16:3-36.

Kugler, J., and F. Zagare, eds. 1987. *Exploring the Stability of Deterrence*. Boulder: Lynne Rienner.

Kugler J., and S. Werner. "Power Transitions and Military Buildups: Resolving the Relationship between Arms Buildups and War." In *Parity and War*, ed. J. Kugler and D. Lemke. Ann Arbor: The University of Michigan Press.

Kuznets, S. 1971. *The Economic Growth of Nations*. Cambridge: Harvard University Press.

Kydland, F., and E. Prescott. 1977. "Rules Rather than Discretion: The Inconsistency of Optimal Plans." *Journal of Political Economy* 85:473-93.

Laney, L. O., and T. D. Willett. 1983. "Presidential Politics, Budget Deficits, and the Money Supply in the United States, 1960-1970." *Public Choice* 60:53-69.

Lasswell, H. 1958. *Politics: Who Gets What, When, How*. Cleveland: Meridian Books.

Laughlin, B. 1981. *Black Markets around the World*. Mason, Mich.: Loompanics Unlimited.

Leblang, D. 1996. "Property Rights, Democracy, and Economic Growth." *Political Research Quarterly* 49:5-26.

Lemke, D. 1991. "Predicting Peace: Power Transitions in South America." Paper presented at the annual meeting of the International Studies Association, Vancouver, British Columbia.

Levi, M. 1988. *Of Rule and Revenue*. Berkeley and Los Angeles: University of California Press.

Levine, D. 1986. "Review Symposium of The Decline of Fertility in Europe." *Population and Development Review* 12(2).

Levine, R., and D. Renelt. 1991. "Cross-Country Studies of Growth and Policy: Methodological, Conceptual, and Statistical Problems." *Working Paper No. 608,* World Bank.

_____ 1992. "A Sensitivity Analysis of Cross-Country Growth Regressions." *American Economic Review* 82(4):942-63.

Levis, M. 1979. "Does Political Instability in Developing Countries Affect Foreign Investment Flow? An Empirical Estimation." *Management International Review* 19:59–68.

Lindert, Peter H. 1991. *International Economics.* 9th ed. Burr Ridge, Illinois: Irwin.

Lipset, S. M., and S. Rokkan. 1967. *Party Systems and Voter Alignments.* Part I. New York: Free Press.

Londregan, J. B., and K. T. Poole. 1990. "Poverty, the Coup Trap, and the Seizure of Executive Power." *World Politics* 42 (January): 151-83.

Lotz, J., and E. Morss. 1971. "Measuring 'Tax Effort' in Developing Countries." *International Monetary Fund Staff Papers* 14:478-79.

Lucas, R. 1986. "Principles of Fiscal and Monetary Policy." *Journal of Monetary Economics* 17:117-34.

_____ 1988. "On the Mechanics of Economic Development." *Journal of Monetary Economics* 22:3-42.

Lust-Okar, E. and A. F. K. Organski. 1997. *Forms of Government and the Costs of Resources.* forthcoming.

Lutz, W. 1994. *Population Bulletin: The Future of World Population.* Population Reference Bureau, Inc., 49(1).

Maddala, G. S. 1983. *Limited Dependent and Qualitative Variables in Econometrics.* London: Cambridge University Press.

Madison, A. 1988. *The World Economy in the 20th Century.* Development Centre Studies. Paris: OECD.

Madison, A. 1991. *Dynamic Forces in Capitalist Development: A Long-Run Comparative View.* New York: Oxford University Press.

Manikow, N. G. 1987. "The Optimal Collection of Seigniorage: Theory and Evidence." *Journal of Monetary Economics* 20:327-41.

Mayer, Thomas, ed. 1990. *The Political Economy of American Monetary Policy.* Cambridge: Cambridge University Press.

Mayhew, D. R. 1974. *Congress: The Electoral Connection.* New Haven, Conn.: Yale University Press.

Midlarsky, M. I. 1982. "Scarcity and Inequality." *Journal of Conflict Resolution* 26.

_____ 1988. "Rulers and the Ruled: Patterned Inequality and the Onset of Mass Political Violence." *American Political Science Review* 82(2).

Migdal, J. S. 1988. *Strong Societies and Weak States: State-Society Relations and State Capabilities in the Third World.* Princeton: Princeton University Press.

Miller, G., and J. Oppenheimer. 1982. "Universalism in Experimental Committees." *American Political Science Review* 76:561-74.

Minor, M. 1987. *Explaining Changes in the Propensity of Developing Countries to Expropriate Foreign Direct Investment.* Ph.D. diss., Vanderbilt University.

Mishkin, F. S. 1984. "Causes of Inflation." In *Price Stability and Public Policy,* proceedings of a symposium sponsored by the Federal Reserve Bank of Kansas City, Jackson Hole, Wyoming.

Mueller, Dennis. 1979. *Public Choice*. Cambridge: Cambridge University Press.

Mueller, D., R. Tollison, and T. Willett. 1976. *"Solving the Intensity Problem in Representative Democracy,"* In *The Economic Approach to Public Policy*, ed. R. Amacher, R. Tollison and T. Willett, 444-73. Ithaca: Cornell University Press.

Muller, E., and M. Seligson. 1987. "Inequality and Insurgency."*American Political Science Review* 81(2).

Musgrave, R. 1961. "Approaches to a Fiscal Theory of Political Federalism." In *Public Finances: Needs, Sources, and Utilization*. Princeton: National Bureau of Economic Research.

Mussa, M. 1982. "Empirical Regularities in the Behavior of Exchange Rates and Theories of Foreign Exchange Markets." In *Economic Policy in a World of Change*, ed. Karl Brunner and Alan N. Meltzer. Amsterdam: North Holland.

Myrdal, G. 1968. *Asian Drama: An Inquiry into the Poverty of Nations*. Vol. 2. New York: Twentieth Century Fund.

Nam, C. B., and S. G. Philliber. 1984. *Population: A Basic Orientation*. Englewood Cliffs, N. J.: Prentice-Hall.

Nelson, J. M., ed. 1990. *Economic Crisis and Public Choice*. Princeton: Princeton University Press.

_____ 1991. "A Critique by Political Scientists." In *Politics and Policy Making in Developing Countries*, G. M. Meier. San Francisco: ICS Press.

Nelson, J., et al. 1989. *Fragile Coalitions: The Politics of Economic Adjustment*. New Brunswick: Transaction Books.

Ness, G., and H. Ando. 1984. *The Land is Shrinking: Population Planning in Asia*. Baltimore: Johns Hopkins University Press.

Newy, W., and K. West. 1987. "A Simple Positive Semi-Definite, Heteroscedasticity and Autocorrelation Consistent Matrix." *Econometrica* 55:703-08.

Nigh, D. 1985. "The Effect of Political Events on United States Direct Foreign Investment: A Pooled Time-Series Cross-Sectional Analysis." *Journal of International Business Studies* 16:1–17.

Nordlinger 1981. *On the Autonomy of the Democratic State*. Cambridge: Harvard University Press.

North, D. C. 1981. *Structure and Change in Economic History*. New York: Norton.

_____ 1990. *Institutional Change and Economic Performance*. Cambridge: Cambridge University Press.

North, D. C., and B. R. Weingast. 1989. "Constitutions and Commitment: The Evolution of Institutions Governing Public Choice in Seventeenth-Century England." *The Journal of Economic History* 49:803-32.

Notestein, F. 1945. "Population, The Long View." In *Food For The World*, ed. T.W. Schultz, 36-57. Chicago: Chicago University Press.

Oates, W. A. 1972. *Fiscal Federalism*. New York: Harcourt Brace Javonovich.

_____ 1985. "Searching for Leviathan: An Empirical Study." *American Economic Review* 75:4.

O'Donnell, G. 1978. "Reflections on the Patterns of Change in the Bureaucratic Authoritarian State." *Latin American Research Review* 13(1):3-38.

O'Donnell, G., and P. C. Schmitter. 1986. "Tentative Conclusions about Uncertain Democracies." In *Transitions from Authoritarian Rule.*, ed. G. O'Donnell, P. G. Schmitter, and L. Whitehead, 3-78. Baltimore: The John Hopkins University Press.

OECD. 1991. *The Role of Tax Reform in Central and Eastern European Economies*. Paris: OECD.

Organski, A. F. K. 1958. *World Politics*. New York: Alfred Knopf.

_____ 1965. *Stages of Political Development*. New York: Alfred Knopf.

Organski, A. F. K., and M. Arbetman. 1993. "The Second American Century: The New International Order." In *Behavior, Culture, and Conflict in World Politics*, ed. W. Zimmerman and J. Jacobson. Ann Arbor: University of Michigan Press.

Organski, A. F. K., B. Bueno de Mesquita, and A. Lamborn. 1972. "The Effective Population in International Politics." In *Governance and Population: The Governmental Implications of Population Change*, ed. Keir Nash. Washington D. C.: U. S. Government Printing Office.

Organski, A. F. K., and J. Kugler. 1978. "Davids and Goliaths: Predicting the Outcomes of International War." *Comparative Political Studies* 11(1).

_____ 1979. "Technical Report: A Program of Research of National Estimates." Defense Advanced Research Projects Agency. U.S. Department of Defense. Contract #N00014-78-C-0247.

_____ 1980. *The War Ledger*. Chicago: University of Chicago Press.

_____ 1982. *Program on National Estimates: Final Report*. Defense Advanced Research Projects Agency. U.S. Department of Defense (February).

Organski, A. F. K., J. Kugler, T. Johnson, and Y. Cohen. 1984. *Births, Deaths and Taxes*. Chicago: University of Chicago Press.

Organski, A. F. K., J. Kugler, and M. A. Abdollahian. 1995. "The Mosaic of International Power: Reflections on General Trends." In *Toward an International Economic and Social History*, ed. B. Etamad, J. Batou, and T. David, 169-92. Geneva: Passe Present.

Osborne, D. 1988. *Laboratories of Democracy*. Boston: Harvard Business School Press.

Owens, J. R., and L. Wade. 1984. "Federal Spending in Congressional Districts." *Western Political Quarterly* 37:404-23.

Page, B. 1984. *Who Gets What From Government?* Berkeley and Los Angeles: University of California Press.

Pahr, R., and P. Papayanou. 1996. "Inside Out: A Theory of Domestic Institutions and International Politics." Paper presented at the annual meeting of the American Political Science Association.

_____ *New Games in International Politics*. Forthcoming.

Pastor, M., Jr., and E. Hilt. 1993. "Private Investment and Democracy in Latin America." *World Development* 21(4):489-507.

Perron, P. 1988. "Trends and Random Walk in Macroeconomic Time Series: Further Evidence from a New Approach." *Journal of Economic Dynamics and Control* 12:297-332.

Persson, T., and S. Svensson. 1989. "Why Would a Stubborn Conservative Run a Deficit." *Quarterly Journal of Economics* 104(2).

Pettenati, P. 1979. "Illegal and Unrecorded Employment in Italy." Monte dei Paschi di Siena. *Economic Notes* 8(1).

Pfeffermann, G. P., and A. Madarassy. 1989. "Trends in Private Investment in Thirty Developing Countries." International Financial Corporation Discussion Paper No. 6. Washington, D.C.: World Bank.

Phelps, E. 1973. "Inflation in the Theory of Public Finance." *Swedish Journal of Economics* 75:67-82.

Phillips, J., J. Bongaarts, and W. P. Mauldin. 1990. "The Demographic and Impact of Family Planning Programs." Working Paper No. 17 Research Division, The Population Council, New York.

Phillips, R. J. 1988. "'War News and Black Market Exchange Rate Deviations from Purchasing Power Parity: Wartime South Vietnam." *Journal of International Economics* 25:373-78.

Pigou, A. C. 1947. *A Study in Public Finance*. London: Macmillan.

Pindyck, R. 1988. "Irreversible Investment, Capacity Choice, and the Value of the Firm." *American Economic Review* 78:969-85.

Pitt, M. M. 1984. "Smuggling and the Black Market for Foreign Exchange." *Journal of International Economics* 16:243-57.

Polachek, S. W., and B. J. Yoon. 1987. "A Two-Tiered Earnings Frontier Estimation of Employer and Employee Information in the Labor Market." *Review of Economics and Statistics* 69:296-302.

Polanyi, K. 1944. *The Great Transformation*. Boston: Beacon Press.

Political Risk Services. Various issues. *The Political Risk Yearbook*. Syracuse: Frost and Sullivan Inc.

Portes, A. 1984. "Latin American Class Structures: Their Composition and Change During the Last Decades." Occasional Paper No. 3, School of Advanced International Studies, The Johns Hopkins University.

Portes, A., S. Blitzer, and J. Curtis.1986. "The Urban Informal Sector in Uruguay: Its Internal Structure, Characteristics, and Effects." World Development 14(6).

Poterba, J. M., and J. J. Rothemberg. 1990. "Inflation and Taxation with Optimizing Governments." *Journal of Money, Credit, and Banking* 22(1):1-18.

Pressman, J. L. 1975. "Political Implications of the New Federalism." In *Financing the New Federalism*, ed. W. Oates. Baltimore: Johns Hopkins University Press.

Protopapadakis, A., and J. Siegel. 1987. "Are Money Growth and Inflation Related to Government Deficits? Evidence from Ten Industrialized Countries." *Journal of International Money and Finance* 6:31-48.

Przeworski, A., and F. Limongi. 1993. "Political Regimes and Economic Growth." *Journal of Economic Perspectives* 7:51-69.

Ramsey, F. P. 1927. "A Contribution to the Theory of Taxation." *Economic Journal* 37:47-61.

Ranis, G. 1990. "Contrasts in the Political Economy of Development Policy Change." In *Manufacturing Miracles: Paths of Industrialization in Latin America and East Asia*, ed. G. Gereffi and D. L. Wyman. Princeton: Princeton University Press.

Ray, B. A. 1980. "Congressional Losers in the U.S. Federal Spending Process." *Legislative Studies Quarterly* 3:359-72.

Reid, J. N. 1980. "Politics, Program Administration, and the Distribution of Grants in Aid: A Theory and a Test." In *Political Benefits*, ed. B. S. Rundquist. Lexington, Mass.: Lexington Books.

RFERL. Oct. 1992-Dec. 1993. *RFERL Daily News Report*. Munich: RFERL.

Rich, M. J. 1989. "Distributive Politics and the Allocation of Federal Grants." *American Political Science Review* 83:193-213.

Richards, T. 1977. "Fertility Decline in Germany: An Econometric Appraisal." *Population Studies* 31(3).

Riker, W. 1964. *Federalism: Origin, Operation, and Maintenance.* Boston: Little Brown.

Riker, W. H., and D. L. Weimer. 1993. "The Economic and Political Liberalization of Socialism: The Fundamental Problem of Property Rights." *Social Philosophy and Policy* 10(2):78-102.

Rodrik, D. 1991. "Policy Uncertainty and Private Investment in Developing Countries." *Journal of Developmental Economics* 36(3):229-42.

Rokkan. S., A. Campbell, P. Torsvile, and H. Valen. 1970. *Citizens' Election Parties.* Part II. New York: David McKay Co.

Romer, P. M. 1986. "Increasing Returns and Long-Run Growth." *Journal of Political Economy* 94:1002-37.

_____ 1990. "Endogenous Technological Change." *Journal of Political Economy* 98:s71-s102.

Romer, T., and H. Rosenthal. 1979. "Bureaucrats vs Voters." *Quarterly Journal of Economics,* November.

Root, F. R. 1968. "Attitudes of American Executives towards Foreign Government and Investment Opportunities." *Economic and Business Bulletin* 2.

Root, F. R., and A. Ahmed. 1979. "Empirical Determinants of Manufacturing Direct Investment in Developing Countries." *Economic Development and Cultural Change* 27(4):751-57.

Roubini, N. 1991. "Economic and Political Determinants of Budget Deficits in Developing Countries." *Journal of International Money and Finance* 10:549-72.

Roubini, N., and J. Sachs. 1989. "Government Spending and Budget Deficits in Industrial Countries." *Economic Policy* 8:100-32

Rouyer, A. 1987. "Political Capacity and the Decline of Fertility in India." *American Political Science Review* 81(2).

Rueschemeyer, D., and P. B. Evans. 1985. "The State and Economic Transformation. Toward an Analysis of Conditions Underlying Effective Intervention." In *Bringing the State Back In,* ed. P. Evans, D. Rueschemeyer, and T. Skocpol. New York: Cambridge University Press.

Sachs, J., ed. 1989. *Developing Country Debt and Economic Performance.* Chicago: Chicago University Press.

Saltzstein, A. 1977. "Federal Categorical Aid to Cities: Who Needs It Versus Who Wants It." *Western Political Quarterly* 30:377-83.

Samuelson, P. A. 1954. "The Pure Theory of Public Expenditure." *Review of Economics and Statistics* 36:387-89.

Sargent, T., and N. Wallace. 1981. "Some Unpleasant Monetarist Arithmetic." *Quarterly Review* 1-17, Federal Reserve Bank of Minneapolis.

Sayrs, L. W. 1989. *Pooled Time Series Analysis.* Beverly Hills: Sage.

Schmidt, P., and C. A. Lovell. 1979. "Estimating Technical and Allocative Inefficiency Relative to Stochastic Production and Cost Frontiers." *Journal of Econometrics* 9:343-66.

Schneider, F., and B. S. Frey. 1985. "Economic and Political Determinant of Foreign Direct Investment." *World Development* 13:161-75.

Schreiber, J. S. 1970. *U.S. Corporate Investment in Taiwan.* New York: University Press of Cambridge.

Schultz, K., and B. Weingast. 1995. "Limited Government, Powerful States." Mimeo.

Scmidt, P., and R. Sickles. 1984. "Production Frontiers and Panel Data," *Journal of Business and Economic Interests.* 2(4):367-73.

Scully, Gerald W. 1992. *Constitutional Environments and Economic Growth.* Princeton, NJ: Princeton University Press.

Segura, G., and J. H. Kuklinski. 1995. "Of Endogeneity, Time, and Space: Public Opinion and Political Representation." *Legislative Studies Quarterly* 20(1): 3-22.

Sharkansky, I. 1968. *Spending in the American States.* Chicago: Rand McNally.

_____ 1969. *The Politics of Taxing and Spending.* New York: Booth Merrill.

Sharp, E. B., and D. Elkins. 1987. "The Impact of Fiscal Limitation: A Tale of Seven Cities." *Public Administration Review* 47:385-92.

Sinding, S., J. Ross, and A. Rosenfield. 1994. "Seeking Common Ground: Unmet Need and Demographic Goals." *International Family Planning Perspectives* 20 (March 1, 1994):23-28.

Singer, J. D., and M. Small. 1972. *The Wages of War, 1816-1965: A Statistical Handbook.* New York: John Wiley.

Skocpol, T. 1986. "Bringing the State Back In: Strategies of Analysis in Current Research." In *Bringing the State Back In,* ed. P. .B. Evans, D. Rueschemeyer, and T. Skocpol. Cambridge: Cambridge University Press.

Skolka, J. 1987. "A Few Facts about the Hidden Economy." In *The Unofficial Economy,* ed. S. Alessandrini and B. Dallago. Hants, England: Gower Publishing Company.

Smith, S. 1986. *Britain's Shadow Economy.* London: Oxford University Press.

Snider, L. M. 1986. "Political Capacity and Political Risk: The Development and Validation of a Measure." In *Global Risk Assessment: Issues, Concepts and Applications,* ed. J. Rogers. Vol. 2, 152–79. Riverside, Calif.: Global Risk Assessment Inc.

Snider, L. W. 1988. "Political Strength, Economic Structure, and the Debt Servicing Potential of Developing Countries." *Comparative Political Studies* 20(4).

_____ 1990. "The Political Performance of Third World Debt: Governments and the Debt Crisis." *American Political Science Review* 84(4):1263-80.

_____ 1996. "The Political Strength of Nations and the Third World Debt." Boulder, Colo.: Westview Press.

Stanley, H. W., and R. G. Niemi. 1992. *Vital Statistics on American Politics.* Washington, D.C.: CQ Press.

Stein, R. 1979. "Federal Categorical Aid: Equalization and the Application Process." *Western Political Quarterly* 32:396-408.

_____ 1981. "The Allocation of Federal Aid Monies: The Synthesis of Demand Side and Supply Side Explanations." *American Political Science Review* 75:334-43.

Stimson, J. A. 1985. "Regression in Time and Space." *American Journal of Political Science* 29:914-47.

Stobaugh, R. B. "How to Analyze Foreign Investment Climates." *Harvard Business Review* September-October:100–08.

Stockman, A. 1981. "Anticipated Inflation and the Capital Stock in a Cash-in-Advance Economy." *Journal of Monetary Economics* 8:387-93.

Summers, R., and A. Heston. 1988. "A New Set of International Comparisons of Real Product and Price Level Estimates for 130 Countries, 1950-1985." *Review of Income and Wealth* 25:1-25.

_____ 1991. "The Penn World Table (Mark 5): An Expanded Set of International Comparisons, 1950-1988." *Quarterly Journal of Economics* 56:327-68.

Tabellini, G., and A. Alesina. 1990. "Voting on the Budget Deficit." *American Economic Review* 80:37-49.

Tait, A., W. Gratz, and B. Eichengreen. 1979. "International Comparisons of Taxation for Selected Developed Countries, 1972-76." *International Monetary Fund Staff Papers* 26:123-156.

Tanzi, V. 1991. "Is There a Limit to the Size of Fiscal Deficits in Developing Countries?" In *Public Finance in Developing Countries*, ed. V. Tanzi. Washington, D.C.: International Monetary Fund.

Taylor, C. L. 1985. *ICPSR Data Set*. Ann Arbor: University of Michigan, Inter-University Consortium for Political and Social Research

Taylor, C. L., and. D. A. Jodice. 1983. *World Handbook of Political and Social Indicators,* 3rd ed. Vol. 2. New Haven: Yale University Press.

_____ 1988. *World Handbook of Political and Social Indicators, 1988.* New Haven: Yale University Press.

_____ 1993-1994. *World Handbook of Political and Social Indicators III: 1948-1982.* Ann Arbor, Michigan. Inter-University Consortium for Political and Social Research.

Taylor, L. 1988. *Varieties of Stabilization Experience.* Oxford: Clarendon Press.

Taylor, M. P. 1988. "An Empirical Examination of Long Run Purchasing Power Parity Using Co-Integration Techniques." *Applied Economics* 20:1369-82.

Thomas, A. 1948. *The Industrial Revolution.* New York: Oxford University Press.

_____ 1955. *An Economic History of England, The 18th Century.* Methane.

Thompson, W. S. 1929. "Population." *American Journal of Sociology* 34:959-75.

Tiebout, C. M. 1956. "A Pure Theory of Local Expenditures." *Journal of Political Economy* 64:416-424.

Tilly, C. 1975. *The Formation of National States in Western Europe.* Princeton: Princeton University Press.

_____ 1978. *From Mobilization to Revolution.* Reading, Mass.: Addison-Wesley Press.

_____ 1986. "Review Symposium of The Decline of Fertility in Europe." *Population and Development Review* 12(2).

Tokman, V. E. 1982. "Unequal Development and the Absorption of Labour, Latin America 1950-1980." *Cepal Review* 17(August).

_____ 1985. *Beyond the Crisis.* PREALC. Geneva: International Labour Organization.

Toynbee, A. 1956. *The Industrial Revolution.* Boston: Beacon Press.

Tsui, A., and D. J. Bogue. 1978. "Declining World Fertility: Trends, Causes, Implication." *Population Bulletin* 33(4).

United Nations. 1978. *Population Trends and Prospects by Country, 1950-2000: Summary Report of the 1978 Assessment.* New York: United Nations.

_____ 1990. *United Nations Demographic Yearbook.* New York: United Nations.

United Nations Center on Transnational Corporations. 1991. *Government Policies and Foreign Direct Investment.* New York: United Nations.

United States Advisory Commission on Intergovernmental Relations. 1990. *Significant Features of Fiscal Federalism, 1990.* Washington, D. C.

Van de Kaa, D. 1987. "Europe's Second Demographic Transition." *Population Bulletin* 42(March 1).

Van den Broek, J., F. R. Forsund, L. Hjalmarsson, and W. Meeusen. 1980. "On the Estimation of Deterministic and Stochastic Frontier Production Functions." *Journal of Econometrics* 13:117-38.

Vasquez, J. 1994. *The War Puzzle*. Cambridge Studies in International Relations, Vol. 27. Cambridge: Cambridge University Press.

Verba, S., N. Nie, and J. R. Petrocik. 1976. *The Changing American Voter*. Cambridge: Harvard University Press.

Verspagen, B. 1992. "Endogenous Innovation in Neo-Classical Growth Models: A Survey." *Journal of Macroeconomics* 14:631-62.

Watson, W. 1977. *Family Planning in the Developing World*. New York: Population Council.

Webber C., and A. Wildawski. 1986. *History of Taxation and Expenditure in the Western World*. New York: Simon and Schuster.

Weede, E. 1984. "Political Democracy, State Strength, and Economic Growth in LDCs: A Cross-National Analysis." *Review of International Studies* 10:297-312.

White, H. 1980. "Heteroskedasticity-Constant Covariance Matrix Estimator and a Direct Test for Heteroskedasticity." *Econometrica* 48:817-38.

Whiteley, P. 1986. *Political Control of the Macroeconomy*. Calif.: Sage Publications.

Wildavsky, A. 1984. "Federalism Means Inequality: Political Geometry, Political Sociology, and Political Culture." In *The Cost of Federalism*, ed. R. Golembiewski and A. Wildavsky. New Brunswick: Transaction Books.

Willett, T. D., ed. 1988. *Political Business Cycles: The Political Economy of Money, Inflation, and Unemployment*. Durham, N. C.: Duke University Press.

Willett, T. D., K. Banaian, L. O. Laney, M. Merzkani, and A. D. Warga. 1988. "Inflation Hypotheses and Monetary Accomodation: Post War Evidence from the Industrial Countries." In *Political Business Cycles: The Political Economy of Money, Inflation, and Unemployment*, ed. T. D. Willett. Durham, NC: Duke University Press.

Willett, T. D., et al., eds. 1995. *Establishing Monetary Stability in Emerging Market Economies*. Boulder: Westview Press.

Willett, T. D. 1995. *"The Public Choice Approach to International Economic Relations."* Tenth Annual Virginia Political Economy Lecture. Center for the Study of Public Choice, George Mason University.

Wolfram, F., and P. Lundgreen. 1975. "The Recruitment of Administrative and Technical Personnel." *The Making of Western States in Western Europe*, ed. C. Tilly. Princeton: Princeton University Press.

Woods, A. 1988. *Global Trends in Exchange Rates, 1960-1984*. World Bank Discussion Paper No. 35. Washington, D.C.

Woodward, P. D., and R. J. Rolfe. 1993. "The Location of Export Oriented Foreign Direct Investment in the Caribbean Basin." *Journal of International Business Studies* First Quarter: 121–44.

World Bank. 1989. *World Development Report*. New York: United Nations.

_____ 1992a. *Social Indicators of Development 1991-92*. Washington, D.C.: The International Bank for Reconstruction and Development.

_____ 1992b. *Statistical Handbook. States of the Former USSR*. Washington, DC: The World Bank.

_____ Various issues. *World Debt Tables*. Washington, D.C.: The World Bank.
_____ Various years. *World Development Report*. Oxford University Press.
Young, A. 1992. "A Tale of Two Cities: Factor Accumulation and Technical Change in Hong Kong and Singapore." *NBER Macroeconomic Annual*. National Bureau of Economic Research.
Yue, C. S. 1993. "Foreign Direct Investment in ASEAN Economics." *Asian Development Review* 11(1):60–102.

Index

About the Book and Editors

Given today's heightened competition between national economies in the global marketplace, many have come to believe that government intervention is needed in order for a country to maximize its economic well-being. But to what extent can even the most capable government act to attract investment and enhance economic growth without creating or exacerbating conflicts in society—especially when unpopular measures, such as those aimed at controlling inflation and population growth, must be implemented?

This timely book by an international team of economists and political scientists tackles that question head on. The contributors draw on theory and empirical data to provide a framework for measuring governments' ability to gather material resources and mobilize populations. They analyze a variety of policy choices made in the United States and in other nations around the world during the past fifty years, showing how states can increase their political capacity and thereby reduce economic transaction costs and domestic resistance to government goals.

Marina Arbetman is assistant professor of political science and political economy at the Murphy Institute of Political Economy, Tulane University, and at the City University of New York. **Jacek Kugler** is Elisabeth Helm Rosecrans Professor of International Relations at the School of Politics and Economics, the Claremont Graduate University.